PANPIPES & PONCHOS

Currents in
Latin American
& Iberian Music

ALEJANDRO L. MADRID, SERIES EDITOR
WALTER AARON CLARK, FOUNDING SERIES EDITOR

Panpipes & Ponchos

MUSICAL FOLKLORIZATION AND THE RISE OF THE ANDEAN
CONJUNTO TRADITION IN LA PAZ, BOLIVIA

Fernando Rios

OXFORD
UNIVERSITY PRESS

OXFORD
UNIVERSITY PRESS

Oxford University Press is a department of the University of Oxford. It furthers
the University's objective of excellence in research, scholarship, and education
by publishing worldwide. Oxford is a registered trade mark of Oxford University
Press in the UK and certain other countries.

Published in the United States of America by Oxford University Press
198 Madison Avenue, New York, NY 10016, United States of America.

Library of Congress Cataloging-in-Publication Data
Names: Rios, Fernando, author.
Title: Panpipes & ponchos : Musical folklorization and the rise of the Andean conjunto tradition
in La Paz, Bolivia / Fernando Rios.
Description: New York : Oxford University Press, 2020. |
Series: Currents in Latin American and Iberian music |
Includes bibliographical references and index.
Identifiers: LCCN 2019053179 (print) | LCCN 2019053180 (ebook) |
ISBN 9780190692278 (hardback) | ISBN 9780190692285 (paperback) |
ISBN 9780190692308 (epub) | ISBN 9780190692315 (on-line)
Subjects: LCSH: Folk music—Bolivia—La Paz—History and criticism. |
Creoles—Bolivia—La Paz—Music—History and criticism |
Mestizos—Bolivia—La Paz—Music—History and criticism
Classification: LCC ML3575.B68 L363 2020 (print) | LCC ML3575.B68 (ebook) |
DDC 781.62/688408412—dc23
LC record available at https://lccn.loc.gov/2019053179
LC ebook record available at https://lccn.loc.gov/2019053180

9 8 7 6 5 4 3 2

Paperback printed by Marquis, Canada
Hardback printed by Bridgeport National Bindery, Inc., United States of America

For Thalia

Contents

Acknowledgments

SEVERAL YEARS BEFORE I had a clear idea of what ethnomusicology was, I spent a summer in Bolivia, where I planned to expand my knowledge of Bolivian folkloric music and other facets of "my cultural roots" beyond what I had learned growing up as a Bolivian-American in the Midwest, and in the two years that had I lived in Bolivia while still in primary school. On my way to an arts fair in the city of Cochabamba, a chance meeting with Ramiro de la Zerda—an ex-member of Los Kjarkas (one of Bolivia's most popular folkloric groups since the 1980s) and then-director of Fortaleza—proved to be fortuitous. Ramiro, after hearing of my musical interests, invited me to watch Fortaleza's concert at the fair and offered to give me music lessons at a later date. I eagerly accepted on both fronts.

At one of our weekly sessions at his house, we listened to Los Jairas' classic 1966 recording of the *yaraví* "El Llanto de Mi Madre" (The tears of my mother), so that Ramiro could transcribe for me the lyrics set in the Quechua language. I had been captivated by the text since I had first heard this album, which figured among the handful of Bolivian music recordings in my possession prior to this trip. The *kena* solo on this track also had caught my attention. To my then untrained ears, the kena player's plaintive lines, full of vibrato, evoked the essence of traditional Andean indigenous music. Ramiro, too, admired the skills of the wind soloist, whom he ranked as one of the best kena players to perform in Bolivia. When he pointed out to me that the instrumentalist was a Swiss musician, Gilbert "el gringo" Favre, I was surprised, because the album cover—which features colorfully dressed highland indigenous musicians—had led me to assume that Bolivian artists performed on the recording. Though intrigued by this discovery, I did not know what to make of this information. Little did I know that my early questions about Los Jairas, and the history of the Bolivian folkloric music movement in general, would eventually lead me to conduct the research that forms the basis of this book.

A few years after this trip, I applied to the ethnomusicology program at the University of Illinois at Urbana-Champaign, expressly to study under Thomas Turino, whose writings on Peruvian music had prompted a major shift in my understanding of the music-dance practices of the Southern Andean region. I am grateful to this day that the graduate committee accepted me into the program, as I consider my education at Illinois to be a life-changing one that not only provided me with a solid foundation for my professional life, but also had a deep impact on my worldview. In addition to Tom, I would like to thank Donna Buchanan, Charles Capwell, the late Bruno Nettl, and Gabriel Solis, each of whom taught me much about the field of ethnomusicology. My training as a budding Andeanist at Illinois was greatly enhanced by the courses that I took with Bolivianist anthropologist Andrew Orta, Peruvianist historian Nils Jacobsen, and Quechua teacher Clodoaldo Soto. Of my fellow graduate students, I would like to acknowledge the friendship and encouragement of Joanna Bosse, Angelina Cotler, Greg Diethrich, Adriana Fernandes, Stefan Fiol, Eduardo Herrera, Ladona Martin-Frost, Dave McDonald, Derek Pardue, Tony Perman, Chris Scales, and Anna Schultz. My education and fieldwork in my time at Illinois were supported by a Graduate College Fellowship, Illinois Consortium for Educational Opportunity Fellowship, Foreign Language Area Studies Summer Fellowship, and Tinker Summer Field Research Grant.

This book would not have been possible without the help of numerous individuals. First of all, I wish to thank the staff at La Paz's Biblioteca del Congreso, Biblioteca Municipal, and Universidad Mayor de San Andrés, and in Cochabamba, Universidad de San Simón, for granting me access to newspaper collections and other archival materials, because this book draws heavily on primary historical sources—a methodology consistent with the book's major goals. I also wish to thank the many individuals involved in the Bolivian folklore movement who took the time to speak with me and often graciously shared their personal libraries of concert programs, newspaper clippings, photographs, and music scores. Many also allowed me to dub recordings that were otherwise difficult to obtain. While it is not possible to list everyone here, I would like to especially recognize José Aramayo Martínez, Leni Ballón, Norah and María Luisa Camacho, Ernesto Cavour, the late Waldo Cerruto, the late Carola Cobo de Ruíz, Hery Cortéz, Manuel Cruz, Xavier Díaz Torres, Marcelino Fernández, Julio Godoy, Jaime Lafuente, Willy Loredo, Augustín "Cacho" Mendieta, Jorge Miranda, Tito Morlán, Pepe Murillo, Julio César Paredes Ruiz, the late Tito Peñarrieta, Germán Rivas, the late Orlando Rojas, Mario Hugo Romero, Alfredo Solíz Bejar, María Luisa and Elsa Tejada, the late Chela Urquidi, and Irma Vásquez de Ronda. When I spent time in Paris investigating Europe's Andean music scene, the late Carlos Ben-Pott, the late Carlos Cáceres, the late Héctor Miranda, José Mendoza, Cristóbal Soto, and Jean Vidaillac provided me with invaluable assistance. On the Buenos Aires leg of my research project, I gained much from the insights of the late Víctor "Vitillo" Ábalos, Perla Aguirre, Fernando

Barragán, Rodolfo Dalera, the late Raúl Shaw, the late Arnoldo Pintos, and the late Jaime Torres.

The friendships I have made through the Society for Ethnomusicology, particularly with my fellow Latin Americanists, have helped sustain me through the years. Jonathan Ritter has been one of my strongest supporters and is one of the most generous people I know. I also find myself lucky to count as colleagues and friends Ana Alonso-Minutti, Jacky Ávila, Sean Bellaviti, Michael Birenbaum Quintero, Juan Diego Díaz, León García Corona, Eduardo Herrera, Joshua Katz-Rosene, Javier León, Alejandro Madrid, Hettie Malcomson, Ian Middleton, Robin Moore, Michael O'Brien, Sergio Ospina-Romero, Daniel Party, Marysol Quevedo, Greg Robinson, Henry Stobart, Susan Thomas, Joshua Tucker, Patricia Vergara, Jud Wellington, Juan Eduardo Wolf, and Ketty Wong.

At the University of Maryland, thanks in particular go to musicologist Pat Warfield for his camaraderie, steadfast support, good humor, and intellectual interchanges on curricular design. Siv Lie has been the ideal ethnomusicology colleague, and I greatly appreciate her friendship, vision, and strong commitment to mentoring students. My appreciation also goes to the other members of the Division of Musicology and Ethnomusicology: Barbara Haggh-Huglo, Olga Haldey, Richard King, Will Robin, and Larry Witzleben. Thanks also to my current and former advisees in the graduate program, Elizabeth Goldman, Víctor Hernández-Sang, Ben Jackson, Alice Rogers, Jennie Terman, Patricia Vergara, Mariángel Villalobos Benavides, and Max Yamane, for their enthusiasm about ethnomusicology and for inspiring me to become a better mentor and teacher. I would also like to thank graduate assistant Matthew Samson from the Division of Music Theory and Composition for his help with the transcriptions that appear in this book.

At Oxford University Press, Alejandro Madrid and Suzanne Ryan deserve my enduring appreciation for believing in this project from the beginning and seeing it through to completion. I also thank the press's anonymous reviewers for their insightful comments on the manuscript. Early versions of the main case studies in Chapter 3 previously appeared in the 2017 essay "Las Kantutas and Música Oriental: Folkloric Music, Mass Media, and State Politics in 1940s Bolivia," and 2018 article "From Elite to Popular: Estudiantinas in La Paz, Bolivia, 1880s–1940s." I thank the journals *Resonancias: Revista de Investigación Musical*, and *Diagonal: An Ibero-American Music Review*, respectively, for permission to use portions of these essays. Thanks also go to the Society for Ethnomusicology for allowing me to incorporate parts of my 2010 *Ethnomusicology* article "Bolero Trios, Mestizo Panpipe Ensembles and Bolivia's 1952 Revolution: Urban La Paz Musicians and the Nationalist Revolutionary Movement" into Chapter 5.

Finally, I reach the most important part. I cannot even begin to adequately express my heartfelt gratitude to my wife, Thalia, who has been on this journey with me from my pre-ethnomusicology days as a master's student in classical guitar performance. She thus has been with me throughout all of the highs and lows of graduate school, and the challenges of navigating the job market. During all of my research trips (in which she helped me with archive collection) she accompanied me. She has also spent countless hours listening to me brainstorm ideas, reading everything I have written, and offering invaluable suggestions. For these reasons, and a multitude more, I have always dedicated my works to her, and this book is no exception. Without her constant, nurturing presence and unconditional love, I would not have been able to achieve what I have so far. My life is not complete without her, and I look forward to our future together, always.

1

INTRODUCTION

MELODIOUS PANPIPES AND kena flutes. The shimmering strums of a *charango*. Poncho-clad musicians playing "El Cóndor Pasa" (The condor passes) at subway stops or street corners while selling their recordings. These sounds and images no doubt come to mind for many "world music" fans when they recall their early encounters with Andean folkloric music groups. Termed "Andean conjuntos" in this book and "pan-Andean bands" in other scholarship,[1] ensembles of this type have long formed part of the "world music" circuits of Paris, Hamburg, Amsterdam, Vienna, New York, Boston, San Francisco, Tokyo, and other cosmopolitan hubs of the Global North. In the metropolitan centers of Latin America, too, colorfully dressed Andean conjuntos have been present in the music scene for decades, not only in Bolivia, Ecuador, and Peru as would be expected (i.e., in the Andean countries), but also in Argentina (see Portorrico 2004), Chile (see González Rodríguez, Rolle, and Olsen 2009), and Colombia (see Katz-Rosene 2015), and even as far away from the Andean mountain range as Mexico (see Arana 1988; Zolov 1999, 225–33). Unquestionably, no other Andean-associated musical tradition has experienced such broad dissemination from the 1960s to the present day.

Andean conjuntos sonically and visually foreground signifiers of indigeneity (e.g., through their instrumentation, repertoire, ensemble names, and performance attire), so much so that fans often mistakenly believe that the music that these groups play is solidly based in rural indigenous highland traditions. To be sure, Andean conjunto artists perform on musical instruments of Andean indigenous origin or

Panpipes & Ponchos. Fernando Rios, Oxford University Press (2020). © Oxford University Press.
DOI: 10.1093/oso/9780190692278.001.0001.

association, namely, the *zampoña* (panpipe), kena (end-notched flute), charango (mandolin-sized chordophone), and *bombo* (bass drum), but with versions of these instruments that differ substantially in their construction and tuning from typical rural indigenous models. Additional defining characteristics of the Andean conjunto tradition, such as the ensembles' mixed-instrument lineup of four to six musicians (which includes at least one guitarist), expansive repertoire of genres (e.g., *huayño, cueca, bailecito, yaraví, taquirari, carnaval, morenada, tinku, chuntunqui, tobas, caporal-saya*), and preferred performance contexts (folklore shows and recitals), similarly do not have a foundation in the customary musical practices of Southern Andean indigenous communities.

Urban *criollo* and *mestizo* folkloric artists,[2] rather than rural indigenous musicians, created and consolidated the Andean conjunto tradition, and accordingly they served as the principal figures in its early trajectory as a mass-mediated musical expression in the Andean region and abroad. Even more counterintuitively, it was Argentine musicians who played the lead role in the initial transnational diffusion of Andean conjunto music. With Paris as their base of operations, the Argentine-led bands Los Incas and Los Calchakis introduced "El Cóndor Pasa" and other highly stylized folklorizations of Andean indigenous music to European audiences in the 1950s and 1960s, thereby opening the door to the European market for Andean folklore acts from other Latin American countries (Rios 2008).

The Chilean *nueva canción* (new song) groups Inti-Illimani and Quilapayún spearheaded the next wave of European fascination with Andean folkloric music, which emerged in the 1970s and lasted into the following decade. In the Latin American context (with the exception of Bolivia), Inti-Illimani and Quilapayún also represented the ensembles most responsible for popularizing the Andean conjunto format and its associated musical style in the late 1960s and 1970s, and in shaping the primary meanings that musicians and audiences initially attached to this type of Andean music.[3]

In Bolivia, the late 1960s marks the moment when, for the first time, the Andean conjunto became a commonly used ensemble configuration. This new development in the field of Bolivian folkloric-popular music (i.e., mass-mediated folkloric music) intersects with the beginnings of Chilean nueva canción, and the initial phase of Paris's Andean music scene, through the intriguing figure of Gilbert Favre. A kena soloist and Dixieland-style clarinetist from Switzerland, Favre frequently crossed paths with Los Incas and Los Calchakis in Paris's Left Bank in the early-to-mid-1960s, and found inspiration in their interpretive approaches. After devoting about three years to adapting his clarinet technique to the kena, Favre made his first trip to Bolivia in 1966. Within a few months, he founded the band Los Jairas with three La Paz criollo-mestizo musicians: Ernesto Cavour (charango), Julio Godoy (guitar), and Edgar "Yayo" Joffré (lead vocals, *bombo legüero*). One of Bolivia's most influential ensembles of the 20th century, Los Jairas is widely credited, by scholars and local musicians alike, with canonizing the Andean conjunto as Bolivia's preeminent ensemble format for interpreting *música folklórica nacional* (national folkloric music) (e.g., see Céspedes 1984; Arauco 2011; Bigenho 2012; Sánchez Patzy 2017).

Favre also set into motion the founding of the venue Peña Naira, where Los Jairas functioned as the house band from mid-1966 until the members departed for Europe in late 1969. A then unusual type of locale in the La Paz setting, because it exclusively presented folkloric artists and catered to an upscale clientele, Peña Naira rapidly became the epicenter for the Bolivian folklore movement.[4] By 1969, numerous establishments of this kind had sprouted up in La Paz, initiating a process that, once it had spread to the country's other major cities, established the peña as a Bolivian cultural institution. The peña circuit, in turn, offered employment opportunities to musical acts in the same vein as Los Jairas, that is, Andean conjuntos, and consequently spurred the formation of new ensembles of this variety. Given the important role that local peñas enacted in Bolivia's folklore movement, it is notable that Favre's source of inspiration for Peña Naira was a Chilean venue, Santiago's famed La Peña de los Parra (The peña of the Parra family).

Yet despite this direct link between the Bolivian and Chilean folklore scenes of the 1960s, musicians and audiences in the two countries ascribed vastly divergent meanings to the Andean conjunto. In Chile, the musical and political activities of nueva canción artists fostered unprecedented public interest for folklorized renditions of Andean indigenous music (particularly of Bolivian and Peruvian musical traditions), and as a result, by the early 1970s Chileans strongly associated Andean conjunto music with nueva canción's leftist politics of pan–Latin Americanism. A similar development occurred in Peru, Ecuador, Colombia, Mexico, and elsewhere in Latin America where the first generation of locally based Andean conjuntos modeled themselves after Chilean nueva canción groups (see Oliart and Llórens 1984; Arana 1988; Peralta 2003; González Rodríguez, Rolle, and Olsen 2009; Tucker 2013; Katz-Rosene 2015). For Bolivians of the same period, in contrast, the Andean conjunto's characteristic ensemble format and musical style had nothing to do with pan–Latin Americanism. Instead, they generally regarded the Andean conjunto tradition as a "national" musical expression, one that exhibited significant continuities with earlier Bolivian criollo-mestizo forms of folkloric music making.

A major goal of this book is to illuminate how urban La Paz[5] folkloric musical trends, practices, and initiatives of the early-to-mid 20th century paved the way for Los Jairas' dramatic ascent to national stardom and facilitated Bolivia's ensuing canonization of the Andean conjunto tradition. Notwithstanding Los Jairas' significant impact on contemporaneous as well as future Bolivian currents in música folklórica nacional, when the group arrived on the urban La Paz music scene in 1966, their interpretive approach, instrumentation, and repertoire did not represent a radically new direction for the Bolivian folklore movement. In the 1950s and early 1960s, the musical acts Conjunto 31 de Octubre, Conjunto Kollasuyo, and Armando Valdéz y su Conjunto Andino had already used similar musical practices (Chapter 5). Ensembles from even earlier periods, such as Lira Incaica, which was active in the 1920s and 1930s, had also adapted Andean indigenous tunes in a manner that bears a striking resemblance to how Andean conjuntos would later folklorize highland indigenous musical expressions (Chapter 3). As this book reveals, then, Los Jairas made popular

in Bolivia a style of musical interpretation with substantial roots in the folklorization practices developed by previous generations of urban criollo-mestizo musicians.

Panpipes & Ponchos examines not only the Andean conjunto tradition and its most
direct stylistic precursors, but also a diverse range of other musical expressions. In
the chapters that follow, the book devotes ample attention to *estudiantinas* (plucked
string orchestras), female vocal duos (e.g., Las Kantutas), male *tríos románticos*
(whose hallmark genre was the Cuban-derived *bolero*), art-classical compositions
(e.g., *Amerindia*), urban mestizo panpipe ensembles (e.g., Los Choclos), and rural
indigenous wind bands (especially groups specializing in the regional panpipe consort styles known as "Sikuris de Italaque" and "Kantus de Charazani"), thereby offering a broad perspective on the La Paz music scene from the 1920s to 1960s. Another
important advantage of this approach is that it uncovers the precise ways in which
Los Jairas' meteoric success represented the culmination of over four decades of
Bolivian musical currents in various spheres of artistic practice.

The second principal aim of this book is to detail and shed light on the Bolivian
state's role in fostering the folkloric music movement in the urban La Paz setting,
from the period when the Bolivian variant of Latin American *indigenismo* (indigenism) initially became an important influence on La Paz criollo-mestizo artists (i.e., the
1920s), to the boom decade of the folklore movement (i.e., the 1960s). Over this pivotal
era, Bolivian state-funded folkloric musical practices at times aligned with, and in
other cases contradicted, the presiding administration's political priorities and official ideologies in the area of nation-building. Nonetheless, Bolivian state agencies and
officials regularly provided logistical and financial support for folkloric musical performances and initiatives in this period, and for this reason the Bolivian government
constituted an important player in the trajectory of the folkloric music movement.

The book's third major goal is to elucidate how stylistic trends in folkloric interpretation among La Paz criollo-mestizo musicians articulated with non-Bolivian musical currents. Perhaps surprisingly to many readers of this book, given Bolivia's image
internationally as one of the most "Indian" and culturally traditional countries of
Latin America, the Bolivian folkloric music movement developed in close dialogue
with transnational artistic trends from the 1920s to 1960s. By extensively document-
ing how leading La Paz criollo-mestizo folkloric musicians borrowed practices and
ideas from foreign artists, especially Peruvian, Argentine, Chilean, and Mexican
musicians, this book corroborates ethnomusicologist Thomas Turino's observation,
based on his research on Zimbabwean popular music (Turino 2000), that cosmopolitanism underpins musical nationalism, a provocative argument that runs counter to
the conventional view that cosmopolitanism and nationalism constitute fundamentally opposed cultural orientations.[6]

For Latin Americanist scholarship on music and nationalism, this book adds to
the body of historical research that details the artistic and sociopolitical processes
through which the politically dominant sectors gradually came to imagine certain
locally distinctive musical practices as paramount forms of national culture (e.g.,
Raphael 1990; Austerlitz 1997; Moore 1997; Scruggs 1999; Vianna 1999; Wade 2000;

Jáuregui 2007; Wong 2012) and, more specifically, to investigations that explore the canonization of "folkloric" musical expressions (discussed in the next section). The book's most significant contribution, however, is to the field of Bolivian music studies. Although a number of scholars have explored the subject of Bolivian folkloric music, *Panpipes & Ponchos* is the first book-length study that chronicles how Bolivia's folkloric music movement articulated, on the one hand, with Bolivian state projects, and on the other, with transnational or cosmopolitan artistic currents, throughout the key period spanning the 1920s to 1960s.

MUSIC AND FOLKLORIZATION, AND PLAN OF THE BOOK

The performance practices of Andean conjuntos represent a classic example of what ethnomusicologists, folklore studies researchers, anthropologists often conceptualize as "folklorization."[7] Music scholars generally use this term when discussing highly stylized, recontextualized, and resignified enactments of rural music-dance practices that in these new versions tend to be more "presentational" (i.e., geared toward contexts where the performers entertain a largely passive audience) than the "root" traditions (which in contrast usually exhibit more of a "participatory" nature).[8] Even though folkloric musicians typically portray their artistic efforts as acts of cultural preservation, then, folklorization results in the creation of new cultural practices, ones with highly varying degrees of fidelity to the folklorist's rural sources of inspiration (see Rios 2012).

In Latin America, the folklorization of local music-dance expressions initially gained momentum in the early-to-mid-20th century, as part of broader folklore movements that in turn had assorted connections with state projects of nation-building and modernization (Rowe and Schelling 1991, 1–8; Mendoza 2000, 48–55; Turino 2003; Chamosa 2010; Hellier-Tinoco 2011).[9] Persons of elite and middle-class socioeconomic status, rather than "folk" community members, generally led Latin America's folklore movements in this period, and as a result, elite and middle-class agendas constituted the driving force behind most folklorization initiatives.

Folklore movements are primarily identified with nationalism and related political projects such as regionalism, but not commonly with cosmopolitanism. Yet it is indisputable that national and regional folklore movements represent local variants of transnational sociopolitical and artistic currents. The consolidation of criollo-mestizo indigenismo within the folklore movements of multiple Latin American countries in the early 20th century (see Earle 2007), and the ways in which the national scenes freely adapted indigenista concepts and practices that circulated internationally, exemplifies the cosmopolitan character of Latin American folklore movements.

Bolivian indigenismo, for instance, was heavily indebted to its Peruvian counterpart from the 1920s to 1940s, the very period when La Paz criollo-mestizo artists, politicians, and writers increasingly aligned themselves with this elite and middle-class form of nativism (Part I: Chapters 2 and 3). Peruvian indigenista musicians, scholars, and "Inca theater" troupes traveled to La Paz with some frequency in this era and experienced a welcome reception, in large part because La Paz criollo-mestizo society had developed a fascination with the Incas of Cuzco and legacies of their civilization. Following in the footsteps of Peruvian indigenismo, La Paz–based indigenista musicians authored compositions that evoked the pre-Columbian age of the Inca Empire (e.g., Velasco Maidana's "Inca ballet" *Amerindia*), and many selected names for their musical acts that unambiguously conjured up this imagery (e.g., estudiantina Lira Incaica). Although the long vanquished Inca Empire initially constituted the main object for La Paz's indigenista movement, contemporary indigenous communities also interested prominent paceño indigenistas, such as Antonio González Bravo (often termed Bolivia's first ethnomusicologist).

La Paz indigenistas organized the earliest Bolivian folklore festivals that showcased Andean rural indigenous ensembles (Chapter 2). In the Americas and beyond, folklore festivals (which differ from rural festive events of a more traditional nature, such as fiestas)[10] function as important mechanisms for altering the practices and meanings of local music-dance traditions, normally to make them better correspond with the aesthetic criteria of prize committees and tenets of nationalist ideology (for insightful studies of Bolivian folklore festivals, see Rockefeller 1999; Bigenho 2002; Solomon 2014). In the period that this book covers, La Paz folklore festivals that featured rural indigenous or "autochthonous" Andean wind bands took place in large public spaces such as the local stadium, and in most cases were state-sponsored occasions (Chapters 2, 4, and 6). These spectacles exposed urban La Paz audiences to a number of the *tropa* (Andean indigenous wind consort) genres that indigenous community musicians customarily played at fiestas in the small highland towns of the *departamento* (equivalent to a US state) of La Paz. Through various means, Bolivian state-sponsored folklore festivals portrayed these traditional forms of Andean indigenous music-dance expression as the roots of Bolivian national music, a nativist notion that represents one of the principal discourses of Bolivia's folklore movement.

Criollo-mestizo musicians participated as well in Bolivian folklore festivals, from the advent of indigenismo, to the 1960s folklore boom. Many of these artists incorporated facets of Andean indigenous musical practices into their folkloric numbers (especially melodies, and secondarily instruments), to imbue them with locally distinctive elements. Folklore company productions, such as the choreographed revues presented by the state-funded Ballet Folklórico Oficial and Academia de Danzas, stylized Andean indigenous musical traditions as well, to cater to the aesthetic expectations of mainstream criollo-mestizo audiences (Chapter 4). Los Jairas' interpretive approach similarly integrated surface aspects of Andean indigenous expressive practices into a criollo-mestizo musical framework (e.g., equal temperament, tertian triad-based chords), an unequal blending that henceforth would largely define

Bolivian national folkloric-popular music. Although Los Jairas seldom performed in Bolivian folklore festivals or folklore company revues, the shows of Peña Naira—the band's principal venue from 1966 to 1969—adhered to most of the conventions that these state-funded productions had established in the 1950s, as held true for the Bolivian peña scene in general by the late 1960s (Chapter 7).

In the early decades of the Bolivian folklore movement, radio stations served as the primary vehicles for diffusing folkloric music through the local mass media, because Bolivia's first record company would not appear until 1949 (Discos Méndez), and television channel until 1969 (Televisión Boliviana). State-run Radio Illimani, which was founded in 1933, during the Chaco War, enacted an especially important role in normalizing the concept of the "Bolivian folklore star" in the 1930s and 1940s, by promoting musical acts such as the female vocal duos Las Kantutas and Las Hermanas Tejada (Chapter 3). Orquesta Típica La Paz, a state-funded estudiantina that played indigenista repertoire, is another local ensemble that reached a wide audience by regularly performing on the programs of a state-owned station, in this case Radio Municipal in the mid-1940s (Chapter 3). A couple of years after the 1952 Revolution—the momentous event that initiated the twelve-year period of rule by the Movimiento Nacionalista Revolucionario (Nationalist Revolutionary Movement) or MNR, Conjunto 31 de Octubre debuted on Radio Illimani, as the station's latest house band. The brainchild of an MNR official, Conjunto 31 de Octubre represents an intermediate step, in its instrumentation and other aspects of the group's performance practices, between La Paz's indigenista estudiantinas of the late 1930s and 1940s, and the Andean conjuntos that appeared on the scene in the 1960s (Chapter 5).

When Radio Illimani added Conjunto 31 de Octubre to its lineup in 1954, Discos Méndez of La Paz had been issuing releases for almost five years. Prior to the label's founding in 1949, Bolivian musicians who wished to make recordings had only been able to do so abroad; Buenos Aires, Argentina was their usual destination (Chapter 3). With the appearance of Discos Méndez, La Paz–based artists thus had much easier access to a recording studio, and before long, the quantity of Bolivian folkloric music recordings that were available to local consumers greatly increased. Discos Méndez's modest output, though, lessened the impact that its releases had in shaping musical trends. Because no other Bolivian label surfaced in the 1950s, the local recording industry's influence on folkloric musical practices was relatively limited up to this point, compared to the situation in most other Latin American countries (for Mexico, see Sheehy 1997).

Discolandia of La Paz and Lauro Records of Cochabamba relegated Discos Méndez to a subordinate position in the Bolivian market in the 1960s. By the middle of the decade, the local recording industry had experienced major growth, and partly as a result, criollo-mestizo musicians who had formerly specialized in popular music genres of non-Bolivian association, such as the bolero, increasingly reinvented themselves as folklorists (Chapter 6). As this development illustrates, mass-communication industries often attempt to exploit the national market by encouraging the commodification of regionally distinctive musical practices, a process that frequently leads musicians to folklorize traditional local genres (see Turino 2003); the dynamics of Bolivia's tourism industry began to have a similar effect on rural indigenous musicians in the mid-1960s (Chapter 6).

For many La Paz–based musicians who came of age as folklore artists in the mid-to-late 1960s, the possibility of earning a spot on one of the "national" music-dance delegations that would represent Bolivia at Argentina's Festival Latinoamericano de Folklore (Festival of Latin American Folklore) is what had initially led them to focus their energies on folkloric interpretation (Chapters 6 and 7). From 1965 to 1967, the Festival Latinoamericano de Folklore took place annually in the Salta region, the birthplace of most of the stars of the Argentine folkloric music movement. The *zamba* hits of Los Chalchaleros, Los Fronterizos, and many other internationally acclaimed Salta acts enjoyed a high level of popularity in Bolivia, so much so that the Argentine folklore movement constituted a major stylistic influence on La Paz criollo-mestizo musicians in the 1960s. Paceño artists' lofty estimation of Argentina's folklore scene heightened their enthusiasm for taking part in Salta's Festival of Latin American Folklore.

It is also true, though, that from the early 20th century onwards, Bolivian musicians often had aspired to secure performance and/or recording opportunities abroad, in the knowledge that those who realized this objective almost invariably saw their standing as artists rise to new heights at home. *Panpipes & Ponchos* documents numerous examples of this phenomenon, including Velasco Maidana's 1938 concert engagements in Berlin (Chapter 2); Las Kantutas and Las Hermanas Tejada's 1942 trip to Buenos Aires (Chapter 3); the *Fantasía Boliviana* troupe's 1959 tour of China, Czechoslovakia, and the USSR (Chapter 4); bolero act Raúl Shaw Moreno y Los Peregrinos' stay in Mexico City in the late 1950s (Chapter 5); the Bolivian delegation's award-winning performances at the first edition of Salta's Festival Latinoamericano de Folklore (Chapter 6); and Los Jairas' time in Europe from 1969 to 1973 (Chapter 7). The Bolivian case thus illustrates how navigating the expectations of foreign audiences and record labels often can play an essential role in the trajectories of national music artists.

As a general rule, the musical expressions that mainstream society views as nationally characteristic tend to embody core principles of nationalist ideology. From the 1920s to 1940s, La Paz–based criollo-mestizo nationalists of nativist inclination promoted or at least expressed support for indigenismo (Part I: Chapters 2 and 3), while in the MNR period (1952–1964), the Bolivian state officially championed another nativist-nationalist ideology with implications for the cultural sphere, *mestizaje* (ethnic-cultural fusion) (Part II: Chapters 4 and 5). Even though indigenismo focused on the "Indian" (usually in a patronizing way), and MNR discourse about mestizaje invoked an idealized mestizo, these nationalist ideologies were not incompatible. Indeed, Bolivian national musical practices often articulated with indigenismo *and* mestizaje. The interpretive approaches of Bolivia's Andean conjuntos represent a prime example.

During Los Jairas' period of activity in Bolivia (1966–1969), the public responded enthusiastically to the group, in part because many listeners, especially youths and young adults, regarded it to be an up-to-date, or hip, musical act. Los Jairas' fashionable image stemmed from the ensemble's association with the major new developments in the Bolivian folkloric music scene, such as the appearance of peñas, and controversy over "neo-folklore." From the 1970s onward, Bolivian Andean conjuntos would more overtly foreground "modern" signifiers, through their use of pop ballad conventions (e.g., Los Kjarkas), and by adding the electric bass and trap-set to their instrumentation (e.g., Ch'ila Jatun). (Chapter 8: Postlude). By blending "traditional" and "modern" signifiers in this way, these musical acts have been able to preserve the Andean conjunto's standing as Bolivia's preferred ensemble format for mass-mediated música folklórica nacional, in a manner that parallels how in other Latin American countries popular music artists that specialize in "national" genres have been able to reach a broad national audience (see Moore 1997 for Cuban *son*; Austerlitz 1997 for Dominican *merengue*).

Regardless of the country, folklore movements strive to bridge the divide between the nation's urban and rural populations, usually by persuading urban residents to reimagine provincial customs as their own cultural heritage, along with stylized folkloric enactments of these so-called folk traditions. The urban-rural cultural gulf, though, often tends to hamper the folklore movement's initial attempts to convince a majority of urban mainstream society to identify with "folk culture." In Latin America, this nativist endeavor initially faced additional, significant obstacles when the folklorization process centered on indigenous cultural expressions. These obstacles stemmed from the politically dominant sector's long-standing hostility toward "Indians" and indigenous-associated traditions, and the elite's maintenance of a racialized or ethnicized social hierarchy that relegated indigenous people to second-class status (see Urban and Scherzer 1991; Earle 2007). It was largely for these reasons that, prior to the rise of Bolivian indigenismo in the early 20th century, Bolivian criollos and mestizos had expressed negligible interest in Andean rural indigenous music-dance traditions, as the next two sections explain.

CRIOLLO-INDIGENOUS RELATIONS IN 19TH-CENTURY BOLIVIA

On July 16, 1809, a group of La Paz criollos ("criollo" then mainly referred to persons of Spanish ancestry born in the Americas), led by Pedro Domingo Murillo, brazenly announced their plan to found an independent republic that would govern the Spanish colonial territory known as the Real Audiencia de Charcas, or Alto Perú (which largely coincides with present-day Bolivia). It was one of South America's earliest formal declarations for political independence to take place in the colonial period. In response, the Spanish Crown dispatched a royalist army that swiftly ended the uprising by executing its leaders, including Murillo. Alto Perú (Upper Peru) would ironically end up being the last of Spain's South American territories to earn sovereignty: the region remained under royalist control until finally achieving independence in August 1825. (Soon afterwards the country was renamed the Republic of

Bolivia, in honor of Simón Bolívar.) Despite the actions of Murillo and his fellow conspirators in 1809, the local criollo class expressed only tepid support for the Wars of Independence while the conflict raged through much of the continent in the 1810s and 1820s. Most Upper Peruvian criollos preferred to back the royalist cause instead. It was only in the closing stages of the independence struggle, when Colombian and Venezuelan armies were on the verge of defeating the Spanish forces entrenched in Upper Peru, that the local elite definitively shifted its allegiance to the patriot side (Arnade 1970; Klein 1992, 89–98).

There are many reasons why the criollo class of Upper Peru remained largely on the sidelines of South America's 19th-century independence movements. One of the most important factors, though, was this sector's fear that a prolonged war in the region might inadvertently provide the Andean indigenous masses with the opportunity to launch their own insurrections. This apprehension was not unwarranted. Only a few decades earlier, in the 1780s, the indigenous mobilizations headed by La Paz's Túpaj Katari, Potosí's Tomás Katari, and Cuzco's Túpaj Amaru II had seriously threatened to overturn the political order in the Southern and Central Andes. Although these insurrections failed, they underscored the precarity of criollo political dominance in a region where indigenous people represented the vast majority of the population (Larson 2004, 34–37).

For La Paz's criollo class, the memory of Túpaj Katari's siege of the city loomed large in the years of the Wars of Independence. For about six months in late 1780 and early 1781, Katari's Aymara army had blockaded the city and warned its inhabitants that it would massacre them unless they surrendered. Unable to access their usual food supplies in the countryside, the criollo and mestizo residents were "reduced to eating horses, mules, dogs, cats, even animal skins and praying to the Virgin for succor" (Thomson 2002, 5). Luckily for them, royalists forces sent from Buenos Aires ultimately defeated the rebels. Not content with simply executing Katari, the authorities also had him quartered, to send an unambiguous message to future insurgents. In a gruesome spectacle, the Aymara leader's "head and limbs were then distributed for prominent display in the areas where his influence had been greatest" (Thomson 2002, 18). The 1780s was not the last time that the inhabitants of La Paz city would experience a large-scale indigenous uprising, however. Two years after Murillo's 1809 cry for independence, Andean indigenous people cut off La Paz from the surrounding towns for four months, until a royalist army once again violently quashed the revolt (Arze Aguirre 1979, 157–203).

In the early independence period, Bolivia's politically dominant criollo sector remained wary of the indigenous population, whom they consigned to second-class status through a legal system that recycled the principles of the Spanish colonial framework of "two republics": "The Republic of Spaniards" (which besides Spaniards had also included criollos and mestizos), and "The Republic of Indians" (Larson 2004, 40). Consistent with this strategy, in 1826 Bolivian state officials reinstituted the "Indian tax," which had operated as the "juridical keystone of Spanish policy of racial hierarchy and segregation" in the colonial era (Larson 2004, 40). The Bolivian government relied heavily on this source of revenue from the late 1820s to 1860s, to make up for the declining profitability of the country's mining exports (Klein 1992, 104–6).

The city of La Paz—the administrative center for the departamento with the largest number of indigenous inhabitants (i.e, the departamento of La Paz)—rose in its economic and especially political importance over the course of the 19th century, as a direct result of the Bolivian state's dependence on the "Indian tax" (Barragán 1990, 23–25). Urban La Paz would increasingly vie with Sucre—the original and still official national capital—for the status of Bolivia's center of political power as the century wore on, a rivalry that would escalate in the run-up to the 1898–1899 Civil War (Chapter 2).

By the late 1860s, the criollo class was increasingly pressing for the abolition of indigenous tribute payments, seldom from any empathy with indigenous people, but rather as a way for criollos to exploit *ayllu* (Andean indigenous community) lands that the government had deemed off limits to capitalist speculators as long as the community members paid the "Indian tax" (Platt 1982; Klein 1992, 151; Larson 2004, 214–17). Faced with criollo attempts at usurping ayllu properties, indigenous communities challenged these "free trade" actions through legal channels and, when that approach failed, through insurrection movements. From 1869 to 1871, indigenous uprisings surged once again in the highlands and culminated in another siege of La Paz city, thus temporarily halting criollo efforts to privatize communal ayllu lands (Klein 1992, 151–52; Larson 2004, 218).

Given the 19th-century Bolivian elite's antagonistic relationship with the Andean indigenous population, it is hardly surprising that criollo imaginings of the nation then rarely invoked the traditions and legacies of highland indigenous people (Demelas 1981; Larson 2004). Yet Peru had similarly experienced large-scale indigenous rebellions in the late Spanish colonial period (e.g., Túpaj Amaru II's insurrection in Cuzco and neighboring areas), but Lima's upper class nevertheless used Inca symbolism for nationalist purposes in the early independence period (Earle 2007, 21–22, 60–67, 124, 127–28). Notably, the text for the original 1821 version of the Peruvian national anthem poetically depicts the new republic as "a (metaphorical) reincarnation of the Inca Empire" (Earle 2007, 74).[11]

In contrast, Bolivia's national anthem (composed in 1845) contains no textual references to the Inca Empire, or to any other pre-Columbian Andean civilization, not even Tiwanaku (whose ceremonial center had been located in the La Paz region). With few exceptions, 19th-century Bolivian criollos avoided drawing parallels between their republic and the indigenous political entities that had preceded it.[12] Their anxiety over the prospect of future indigenous mobilizations, and recognition that indigenous people still greatly outnumbered criollos in the Bolivian Andes, largely explain the local criollo sector's reluctance to make historical comparisons of this sort.[13] Peruvian criollos of course also worried about the possible outbreak of Andean indigenous revolts in the 19th century. Unlike urban La Paz, however, Peru's capital city of Lima had not recently undergone an indigenous-led blockade that had threatened the survival of its criollo inhabitants. In any event, and for a variety of reasons, Peruvian indigenismo would develop into a major artistic-political-intellectual current among the elite class and middle class in Lima, Puno, and especially Cuzco by the end of the 19th century, several decades before Bolivian indigenismo would develop into a full-fledged movement. Urban La Paz criollo and mestizo musicians could therefore look to their Peruvian counterparts for inspiration when the Bolivian indigenista movement ultimately took shape in the early 20th century, something they would in fact do, and to such an extent that early Bolivian musical indigenismo would exhibit a remarkable degree of Peruvian influence (Chapter 2).

MUSIC IN LA PAZ CITY IN THE 19TH CENTURY

In 1548, the Spaniard Alonso de Mendoza and his entourage founded the settlement of Nuestra Señora de La Paz (Our Lady of Peace) on the site of the Aymara village of Chuquiago Marka (one of many spellings). Eventually known simply as La Ciudad de La Paz (The city of La Paz), it was segregated according to Spanish caste-racial categories in the colonial period. The end of Spanish rule did not end this arrangement. After 1825, criollos and mestizos continued to monopolize the residences located in the most prestigious part of town, the three-block radius surrounding Plaza 16 de Julio (July 16)—rechristened in 1902 as "Plaza Murillo" (after the patriot-martyr Pedro Domingo Murillo). The Presidential Palace and other government offices were erected in this zone (Barragán 1990). In the 19th century, and even the early 20th century (see Chapter 2), Bolivian state officials passed various laws and decrees aimed to deter indigenous people from passing through this central district of the city (Sierra 2013).

Indigenous people who lived in the urban La Paz area were then largely restricted to the *barrios de indios* (Indian neighborhoods), of which three existed in the mid-1800s: San Pedro (Saint Peter), San Sebastián (Saint Sebastian), and Santa Bárbara (Saint Barbara). Agricultural work represented the main livelihood for the residents. As the century advanced, San Sebastián and Santa Bárbara transformed into predominantly mestizo or criollo-mestizo neighborhoods, while indigenous people found themselves compelled to move to areas farther away from the city limits (Barragán 1990; Sierra 2013).

The music-dance activities that took place in the barrios de indios appear to have followed the conventions that have long characterized indigenous music making in the ayllus of the Southern Andes. In the course of a year, the residents of these neighborhoods celebrated a succession of fiestas that, in a syncretic manner, commemorated Catholic patron saint holidays and the agricultural cycle (Soux 2002, 251–56). The tropa was the standard ensemble format for these festive occasions (Soux 2002). A type of same-instrument wind band or consort, tropas employ either one variety of panpipe (e.g., *siku, ayarachi*), end-notched flute (e.g., kena, *kena-kena, choquela*), duct flute (e.g., *pinkillu, tarka*), or side-blown flute (known variously as the *flauta traversa, phala, pífano,* or *pitu*), usually with multiple sizes of the wind instrument. These ensembles often include percussion instruments as well (e.g., bombo, *wankara, caja*). Unfortunately, contemporaneous writers seldom provide details on tropa performance practices of the La Paz area. It is probable, though, that the musicians who played in the ensembles rendered melodies in monophony (unison and octaves), or parallel polyphony (e.g., fourths and fifths, along with unison and octaves), in a manner comparable to that of their 20th- and 21st-century counterparts.

Paceños (urban La Paz residents) of the criollo class generally viewed indigenous forms of music and dance with pronounced indifference in the 19th century. This stance reflected their belief that criollos not only were culturally distinct from indigenous people, but also belonged to another "race," that is, the "white race" (Barragán 2011). The members of this elite sector made a living as government officials, lawyers, or owners of commercial enterprises, or in other white-collar occupations. Many supplemented their incomes as absentee owners of haciendas (rural estates) (Barragán 1990). Culturally, 19th-century La Paz criollos eagerly imitated European trends, from clothing and hairstyles to the arts. Their favorite musical expressions accordingly adhered to the latest European fashions. In the art-classical music sphere, Italian operas and Spanish *zarzuelas* (a type of operetta) represented their music of choice, along with European orchestral compositions (mainly in the form of piano reductions). Even more popular among this sector were dance genres such as the waltz, polka, Spanish paso doble, Polish mazurka, Italian cavatina, and Cuban habanera, as played by brass bands, pianists, and plucked-string ensembles. The center of musical life for paceño criollos, meanwhile, was the Teatro Municipal (Municipal Theater), a European-style concert hall built in 1845 (Soux 1992, 87–125, 194–201).

It was in less formal settings, such as private parties, and the brass band *retretas* (retreats) offered weekly at the main boulevard of the city, El Prado, that urban La Paz criollos most often heard performances of regionally distinctive South American genres, especially the cueca, bailecito, yaraví, and huayño (Soux 1992, 237–39, 263; González Bravo 1961b, 93). By the late 1800s (if not sooner), the elite and middle class classified these four criollo-mestizo genres as the principal forms of Bolivian national music. The cueca, bailecito, yaraví, and huayño would maintain their place in the "national music" repertoire of La Paz criollo and mestizo artists in the 20th century, representing the staple genres for leading figures in the folklore movement.

The cueca and bailecito initially became part of Bolivian criollo and mestizo music making in the years of the Wars of Independence, when troops from other South American territories who were stationed in the country popularized the genres locally (Rossells 1996, 60–61). Derived from the Peruvian-Chilean *zamacueca* (which in turn sprang from the Spanish *jota*; Vega 1953), Bolivia's regional variants of the cueca and bailecito exhibit the *sesquiáltera* hemiola (interplay between $\frac{3}{4}$ and $\frac{6}{8}$ meters) that is present in many other Latin American music-dance genres of Spanish derivation (e.g., Mexican *son jarocho*, Colombian *bambuco*, Argentine zamba). In terms of their musical structure, Bolivian cuecas and bailecitos use AABA sectional form. The two genres differ primarily in their repetition schemes (Bolivian musicians play the entire tune twice when performing cuecas, whereas they realize the melody three times on bailecitos), tempos (in Bolivia, bailecitos are played at a slightly faster speed than cuecas), and accent patterns.[14]

The yaraví also entered the repertoire of Bolivian criollo-mestizo musicians in the 19th century (Cárdenas 2015, 72–75). Usually in $\frac{6}{8}$ meter (although Bolivian yaravís often are in $\frac{2}{4}$ or $\frac{4}{4}$; see Chapter 7), this musical form seems to have originated in Peruvian (i.e., Lower Peruvian) criollo-mestizo society in the late colonial era, most likely in the Cuzco area (Pagaza Galdo 1960–1961; Varallanos 1988). Bolivian indigenista writers often assert that the yaraví is derived from a pre-Columbian genre, the *harawi* (e.g., Paredes 1913, 187–88; Anaya de Urquidi 1947, 80; Lara 1960, 114–16). Peruvian scholars, though, have debunked this scenario (Pagaza Galdo 1960–1961; Varallanos 1988). In any case, by the mid-1800s Peru's yaraví tradition had spread not only to Bolivia but also to Argentina, Chile, Ecuador, and Uruguay (Vega 1962a). In urban La Paz, serenades represented a key performance context for yaravís in the 19th century (Soux 1992, 239). Befitting this social function, and in accordance with the yaraví's alternate name, *triste* (Spanish for "sad"), musicians traditionally perform the genre at a languid tempo, while the texts they interpret usually convey sorrowful emotions.[15]

The huayño is a simple-duple-meter dance genre ($\frac{2}{4}$ or $\frac{4}{4}$ meter) in sectional form (e.g., AABB, AABBCC) that often features pentatonically oriented melodies. A galloping pulse, which stresses the offbeat, constitutes the genre's most distinctive musical characteristic. Scholars have yet to establish the origins of the huayño (alternately spelled wayñu, wayño, guaiño, and many other ways—and with or without the tilde placed above the "n"). References to the genre appear from time to time in Spanish colonial writings, but not with detailed descriptions of the tradition's musical aspects. It is therefore unclear if these accounts refer to expressive practices that resemble the genre currently known in Bolivia and Peru as the huayño (Romero 2002, 41–42; Tucker 2013, 190). Complicating this issue further is that highland indigenous people often have used essentially the same designation (e.g., wayñu) as a label for community-specific forms of music and dance in the Southern Andes (see Turino 1993; Solomon 1997; Stobart 2006).

Within the sociocultural hierarchy of 19th-century Bolivia, in which criollos placed themselves at the top and indigenous people at the bottom, mestizos occupied an intermediate position (Harris 1995). A Spanish colonialist invention, the "mestizo" category originally denoted persons of mixed Spanish and indigenous ancestry. By the early republican era, however, in La Paz city and other Bolivian sites mestizo status had come to be defined chiefly by an individual's profession. Artisans, retail workers, domestic laborers, and persons working in other traditional blue-collar occupations made up most of the mestizo class in 19th-century urban La Paz, as censuses from this period document. The designation "cholo," meanwhile, represented a derogative term that the criollo class used when they were referring to mestizos of the lowest socioeconomic rank (Barragán 2011).

Mestizos negotiated their intermediate standing in paceño society through various means, including the performance of music and dance traditions. The members of this sector tended to use expressive practices to demonstrate their cultural affinity with criollos, and distinction from indigenous people. This relational dynamic explains why urban La Paz mestizos and criollos interpreted many of the same genres in this period (e.g., cueca, bailecito, yaraví, huayño), and also favored the same instruments, namely, the guitar, *bandurria* (a Spanish stringed instrument similar to the mandolin), piano, and brass band instruments (Soux 1992, 240).

Yet paceño mestizo musicians then also played the charango, even though La Paz criollos did not customarily do so at the time, apparently because of the instrument's associations with cholos and indigenous people, that is, the so-called lower-classes (Soux 2002, 258). Approximately the size of a Hawaiian ukulele and fitted with a variable number of courses (sets of adjacent strings), the charango is an Andean version of Spanish plucked-stringed instruments (e.g., bandurria, *vihuela*). It therefore is analogous to the Colombian *tiple*, Cuban *tres*, Mexican *jarana*, Venezuelan *cuatro*, and numerous other regionally distinctive Latin American chordophones that originated in Spanish colonial times and became associated with national or regional identity in the 20th century.

La Paz mestizos' identification with the *callahuaya* (or *kallawaya*) music-dance genre constitutes the second notable exception to this sector's usual avoidance of Andean indigenous-associated expressive practices in the 19th century. A parade tradition, the callahuaya genre evokes the mystique surrounding the Andean indigenous ritual healers from the Charazani Valley (Bautista Saavedra Province, La Paz) widely known as the Callahuaya or Kallawaya, whose fame dates to the epoch of the Inca Empire (Bastien 1978, 23–25). In the mid-to-late 1800s, La Paz callahuaya dancers wore indigenous-style striped ponchos and *lluchus* (wool caps with ear flaps), and carried a medicinal pouch on their sides (Soux 2002, 257). Callahuaya dancers' mimesis of Andean indigenous cultural traditions represents a harbinger of future trends in urban La Paz mestizo and criollo music-dance practices in the realm of folkloric expression.

The callahuaya genre, though, was an outlier in 19th-century paceño cultural life. It is worth underscoring that in this period neither the criollo nor mestizo residents of La Paz city played the musical instruments most identified with the region's indigenous population, that is, tropa instruments such as the siku (or other types of panpipes), kena (or other end-notched flutes), and bombo. Nor did they coordinate "folklore festivals" for Andean indigenous musical ensembles. If they had organized cultural exhibitions of this type, it would have meant that criollo-mestizo society generally regarded Andean indigenous expressive practices as the roots, or at least a characteristic facet, of Bolivian national culture. There is no evidence that these notions were prevalent at the time in urban La Paz criollo-mestizo society (Soux 1992, 268–69).

In the sphere of paceño art-classical music, meanwhile, compositions that musically or textually referenced "indigenous culture" were exceedingly rare in the 19th century. Among the few examples are Adolfo Ballivián's opera *Atahualpa* (named after the last sovereign ruler of the Inca Empire), and Modesta Sanjinés's piano piece *Zapateo Indio: Baile de los Indígenas de los Alrededores de la Ciudad de La Paz* (Indian zapateo: Dance of the indigenous people from the outskirts of the city of La Paz) (Soux 1992, 172–76, 177–78). Ballivián and Sanjinés moved in the upper echelons of La Paz society, as they were members of extremely wealthy families. It appears that their privileged positions afforded them a degree of freedom to depart from the conventions that otherwise discouraged criollo musicians from taking inspiration from the cultural practices and historical legacies of Andean indigenous people. Sanjinés, a skilled pianist who spent the final years of her life in France and published many of her scores there, incorporated melodies of Andean indigenous origin or derivation into *Zapateo Indio*, while Ballivián, a former president of Bolivia, looked to the legends surrounding the life and tragic death of the last Inca Emperor when he wrote *Atahualpa* (whose score unfortunately has not survived). By taking inspiration from pre-Columbian civilizations and present-day indigenous traditions, respectively, *Atahualpa* and *Zapateo Indio* foreshadow the two major trends in La Paz criollo-mestizo indigenista music making that would emerge in the early-to-mid-20th century, as the following chapters document.

NOTES

1. US-based scholars of Andean music normally use the term "pan-Andean band" when referring to this type of Andean folkloric-popular music group (e.g., Mendoza 2000; Bigenho 2012; Tucker 2013). In Bolivia, there is no agreement on the name of this ensemble format. Local musicians and audiences use various descriptors for it, such as *conjunto de música folklórica nacional* (national folkloric music group). They seldom employ the term "pan-Andean group," however, because unlike elsewhere in Latin America, Bolivians associate this variety of musical ensemble with national identity rather than pan-national forms of identification (as this chapter explains). In the absence of another suitable designation, in this book I use the designation "Andean conjunto" for ensembles that adhere to the tradition's characteristics as outlined in this chapter (e.g., instrumentation, repertoire).

2. I briefly discuss the sociocultural categories of criollo, mestizo, indigenous, and *cholo* at a later point in this chapter, focusing on their usage by La Paz city residents. When employing these ethnic labels to classify someone, Bolivians take into account various factors that often include the individual's socioeconomic standing, occupation, customary attire, formal education, place of residence, surname, and phenotype. Complicating matters further, the social context influences how Bolivians apply these ethnicized descriptors to categorize themselves and others (see Canessa 2006, 2007; Albó 2008; Toranzo 2008). Following Bolivianist convention, in this book I employ the compound term "criollo-mestizo" when it is unclear if the persons or groups being discussed identify as criollos or mestizos. I mainly use the designation "indigenous people" when referring to members of indigenous communities (*ayllus*).

3. For an overview of Chile's nueva canción movement, see Morris 2014.

4. Throughout the book, I use the designations "Bolivian folklore movement" and "Bolivian folkloric music movement." I do not mean to imply, though, that the wide array of

Bolivian folkloric musical activities and projects that this book discusses for the 1920–1970 period represented a highly unified movement.

5. For variety, I use "urban La Paz" as a synonym for "La Paz city." This term also differentiates Bolivia's acting capital city from the rest of the departamento (i.e., state) of La Paz, which largely consisted of small towns in the time period this book covers.

6. It should be pointed out, though, that Turino's conceptualization of "cosmopolitanism" differs significantly from the standard definition of the term (see Turino 2000: 6–12).

7. Since the 1990s, Latin Americanists have produced numerous studies on musical folklorization (e.g., Turino 1993; Sheehy 1997; Scruggs 1998; Rockefeller 1999; Guss 2000; Mendoza 2000; Hagedorn 2001; Bigenho 2002; Ritter 2002; Feldman 2006; Hutchinson 2009; McDowell 2010; Hellier-Tinoco 2011; Rios 2012; Solomon 2014). Europeanists also have given considerable attention to this subject (e.g., Hafstein 2018), although many use an alternate term, "folklorism" (e.g., Olson 2004). It appears that scholars who study similar phenomena in other world areas infrequently conceptualize it as folklorization (exceptions include Fiol 2017).

8. In *Music as Social Life* (2008a), ethnomusicologist Thomas Turino lays out the characteristics of participatory and presentational music making: "Broadly defined, *participatory performance* is a special type of artistic practice in which there are no artist-audience distinctions, only participants and potential participants performing different roles, and the primary goal is to involve the maximum number of people in some performance role. *Presentational performance*, in contrast, refers to situations where one group of people, the artists, prepare and provide music for another group, the audience, who do not participate in making the music or dancing" (Turino 2008a, 26).

9. Eighteenth- and 19th-century European intellectuals first elaborated the concepts of "the folk" (or *volk*), "folklore," and "folk music." For an insightful discussion of the emergence of these concepts in the European setting, see Gelbart (2007).

10. Following Rockefeller (1999) and Solomon (2014), I reserve the term "folklore festival" for criollo- or mestizo-coordinated (and in most cases state-funded) music-dance events that the organizers explicitly frame as "folklore" exhibitions, while I use the designation "fiesta" to refer to traditional Andean indigenous community celebrations.

11. In 1901, though, Peruvian state representatives "ordered the lyrics [of the national anthem] to be changed . . . [to] something more elevating" (Earle 2007, 74). The new text, by the poet José Santos Chocano, no longer mentions the Inca Empire (Earle 2007, 74).

12. In a rare departure from the 19th century La Paz elite's usual indifference toward pre-Columbian civilizations, in the 1840s Bolivian state officials established a small museum to house artifacts collected from the ruins of Tiwanaku (Qayum 2011, 165).

13. Twenty-one years after the founding of the Republic of Bolivia, indigenous people represented about 80% of the population, according to the 1846 census (Larson 2004, 204).

14. Since at least the mid-20th century, Bolivian musicians typically have accented the "*and* of 2" and "3" when they perform the cueca, if the genre is counted in $\frac{3}{4}$ meter (rather than $\frac{6}{8}$). For a bailecito, the stressed beats fall on the "2" and "3" (also in $\frac{3}{4}$ meter). Scholars have yet to determine when these practices became standardized in Bolivia.

15. The terms "yaraví" and "triste" refer to the same genre. Some scholars, though, treat the yaraví and triste as distinct albeit related musical forms (e.g., Cárdenas 2015).

Foundations of the Bolivian Folkloric Music Movement

MUSICAL DIMENSIONS OF INDIGENISMO

PERU AND MEXICO represented the vanguard of Latin American indigenismo when the two countries commemorated their first centennials of political independence in 1921.[1] In Lima, Peruvian state authorities had recently unveiled a statue of the mythical founder of the Incan royal family, Emperor Manco Capac. The legendary pre-Columbian ruler also served as the inspiration for the picturesque "Manco Capac float" that ambled through downtown Lima during the centennial events, and in which a group of "individuals dressed as Incas posed against an Inca-style archway" (see Earle 2007, 193–94). In Mexico City, meanwhile, a re-enactment of an Aztec ceremonial rite, devoted to the goddess Xochitlquetzalli (the patroness of artists) and complete with the vivid spectacle of a simulated human sacrifice, represented one of the principal attractions at Mexico's 1921 centennial (Gonzales 2009, 260).

That likenesses of pre-Columbian "Indians" had pride of place in Peru and Mexico's national remembrances is as would have been expected. The leading indigenista figures of both countries, like their counterparts elsewhere in Latin America, preferred to extol indigenous societies of the distant past over those of the present, thereby minimizing the chance that criollo-mestizo indigenista activities would empower indigenous communities, a cultural appropriation strategy with roots in 19th-century Latin American elite nationalism (Earle 2007). Yet as the 20th century advanced, Mexican and Peruvian indigenistas selectively valorized the present-day cultural expressions of indigenous people (De la Cadena 2000; Earle 2007, 184–212; Mendoza 2008). Mexico's 1921 centennial reveals this emergent trend, because two of the most

Panpipes & Ponchos. Fernando Rios, Oxford University Press (2020). © Oxford University Press.
DOI: 10.1093/oso/9780190692278.001.0001.

attended events in Mexico City, the Exposición de Artes Populares (Exhibition of Popular Arts) and Noche Mexicana (Mexican Night), showcased actual indigenous musicians and dancers (López 2006; Gonzales 2009, 262–64; Hellier-Tinoco 2011, 65–67).

Four years later in La Paz city, Bolivians observed the hundred-year anniversary of the birth of their republic, but in striking contrast to the nativist tone of the commemorations in Mexico and Peru, Bolivia's official 1925 celebration was almost entirely devoid of expositions and performances that could be labeled as indigenista.[2] President Bautista Saavedra, then in the final months of his term (1921–1925), used the occasion to disseminate his vision of a modern Bolivia, one in which there was little place for indigenismo and especially indigenous people (Cristelli 2004). Indeed, the regime went to great lengths to ensure that indigenous music-dance styles, and even typically dressed indigenous people themselves, would be nowhere to be found in the city's downtown when the centennial events took place there. As historian Luis Sierra (2013) documents, the Saavedra administration "dusted off and reemployed local nineteenth-century laws" (Sierra 2013, 69) to craft the illusion, chiefly for the foreign visitors who were in town for the centennial (Albó and Preiswerk 1986, 29), that the central district of La Paz represented a "white" space that was free of "Indians" (Sierra 2013, 57–59, 68–70).

The musical offerings that animated the proceedings in La Paz city aligned with Saavedra's Eurocentric criollo nationalism. Orchestral and brass band renditions of the Bolivian National Anthem punctuated state ceremonies, while the concerts that formed part of the official festivities presented solo and ensemble performances of the classic works of Beethoven, Schumann, Schubert, Chopin, Liszt, Verdi, and other famed European art-classical composers (Crónica del Primer Centenario de la República, 1825–1925, Bolivia 1926, 87, 89; MacLean y Esteros 1926, 113, 193–95, 213). It fell to a visiting Peruvian dancer, Elena Graña Garland, to interject some indigenista entertainment into the commemorative activities. At a show staged at La Paz city's International Exposition, Graña Garland interpreted "La Danza del la Honda" (Dance of the sling)—supposedly an "Incan dance," reprising the performance that she had given of this dance number a few years earlier in Lima for Peru's centennial events (MacLean y Esteros 1926, 206).

Twenty-three years after Bolivia's 1925 centennial, urban La Paz hosted another lavish commemoration, this time to honor the city's 400th anniversary. But, in a clear departure from the 1925 event, the 1948 celebration included a "folklore" festival that was wholly devoted to Andean indigenous music-dance performances, the Concurso Folklórico Indígena del Departamento (El Diario [The daily, a La Paz newspaper, hereafter ED], Nov. 24, 1948). The audience who attended the Concurso witnessed a diversity of tropa (indigenous wind consort) traditions, from relatively well-known ones, including the panpipe style of Los Sikuris de Italaque, to those that not even Bolivia's foremost scholars of indigenous music knew existed, such as Kantus de Charazani.

As the 1948 Concurso Folklórico Indígena del Departamento's inclusion in La Paz's 400-year anniversary celebration suggests, mainstream paceño criollo-mestizo views about the cultural value and meanings of the La Paz region's Andean indigenous music-dance practices had undergone a significant transformation in the twenty-three years following the 1925 centennial. This chapter elucidates this major shift, by exploring key developments in the paceño indigenista musical scene that transpired in the period from the 1920s to 1940s.[3] Chapter 3 complements this line of investigation, with extended treatments of the activities of La Paz estudiantinas and superstar female vocal duos in roughly the same era.

Throughout Latin America, elite and middle-class interest in regionally distinctive music-dance expressions reached new heights in the early decades of the 20th century, as part of a quest among a varied cast of politicians, writers, and artists for local traditions that unmistakably demonstrated the nation's cultural uniqueness. Indigenismo represented a manifestation of this phenomenon. The Bolivian variant of this movement took inspiration from indigenista currents radiating from other Latin American countries, including Mexico and Argentina, but above all else from Peru. As this chapter reveals, Peruvian indigenista musicians, scholars, and "Inca Theater" troupes regularly visited La Paz from the 1910s to 1940s, and greatly influenced the local indigenista musical scene during this critical period in its development.

Bolivian indigenismo articulated in various ways with Bolivian state agendas, including criollo politicians' mounting use of nationalist rhetoric and gestures to expand their popularity among non-elite sectors. On a number of occasions, moreover, political regimes provided financial and logistical assistance for paceño indigenista artistic endeavors. No single party or administration guided the development of the Bolivian indigenista movement to a significant degree, however, unlike what occurred in the better-known cases of Peru and Mexico (Gotkowitz 2011, 19; Qayum 2011, 161). This type of scenario would not have been possible, anyway. Bolivia experienced numerous abrupt changes of government and concomitant shifts in official state ideology in the 1930s and 1940s, the very period when indigenismo reached its consolidation in La Paz city. Yet Bolivian state sponsorship of indigenista music-dance events remained relatively consistent, whether the ruling party or regime branded itself as leftist-populist, as was true of the Toro-Busch "military socialist" administration (1936–1939) and RADEPA-MNR coalition government (1943–1946), or alternately as reactionary-conservative, such as the regimes of General Enrique Peñaranda (1940–1943) and Dr. Enrique Hertzog (1947–1949). In this volatile period of Bolivian political history, the support that state-affiliated agencies conferred to La Paz criollo-mestizo musical activities of an indigenista orientation therefore represents a rare point of continuity.

THE EMERGENCE OF MUSICAL INDIGENISMO IN LA PAZ

In 1899, the La Paz–based Liberal Party and its Andean indigenous allies ousted from power the Sucre-centered Conservatives (who had ruled since 1884), after emerging triumphant on the battle front in the Civil War (also called the Federal War). Liberal

Party–led regimes would govern the country for the next twenty-one years (1899–1920). It was in this period that La Paz city definitively replaced Sucre (the capital of the departamento of Chuquisaca) as Bolivia's seat of government or acting national capital, and shed its former status as a "large village" (Sanjinés 2004, 32). The era of Liberal rule also saw the rise of a cohort of urban La Paz–based criollo-mestizo writers, scholars, and artists who increasingly made the case that all Bolivians should regard the indigenous traditions and legacies of the La Paz region's Aymara population as characteristic expressions of national culture (Qayum 2002, 2011).

The Liberal governments' shockingly hostile actions toward the indigenous troops who had fought alongside them in the conflict greatly complicated the efforts of La Paz's pioneer indigenistas. Once the Civil War had concluded, the Liberals made it clear that they would be terminating their cross-ethnic political coalition, by placing under arrest hundreds of the party's wartime comrades among the rural indigenous sector, most of whom hailed from Aymara-speaking districts in the departamento of La Paz. The principal commander of the indigenous armies, Pablo Zárate Willca, along with approximately 289 additional Aymara veterans of the Civil War, suffered the indignity of a show trial that "incubated multiple racist theories explaining the biological and social origins of Indian inferiority" before being executed by the Bolivian state (Larson 2004, 239). To further discredit their former allies, the Liberals fueled the resurgence of criollo-mestizo stereotypes about the purportedly "bloodthirsty nature" of Aymara Indians and their irrational desire to exterminate "the white race" (Demelas 1981, 70–76; Kuenzli 2010, 254).

The early figures of Bolivian indigenismo undoubtedly faced a delicate balancing act in the country's new power center of urban La Paz. At first, they focused their energies on praising the Tiwanaku civilization, which they portrayed as vastly superior to contemporary Andean indigenous societies (Qayum 2002, 2011). Some of these paceño indigenistas, as well as foreign writers, even dismissed the idea that the pre-Columbian ancestors of Bolivia's present-day Aymara population had been responsible for building the Tiwanaku ruins, and instead credited distant and long-vanished "white" civilizations, as far-fetched as Atlantis (Gildner 2013).

Also to circumvent the heated debates brewing in elite and middle-class society over the supposedly inferior cultural level and evolutionary stage of the Aymara, La Paz's indigenistas selected the Incas to serve as their movement's "preferred Indian" image (Kuenzli 2013). That the Incas spoke Quechua, not Aymara, and hailed from Peru's Cuzco area made it possible for Bolivians to exalt this type of "Andean Indian" without eliciting major controversy or moral panics in the Liberal period (Kuenzli 2013). It was hardly an original strategy. After all, Peruvian indigenistas had long made the "cult of the Incas" a centerpiece of their movement (see De la Cadena 2000; Mendoza 2008).

Given the Bolivian indigenista movement's fascination with the Inca Empire, Peruvian indigenistas whose cultural productions made extensive use of Incan-esque imagery could expect a favorable reception in La Paz. Daniel Alomía Robles was among the first to experience this reaction. Author of the music featured in the Peruvian *zarzuela*, or Spanish-language operetta, "El Cóndor Pasa" (premiered in Lima in 1913)—whose *kashua* movement would form the basis of the Andean conjunto staple piece bearing the same name (Chapter 7)—he traveled to La Paz city in 1915 to conduct excerpts from his acclaimed "Inca opera" *Illa Cari* (Quechua for "God of lightning"). Alomía Robles also presented his orchestral arrangements of the yaraví "Manchaypuito"[4] and an unidentified "Bolivian air," along with other indigenista numbers (Rossells 1996, 95–96). Paceño music critics raved over his artistry, while the exclusive Club de La Paz organized an elite society gala for him, using the occasion to bestow Alomía Robles with a medal of appreciation "for having valorized the cultivation of autochthonous music" (Rossells 1996, 96). During his stay, Alomía Robles also gave a lecture, in which he argued that Incan music was fundamentally pentatonic (Wahren 2014, 71), echoing an erroneous belief that Peruvian and foreign researchers held at the time (see Romero 2016, 81–82, 88–89, 91). The presentation nevertheless fired up the imagination of the new director of the National Conservatory of Music, Antonio González Bravo, who would become one of Bolivia's most prominent scholars in the field of Andean music research (as discussed later in this chapter).

In the next ten years, Peruvian "Inca theater" companies regularly treated paceño audiences to elaborately mounted productions that invariably featured music and dance sketches. In 1917 alone, three of these troupes graced the city's principal stages (Itier 2000, 49, 52–53), indicating that there was considerable demand for this type of entertainment in elite and middle-class paceño society. This popularity does not mean, however, that a significant proportion of this sector had yet warmed to the idea that the actual musical traditions of the La Paz region's highland indigenous inhabitants had artistic merit. The following year, in fact, the Municipality of La Paz would pass a law that regulated and taxed the local Aymara population's use of traditional masks and associated regalia in celebratory occasions, to dissuade indigenous people from performing their music-dance expressions within the city limits (Sierra 2013, 48).

The Compañía Dramática Incaica Cuzco was the first of the three Peruvian "Inca theater" companies to visit La Paz city in 1917. In January the troupe, led by Luis Ochoa, interpreted Peru's best-known theatrical work of the indigenista variety, *Ollantay*, at its La Paz concert.[5] A critic for the newspaper *El Siglo* (The century) characterized the performance as "a colossal success . . . worthy of headlining the program in any theater in the Americas" (quoted in Itier 2000, 49). Five months later, Calixto Pacheco's Compañía Lírica Incaica Ccorillacta ("Ccorillacta" is Quechua for "Hometown of gold"), which also was from Cuzco, stopped in La Paz.[6] The ensemble recalled the glories of the Incan epoch with *Yawarwaqaq* (Quechua for "The one who cries blood"), a vividly titled production that was set to the music of Peruvian composer Manuel Monet. Before leaving La Paz city, the Compañía Lírica Incaica Ccorillacta unveiled another work, *Wayna Qhapaq* (Itier 2000, 52–53). It told the story of the Incan Emperor of the same name (also spelled Huayna Capac, and many other ways), whose untimely death, around 1525, occurred on the eve of Francisco Pizarro's initial campaigns in the Andean region—which would culminate with the Spanish *conquistador*'s capture and execution of the last sovereign ruler of the Inca Empire, Wayna Qhapaq's son, Atahualpa.

In 1923, one of Latin America's most celebrated indigenistas, the Peruvian writer, historian, and choreographer Luis E. Valcárcel, brought to La Paz his forty-seven-member Cuzco folklore troupe, the Misión Peruana de Arte Incaico. At this moment in the group's trajectory, its musical repertoire ranged from "more harmonized and orchestrated compositions" such as the already classic Peruvian indigenista works "Himno del Sol" (Hymn to the sun; arranged by Daniel Alomía Robles) and "Ollantay" (Manuel Monet's version) (Mendoza 2008, 25), to harmonically sparse arrangements of Andean indigenous tunes that the members of the troupe realized on the kena, charango, bombo, and other typical instruments of the Central and Southern Andean regions (Valcárcel 1981, 218–19; Mendoza 2008, 25–34).

The Misión Peruana de Arte Incaico frequently depicted contemporary Andean indigenous musical expressions as if they represented Incan survivals (see Mendoza 2008, 17–34). Peruvian as well as Bolivian indigenistas often conflated the two. This misconception stemmed from their conviction, derived from social evolutionism, that indigenous musical practices had largely remained static since the pre-Columbian age. The scarcity of information about Incan music then available to scholars and the broader public, beyond the tidbits found in the 16th- and 17th-century writings of Garcilaso de la Vega, Felipe Guamán Poma de Ayala, and other Spanish chroniclers of the early colonial period (Romero 2016, 76–79), also partially accounts for the indigenista tendency to confuse Andean indigenous music of the distant past with that of the present day.[7]

Poetry recitations represented an additional medium through which the members of Valcárcel's ensemble creatively evoked the times of the Incas. At the troupe's recitals in La Paz, which took place at the Municipal and Princesa Theaters, Luis Ochoa (formerly of Compañia Dramática Incaica Cuzco) declaimed Quechua poems, while outfitted as Inca nobility. Not content to just witness the spectacle, several Bolivian musicians and poets joined forces on the stage with the Misión Peruana de Arte Incaico, entertaining the upper crust of paceño society in attendance (Itier 2000, 75–76).

Even President Bautista Saavedra (term in office: 1921–1925) took the time to catch the shows (Valcárcel 1981, 218–19). The leader of the Republican Party—whose ideology differed minimally from that of the Liberals (Klein 1969; 64–71), Saavedra had recently sanctioned "brutal anti-Indian repression" to quell strikes and other indigenous mobilizations in rural areas (Gotkowitz 2007, 58). The most infamous example of this policy was the Bolivian military's 1921 massacre of Aymara indigenous people in the La Paz town of Jesús de Machaca (Choque 1986). As with the case in Peru (see De la Cadena 2000), criollo-mestizo appreciation of indigenista cultural productions and discrimination against indigenous people often coexisted, disturbingly, among the same individuals in Bolivia. President Saavedra, for one, apparently enjoyed the concert that the Misión Peruana de Arte Incaico offered in La Paz, so much so that he made a donation to the troupe to help defray its travel expenses to Buenos Aires (Valcárcel 1981, 218–19).

Under the sway of Peruvian indigenismo, in the early 1920s Bolivian criollo-mestizo musicians increasingly tried their hand at authoring indigenous-themed works. Biographical sketches of a few notable paceño artists who formed part of this emergent trend appear in J. Ricardo Alarcón's edited volume *Bolivia en el Primer Centenario de Su Independencia* (1925), which was issued in the run-up to the national centennial. Eduardo Calderón Lugones and Manuel Norberto Luna figure among those listed. A professor at the National Conservatory of Music, Calderón Lugones established his name as an artist through his virtuosic violin playing, and secondarily via his musical creations. By 1925, Calderón Lugones had begun his forays into indigenista composition, as his oeuvre included violin works with "Aymara motives" (Alarcón 1925, 376). For Manuel Norberto Luna, meanwhile, the piece "Choqueyapu," which he termed an "indigenous *pasacalle*,"[8] represented his main contribution to musical indigenismo. Named after the river that then traversed (and nowadays crosses under) La Paz city, "Choqueyapu" earned Luna a degree of local fame, although his reputation as a composer was based primarily on his religious works, such as masses (Alarcón 1925, 391).

The 1920 Misión de Arte y Propaganda Nacional Boliviana (Mission of Bolivian National Art and Propaganda), an early instance of Bolivian state-sponsored folklorization that unambiguously framed Andean indigenous music as a defining component of national music (Rossells 1996, 108–9), provides additional evidence that indigenista musical activities were gaining favor in Bolivia. Spearheaded by Raúl Jaimes Freyre (brother of the celebrated modernist writer Ricardo Jaimes Freyre), in his capacity as Director de Conferencias y Propaganda Industrial for the Liberal Party regime of José Gutiérrez Guerra (term in office: 1917–1920), the 1920 Misión toured the major cities of Bolivia, with the purpose of fostering national sentiment. Sucre's Belisario Zárate and Potosí's Simeón Roncal, along with other criollo-mestizo musicians similarly acclaimed as "specialists in the interpretation of genuinely national airs," formed part of the entourage (Rossells 1996, 108). Key to the artists' credentials was their avid cultivation of "Incan music," a repertoire that they ostensibly had collected "in the countryside" after hearing Andean indigenous musical ensembles perform traditional numbers (Rossells 1996, 108).

Film is another area of cultural production in which Bolivian artists explored indigenista subject matter in the 1920s. The country's first feature film, *Corazón Aymara* (Aymara heart/soul), exemplifies this current. Released in July 1925—a few weeks before the Saavedra government would stage the national centennial commemoration—*Corazón Aymara* depicts the struggles of a fictional indigenous woman named Lurpila, as a window into the plight of the Aymara population. The film earned positive reviews from critics in the major La Paz newspapers, indicating that an influential sector of paceño society appreciated cultural productions that sought to portray the lives of rural indigenous people (see Himpele 2008, 100–101, 104–6).

To animate this silent movie, Adrián Patiño Carpio composed and/or arranged "passages of indigenous music"; a pianist performed these pieces at the film's screenings in La Paz (Susz 1990, 40–41).[9] Patiño Carpio was a well-known paceño brass band director and prolific composer, who in his career would author numerous *fox incaicos*, or Incan foxtrots (Rojas Rojas 1989, 51–54). Fusing stylistic features of the US foxtrot with the imagery of indigenismo (primarily in the titles of pieces), the Incan foxtrot, a genre of Peruvian origin (Lloréns Amico 1983, 97–116), represented a mainstay for La Paz criollo-mestizo ensembles in the 1920s and 1930s, particularly for estudiantinas (Chapter 3) and brass bands. The genre's local popularity thus further substantiates Peruvian indigenismo's influence in this period on Bolivian musicians. Patiño Carpio's musical contributions to *Corazón Aymara*, meanwhile, probably include Incan foxtrots, because by 1920 he had turned his attention to the genre (see Cárdenas 1986, 57–58).

Also in 1925, José María Velasco Maidana, then a budding art-classical musician (profiled later in this chapter), was primed for the La Paz debut of his film *La Profecia del Lago* (The prophecy of the lake), which "tells of an elite woman in La Paz who falls in love with an Indian domestic servant (*pongo*) on her hacienda" (Himpele 2008, 99). To the great dismay of Velasco Maidana, Saavedra regime officials deemed *La Profecia del Lago*'s treatment of interethnic romance to be so inflammatory that they prevented its screening in La Paz theaters. The authorities even went so far as to order Velasco Maidana to "surrender the film," so that they could burn it (Himpele 2008, 99–100).

Despite the absence of Bolivian indigenista artistic creations at the official events of the national centennial (as noted in the opening pages of this chapter), paceño interest in indigenismo clearly was on the upswing by 1925. The Bolivian state's banning of Velasco Maidana's *La Profecia del Lago*, though, indicates that in socially conservative elite sectors it was still strongly believed that the ethnicized social hierarchy should remain intact. Seen in this light, the Saavedra government's successful efforts at limiting the presence of typically dressed Andean indigenous people at the official centennial events constitute an analogous, reactionary elite attempt to uphold traditional sociocultural boundaries, at a time when Bolivian and Peruvian indigenista productions valorizing Andean indigenous cultural expressions potentially undermined the ideological basis of discriminatory criollo-mestizo attitudes toward rural indigenous people.

THE FIRST INDIANIST WEEK

Indigenista exhibitions became more frequent in urban La Paz by the end of the decade, largely through the efforts of the civic association Los Amigos de la Ciudad (Friends of the city). Organizing these events formed part of the group's agenda of fortifying La Paz's supremacy among Bolivia's cities (Wahren 2014). Predominantly of elite membership, Los Amigos de la Ciudad was founded in 1916, but as Grupo

Cívico Tahuantinsuyu. The organization's original name offers another example of Bolivian indigenismo's initial Inca-centrism; "Tahuantinsuyu" (Quechua for "The four regions") is the term that the Incas had used to refer to their empire. In 1928, Grupo Cívico Tahuantinsuyu rebranded itself as "Los Amigos de la Ciudad," and for the next six years, the association maintained close ties with the Republican Party (Wahren 2014, 92–93), which dominated the Bolivian political system from 1926 to 1934 (Klein 1969, 64–199).

In 1929, 1930, and 1931, Los Amigos de la Ciudad took it upon themselves to coordinate the music and dance activities for Fiestas Julianas (July Festivities) (Wahren 2014, 83–88). Since the 1880s—when tensions between La Paz– and Sucre-based political parties had begun to escalate—Fiestas Julianas had been the principal time of year for large-scale cultural expositions of regionalist or nationalist orientation in the urban La Paz setting (Bridikhina, Vera Cossío, Rojas, Mamani Iñiguez, and et al. 2009). The holiday memorializes the ultimate sacrifice of La Paz's favorite son, the patriot Pedro Domingo Murillo, who died at the hands of royalist forces for his leadership role in the July 16 (1809) declaration of national independence (see Chapter 1).

Criollo, mestizo, and indigenous music-dance expressions animated the Fiestas Juliana celebrations of 1929, 1930, and 1931, with the events taking place at two venues, the Municipal Theater and Hipódromo Nacional (National Racetrack) (Wahren 2014, 84–88). Criollo and mestizo artists performed at both sites. Indigenous ensembles such as Los Sikuris de Italaque, in contrast, were restricted to the National Racetrack, whose location in the outskirts of the city placed it far away from the central district—still an unwelcome area of urban La Paz for Andean indigenous people. To avoid scandalizing socially conservative elite and middle-class paceños, a spokesperson for Los Amigos de la Ciudad assured them in the pages of *La Razón* that the indigenous musicians and dancers taking part in the festivities would not be displaying their traditions in the streets of the downtown (Wahren 2014, 85–86).

Five months after 1931's Fiestas Julianas, in the Christmas season, Los Amigos de la Ciudad staged Bolivia's first large-scale exhibition of indigenismo, a week-long event that the association designated, appropriately enough, the Semana Indianista (Indianist Week) (Wahren 2014, 92–109). The proceedings encompassed musical performances, visual art showings, conference presentations, radio broadcasts, and theater productions, along with day trips to the Warisata *escuela-ayllu* (a pioneering indigenous community school discussed later in this chapter) and Tiwanaku ruins. Forging "an authentic Bolivian culture with Amerindian roots" was the primary goal of the Semana Indianista, explained its organizer, Alberto de Villegas (Wahren 2014, 93).

Reflecting Los Amigos de la Ciudad's estimation of Peru's indigenista movement, the group invited Peruvian "artists of Indianist tendency" to participate in the Semana Indianista, by sending a message to that effect to the governors of Cuzco, Arequipa, and Puno (Wahren 2014, 106–7). The traveled Cuzco musician Pancho Gómez Negrón accepted the invitation. He performed at the closing concert of the Indianist Week, the Velada Indianista (Indianist Exhibition) held at the Municipal Theater. Donning

Andean indigenous-style garb, Gómez Negrón—whose charango skills earned him the nickname of *saqra charango*, or "devil charango," in Peru (Mendoza 2008, 96, 100–104)—wowed the spectators in La Paz with his musical virtuosity and interpretive flair on the charango, guitar, and kena (*La Razón*, Jan. 5, 1932; *ED*, Jan. 5, 1932).[10]

Gómez Negrón's set was far from being the lone segment in the concert that evinced the influence of Peruvian indigenismo. For the opening selection, paceño folklorist Dr. Luciano N. Bustíos's mixed-gender choir, Nina Inti, whose name referenced the Incas' primary devotion to the Inti (Sun) deity, sang a Peruvian indigenista staple that evoked the same image, Alomía Robles's "Himno del Sol" (Hymn to the sun), in an arrangement by Sucre art-classical musician Manuel José Benavente.[11] Later in the program, Bolivian pianist Cira Villalobos Dupleich displayed her musicianship with a solo fantasia named after Cuzco's Sun Festival, "Inti Raymi," while at another point in the program, Bolivian singer Berta Elías interpreted "Noche de Luna en Cuzco" (Moonlit night in Cuzco) (*La Razón*, Jan. 5, 1932; *ED*, Jan. 5, 1932). Even an indigenous *cuzqueña* (woman from Cuzco), or actually a paceña dressed as one, took part in the event, in the dance-fashion segment of the Velada Indianista. Antonio González Bravo choreographed this portion of the program, in which young women of elite socioeconomic background masqueraded as indigenous Andean peasants (*La Razón*, Jan. 5, 1932; *ED*, Jan. 5, 1932).

Indigenous people themselves, though, were not present at the Velada Indianista, either as performers or audience members, no doubt because of its setting in the sacrosanct space of the Municipal Theater. Yet the proceedings of the Semana Indianista did not completely exclude Andean indigenous musicians. Indigenous schoolchildren from the La Paz town of Caquiaviri performed the choral work "Cóndor Mallku" ("Indigenous leader" in Aymara and Quechua) and other criollo-mestizo indigenista vocal numbers on the live program that Radio Nacional—then Bolivia's sole radio station (founded in 1928)—transmitted as part of the Indianist Week (Stefanoni 2012, 59). And on another Radio Nacional broadcast that aired this week, a panpipe tropa from Ch'ijini, a working-class La Paz neighborhood then inhabited mainly by indigenous people and cholos, played "Aymara music" (Stefanoni 2012, 59).[12] It was at the events staged in Tiwanaku, which for many attendees represented the highlight of the Semana Indianista, that indigenous people and traditional indigenous expressive practices had the most prominent as well as visible role. While wearing "native regalia," Andean tropas of assorted varieties performed typical genres for those who made the trek to the Tiwanaku ruins (Wahren 2014, 99).

In La Paz's estudiantina scene, by this time many groups no longer focused on European musical works (as they had in prior decades), and instead favored indigenista repertoire (Chapter 3). Filarmónica 1° de Mayo (May 1st philharmonic) represented this artistic current at the Semana Indianista's inaugural concert. In its set, the ensemble interpreted "arrangements of indigenous melodies" (Wahren 2014, 103), including one of "Irpastay" (Stefanoni 2012, 58–59), a future folkloric classic (also spelled "Hirpastay") that is purportedly based on the music of an Aymara courtship ritual bearing the same name. The printed program does not describe

Filarmónica 1° de Mayo's instrumentation. It is likely, though, that a charango player, or perhaps even several, formed part of the group. Paceño estudiantinas of the day often included charanguistas (as did Peruvian estudiantinas), as a way of localizing their traditional ensemble lineups of European plucked string instruments (i.e., mandolins, guitars, *laúdes* [the Spanish term for lutes], and bandurrias).

A charango soloist, Mauro Núñez, performed on the 1931 Radio Nacional show in which the Ch'ijini panpipe tropa presented its numbers (Stefanoni 2012, 59). From the Chuquisaca town of Villa Serrano, Núñez had been living in La Paz city since 1927 (Torres 2006, 186). He was a relatively unknown folklore artist in this period, but he would go on to become one of Bolivia's most acclaimed charango virtuosos amid the 1960s folklore boom, after having spent two and a half decades of his life outside of the country, mainly in the capitals of Peru and Argentina (Chapters 3 and 7). On the 1931 Radio Nacional program, Núñez offered the station's listeners a taste of the Andean indigenous musical expressions practiced in the Chuquisaca region, by recreating them in stylized form with the charango, as well as other traditional instruments (Stefanoni 2012, 59).

The proceedings of the Indianist Week reveal that, by 1931, the musical dimensions of the paceño indigenista scene exhibited many of the characteristics that would define Bolivia's folkloric music movement from the 1960s onward. Given the criollo-mestizo sector's long-standing disparagement of, and continued discrimination against, indigenous people, however, only a small part of urban La Paz's criollo-mestizo population in all likelihood considered folkloric enactments of Andean indigenous music to represent *the* paramount forms of Bolivian "national music" in the early 1930s. As is the case around the world, individuals and groups regularly attach new meanings to local musical practices (e.g., from "their" to "our" musical traditions), but the older associations usually linger on. For a generation of Bolivians, the Chaco War experience fostered a heightened sense of nationalism, which had important ramifications for the field of national music.

THE CHACO WAR YEARS, AND SECOND INDIANIST WEEK

Six months after the 1st Indianist Week, President Daniel Salamanca (term in office: 1931–1934) used the recent skirmishes between Bolivian and Paraguayan troops stationed in the desolate and sparsely populated Chaco region as a pretense to plunge Bolivia into the Chaco War (1932–1935). Salamanca had become exasperated by his Republican administration's lack of notable political successes on the domestic front, and arrived at the deluded conclusion that "all his personal glory and promise of future greatness could at last find unfettered expression" in a war effort (Klein 1969, 152). The "deadliest interstate conflict in twentieth-century Latin America" (Shesko 2015, 301), the Chaco War set into motion a number of political changes in Bolivia, from Salamanca's ouster in 1934, to the post-1936 delegitimization of the

Liberal and Republican parties, to the rise of a new cohort of political actors who became known as the Chaco Generation.[13]

Bolivia obtained its first state-operated radio station, Radio Illimani of La Paz, less than a year into the Chaco War, in 1933. Named after the spectacular, snow-peaked mountain overlooking the city, the station was equipped with a powerful signal, so that the broadcasts could reach listeners countrywide and thereby effectively bolster Bolivian patriotism, while at the same time thwart the rival media campaign of Paraguayan radio stations (De la Quintana and Duchén 1986, 11–12). Radio Illimani's musical programming in the war years contributed to the Bolivian state's efforts to intensify national consciousness. Alongside government propaganda about the Chaco conflict, the station transmitted recordings and live performances of Bolivian indigenista art-classical compositions (mainly orchestral and piano pieces) and traditional Andean criollo-mestizo music-dance genres (e.g., huayño, cueca, bailecito, yaraví), which solidified the national associations of these musical expressions for the Bolivian public (Cárdenas 1986, 50, 66–67; De la Quintana and Duchén 1986, 40–43; Fernández Terán 2002, 235–36).[14]

José Salmón Ballivián's *Suite Aymara*, one of Bolivia's most celebrated art-classical music compositions (Rivera de Stahlie 1995, 73–76; Bigenho 2002, 114–21), figures among the indigenista works that Radio Illimani broadcast on a regular basis during the Chaco War, along with Belisario Zárate's *Serenata Campestre–Tres Motivos Indianistas* (Countryside serenade–Three Indianist motives), Eduardo Calderón Lugones's *Canción de la Puna* (Song of the mountain), and Jorge Parra's *Plegaria al Sol* (Prayer to the sun) (see Cárdenas 1986). *Suite Aymara* consists of three movements: "Danza Guerrera" (War dance), "Danza Religiosa" (Religious dance), "Auki Auki"[15] ("The old men" in Aymara), and "Cuando Florecen las Habas" (When the beans flower). As the title *Suite Aymara* suggests, by the early 1930s Bolivian art-classical composers of indigenista orientation drew inspiration from Aymara cultural expressions of the La Paz region, although the Incas of Cuzco continued to represent popular subject matter in their musical works.

According to Salmón Ballivián (see Rivera de Stahlie 1995, 74), *Suite Aymara* "reconstructs the pre-Hispanic social world of the Andean region." Yet Bolivian and Peruvian indigenistas of the early-to-mid 20th century knew exceedingly little about pre-Columbian Andean music, because of the lack of reliable historical sources, as previously noted. Salmón Ballivián's solution to this predicament? Similar to many of his Latin American contemporaries in the field of "nationalist" art-classical music (see Béhague 2006), he simply collected tunes from present-day indigenous ensembles, and used them as motives in his own works (Rivera de Stahlie 1995, 74).[16]

Suite Aymara initially attained lauded status in the Chaco War years. In 1933, as a result of a Radio Illimani initiative, the United States' National Broadcasting Company (NBC) aired an orchestral rendition of the work (De la Quintana and Duchén 1986, 43), which conferred it unprecedented international exposure for a Bolivian musical composition of any kind. The NBC transmission helped canonize *Suite Aymara*, as did Salmón Ballivián's upper-class background and personal connections.[17] From this point onward, *Suite Aymara* would represent an obligatory "national" number for Bolivian symphony orchestras. It would also find its way into the repertoire of La Paz estudiantinas such as Filarmónica 1° de Mayo (Chapter 3). As for Salmón Ballivián, he would play an important role in the Bolivian folkloric music movement during the 1940s, through his service on folklore festival committees (as discussed in a later section) and involvement in other high-profile indigenista initiatives, such as the creation of the Orquesta Típica La Paz (Chapter 3).

Two years after NBC's transmission of *Suite Aymara*, the Chaco War concluded, with the Paraguayan forces declaring victory. On the Bolivian side, 50,000 to 60,000 troops perished in the conflict, almost one of every four combatants, with a large proportion dying from non-combat-related causes, especially dehydration, starvation, and disease (Shesko 2015, 304). Bolivia's number of casualties in the war, relative to the total population, was therefore comparable to the massive fatalities that many European countries had suffered during World War I (Klein 1992, 194). Bolivia's territorial losses also were stark. Once the final treaty had been signed in 1938, Bolivia possessed "far less land [in the eastern lowlands] than it had held before its leaders provoked the war," while Paraguay ended up with "three-quarters of the Chaco" region (Shesko 2015, 303).

A devastating and humiliating experience, Bolivia's Chaco War defeat to Paraguay provoked widespread outrage over the conduct of the country's political leaders, and soul searching about the nation's future. It also prompted criollo-mestizo intellectuals, novelists, artists, and politicians to revisit and debate the issues surrounding the so-called Indian problem (see Salmón 1997; Bigenho 2002, 25–28, 130; Sanjinés 2004, 107–36), in large part because Andean indigenous people "constituted the largest single group in Bolivia's army" (Shesko 2015, 307).[18] Decades earlier, Peru's defeat to Chile in the Pacific War (1879–1883) had similarly revived local interest in addressing its "Indian problem" and given a major boost to Peruvian indigenismo (De la Cadena 2000).[19]

Six months into the post–Chaco War era, in January 1936, Los Amigos de la Ciudad put on a second Semana Indianista. Its raison d'être was the same as that for the first edition, because the 1936 event's organizers intended to display "the enormous richness of the vernacular themes upon which will be based the national art of the future" (*ED*, Jan. 5, 1936). This nationalist endeavor obtained the support of the Liberal Party administration of President José Tejada Sorzano (term in office: November 1934–May 1936). The regime allowed Los Amigos de la Ciudad to use the Army Officers' Social Club for several of the event's principal attractions, such as the art exhibitions (for painting, sculpture, and decorative art), conference lectures, and book displays. Musical performances also took place at this state-owned space as part of the Semana Indianista (*ED*, Jan. 6, 1936).

The major paceño newspapers and radio stations gave ample coverage to the proceedings, informing Bolivians across the country about the happenings. In addition,

Radio Illimani and Radio Nacional broadcast "native music" programs to coincide with the Indianist Week (*ED*, Jan. 5 and 13, 1936), while *El Diario* published a string of indigenista-themed articles (e.g., "Our Duty to the Indian"), including an essay by Peruvian writer Belisario Cano on Aymara history (*ED*, Jan. 5, 1936). As had been the case at the 1st Semana Indianista, the 1936 iteration culminated with a Municipal Theater recital featuring choral works, vocal solos and duets, estudiantina pieces, dance sketches, and poetry readings, as well as a fashion show in which "distinguished society ladies" modeled the "typical" outfits of rural highland indigenous people (*ED*, Jan. 11, 1936).

The 2nd Semana Indianista thus greatly resembled its antecedent. References to the Incas still abounded in the recital programs, and also in the names of some of the acts, such as charango soloist Manco Kapaj, Trío Yupanqui, and estudiantina Lira Incaica. Led by Alberto Ruiz Lavadenz (profiled in Chapter 3), Lira Incaica interpreted his composition "Capricho Incaico" (Incan capriccio), and three pieces that he based on Andean indigenous tunes, "Huacacari" (Quechua for "Sacred plant"), "Motivo Vernacular" (Vernacular motif), and "Danza de Cullawas" (see *ED*, Jan. 11, 1936). For "Danza de Cullawas," Lira Incaica set aside their usual mandolins, guitars, bandurrias, and charangos for a tarka tropa and caja drums, to emulate the festive style of highland indigenous music making in the Carnival season (*ED*, Jan. 11, 1936).[20] It was apparently the sole criollo-mestizo musical number presented at the 2nd Indianist Week that attempted to enact the performance practices of Andean indigenous community ensembles. Rural indigenous musicians, meanwhile, played no part in any of the events.

Antonio González Bravo's musical arrangements and dance sketches comprised most of the program at the concert that closed the Second Indianist Week. The choir that performed at the recital, for instance, interpreted his settings of "Sikuri de Italaque No. 3" and *Dos Melodías de Italaque* (Two Italaque melodies), which incorporate panpipe tropa tunes that he had collected in the district surrounding the town of Italaque in La Paz's Camacho Province. As the next section details, by 1936 González Bravo was well on his way to becoming an advocate for "Los Sikuris de Italaque"—as the indigenous siku tradition of this region had long been known in criollo-mestizo circles.[21] González Bravo had also established himself by then as an authority on Andean indigenous music, a reputation that he would retain in the post-1952 era (Chapters 4 and 5). The following section introduces this key figure in La Paz's indigenista music scene, with special attention given to his involvement with one of Bolivia's most acclaimed and widely-recognized indigenous panpipe tropa expressions.

ANTONIO GONZÁLEZ BRAVO AND LOS SIKURIS DE ITALAQUE

Born in 1885 in the La Paz town of Laja, González Bravo descended from a *vecino* (criollo-mestizo town resident) family of Aymara *cacique*, or native lord, lineage (Paredes Candia 1967, 17, 56–57). In his youth, his family sent him to live in La Paz city for a proper formal education, as was customary for the children of vecinos. When he reached his late teens, González Bravo enrolled at the Universidad de San Andrés, and studied Western art-classical music at the nearby National Conservatory of Music. He assumed the directorship of the latter institution in 1915 and held this post for the next three years. He served a second term as head of the National Conservatory from 1922 to 1923, and a third stint from 1935 to 1942 (Alejo 1925, 360; *ED*, Sept. 30, 1945; Paredes Candia 1967, 24–26).

González Bravo was heavily involved in the indigenista movement by the early 1930s. He became a founding member of the Sociedad Arqueológica de Bolivia (Bolivian Society for Archeology) in 1930, along with the organizer of the 1st Indianist Week, Alberto de Villegas, and other indigenista figures (Browman 2007, 36). Three years later, González Bravo joined the teaching staff at the Warisata ayllu-school, which was known for its bold indigenista curriculum (discussed later in this chapter). It was also in the 1930s that González Bravo gained an international reputation as Bolivia's leading scholar of Andean indigenous music. Shortly after the 2nd Indianist Week, his article "Sicus" (alternate spelling for "sikus") appeared in the *Boletín Latino Americano de Música* (Latin American music bulletin) (González Bravo 1936), which at the time was considered one of South America's most respected music journals (see Romero 2016, 83–84). In the next couple of years, the Boletín printed two additional essays by González Bravo, "Kena, Pincollos[22] y Tarkas," and "Trompeta, Flauta Traversa, Tambor y Charango" (Trumpet, transverse flute, drum, and charango) (González Bravo 1937, 1938).

An avid, and apparently self-trained, researcher, González Bravo is often characterized as Bolivia's first ethnomusicologist (e.g., Céspedes 1984, 222; Auza León 1989, 47; Gobierno Municipal de la Ciudad de La Paz Oficialia Mayor de Cultura 1993, 19). In 1915, at the outset of his professional career, González Bravo attended a lecture that would make a major impression on him, one by Peru's Daniel Alomía Robles. As previously explained, Alomía Robles had traveled to La Paz that year, primarily to showcase his musical works. The (supposed) pentatonicism of Incan music was the subject of Alomía Robles' lecture (Wahren 2014, 71), unsurprisingly, given that this topic intrigued him (see Romero 2016, 81). Ten years later, González Bravo characterized Alomía Robles's findings on Incan music as a "great revelation," in his derivatively titled article "The Pentatonic Mode in National Music" (Wahren 2014, 71).[23]

González Bravo eventually made an excursion to Peru, in the late 1920s or early 1930s, where his itinerary included stops in Cuzco city and, in the departamento of Puno, the districts of Lampa and Santiago de Pupuja (González Bravo 1936, 255–56; 1938, 172; *ED*, Dec. 18, 1939; Paredes Candia 1967, 79). While in Puno, he might have heard about the novel indigenous ensemble Qhantati Ururi ("Dawning star" in Aymara).

Around 1929, in the Puno district of Conima, the vecino landowner and indigenista Natalio Calderón established Qhantati Ururi, whose performance practices differed greatly from those of traditional indigenous ensembles of the region (Turino 1993, 127–131). One of the most striking ways in which Calderón's vision for Qhantati

Ururi broke from local indigenous practice was his prioritization of sound quality (defined according to his cultural-outsider perspective as a mestizo) over the egalitarian Aymara ethos of maximizing musical participation. As the self-appointed director and president of Qhantati Ururi, Calderón also diverged from local indigenous custom by incorporating the "best" musicians from different ayllus into the group, adopting the commanding style of a musical conductor (rather than the indirect manner of a traditional *guía*, or guide), holding regular and mandatory rehearsals, giving the ensemble a non-ayllu name (i.e., Qhantati Ururi instead of, say, Sikuris de Ayllu Sulcata), and instituting a new harmonic siku tropa style consisting of nine voices in parallel thirds (local siku groups previously had performed solely in unison and parallel octaves). In the years of Calderón's leadership, the ensemble often performed for vecino audiences, mainly in Puno. In 1939, Qhantati Ururi marked a milestone in its trajectory, when the group traveled to the city of Lima for a state-funded folklore contest, the Fiesta de Amancaes (Turino 1993, 127–131).

Calderón's role in Qhantati Ururi might have inspired González Bravo to develop close ties with Los Sikuris de Italaque. Yet it is also possible that it was the other way around, and/or that Calderón and González Bravo mutually influenced each other. Whatever the case, in roughly the same period, the two vecino indigenistas became deeply involved with Aymara tropa traditions practiced in adjacent regions on the Peru-Bolivia border: Puno's Huancané province (which includes the district of Conima) and La Paz's Camacho province (which contains the town of Italaque and the surrounding area). For both individuals, moreover, the siku tropa represented their favored Andean rural indigenous ensemble format.

The departamentos of Puno and La Paz are home to a vast array of Andean indigenous wind-consort traditions, so it is worth considering why González Bravo and Calderón were so drawn to the siku tropa. Typically, indigenous musicians of the Southern Andes generate a lower tessitura (musical pitch range) and far less strident timbre when they perform on the siku (which is played with a hocketing technique), compared to the quality of sound they normally produce on other tropa wind instruments, that is, end-notched flutes (e.g., kenas, choquelas), duct-flutes (e.g., pinkillus, tarkas), and transverse flutes (known as flautas traversas, phalas, pífanos, pitus, and other names), as well as non-siku iterations of the Andean panpipe (e.g., the non-hocketed ayarachi).[24] Largely for aesthetic reasons, criollos and mestizos usually regard siku music as the most sonically pleasing (or least objectionable) form of indigenous tropa music. Turino's research on Peruvian music offers clear examples of this phenomenon (Turino 1993, 153–55).

A similar pattern holds true for Bolivia, as this book documents. An early example of this pro-siku bias appears in Rigoberto Paredes's 1913 essay "El Arte en la Altiplanicie" (Art in the altiplano), in which he states, "the music of siku ensembles is the best kind [of music] that indigenous people have, not only for its musical variety, but also for its harmonious execution" (Paredes 1913, 158). González Bravo, for his part, believed that the skills of indigenous siku makers partially accounted for the (supposed) superiority of siku music relative to other Andean tropa traditions. In the

1937 article "Kenas, Pincollos y Tarkas" (1937, 31), he claims that siku construction techniques had reached such a level of excellence among indigenous artisans in the highlands that improvements were unnecessary, whereas in his view, kena, pinkillu, and tarka makers still needed to "perfect" their craft.

Paredes singles out the abilities of Italaque siku musicians in "Art in the Altiplano," calling them "the best" players of the instrument (Paredes 1913, 158). He also remarks that Italaque siku tropas "do not restrict themselves to national airs, as the Indians possess a fine ear and true musical talent, they perform songs and foreign waltzes with much conviction" (Paredes 1913, 158). These comments, which Paredes first made in an 1898 publication (Paredes 1898, 34), constituted high praise for him. A prolific indigenista writer of vecino heritage who, like González Bravo, traced his ancestry to Aymara caciques (Kuenzli 2013, 79–83), Paredes in his writings seldom had anything positive to say about Andean indigenous music. That he nonetheless found Italaque sikuri music to be redeeming suggests that when ensembles of the region performed for criollo-mestizos, they may have modified their usual musical style to fit this audience's aesthetic preferences. Offering additional evidence of this practice is the repertoire of sikuri groups from Italaque, namely, its inclusion of "foreign waltzes" (Paredes 1913, 158). To my knowledge, traditional indigenous panpipe genres of the La Paz region rarely if ever adhere to simple-triple meter, that is, the characteristic meter of the waltz.

In 1906, another paceño writer and ethnologist, Fenelón Eguino, praised the siku tradition of Italaque. In a lecture on Andean indigenous music that he presented at the Bolivian consulate in Buenos Aires, Argentina, Eguino stated that Italaque musicians "enjoy the reputation of being excellent panpipe players" (Eguino 1906, 4). He also informed the public that in the past, Bolivian presidents such as Manuel Isidoro Belzú (term in office: 1848–1855) had celebrated birthdays and political anniversaries with Italaque siku tropa performances (Eguino 1906, 4–5). In 1885, the Santa Cruz newspaper *La Estrella del Oriente* (The star of the orient/east) printed an article that corroborates Eguino's assertion that Sikuris de Italaque ensembles were known to entertain presidents with panpipe music. A satirical piece, it mocks this tradition, no doubt reflecting the eastern lowland criollo sector's well-known resentment of the western highland region's political dominance nationally (*La Estrella del Oriente*, June 10, 1885).

Scholars have yet to publish detailed historical studies that illuminate the Italaque siku tradition's trajectory in criollo-mestizo circles in the 19th and early 20th centuries. It is evident, though, that by the early 1900s Italaque panpipe tropas possessed name recognition outside of their home province to a degree that was unusual at the time in Bolivia for Andean indigenous musical ensembles, and at least a few decades before Conima's sikuri group Quantati Ururi would achieve a comparable reputation in Peru. When Natalio Calderón created Quantati Ururi circa 1929, then, it is highly possible that the earlier example of Los Sikuris de Italaque weighed on his mind.[25]

González Bravo, meanwhile, visited Italaque for the first time in June 1925, while conducting his initial fieldwork expedition in the La Paz countryside (González Bravo

1938, 172; *ED*, Dec. 18, 1939; González Bravo 1958). Over a decade later, he described his early experiences in the Italaque region as "unforgettable" (González Bravo 1938, 172). Within a few years of this 1925 excursion, González Bravo had additional chances to hear the music of Sikuris de Italaque groups, without having to leave his home base.

In 1929, 1930, and 1931, Italaque panpipe tropas journeyed from Camacho Province to the city of La Paz, to compete in the indigenous music contests that Los Amigos de la Ciudad held at the National Racetrack for Fiestas Julianas (previously described).[26] Of the various ensembles that performed in these festivals, it was Italaque's sikuris who consistently earned the most accolades from prize committees and newspaper writers (Wahren 2014, 85, 88). The Italaque group's participation in the first edition of the competition was not of their own free will, but the result of pressure from local vecino authorities, as the musicians explained in the complaint they relayed to Los Amigos de la Ciudad (Wahren 2014, 88). Vecinos therefore had some degree of involvement in, and influence over, the Sikuris de Italaque tradition, perhaps in a form akin to Calderón's leadership role in nearby Conima with Qhantati Ururi.

By 1935 (if not earlier), González Bravo had established a relationship with Italaque panpipe musicians; he is listed as the "artistic director" of "the famous" Sikuris de Italaque group that played a few numbers at Hernando Siles Stadium[27] for 1935's Gran Festival Folklórico Boliviano-Chileno (Grand Festival for Bolivian and Chilean Folklore) (*La Razón*, Sept. 23, 1935). According to the program notes, which González Bravo wrote, the participating Italaque ensemble already "had earned the top prizes in several music contests" (*La Razón*, Sept. 23, 1935). Two paceño estudiantinas with Incan names, Tahuantinsuyu (led by composer Julio Martínez Arteaga) and Lira Incaica, also took part in the one-day festival, as did Chilean folkloric group Los Huasos.[28] Yet Los Sikuris de Italaque closed both halves of the concert and was thereby afforded the most prominent slots, a scenario that probably owed much to the influence of González Bravo.

From this point onward, González Bravo would often employ the medium of his writing, in scholarly and public sector forums, to champion the musical prowess of Los Sikuris de Italaque, in a manner reminiscent of Peruvian anthropologist and indigenista novelist José María Arguedas's advocacy for Cuzco charango player Julio Benavente Díaz and Ayacucho guitar soloist Raúl García Zárate (see Mendoza 2008, 120–21; Tucker 2013, 123–24). González Bravo's article "Sicus," which he submitted to the *Boletín Latino Americano de Música* two months after the 1935 Gran Festival Folklórico Boliviano-Chileno (see González Bravo 1936, 256), is an early example. On the final page, besides once again characterizing Sikuris de Italaque ensembles as "famous," he explains to his readers that the variety of bamboo cane that Italaque siku manufacturers employ is thinner than that which is typically used in other regional panpipe traditions of greater La Paz, and that it is partly for this reason that Italaque siku ensemble music (supposedly) exhibits a "sweeter and more harmonious timbre" (González Bravo 1936, 256). The 1937 article "Kenas, Pincollos y Tarkas" also illustrates González Bravo's fascination with Italaque's sikuris. The Andean panpipe instrument family is clearly not the subject of this essay, given its title, but nonetheless, a photo of an Italaque siku tropa adorns the opening page of "Kenas, Pincollos y Tarkas" (González Bravo 1937, 25).

González Bravo does not appear to have ever taken up permanent residence in Italaque or nearby areas. His interaction with the region's sikuris consequently seems to have been sporadic, unlike the continuous relationship Natalio Calderón maintained with Qhantati Ururi in Puno. Accordingly, the La Paz educator probably wielded less of an influence in shaping Italaque's siku tropa style than his Peruvian counterpart did with the Conima tradition. In another difference, Los Sikuris de Italaque had gained recognition beyond their home region many years before González Bravo came into contact with local groups, whereas Conima's siku tropas began to attain this status only in the 1930s, following Calderón's involvement. González Bravo thus might have felt less of a need, or thought it was inappropriate, to radically modify Italaque siku groups' harmonic framework (which consists of unison and parallel octaves) or other traditional practices. Calderón felt no such compunction, because he went so far as to create the unorthodox harmonic framework of parallel thirds that henceforth would sonically define Conima's sikuri style.

As a public intellectual, González Bravo had a national status in Bolivia, which far superseded Natalio Calderón's more limited, regional profile in Peru. From the 1930s to 1950s, González Bravo's writings regularly appeared in Bolivia's major newspapers, and therefore were available to, and potentially influenced, the national readership. Folklore festival juries represented another important avenue through which González Bravo made his views known regarding indigenous musical traditions. Through his leadership position on these committees (see the final section of this chapter, and Chapter 4), he contributed to Los Sikuris de Italaque's canonization as one of Bolivia's preeminent indigenous panpipe tropa styles (a status the tradition has maintained as of 2020). From time to time, González Bravo also facilitated the participation of Italaque siku tropas in indigenista exhibitions held in La Paz city, such as the inaugural commemoration of Day of the Indian.

INDIGENOUS MUSICIANS IN THE MUNICIPAL THEATER: THE FIRST DAY OF THE INDIAN

In May 1936, four months after the 2nd Indianist Week, Colonels David Toro and Germán Busch ousted the unpopular Liberal Party leader José Tejada Sorzano from the presidency through a military coup d'état. Toro served as president for the next fourteen months, while Busch played the part of "the power behind the throne" (Klein 1992, 201). The two colonels declared that Bolivia would be ruled under the principle of "military socialism," even though neither leader intended to transform Bolivia into a socialist state. In the aftermath of the Chaco War debacle, the public demanded radical change in the political system, something Toro and Busch knew full well when they branded themselves as military socialists (Klein 1992, 199–210).

The Toro-Busch coalition was fleeting. Busch resigned from the administration in early 1937, and later in the year, during Fiestas Julianas, masterminded a successful coup against his former ally. The Busch presidency lasted until August 1939, when, stunning his supporters and foes alike, the increasingly erratic, and paranoid, Bolivian head of state committed suicide (Klein 1969, 309–20).

The military socialist era (1936–1939) represents a critical conjuncture for the establishment of moderate and radical-leftist parties in Bolivia, and expansion of political participation beyond the elite class (Klein 1992, 321–22). In the area of state-indigenous relations, amid mounting criollo-mestizo debates over how to best integrate the indigenous masses into "the active life of the nation" (Larson 2003, 191), the Toro and Busch regimes lent their support to the innovative *núcleos escolares*, which were rural vocational schools that instructed indigenous students in their home provinces. In 1931, leftist mestizo teacher Elizardo Pérez and Aymara education activist Avelino Siñani had founded the earliest, and most famed, núcleo escolar in the La Paz town of Warisata, in consultation with indigenous community members. Known as the Warisata ayllu-school, it was run according to traditional Aymara egalitarian and communitarian principles. The institution pioneered a host of socially progressive initiatives, from bilingual education in Aymara and Spanish, to an inter-cultural curriculum (Pérez 1962; Salazar Mostajo 1997; Larson 2003, 193–203).

Busch paid homage to the Warisata ayllu-school in August 1937, one month into his presidency, when he chose August 2—the núcleo escolar's founding date—to be the time of year that Bolivians henceforth would celebrate a new national holiday, Día del Indio (Day of the Indian).[29] To mark the inauguration of Day of the Indian, the Ministry of Education coordinated three Municipal Theater recitals that showcased student performers from the núcleos escolares of Caquiaviri (Pacajes Province, La Paz) and Warisata (*ED*, July 21, 24, and 27, 1937). In the two concerts the Caquiaviri contingent offered at the venue, the schoolchildren sang indigenista choral works such as "Cóndor Mallku" (Caquiaviri students had performed the same work at the 1st Indianist Week, as previously noted); recited nativist poems, including "Elogio de las Manos del Indio" (Elegy to the hands of the Indian); and danced stylized versions of the *chiriwanos* panpipe genre (also spelled *chiriguanos*) and other Andean indigenous expressive practices, to the accompaniment of a pianist, or seven-member tarka tropa (*ED*, July 24 and 26, 1937). The Warisata schoolchildren's recital at the Municipal Theater took place two days later and featured a similar repertoire. But instead of a tarka tropa, a Sikuris de Italaque group performed, to open each segment of the three-part program (*ED*, July 27, 1937).

González Bravo served as the musical director and conductor for the Warisata delegation at this concert. His prominent role in the proceedings surely explains the presence of an Italaque sikuri tropa at an event otherwise devoted to Warisata's núcleo escolar (Italaque did not possess this type of institution at the time, to my knowledge). The choral repertoire the schoolchildren interpreted, meanwhile, drew entirely from González Bravo's 1934 collection, *Lírica de Warisata: 6 Canciones Aimaras* (Lyric poetry of Warisata: 6 Aymara songs). During his tenure as a music and physical education teacher at the Warisata ayllu-school (1933–1934), he had transcribed and harmonized indigenous tunes of the region, added his own poetic Aymara lyrics, and taught these musical selections to his students, to instill local pride in Aymara culture (González Bravo 1957; Pérez 1962, 154–56; Salazar Mostajo 1997, 29, 193–98, 273–87). Given the scarcity of vocal musical traditions in the areas of the rural Andes where Aymara speakers predominate (see González Bravo 1948, 422), González Bravo unsurprisingly based his 1934 setting of local indigenous melodies on instrumental pieces.

Panpipe tropa traditions were the source of four of the six tunes in *Lírica de Warisata* (genres: *marcha del inca,* chiriwanos, *laquitas,* and *palla pallas*). The radical-leftist ideological currents that infused the philosophy of the Warisata ayllu-school probably strengthened González Bravo's long-standing preference for the siku. Notably, one year before 1937's Day of the Indian recital, González Bravo pronounced, in the article "Sicus" that appears in the *Boletín Latino Americano de Música,* that the siku "best expressed" the "communist" values of ancient and contemporary Andean indigenous societies (1936, 255). He arrived at this conclusion, no doubt, because sikuri musicians employ a hocketing technique that renders solos impossible. As for his assumption that indigenous Andeans traditionally practiced a form of communism, this view had been widespread in intellectual circles in the Andes and beyond since the 1920s. Bolivian writer Tristán Marof (whose early works include 1926's *La Justicia del Inca* [Justice of the Inca]), France's Louis Baudin (author of 1928's *L'Empire Socialiste des Inka* [The Socialist Empire of the Incas]), Peru's José Carlos Mariategui (the founder of Peru's Communist Party), and Luis E. Valcárcel (discussed previously) figure among the influential European and Latin American intellectuals active in the 1920s who characterized the Inca Empire as a communist or socialist-style state, either to criticize or idealize the Incan system of governance (Davies 1995, 7; John 2009, 36–38; Smale 2010, 167, 223).

At its Día del Indio concert, the Warisata choir opened with the first selection from *Lírica de Warisata,* "Marcha de los Cóndores" (March of the condors), which incorporates a marcha del inca panpipe melody (Salazar Mostajo 1997, 273–77). Before the singers took center stage, the student Pedro Miranda declaimed the poetic lyrics of this song, setting a serious tone for the recital.[30] The vocalists, meanwhile, realized a two-part harmonic texture (primarily in the intervals of thirds and sixths), while a pianist accompanied them, on each of their musical numbers (*ED,* July 27, 1937).

Overall, the students' rendering of *Lírica de Warisata* seems to have adhered to criollo-mestizo music performance conventions, from the tertian-triadic harmony, to the poetic texts and piano accompaniment. In keeping with his Western art-classical training, González Bravo must have believed that *Lírica de Warisata* represented a good faith (rather than ethnocentric) attempt on his part to raise indigenous music to the so-called universal standard. Regardless of his intentions, the schoolchildren's interpretation of this work corresponded ideologically with Busch's rationale for establishing the holiday. In the decree instituting Día del Indio, the President stated, patronizingly, that the "social, moral, and cultural level of the autochthonous [i.e., indigenous] masses" needed to be "elevated" (*ED,* July 23, 1937), by which he meant that the indigenous population should look up to, and try to emulate, criollo-mestizo cultural practices. It bears repeating that in the Americas indigenismo encompassed a diverse range of political projects, including ones that mainly upheld, rather than challenged, the traditional social hierarchies (see Gotkowitz 2011, 19–23).

The Warisata students' concert at the Municipal Theater, and the two recitals that the Caquiaviri delegation presented, share many similarities with the program that, the year before, criollo-mestizo artists had offered at the same venue for the 2nd Indianist Week. This is not to say that 1937's Día del Indio recitals did not represent a move toward the greater inclusion of rural indigenous musicians into criollo-mestizo indigenista exhibitions, given that an Italaque siku tropa and Caquiaviri tarka group participated in these Ministry of Education–organized concerts (although not as the main attractions). At the 2nd Indianist Week, in contrast, even though the members of estudiantina Lira Incaica had interpreted a tarka tropa piece with the appropriate indigenous wind and percussion instruments, rural indigenous musicians themselves had not taken part in the proceedings.

In the post–Chaco War era, the Day of the Indian concerts of 1937 appear to represent the earliest instances in which tropas of indigenous membership brought the music of Bolivia's highland villages to the urbane space of the Municipal Theater. It would not be until after the 1952 Revolution, however, that Andean tropa music—albeit as played by mestizo panpipe groups such as Los Choclos and Los Cebollitas—would be heard on a regular basis at La Paz's most esteemed venue (Chapters 4 and 5).

PERUVIAN INDIGENISTAS IN LA PAZ, LATE 1930S TO MID-1940S

In November 1940, González Bravo used the pages of *El Diario* to laud the talk that Peruvian indigenista musician and author Policarpo Caballero Farfán had recently given at the Ministry of Education. He also took the opportunity to remind his readers that more than twenty-five years ago, another Peruvian indigenista figure had left a mark on the paceño scene, Daniel Alomía Robles (*ED*, Nov. 14, 1940). Caballero Farfán returned to La Paz the next year to offer another lecture, but instead of speaking at the Ministry of Education, he gave this presentation in a considerably more prestigious setting, the Palace of Government (*ED*, Feb. 10, 1941), after having received an invitation to do so from President General Enrique Peñaranda (Caballero Farfán 1988, 21).

In the decade and a half after the Chaco War, Peruvian indigenista scholars, artists, and folklore companies continued to influence Bolivian indigenista currents. Most of those who offered recitals and lectures in La Paz hailed from Cuzco. These individuals and groups include, besides Caballero Farfán, the charango player Mamerto Encinas (*ED*, Dec. 25, 1937), trio Huayna Picchu (named after a mountain near the Machu Picchu ruins) (*ED*, Mar. 11, 1943), troupe Sumac Ccosqo (Quechua for "Beautiful Cuzco") (*ED*, Dec. 13, 1944), and, once again, Pancho Gómez Negrón (*ED*, June 29, 1947). Peru's soon-to-be internationally famed "Inca" soprano Zoila Augusta

Emperatriz Chávarri del Castillo, aka "Yma Sumac" (Quechua for "What beauty"), and her husband-manager, Moisés Vivanco, who were from Cajamarca and Ayacucho, respectively, also made their way to the city of La Paz, in 1942 and 1944 (*ED*, June 11, 1942; June 9, 1944).[31]

Bolivia was a stopover on the way to Buenos Aires for Yma Sumac, Vivanco, and many other Peruvian folklorists who performed in urban La Paz in the 1930s and 1940s. Ever since Valcárcel's Mision Peruana de Arte Incaico had presented a critically acclaimed recital series at Buenos Aires' hallowed Teatro Colón in 1923, Peruvian indigenista musical acts often traveled to the Argentine capital (see Mendoza 2008; Kuon Arce, Gutiérrez Viñuales, Gutiérrez, and Viñuales 2009, 199–216). That the US record labels RCA-Victor, Columbia, and ODEON had subsidiaries in Buenos Aires also made the city an attractive destination for Peruvian artists, as did the range of local venues.

These opportunities similarly enticed Bolivian folkloric musicians, such as Alberto Ruiz Lavadenz (of estudiantina Lira Incaica), and female vocal duos Las Kantutas and Las Hermanas Tejada, to undertake the long trek from La Paz to Buenos Aires (Chapter 3). For these artists, much of the allure of participating in the music scene of Buenos Aires—a city then widely perceived as being one of the most culturally sophisticated of Latin America (the so-called Paris of South America)—arose from the well-founded expectation that after doing so their profiles as musicians would receive a major boost back in Bolivia, and perhaps lead to more opportunities to perform abroad and gain additional prestige. Buenos Aires also figures prominently in the careers of José María Velasco Maidana and Eduardo Caba, two highly celebrated Bolivian composers in the field of art-classical music whose trajectories further demonstrate the transnational or cosmopolitan character of Bolivian indigenismo.

JOSÉ MARÍA VELASCO MAIDANA AND *AMERINDIA*, EDUARDO CABA AND *AIRES INDIOS*

Born in Sucre, José María Velasco Maidana initially earned a reputation in La Paz's indigenista scene as a filmmaker. As already noted, his 1925 movie *La Profecía del Lago* (1925) ran afoul of Saavedra officials who regarded the film's depiction of inter-ethnic romance between a criollo woman and an indigenous man to be unacceptable. Velasco Maidana's next feature film, *Wara Wara* (Aymara for "The stars"; 1930), with music by Belisario Zárate, Adrián Patiño Carpio, Simeón Roncal, José Lavadenz Inchauste, Manuel José Benavente, and Teofilo Vargas, once again presents a love story in which the protagonists cross racialized social boundaries. The main characters, though, were a Spanish conquistador and an Incan princess, a scenario that, in patriarchal criollo society, was then viewed as being less controversial (Vargas 2010).

In the mid-1930s Velasco Maidana began to earn critical acclaim for his musical output, starting with *Escenas Indianas* (Indian scenes). An orchestral piece, it is comprised of the movements "Sol de las Cumbres" (Sun of the summits), "Cantando por la Sierra" (Singing for the mountains), "La Leyenda del Yatiri" (The legend of the shaman), and "Danzan los Cusillos" (The Cusillos dance). In 1936, he entered *Escenas Indianas* in a Radio Illimani contest for nativist art-classical musical works and earned the top prize (*ED*, June 6 and 10, 1936). According to an unidentified music critic (*ED*, June 10, 1936), *Escenas Indianas* took after recent currents in European art-classical music composition, such as the primitivist style of Stravinsky's *The Rite of Spring*. The critic also observed, approvingly, that *Escenas Indianas* exhibited far more extensive thematic-melodic development than was generally the case in Bolivian indigenista art-classical works (e.g., Salmón Ballivián's *Suite Aymara*).

A few months after winning the Radio Illimani competition, Velasco Maidana apprised a La Paz newspaper reporter about his latest artistic enterprise, a "folkloric" ballet based on "national motifs" (*ED*, Nov. 20, 1936)—a project that again called to mind Stravinsky's most famous works. Velasco Maidana also informed the journalist that he would soon be leaving for Buenos Aires, where he planned to acquire additional training in music and choreography, and hoped to have his indigenista ballets performed.

In his youth, Velasco Maidana had studied art-classical music in Buenos Aires, at the Fontova Conservatory (Seoane n.d.), an experience that must have made him aware that artists from the Andean countries who presented Incan-themed repertoire attracted a niche audience in the Argentine capital. He also would have known that Buenos Aires–based exponents of the Argentine "nationalist" school of art-classical composition often authored works on Andean or Incan subjects (see Veniard 1986, 2000; Kuon Arce, Gutiérrez Viñuales, Gutiérrez, and Viñuales 2009). For two examples, in 1926, three years after Valcárcel's Misión Peruana de Arte Incaico had performed "Ollantay" at the Teatro Colón, Argentine musician Constantino Gaito premiered his own version of *Ollantay* at the same venue (Caamaño 1969, 285), while in 1934, Alberto Ginastera launched his career as a "nationalist" composer with *Impresiones de la Puna* (Impressions of the high plain) (Stevenson 1968, 259), an Andean-inspired symphony that opens with a movement titled "Quena" (*quena* is a common alternate spelling for kena).

In 1938, Velasco Maidana fulfilled his dream, as it was this year that his "Inca ballet" *Amerindia* (Indian America) debuted in Buenos Aires. Soon afterwards, Argentina's Radio El Mundo transmitted an orchestral rendering of the work's musical selections; radio listeners as far away as Germany heard the broadcast. Unexpectedly, Velasco Maidana received an invitation to conduct *Amerindia* in Berlin, an opportunity he readily accepted (*ED*, May 9, 1938). During his stay in Germany, the Bolivian consulate promoted his compositions, through a Berlin radio show that aired on Bolivian Independence Day; Radio Illimani re-transmitted the program so that the Bolivian public could hear it (*ED*, Aug. 3, 1938). In addition to featuring the music of Velasco Maidana and other renowned Bolivian composers, the broadcast included, curiously, a Peruvian work, Jorge Bravo de Rueda's most popular Incan foxtrot, "Vírgenes del Sol" (Virgins of the sun).

La Paz newspapers ran a stream of articles about *Amerindia* in 1938 and 1939, often portraying the work's reception on the European stage as an extraordinary "national triumph" not only for Velasco Maidana, but also for the Bolivian nation. One writer declared that "this triumph of Velasco Maidana in Germany is of enormous importance for Bolivian art" (*ED*, Feb. 5, 1939), while the following month another journalist predicted that "[u]ndoubtedly, Velasco Maidana has opened a space for Bolivian music, which in its autochthonous form will attract greater interest among the European public" (*ED*, Mar. 7, 1939). Paceños finally had the chance to witness the full production for themselves in 1940, when Velasco Maidana presented *Amerindia*, in its ballet form, at the Municipal Theater (*ED*, May 27, 1940). "[A]n event of magnanimous transcendence in the history of our artistic culture" was how President Peñaranda characterized *Amerindia*'s premiere in La Paz (*ED*, May 28, 1940). Peñaranda, who had only recently been elected to the presidency (term in office: March 1940–December 1943), even felt the need to issue a public apology to Velasco Maidana for having missed the concert, as a consequence of fulfilling his onerous duties as president of Bolivia (*ED*, May 28, 1940).

The next year, Bolivia's leading art-classical musicians sent a petition to Peñaranda in which they urged him to authorize the creation of an official, state-funded Orquesta Nacional de Concierto (National Symphony Orchestra) (*ED*, May 14, 1941). The country had lacked such an ensemble up to this point. The Peñaranda government granted the request and appointed Velasco Maidana to direct the orchestra (*ED*, May 14, 1941; Jan. 1, 1942; Auza León 1985, 119). The regime also funded Velasco Maidana's travels to Lima (Peru), Quito (Ecuador), Cali (Colombia), and Caracas (Venezuela), where he conducted performances of *Amerindia* and other works (*ED*, Apr. 16, May 29, July 26, Sept. 13, 1943). In so doing, the Peñaranda regime became the first Bolivian administration to finance a tour of this international magnitude for a Bolivian art-classical musician.

In his term as National Symphony Orchestra Conductor (1941–1945), Velasco Maidana gave ample publicity to the music of Bolivian composers. Besides his own works, he programmed the indigenista art-classical compositions of his contemporaries, such as those of Eduardo Calderón Lugones, Armando Palmero, and Humberto Viscarra Monje. In addition, the stylized cuecas, bailecitos, and huayños of Adrián Patiño Carpio, Simeón Roncal, Jorge "Chapi" Luna (profiled in Chapter 3), Ismael Zeballos, and other Bolivian criollo-mestizo musicians had a place in the repertoire of the National Symphony Orchestra during Velasco Maidana's tenure with the ensemble (see *ED*, Nov. 11 and 19, 1941). At this key moment in its history, then, the National Symphony Orchestra often performed "national" numbers, as a direct result of Velasco Maidana's strong interest in this form of musical expression.

In 1945, Velasco Maidana relocated to Mexico (soon after, he moved to the United States, where he would live the remainder of his life; Seoane n.d.), at which point Eric Eisner assumed his position as the head of the National Symphony Orchestra.[32] A Czech-Austrian expatriate, who also directed the Orquesta Típica La Paz (Chapter 3), Eisner followed Velasco Maidana's example by regularly including Bolivian indigenista musical works in the programs of the National Symphony Orchestra. He even crafted his own orchestrations of Bolivian compositions, including Eduardo Caba's *Aires Indios* (*ED*, July 18, 1949; Auza León 1985, 128).

Eduardo Caba's local fame and international reputation as a composer can be attributed almost entirely to *Aires Indios* (Indian airs). A solo piano work completed around 1934 (Wahren 2014, 75), it consists of six movements: "Kollavina" (Kolla region), "Korikilla" (Quechua for "Golden moon"), "Flor de Bronce" (Bronze flower), "Flor de Amor" (Flower of love), "Pollera Nueva,"[33] and "La Hilandera" (The spinner). *Aires Indios* features abundant pentatonicism, especially in the motifs, a compositional technique that, worldwide, art-classical musicians often employ to emulate the melodic characteristics of "folk music." The presence of polytonal passages, tertian triads with added ninths, and other hallmarks of 20th-century European art-classical music in *Aires Indios*, though, imparted a "modern" sound to the work, for contemporaneous audiences.

Caba's *Aires Indios* and Velasco Maidana's *Amerindia* most likely share points of stylistic convergence. However, because scholars have yet to locate a copy of the *Amerindia* score (if, in fact, one still exists) and no recording apparently survives of the work's musical passages, establishing the similarities between the two compositions is impossible at this point. Although *Amerindia* has not been performed again, Bolivian music scholars often mention this "Inca ballet," as a stirring example of a Bolivian composer's international "triumph" (e.g., González Bravo 1961, 100; Rivera de Stahlie 1995, 100–101; Becerra 2003, 132). As for *Aires Indios*, the sheet music for this composition has circulated widely in Bolivia and abroad since the 1930s, when an Argentine publishing house, Ricordi, first published it. Generations of Bolivian and non-Bolivian musicians therefore have been able to play Caba's signature piece.

Born in Potosí, Caba spent a formative chapter of his life abroad, like so many of his Latin American peers in the "nationalist" school of art-classical music composition (see Béhague 1979; Schwartz-Kates 2002). From 1925 to 1943, Caba lived in Argentina, Chile, Uruguay, and Spain. He wrote *Aires Indios* in Buenos Aires, where he studied music with Felipe Boero, author of the canonic Argentine nativist opera *El Matrero* (The bandit). In Madrid, Caba composed under the tutelage of Joaquín Turina, whose works frequently derive inspiration from flamenco and other Spanish regional traditions (*ED*, May, 10, 1943; Sept. 30, 1945).

While in Europe, Caba introduced Spanish pianist Ricardo Viñes and French soprano Eugénie "Ninon" Vellin to his compositions, which they in turn performed in multiple countries through their concert tours (*La Razón*, Apr. 5, 2015). Viñes, in particular, popularized the works of many South American composers in his career as an artist (Berrocal 2002). Caba dedicated *Aires Indios No. 5* ("Pollera Nueva") to the Spanish pianist, who debuted it in 1935 in Montevideo, Uruguay (*La Razón*, Apr. 5, 2015). Nemesio Ricoy Soto was another avid interpreter of Caba's music. A pianist from Argentina, Ricoy Soto traveled to La Paz city to offer solo piano recitals in 1938 and 1940, and on both occasions, he played *Aires Indios No. 2* ("Korikilla") and *No. 4* ("Flor de Amor") (*ED*, Sept. 9, 1938; Jan. 7, 1940).

In late 1942, the Bolivian Ministry of Education extended Caba the opportunity to lead the National Conservatory of Music. Then residing in Buenos Aires, he agreed to replace González Bravo as head of the school (*ED*, Apr. 17, 1944; Sept. 30, 1945). During Caba's tenure as director (1943–1944), reports on his musical projects, such as the orchestral piece *El Poema de la Kena* (The poem of the kena)—which Graciela "Chela" Urquidi would use as the musical backdrop for a folkloric ballet in 1951 (Chapter 4)—often appeared in the arts and culture section of La Paz newspapers. These accounts seldom failed to mention that Caba's compositions, especially *Aires Indios*, were highly regarded outside of the country, above all in Argentina (e.g., *ED*, Apr. 5, 1943; Apr. 26 and Aug. 23, 1944). One of Caba's colleagues at the National Conservatory, Luis Paganotto, made a choral arrangement of *Aires Indios No. 1* ("Kollavina") in 1943, which further popularized this movement (*ED*, June 13, Aug. 2, Oct. 17, and Oct. 30, 1943). Paganotto's arrangement would soon become a staple for Bolivian choirs.

A few months into his position at the National Conservatory, Caba served as an adjudicator for a Carnival season music-dance contest held at Hernando Siles Stadium (*ED*, Mar. 13, 1943). Caba's impeccable indigenista credentials made him a logical choice for the role, because the organizers were expecting Andean indigenous ensembles to take part in the event. Recently, the Municipal authorities had passed a decree that explicitly encouraged rural indigenous tropas to perform in urban La Paz's Carnival procession (Gildner 2012, 409). Participation in the festivities—traditionally held in the city's central district—had previously been reserved for criollo and mestizo groups (see Guss 2006; Rossells and Calatayúd 2009). Los Hijos de Sajama (The sons of Sajama [Mountain]) were among the first indigenous ensembles to take advantage of this opportunity. From the La Paz province of Pacajes, the tropa, which an *El Diario* writer described as consisting of "authentic Indians" (Mar. 11, 1943), competed in the 1943 contest that Caba and his fellow committee members evaluated. Los Hijos de Sajama obviously impressed the jury, given that they awarded the first-place trophy to the group (*ED*, Mar. 13, 1943).

In the next two years, Andean indigenous musicians and dancers of rural provenance would increasingly participate in urban La Paz's Carnival (see Rossells and Calatayúd 2009, 47–49, 305–11). The event's growing inclusion of indigenous ensembles provides additional evidence that criollo interest in local indigenous expressive practices was on the rise, a development with many contributing factors, including the acclaim that the music of Caba and Velasco Maidana had garnered in Bolivia. To be sure, Caba's *Aires Indios* and Velasco Maidana's *Amerindia* bore almost nothing in common with Andean indigenous musical styles, but the esteem these works enjoyed in Bolivia must have prodded even socially conservative elite criollos to entertain the possibility that the indigenous expressions that Caba and Velasco Maidana creatively referenced in their music constituted valuable Bolivian national resources. In any case, in the late 1930s and 1940s, Caba and Velasco Maidana represented Bolivian exemplars of indigenismo in the sphere of art-classical music, a status that, as this section has shown, owed much to the trajectory of their signature musical works in elite circles abroad, another illustration of the ways in which Bolivian indigenismo developed in close dialogue with cosmopolitan nativist-artistic currents from other countries.

THE FOUNDING OF BOLIVIAN FOLKLORE DEPARTMENTS

The 1940s saw the establishment of Bolivia's first state-run folklore departments: the Instituto Folklórico Boliviano (*ED*, Sept. 2, 1940), and Departamento de Folklore Boliviano (*ED*, Oct. 1, 1941). The charters of both agencies list "folkloric music" as one of the cultural spheres under their purview. Largely because these bureaus were short lived, though, neither launched music-oriented initiatives of much consequence. Nonetheless, their creation is significant, because it demonstrates that by 1940 the notion that the Bolivian state should fund research on, and encourage the preservation of, "folklore" had gained acceptance at the highest levels of the Bolivian political system (see Gildner 2012).

Also noteworthy is that the Instituto Folklórico Boliviano and Departamento de Folklore Boliviano appeared during the Peñaranda administration. As previously explained, the Peñaranda regime sanctioned the founding of the National Symphony Orchestra (which regularly presented Bolivian indigenista repertoire), and sponsored Velasco Maidana's engagements as a conductor in Peru, Ecuador, Colombia, and Venezuela. It was also in this period that La Paz city's Carnival procession became more welcoming to rural indigenous ensembles. In light of the conservative political views of General Peñaranda (see Klein 1969, 334–68), these developments had little to do with official state ideology, and instead primarily reflected the criollo-mestizo sector's growing interest in Bolivian indigenista cultural productions and rural indigenous expressive practices.

The international context within which Bolivia's earliest folklore departments were launched represents another important conjunctural factor. Many Latin American countries instituted state-run folklore bureaus in the early 1940s, on the heels of the Inter-American Indigenist Institute's 1940 meeting in Pátzcuaro, Mexico (Giraudo and Lewis 2012; Mintz 2015). Elizardo Pérez (of the Warisata ayllu-school) attended this momentous gathering in Mexico, as part of the Bolivian contingent (Gildner 2012, 391). Once again, rather than being an isolated nativist movement, Bolivian indigenismo took its cue from developments that were happening elsewhere in the Americas.

THE VILLARROEL-MNR ADMINISTRATION AND THE 1945 CONCURSO VERNACULAR Y FOLKLÓRICO

By the final months of 1943, the Peñaranda government was in dire straits. Bolivian leftist parties had greatly increased their popular standing in the last three years, often by leveling pointed critiques at the Peñaranda administration, particularly the regime's culpability in instigating the 1942 Catavi Massacre that had left hundreds of striking workers dead in Potosí. The MNR (Movimiento Nacionalista Revolucionario; Nationalist Revolutionary Movement) and PIR (Partido de la Izquierda Revolucionaria; Party of the Revolutionary Left) stood at the forefront of the opposition. Both parties were established in 1941 and enjoyed ample representation in Congress during Peñaranda's term in office. It was in this context that Víctor Paz Estenssoro and Hernán Siles Zuaso (son of ex-President Hernando Siles Reyes)—who would rapidly become two of Bolivia's most influential politicians of the 1940s and beyond—emerged on the national political scene, as founders and leaders of the MNR (Klein 1969, 334–68).

The Peñaranda regime had to deal with another threat as well, coming from a faction of junior-level military officers, many of whom were ex-prisoners of war from the Chaco conflict. Daringly, this group, who operated as a "secret military society" and called themselves Razón de Patria (Cause of the Fatherland) or RADEPA, tried to overthrow the Peñaranda government in November 1943 (Klein 1969, 369). Although the coup failed, the next month they made a second attempt to seize power, but with a new ally, the MNR. This time RADEPA succeeded (Klein 1969, 366–68).

The "inheritors of the title of military socialism" (Klein 1992, 218), RADEPA appointed one of its own, Major Gualberto Villarroel, to the presidency. Setting the tone for his term in office (December 1943–July 1946), Villarroel, at the speech he gave during 1944's Fiestas Julianas, uttered the line for which he would become best known: "We are not enemies of the rich, but we are better friends of the poor" (Peñaloza 1963, 64). A populist and authoritarian regime, the RADEPA-MNR coalition government repeatedly reached out to the urban working class for support, as had the military socialists Toro and Busch. It was in courting the rural indigenous population that the administration broke new ground. Indeed, the RADEPA-MNR government's largely successful efforts at obtaining the backing of indigenous people were unprecedented in Bolivia (see Gotkowitz 2007, 164–232).

Bolivia's first indigenous-coordinated political assembly of national scope, the 1945 Indigenous Congress, took place with the consent of the RADEPA-MNR administration. This groundbreaking event attracted about 1,500 indigenous delegates, many of whom traveled long distances to attend the meeting in La Paz city. At the conclusion of the assembly, President Villarroel, to the delight of the scores of indigenous representatives, and outrage of conservative criollos and mestizos who wished to maintain the status quo, declared that his regime would abolish the highly abusive Bolivian institutions of *pongueaje* and *mitanaje* through which criollo-mestizo owners of large landed estates (i.e., haciendas) had traditionally obligated indigenous farmworkers to provide unpaid personal services for them (Gotkowitz 2007, 192, 219–24).[34]

A few months after the Indigenous Congress, La Paz's Hernando Siles Stadium hosted the Concurso Vernacular y Folklórico (Vernacular and Folkloric Contest). A Fiestas Julianas event, it almost exclusively featured indigenous music-dance styles of the La Paz region. The crowd of 50,000 festival attendees, who included Villarroel, his cabinet, and other high-ranking state officials, witnessed a panorama of Andean tropa traditions, such as the *suri sikuri*, *loco palla palla*, choquela, *waka tokori*, and *auqui*

auqui genres (*ED*, July 16, 1945). To entice indigenous musicians and dancers to participate in the Concurso, the La Paz Municipality had pledged to reimburse the contestants for their travel and lodging expenses, and additionally reward the top groups with cash prizes (*ED*, Mar. 3 and 13, 1945). In total, seventeen troupes, from various La Paz provinces, exhibited their talents at the festival (*ED*, Aug. 5, 1945).

After arriving at Hernando Siles Stadium, the ensembles marched twice around the inner perimeter of the cavernous arena and then faced the festival jury. Indigenista composers José Salmón Ballivián (of *Suite Aymara* fame) and Eduardo Calderón Lugones sat on the committee, with acclaimed indigenista painter Cecilio Guzmán de Rojas (the head of the School of Fine Arts), and Radio Municipal director Luis Lavadenz (Paredes 1949, 32). Upon completing the deliberations, they ranked the ensembles, in five prize categories. Two of the top three awards went to panpipe groups (Loco Palla Pallas de Irupana and Lagua Sikuris de Coroico), reflecting the usual criollo-mestizo preference for indigenous tropas of this variety (*ED*, Aug. 5, 1945).

The contestants had navigated a bold parade route earlier in the day. In the morning hours, they gathered at one of two sites, positioned a couple of miles apart: Plaza Sucre (in the neighborhood of San Pedro) and Plaza Antofagasta (the bus terminal's current location). Then, around noon, while playing their instruments and dancing to the music, the two contingents marched through the heart of the city on their way to the stadium (Paredes 1949, 31–32). The Plaza Antofagasta convoy in particular must have raised eyebrows in conservative elite circles, because it passed within two blocks of the Presidential Palace and Plaza Murillo—an area that within recent memory had been off-limits to indigenous ensembles (as noted at the beginning of this chapter).

At the next Fiestas Julianas, indigenous music and dance traditions of the La Paz region once again occupied center stage at Hernando Siles Stadium (*ED*, July 7 and 12, 1946). This Concurso transpired in the tumultuous final week of Villarroel's presidency, and life. Given the brazen acts of brutality the RADEPA-MNR government's representatives regularly inflicted upon the opposition (see Chapter 3), that the regime came to a violent end is not entirely surprising. Nevertheless, the events of July 21, 1946 stunned even those who longed for the administration's overthrow. On that fateful day, a mob stormed the Presidential Palace, executed Villarroel, and then left his bloodied body hanging in Plaza Murillo, for all to see, on a lamppost (Céspedes 1966, 244–51).

The July 1946 coup d'état represented a victory for the Frente Democrático Antifascista (Democratic Antifascist Front). This coalition encompassed a diverse array of groups on the left and right who temporarily found common cause in their condemnation of the RADEPA-MNR government (Klein 1969, 381–82; Gotkowitz 2007, 233). With the gruesome slaying and postmortem hanging of Villarroel, Bolivia entered a new political era, one characterized by conservative-reactionary regimes that would last until April 1952, and subsequently would be labeled as *el sexenio*, or "the six-year period."

In writings on Bolivian folkloric expressions, the 1945 Concurso Vernacular y Folklórico is often described as a pivotal undertaking in the history of Bolivian state-sponsored folklore festivals involving Andean indigenous tropas (e.g.; Buechler 1980, 339; Paredes Candia 1984, 170; Céspedes 1993, 99; Sánchez C. 1994, 7). Rigoberto Paredes's 1949 book *El Arte Folklórico de Bolivia* (The folkloric arts of Bolivia) enshrined the 1945 Concurso Vernacular y Folklórico's place in Bolivian folklore historiography. In the final pages of the opening chapter, Paredes, after panning the authenticity and musicianship of the festival participants in his usually disparaging, blunt style, reproduces the account of the proceedings that the newspaper *La Razón* had printed in 1945 (Paredes 1949, 30–32). Placing this excerpt in such a prominent spot in the book has ensured that the Concurso has lived on in the tellings of Bolivian folklore researchers and enthusiasts, among whom *El Arte Folklórico de Bolivia* constitutes obligatory reading. Interestingly, by the time the book was available for purchase in 1949, another state-funded festival of indigenous music had taken place in La Paz city, 1948's Concurso Folklórico Indígena del Departamento. Paredes's book does not discuss it, perhaps because he sent the manuscript to the publisher before the festival had transpired. Whatever the case, the Concurso Folklórico Indígena del Departamento's omission from Paredes's book has played a part in the festival's surprising absence from Bolivian and Bolivianist historical narratives about Andean indigenous participation in folklore spectacles.[35]

THE HERTZOG GOVERNMENT AND THE 1948 CONCURSO FOLKLÓRICO INDÍGENA DEL DEPARTAMENTO

In the early months of the sexenio, government agents rounded up and put to death almost 300 Andean indigenous leaders, "for the crime of having remained loyal to Villarroel" (Gotkowitz 2007, 256). Outraged by this shocking action, and by the equally shocking assassination of Villarroel, indigenous-led strikes and other mobilizations broke out in multiple rural sites in early 1947, and soon coalesced into a "cycle of rebellions" (Rivera Cusicanqui 1986, 55–63) that many scholars contend represents "Bolivia's largest rural uprisings of the twentieth century" (Gotkowitz 2007, 234). By June 1947, President Dr. Enrique Hertzog's regime had stamped out most of the revolts, by unleashing the full force of the military and police (Gotkowitz 2007, 256–60). The Hertzog government (Jan. 1947–May 1949) unquestionably was a far cry from the Villarroel presidency in the area of state-indigenous relations. Yet in late 1948, only one year after the Hertzog administration had deployed violent means to stifle indigenous uprisings, fourteen Andean indigenous music-dance ensembles nonetheless journeyed from their provincial La Paz communities to the acting national capital, to compete in the Concurso Folklórico Indígena del Departamento (Folklore Competition for Indigenous Ensembles of the Department).[36]

The festival was one of several cultural exhibitions that the Comité Pro IV Centenario (Pro IV Centenary Committee) arranged in 1948 to commemorate La Paz city's 400-year anniversary. Besides the Concurso Folklórico Indígena del Departamento, the committee organized contests for musical composition (in the categories of música criolla [see Chapter 3], art-classical works, and military band pieces), visual art (for painting, sculpture, and photography), dramatic art (e.g., plays), historical essays, and poetry (*ED*, Aug. 28, Nov. 6 and 24, 1948). The programming must have reminded many paceños of the last local occasion that had involved such an impressive range of cultural activities, the Second Indianist Week of 1936.

The Concurso Folklórico Indígena del Departamento was structured according to musical instrument family, of which there were four categories: dances with siku (open to all Andean panpipe types), dances with pinkillu (and other highland duct-flute traditions, such as the *mohoceño*), dances with kena (kena-kena tropas also competed in this category), and dances with transverse flute (*ED*, Nov. 24, 1948). At the Concurso Vernacular y Folklórico of 1945, in contrast, the participating ensembles had vied against one another without regard to their type of instrumentation.

The format of the 1948 Concurso in all probability reflects the vision of González Bravo (it appears he was not involved in the 1945 festival), who served on the jury with composer Eduardo Caba and music educator Luis Felipe Arce. By organizing the competition around musical instrument families, the Concurso apparently took inspiration from the Andean indigenous musical battles that González Bravo had observed in village fiestas. Nevertheless, the 1948 Concurso diverged substantially from these traditional rural events, which normally are intra-ayllu affairs in which the competing groups not only employ analogous instrumentation, but also use equivalent tropa voicings (e.g., unison and octaves) and perform the same or closely related genres. At the 1948 Concurso, instead, ensembles with little in common stylistically, and whose members hailed from different ayllus, faced off. And they did so in front of a panel of criollo-mestizo judges who ranked the groups without bothering to consult indigenous community members about their aesthetic criteria—a frequent scenario at folklore festivals in the Andean countries (for partial exceptions to this pattern, see Rockefeller 1999 and Ritter 2002).

Presaging the success that Sikuris de Italaque and Kantus de Charazani groups would obtain at MNR government-funded "autochthonous" folklore contests in the mid-1950s (Chapter 4), the committee awarded the first- and second-place trophies to Italaque and Charazani tropas, respectively, in the "dances with siku" category (*ED*, Nov. 24, 1948). The Italaque siku ensemble of course had a key competitive advantage. Compared to other indigenous panpipe groups of the greater La Paz area, sikuris from Italaque had performed far more regularly for urban paceño criollo-mestizos in recent decades and thus had greater experience in catering to the aesthetic preferences of this sector.

González Bravo's presence on the judging panel gave the Italaque sikuris another major advantage. In his most recent article, "Música, Instrumentos y Danzas Indígenas" (Indigenous Music, Instruments and Dances) (published in 1948, but submitted in 1947), he reiterated his esteem for "Los Sikuris de Italaque" by characterizing the tradition's exponents as "the most notable among the siku ensembles" found in the departamento of La Paz (González Bravo 1948, 409). He also described the melodies that the ensembles performed as "very beautiful," and exalted the musicians' creativity (González Bravo 1948, 409). In light of González Bravo's status as the country's leading scholar of Andean indigenous music, his championing of the Italaque siku tradition surely played a part in his fellow jury members' decision to award the top prize in the category for siku tropas to an ensemble that performed this regional style.

According to the committee, the winning Italaque siku tropa was "already famous for their deserved reputation as musicians of pure indigenous essence and artistic perfection" (*ED*, Nov. 24, 1948). The Kantus de Charazani ensemble that earned the runner-up trophy, in contrast, represented something new for the jury. Prior to the 1948 Concurso, the Charazani Valley's indigenous panpipe tropa style had been unknown to most urban La Paz–based indigenista scholars and artists, even to González Bravo. When surveying the La Paz region's Andean indigenous wind-instrument traditions in the article "Indigenous Music, Instruments and Dances" (completed in 1947), nowhere in this lengthy essay does González Bravo mention Kantus de Charazani groups of Bautista Saavedra Province. His earlier publications on Andean music, such as the 1936 article "Sicus," also omit the panpipe ensemble style of Charazani groups.[37] Likewise, Rigoberto Paredes, despite having spent part of his youth not far from Bautista Saavedra Province, in neighboring Camacho Province, does not bring up Kantus de Charazani tropas in his writings on Andean indigenous expressive practices, including 1949's *El Arte Folklórico de Bolivia* (which he most likely submitted to the publisher before the 1948 Concurso, as previously noted).

The harmonies of Kantus de Charazani panpipe music, with its parallel fifths, fourths, and octaves (i.e., parallel polyphony), surely caught González Bravo and the rest of the jury off guard. Indigenous panpipe tropas of the La Paz region traditionally produced a much thinner-sounding, monophonic texture, by performing in unison and octaves (e.g., Sikuris de Italaque groups), or simply in unison (see González Bravo 1948). It appears that Charazani's kantus style originated in the early 20th century (Langevin 1990, 134), probably in emulation of Peruvian siku tropa practices (see Romero Kuljis 2016, 115, 205–11). Charazani vecinos who then regularly traveled to Puno for business purposes seem to have instituted what later became known as the kantus tradition. Interestingly, Conima was one of the districts of Puno that these vecinos often had visited (Romero Kuljis 2016, 115, 205–11). It is thus conceivable that Conima's vecino-led Qhantati Ururi inspired the creation of the Kantus de Charazani style, as both exhibit a highly distinctive harmonic framework that sets them apart from other panpipe tropa traditions in their home regions. Peruvian musical indigenismo's influence on the Bolivian scene therefore may have not been limited to musical practices of criollo-mestizo association, but extended to the indigenous panpipe tropa style characteristic of the Charazani Valley.

The parallel polyphony of Kantus de Charazani music certainly departed from the norm for a Bolivian panpipe ensemble style, although this musical texture was not unheard of in Andean indigenous tropa music that centered on non-panpipe instrument families. In the region of La Paz, for instance, indigenous kena-kena, pusipía, tarka, mohoceño, and transverse-flute ensembles similarly realized melodies in parallel fifths, fourths, and octaves (González Bravo 1948, 414, 417–18). Despite the novelty of Kantus de Charazani music, then, the judges at 1948's Concurso Folklórico Indígena del Departamento could still deem the ensembles' harmonic approach to be traditionally Andean. This in all probability figured into the committee's final decision. After all, the degree to which an indigenous ensembles' musical practices match criollo-mestizo expectations about "authenticity" usually represents an important factor at Bolivian folklore festivals. That paceños had long associated the Charazani Valley with the mysterious Andean indigenous ritual healers known as the Callahuaya or Kallawaya (see Chapter 1) must have added another layer of traditional associations to the music that the kantus group interpreted at the contest, and made it even more intriguing to the judges and spectators. In any case, within a few years of the 1952 Revolution, Los Kantus de Charazani would attain an elevated reputation in the eyes of folklore enthusiasts, that of one of Bolivia's most celebrated indigenous panpipe tropa traditions, thereby becoming the main rival for Los Sikuris de Italaque at state-funded folklore festivals (Chapter 4).

Taken as a whole, the 1948 Concurso Folklórico Indígena del Departamento provides a clear indicator that paceño criollo-mestizo society generally had come to accept the idea—albeit no doubt often reluctantly—that Andean indigenous music-dance styles represented a characteristic facet of the departamento's cultural identity. If that were not true, it is highly unlikely that the IV Centenary committee would have gone against mainstream elite and middle-class opinion and programmed indigenous tropas for the celebration , given the political context. The Hertzog regime, after all, expressed negligible interest in crafting alliances with rural indigenous leaders and communities, and recently had violently repressed indigenous-led mobilizations. That the 1948 Concurso even took place at all, then, is remarkable, and moreover reveals the La Paz elite and middle class's rising estimation of Andean indigenous music-dance traditions.

From the 1920s to late 1940s, mainstream paceño criollo-mestizo views on the cultural value and meanings of Andean indigenous music unquestionably shifted to a significant extent, a development connected to the sociopolitical changes that Bolivia underwent in this often politically turbulent era and, at the same time, to the influence of nativist artistic trends emanating from other Latin American countries, especially the Peruvian variant of indigenismo. The Andean rural indigenous population's standing in paceño society and the Bolivian nation, however, did not experience as dramatic a transformation. In the 1940s, state officials continued to enforce literacy requirements and other discriminatory measures to prevent indigenous people from participating in the official political sphere, and periodically use violent means to halt indigenous political actions. Only after the 1952 Revolution would this disturbing state of affairs undergo major change. But before moving on to the post-1952 Bolivian age of "revolutionary nationalism," the following chapter takes another look at the pre-1952 era, through detailed discussions of the musical activities of estudiantinas and female duos in urban La Paz.

NOTES

1. For an overview of Latin American indigenismo, see Earle 2007, 184–212. For more focused studies, see Brading 1988 for the Mexican case, and De la Cadena 2000 for Peru.

2. Dr. Luciano N. Bustíos mounted a display of Andean indigenous musical instruments and fiesta attire at Bolivia's 1925 centennial festivities (*El Diario*, June 2, 1937; Aldunate viuda de Azero 1994, 11–12), which appears to represent the main exception to the official commemoration's exclusion of indigenista exhibitions. Trained as a lawyer, Bustíos was a major figure in La Paz's emergent indigenista musical scene of the 1920s, as a pianist, a composer, an arranger, and a conductor. In 1929 or 1930, he founded the choir Nina Inti, which performed his musical works (Aldunate viuda de Azero 1994, 13–14). The name of the ensemble, Quechua for "Fire in the Sun," is grammatically awkward, which indicates that Bustíos was not fluent in the language.

3. To my knowledge, this chapter is the first published study on Bolivian indigenismo that provides an overview of the movement's musical dimensions in the urban La Paz setting from the early 20th century to the 1940s. For other work on paceño indigenismo, see Salmón 1997; Qayum 2002, 2011; Bigenho 2005; Kuenzli 2013; and Wahren 2014.

4. In Chapter 7, I discuss "Manchaypuito" (or "Manchay Puito"; the tune also is known as "Dos Palomitas" [Two little doves]) and its link to the Legend of Manchay Puito.

5. For a summary of the plot of *Ollantay*, see Mendoza 2008, 20–21.

6. Nemesio Zuñiga Cazorla's troupe was the third Peruvian indigenista theater company to perform in La Paz city in 1917 (Itier 2000, 53). I have been unable to uncover additional information about the group's activities during its stay in Bolivia.

7. For major studies on Incan musical traditions, see Stevenson 1968; Gruszczyńska-Ziólkowska 1995; Tomlinson 2009; and Stobart 2014.

8. In Bolivia, the term "pasacalle" (literally "pass the street") can refer to a variety of musical genres, although it is most commonly applied to criollo-mestizo traditions.

9. The music score for the film *Corazón Aymara* has unfortunately not survived.

10. Pancho Gómez Negrón's artistic persona in the late 1920s represented a new direction in Peruvian indigenismo, as it emphasized mestizo or cholo cultural practices rather than indigenous traditions (Mendoza 2008, 88–89, 95–96, 100–104). At the Velada Indianista, however, he performed while dressed as an indigenous peasant from Peru.

11. Sucre musician Manuel José Benavente spent much of his career in Buenos Aires, where he interacted with Argentine indigenista artists (see Veniard 1999, 126–28).

12. The Ch'ijini panpipe tropa that performed "Aymara music" on this 1931 Radio Nacional program might have been a misti sikuri, or "mestizo siku," ensemble, given that this tradition had gained a foothold in the Ch'ijini area by the 1920s (see Chapter 5).

13. For scholarship on the Chaco War, see the essays and bibliographies in Chesterton 2016.

14. From Afghanistan to Mexico to Brazil, state-run radio stations have often enacted a key role in fostering nation building (Baily 1994; Hayes 2000; McCann 2004).

15. The third movement of *Suite Aymara*, "Auki Auki" (Aymara for "old men"), is named after an Andean music-dance genre typically performed with flautas traversas (transverse flutes). "Auqui auqui" represents an alternate spelling for the tradition.

16. I have not been able to obtain the original piano or orchestral scores for *Suite Aymara*. Since the 1990s, the Bolivian estudiantina-orchestra Música de Maestros has recorded *Suite Aymara* several times, but with modifications to the composition, including new sections. The ensemble also has often used tropa instruments in its performances of the work (see

Bigenho 2002, 119–20). As a result, Música de Maestros' recorded versions of *Suite Aymara* differ substantially from the composition that Bolivian radio listeners would have heard in the 1930s.

17. Born into an illustrious paceño family whose lineage included presidents, José Salmón Ballivián held high-ranking offices. In the 1930s, he served as Secretary General of the Center of Propaganda and National Defense (one of the entities that founded Radio Illimani), and also Governor and Senator (Auza León 1985, 88–89; Rivera de Stahlie 1995, 71–72; Fernández Terán 2002, 210–14). As a musician, Salmón Ballivián appears to have been largely self-taught. He never learned to read musical notation, so it fell to his daughters to transcribe (and very likely arrange) *Suite Aymara* and other pieces he played for them on the piano, including his popular work *Trilogía India* (Indian trilogy). His familial musical predecessors include Eloy Salmón, who in 1863 composed La Paz's official anthem, *Himno a La Paz* (Rivera de Stahlie 1995, 71–73), and Adolfo Ballivián, the author of the 19th-century opera *Atahualpa* (Chapter 1).

18. Historian Elizabeth Shesko (2015) concurs with the often-repeated claim that Andean indigenous people represented most Bolivian troops in the Chaco War. She maintains, however, that scholars have tended to exaggerate the number and role of indigenous combatants in the war effort, and underplay the participation of other sectors.

19. Even though Bolivia sided with Peru against Chile in the Pacific War (1879–1883), Bolivia's defeat in the conflict did not immediately spur the development of a local indigenista movement comparable in its scope to the one that took hold in Peru (see Demelas 1981).

20. Indigenous musicians, though, traditionally perform the cullawas or *cullaguas* (a huayño-variant also known as *cullawada* or *cullaguada*) with transverse flutes (i.e., pífanos or pitus), not tarkas as Lira Incaica did at the 2nd Indianist Week.

21. "Sikuris de Italaque" is the designation that scholars, folklore artists, and fans normally use to refer to the indigenous panpipe tropa style traditionally practiced in the communities or ayllus located near the La Paz town of Italaque (Camacho Province). As the ensembles do not actually hail from this mestizo-dominated town, however, indigenous musicians of the region generally do not approve of this custom of labeling their sikuri style as "Sikuris de Italaque." Unfortunately, the written historical sources that this chapter relies on employ the umbrella term for this regional panpipe ensemble tradition, rather than specifying the ayllu affiliation of particular groups.

22. Pincollo is a common alternate spelling for pinkillu.

23. González Bravo's 1925 article "El Modo Pentatónico en la Música Nacional" first appeared in *Revista Inti* (Paredes Candia 1967, 79). In 1956, the MNR government's "cultural" magazine, *Khana*, printed a revised version of the essay (González Bravo 1956).

24. For an overview of Bolivia's Andean panpipe traditions, see Cavour 1994, 32–54.

25. To my knowledge, scholars of Peruvian music have not explored this plausible link between the birth of Quantati Ururi and earlier trajectory of Los Sikuris de Italaque.

26. It is possible that in 1926 an indigenous ensemble from Italaque performed at La Paz's Municipal Theater as part of a recital organized by Salmón Ballivián. Teresa Rivera de Stahlie's book *Música y Musicos Bolivianos* (1995, 71) partially reprints Hugo Boero Rojo's recollection of this concert, which he wrote for a 1977 *El Diario* article.

27. Completed in 1931, the Hernando Siles Stadium is named after President Hernando Siles Reyes (term in office: 1926–1930).

28. The Chilean folkloric group "Los Huasos" that performed at the 1935 Gran Festival Folklórico Boliviano-Chileno might have been Los Cuatro Huasos, as this ensemble was active in this period (see González Rodríguez, Ohlsen, and Rolle 2009, 328–29).

29. Peru had instituted its Día del Indio seven years earlier, in 1930 (Earle 2007, 187).

30. Pedro Miranda would go on to become an "Aymará poet" like his mentor González Bravo, as would another Warisata student who recited lyrics at 1937's Dia del Indio concert, Máximo Waiñuco (*ED*, July 27, 1937; Pérez 1962, 302–3; Salazar Mostajo 1997, 31).

31. See Limanksy 2008 for a discussion of Yma Sumac's and Moisés Vivanco's careers.

32. Eric Eisner led the National Symphony Orchestra from 1945 to 1956 (Auza León 1985, 119).

33. The title of the fifth movement of *Aires Indios*, Pollera Nueva, which can be translated as "new skirt," refers to the multilayered skirts traditionally worn by Andean women of the cholo-mestizo class (i.e., *cholas*), such as market vendors.

34. Until after the 1952 Revolution, though, most hacendados ignored the Villarroel regime's 1945 abolition of pongueaje and mitanaje (Gotkowitz 2007, 224–25, 236).

35. Like the case with Rigoberto Paredes's 1949 book *El Arte Folklórico de Bolivia*, González Bravo's 1948 article "Indigenous Music, Instruments, and Dance" does not make reference to the 1948 Concurso Folklórico Indígena del Departamento. On the last page of the essay, it states that González Bravo had submitted the final version to the publisher the previous year (i.e., 1947), which explains this omission. The erasure of the 1948 Concurso from Bolivian popular memory, meanwhile, has had many contributing factors, including the MNR's return to power in 1952. In the ensuing twelve-year period of MNR rule, state officials emphasized the regime's ideological roots in the Villarroel-MNR coalition government (Chapter 4), and downplayed continuities with the 1946–1952 sexenio. Accordingly, the writings of Antonio González Bravo, Antonio Paredes Candia, and other folklorists who worked for MNR government-affiliated "cultural" agencies in the 1952–1964 period (e.g., Department of Folklore) fail to mention the folklore spectacles that took place in La Paz city in the late 1940s.

36. Given the Hertzog regime's violent actions toward Andean indigenous mobilizations in 1947, it seems curious that highland indigenous ensembles performed at the 1948 Concurso. As one of the coordinators, González Bravo might have persuaded some groups to take part, especially those he had long-standing contact with, such as Los Sikuris de Italaque, and perhaps Kena-Kenas de Caquiaviri. Home to an ayllu-school since the 1930s, Caquiaviri represented one of the "core areas of unrest" in the 1947 uprisings (Gotkowitz 2007, 248, 253; also see Rivera Cusicanqui 1986, 59–61).

37. Rectifying this omission, González Bravo made sure to discuss the Kantus de Charazani tradition in his later writings on Andean indigenous musical styles (e.g., Bedregal de Conitzer and González Bravo 1956, 22; González Bravo 1961a, 58). Since this period, Charazani's kantus tradition has been the subject of numerous studies (e.g., Langevin 1990; Templeman 1994; Romero Kuljis 2016).

3

ESTUDIANTINAS AND FEMALE VOCAL DUOS

BOLIVIAN ESTUDIANTINAS OF the 1930s and 1940s—whose members came predominantly from the urban working-class sector, chose ensemble names that often expressed an imagined connection to Andean indigenous culture (e.g., Huiñay Inti, Kollasuyo), performed repertoire that focused on criollo-mestizo "folk" genres and settings of indigenous melodies, and frequently incorporated the kena and charango into their lineups—represent key precursors for the Andean conjuntos that would dominate the national folkloric-popular music scene from the late 1960s onward. When the estudiantina format took root in Bolivia in the late 19th and early 20th centuries, however, local groups of this type followed Spanish estudiantina conventions and thus did not use Andean instruments or have Andean indigenous-sounding ensemble names. The repertoire of these late-19th- and early-20th-century Bolivian estudiantinas, meanwhile, consisted of European or European-derived music, from zarzuela (Spanish operetta) numbers and other "light" art-classical works, to dance genres such as the waltz, Polish mazurka, and Spanish jota. And it was the criollo elite, not the cholo-mestizo working class, who first adopted the estudiantina tradition in Bolivia. The process through which paceño estudiantinas gradually eschewed their original stylistic orientation and elite criollo association, and instead adopted indigenista practices and became strongly identified with cholo-mestizos, is the subject of the first half of this chapter.[1]

The second half examines the careers of the La Paz–based female vocal duos Las Hermanas Tejada (the Tejada Sisters) and Las Kantutas (named

Panpipes & Ponchos. Fernando Rios, Oxford University Press (2020). © Oxford University Press.
DOI: 10.1093/oso/9780190692278.001.0001.

after the national flower, the *kantuta*) from the late 1930s to the run-up to the 1952 Revolution.[2] For much of this period, they stood at the summit of the criollo-mestizo folkloric music movement in the mass-mediated domain, with contrasting specializations. Whereas Las Hermanas Tejada were renowned for their creative renderings of traditional Aymara music, Las Kantutas developed a forte in the carnaval and taquirari genres of the tropical lowlands of eastern Bolivia, a repertoire known as *música oriental*.[3] A look at the trajectories of these superstar duos therefore not only provides another perspective on Bolivian musical indigenismo, but also reveals a concurrent trend in the paceño folkloric music scene, one that then rivaled the popularity of criollo-mestizo folklorizations of Andean indigenous traditions.

By including an extended discussion of the 1940s La Paz vogue for lowland music-dance genres in a book that otherwise concentrates on expressive practices of highland association, this portion of the chapter serves as a partial corrective to the teleological tendency that is often evident in writings that explain the rise of national music traditions, a propensity that can inadvertently reduce the complexity and contradictory impulses of the canonization process to the extent that its outcome appears as an inevitable one. Another reason that the La Paz folklore scene's receptiveness to música oriental merits attention here is its lasting legacy. From the 1940s onward, the overwhelming majority of paceño criollo-mestizo folkloric musicians would supplement their stable of highland genres with the lowland carnaval and taquirari, a practice that laid the groundwork for the Bolivian Andean conjunto tradition's expansive repertoire of distinct music-dance genres.

In many Latin American countries, the estudiantina and female vocal duo formats enjoyed widespread popularity as national folkloric musical ensemble configurations in the early-to-mid-20th century. This chapter therefore offers additional evidence that Bolivian nativist musical currents developed in articulation with transnational artistic movements, and in this sense constituted instances, equally, of cosmopolitanism *and* nationalism. Yet in the case of the estudiantina, Bolivians at first mainly associated the ensemble format with Spanish cultural expressions and more generally with cosmopolitanism, but not with nationalism as well, in keeping with the orientation the tradition exhibited when it arrived in the Americas.

THE SPANISH ESTUDIANTINA AND ITS DISSEMINATION TO LATIN AMERICA

In the mid-19th century, Spanish musicians developed a new form of Carnival-season music making, the estudiantina, which highlighted the sound of plucked stringed instruments and imagery of the mischievous university student groups (*estudiantes* = students) that had enlivened festivities in Renaissance-era Spain (Christoforidis 2017, 2–3). The outfits the members sported accordingly drew on Renaissance models, while their musical instruments of choice were the mandolin-size, double-coursed, steel-string laúd and the bandurria, along with the guitar. The jota, *seguidilla*, and other Spanish "folk" dance genres that zarzuela productions commonly used in the 19th century "to project Spanishness" made up the core of the early estudiantina repertoire, as did the transatlantic habanera (Christoforidis 2017, 3).

Spanish estudiantina practices became more standardized as the century progressed, especially among professional ensembles (Christoforidis 2017, 11). Most groups counted between ten and twenty members, with multiple musicians performing each part of the composition or arrangement. Realizing the melody usually fell to the laúdistas, who with a plectrum often executed rapid, single-note passages to create the illusion of an uninterrupted melodic line (i.e., tremolo effect). The bandurria players used a similar performance style but primarily harmonized with the laúd part. The guitarists, meanwhile, filled out the texture with bass notes or strummed chords, played with finger-style technique. Often complementing the lineup were additional instruments, most commonly the violin, flute, *pandereta* (tambourine), and a set of castanets. On some numbers, estudiantinas accompanied the singing of soloists and/or choirs (Christoforidis 2017, 3).

It was largely through the efforts of Spain's Estudiantina Fígaro that the estudiantina format spread to Latin America (Martín Sárraga 2014; Christoforidis 2017, 11–14). In 1878 in Madrid, Dionisio Granados founded Estudiantina Fígaro, as part of the first wave of touring groups of this type that sought to capitalize on the surging international interest in this ensemble tradition that Estudiantina Española had generated at Paris's third Exposition Universelle (World's Fair) (see Christoforidis 2017, 5–11). To add greater variety to its programs, Granados expanded Estudiantina Fígaro's repertoire to include arrangements of orchestral works (especially overtures and marches), instrumental settings of Italian arias from well-known operas, and non-Spanish dance genres such as the mazurka and gavotte (Christoforidis 2017, 11–14).

In 1880, Estudiantina Fígaro divided into two groups, one of which departed for the Americas that year. By the end of the decade, iterations of the ensemble had entertained audiences in almost every Latin American country (Martín Sárraga 2014). In the majority of these sites, local musicians established their own estudiantinas soon thereafter (for Chile, see Luna Muñoz 1993, 49–65, and Andreu Ricart 1995, 15–169; for Venezuela, see Torres 2007, 21–34; for Colombia, see Rendón Marín 2009, 32–37).

AN ELITE CRIOLLO TRADITION: THE FIRST WAVE
OF BOLIVIAN ESTUDIANTINAS

In 1886, Estudiantina Fígaro landed in Bolivia, where it offered concerts at elite-oriented venues in La Paz, Oruro, and Cochabamba (*El Heraldo* [Cochabamba newspaper], July 31, Aug. 28, 1886). A columnist for the daily *El Heraldo* could barely contain his enthusiasm for the upcoming engagements in Cochabamba city, which the group had added to its itinerary "without prior announcement" (*El Heraldo*, July 13, 1886). The journalist also exclaimed that "we will have the immense pleasure of knowing what an estudiantina is" (*El Heraldo*, July 13, 1886), a comment that reflects the limited exposure that, up to this point, most Bolivians had to Spain's estudiantina tradition.[4]

Even though for Bolivians the plucked-string-orchestra format and Renaissance-inspired attire of Estudiantina Fígaro represented novelties in 1886, the group's repertoire would have been familiar to them, especially to the elite. As Chapter 1 explains, in the 19th century the musical tastes of Bolivia's upper class strongly gravitated toward European dance genres and art-classical works, in part so that this sector could differentiate itself from, and assert its superiority over, the rest of society (i.e., mestizos, cholos, and indigenous people). Estudiantina Fígaro's performance practices thus represented a variety of artistic experience that the Bolivian elite not only appreciated aesthetically but also identified with culturally.

Bolivian estudiantinas began to appear within a few years of Estudiantina Fígaro's brief stay. In La Paz city and elsewhere in the country (e.g., Cochabamba, Sucre),[5] these early groups seem to have drawn their members mainly from the elite criollo sector. This selectivity was true of the paceño estudiantina that played in the 1889 Sociedad Filarmónica (Philharmonic Society) recital held in the run-up to Carnival. The event featured a variety of ensembles and soloists, including a soprano who belted out an aria from Vincenzo Bellini's *La Sonnambula* (The sleepwalker), and a piano-four-hand duo who tackled Louis Moreau Gottschaulk's *Radieuse* (Radiant). Choral works from the zarzuela *El Anillo de Oro* (The golden ring) and the French opéra comique *Haydée, ou Le Secret* (Haydée, or The secret) also formed part of the offerings at this upper-class function (*El Imparcial* [hereafter *EI*], Feb. 21 and 27, 1889).

The estudiantina that took part in the recital was led by a Mr. Polar, who only recently had established the yet-to-be named group. Comprising eleven guitars, six violins, five bandurrias, one mandolin, and a banjo,[6] the twenty-four-member ensemble opened the third portion of the Sociedad Filarmónica's program with a "Král March" (by Prince of Liechtenstein Johann Nepomuk Král). As reported in *El Imparcial*,

[t]he spectators experienced something of a frenzy of delirium: the public shouted, applauded, and even asked for an encore. The estudiantina complied: it repeated the Král March, in the midst of the enthusiasm. (*EI*, Feb. 27, 1889)

By July of the same year, Estudiantina Paceña had emerged on the local scene, under the direction of violinist Zenón Espinoza (*EI*, July 23, 1889). Among La Paz's earliest stable estudiantinas (Alejo 1925, 360), the group initially played repertoire that was very similar to that of Estudiantina Fígaro. At an 1891 event, Estudiantina Paceña began its set with an excerpt from Bellini's opera *Norma*, and followed it up with a polka, two mazurkas, and, as the finale, a "Gran Jota" (*EI*, July 12, 1891).

Estudiantina Verdi and Estudiantina Española La Paz, both founded in the city of La Paz around the turn of the 20th century, also played pieces of Spanish or cosmopolitan association, unsurprisingly, given the names of the groups, and the Spanish

Renaissance-style dress the musicians donned at their performances (see *ED*, July 12, 1904; Apr. 4, 1905). Estudiantina Verdi was even known to play a hallmark Estudiantina Fígaro number, the *fantasía* "Aires Españoles" by Dionisio Granados (*ED*, Apr. 11, 1905).[7] As for Estudiantina Española La Paz, its devotion to European musical forms was such that when the group paid homage to its home city at a 1904 concert attended by President Ismael Montes, the tune it unveiled, "Bella Paceña" (Beautiful La Paz woman), was a mazurka rather than a genre traditionally associated with La Paz (*ED*, Sept. 10, 1904).

In 1904 and 1905, Estudiantina Verdi and Estudiantina Española La Paz displayed their musical artistry and picturesque outfits in La Paz's official Carnival procession (Rossells and Calatayúd 2009, 295). Their participation in the festivities reflects the estudiantina tradition's integration into the cultural life of the paceño upper class, because at the time, La Paz city's Carnival parade remained an exclusively elite affair (see Guss 2006, 299–304; Rossells and Calatayúd 2009). That playing in an estudiantina then represented a respectable pastime in paceño criollo society is also borne out by the number of elite women, most of unmarried status, who joined the ensembles. Indeed, in the 1880s and 1890s several La Paz estudiantinas included a mix of male and female musicians (e.g., *EI*, Dec. 20, 1888; Feb. 21, 1889; Feb. 8 and 26, 1897), while by the early 1900s, all-female estudiantinas existed as well in the city (*ED*, June 7, 1905). Women also had a strong presence in the estudiantina scenes of Chile, Peru, Nicaragua, and Guatemala in roughly the same period, indicating a regional pattern (see Andreu Ricart 1995, 59, 72, 107–11, 119; Rendón Marín 2009, 34). As the 20th century proceeded, elite female participation in estudiantinas appears to have sharply declined in urban La Paz, a development perhaps linked to the cholo-mestizo sector's growing involvement in this ensemble tradition.

NEW DIRECTIONS: 6 DE AGOSTO, FILARMÓNICA 1º DE MAYO, AND ESTUDIANTINA CENTRO ARTÍSTICO HAYDN

The group 6 de Agosto (August 6th; Bolivian Independence Day) formed part of this emergent trend in La Paz's estudiantina scene. Active in the first decade of the 20th century, the ensemble consisted of *obreros* (workers), a designation that in Bolivia mainly refers to urban blue-collar wage laborers of cholo-mestizo cultural background. La Paz newspaper writers repeatedly pointed out the demographic makeup of 6 de Agosto when they were discussing the group (e.g., *ED*, May 31 and June 12, 1908), as this aspect of the estudiantina clearly was seen as unusual at the time. The musicians' ethnic and socioeconomic affiliations, along with the group's overtly patriotic name, caught the attention of the circle of President-Elect Fernando Guachalla in 1908.

Realizing the political benefits of associating the Liberal Party leader with the ensemble, the organizers of Guachalla's 1908 birthday celebration arranged for 6 de Agosto to offer the musical entertainment at his personal residence. In the late hours of May 29, the estudiantina "interpreted beautiful and [tastefully] selected musical pieces" for the incoming head of state and his guests, reported an *El Diario* writer, who moreover claimed that the performance "symbolized the affection that blue-collar youths [*la juventud obrera*] feel toward Doctor Guachalla" (*ED*, May 31, 1908). The journalist also noted that Guachalla, after commending the group's musicianship, implored them to play a few "national airs," to which they obliged (*ED*, May 31, 1908). From the fawning tone of the article, to the very presence of 6 de Agosto at the party, the affair served as a promotional piece for the President-Elect. It also foreshadowed how, in the coming decades, Bolivian political regimes would increasingly assert their leaders' supposed cultural affinities with *el pueblo* (the common people) through populist gestures involving musical performances by urban cholo-mestizo or rural indigenous ensembles.

By the 1920s, working-class estudiantinas like 6 de Agosto no longer were a rarity in La Paz, as documented in photographer Julio Cordero's many vivid portraits of paceño cholo-mestizo musicians, elegantly dressed in European-style suits and ties (which had replaced Spanish Renaissance garb as Bolivian estudiantina attire), posing with their bandurrias, mandolins, laúdes, and guitars (see Cárdenas 1986, 269–71; Cordero 2004, 38–41, 58–59; Stefanoni 2015, 61). For the cholo-mestizo sector, adopting elite cultural expressions represented a long-standing strategy for upward social mobility that enabled members of this intermediate stratum of society to demonstrate their cultural similarities with the upper class, and distinction from indigenous people (Chapter 1). The increasing presence of cholo-mestizo estudiantinas in the La Paz music scene of the 1920s, meanwhile, corresponds with another broader pattern. In Ecuador, the same decade saw the rise of obrero estudiantinas in Quito (Mullo Sandoval 2014), while in Arequipa, Peru, and especially Santiago, Chile, estudiantinas of working-class extraction constituted a major part of the scene by then (Andreu Ricart 1995, 125–28; Cornejo Díaz 2012, 384).

The La Paz ensemble 1° de Mayo (May 1st) represented this new direction. Interestingly, this blue-collar-affiliated group referred to itself as a *filarmónica* (philharmonic) rather than estudiantina, that is, Filarmónica 1° de Mayo, no doubt to underscore the refinement or classiness of their musicianship (additional local synonyms for "estudiantina" then included *orquesta típica, conjunto orquestal*, and *centro artístico*). For music critic Benjamín Alejo, the social-class standing of Filarmónica 1° de Mayo was highly noteworthy. In his 1925 overview of eminent La Paz musical institutions and ensembles—written for the official volume honoring Bolivia's first centennial of political independence—Alejo draws attention to the group's socioeconomic identity twice in the same sentence, first by inserting the word "obrero" into the estudiantina's actual name (i.e., "Filarmónica Obrera 1° de Mayo"), and second by praising the ensemble for its "beautiful cultural work among the obrero sector" (Alejo 1925, 360–61). Paceños evidently still associated estudiantinas primarily with the elite in the mid-1920s, otherwise Alejo would not have felt the need to emphasize the blue-collar status of the members of Filarmónica 1° de Mayo.

Even if Alejo had not mentioned that Filarmónica 1° de Mayo's musicians belonged to the obrero sector, his readers would have assumed it, anyway. The ensemble's name of "May 1st," after all, referenced May Day (also known as International Workers' Day, or Labor Day). Over the last two decades, May Day had become a major celebratory occasion for the labor movement in La Paz city (Klein 1969, 61; Lora 1977, 52, 98) and other urban Bolivian centers (for Oruro, see Smale 2010, 48, 107). In 1926, the Republican regime of Hernando Siles Reyes (1926–1930) instituted May Day as a national holiday, in recognition of the strength of the workers' movement (Smale 2010, 158).[8] Although Filarmónica 1° de Mayo's involvement in organized labor activities has not been documented, it is unlikely that the self-styled "May Day" ensemble refrained from participating in the May Day parades held in La Paz city in the 1920s.[9]

In 1928, over two decades before Bolivia's first record label would appear, Filarmónica 1° de Mayo became one of the earliest (if not *the* earliest) Bolivian estudiantinas to make recordings, when the group taped five tracks for RCA-Victor (in all probability at the Buenos Aires branch of the US-owned company). These selections reveal that the ensemble's mainstays were the huayño, cueca, and Incan foxtrot, a radical departure from the paceño estudiantina tradition's initial focus on genres and musical works that lacked Andean or even Bolivian associations.[10] By 1931, Filarmónica 1° de Mayo also performed settings of Andean indigenous melodies, given that it played this repertoire at the 1st Indianist Week coordinated by Los Amigos de la Ciudad (Chapter 2).

By then, La Paz's Estudiantina Centro Artístico Haydn (Haydn Artistic Center) and its allied symphonic orchestra, Orquesta Centro Artístico Haydn, had made recordings as well for the RCA-Victor label. These releases date from 1930 and comprise forty-six selections.[11] The time the Haydn groups spent in the studio was limited to only a couple of days, making the number of tracks that they completed quite impressive. In the sessions, Estudiantina Centro Artístico Haydn and Orquesta Centro Artístico Haydn exclusively recorded Bolivian criollo-mestizo genres, as Filarmónica 1° de Mayo had done two years earlier. Besides the huayño, cueca, and fox incaico, though, the Haydn ensembles recorded examples of the bailecito (labeled as "*baile*" or "*baile mixto*" [mixed dance]), chuntunqui (a Christmas-season genre practiced mainly in Chuquisaca), and carnaval (an eastern lowland genre from Santa Cruz, i.e., a form of música oriental).

"Ancha Chiri" (Quechua for "Very cold") is one of the tracks that Estudiantina Centro Artístico Haydn recorded in 1930 (RCA-Victor 30202-B). Composed by A. Ferreyra, it follows the traditional musical form of the bailecito, that is, AABA (preceded by a brief introduction), with the entire tune repeated three times. The mandolin and bandurria (and perhaps also laúd) players execute the melody in unison and parallel thirds for much of the piece and, in the signature estudiantina style, tremolo the long notes. The guitarists either strum chords or supply a bass line in the lower register. Dynamic changes offer variety and mark the sections. For the introduction, the ensemble performs at medium volume, before rising to forte for the A section of the principal melody, which they repeat once. The musicians suddenly drop the volume level to piano for the single B section, and unusually for a bailecito, shift to $\frac{2}{4}$ time (which might explain why the tune is identified as a baile mixto on the disc, rather than a bailecito). To conclude, Estudiantina Centro Artístico Haydn plays the last A section back at full volume. If this track is representative of the group's interpretive approach, it strongly resembles that of contemporaneous Peruvian estudiantinas (see Turino 1993, 126; Tucker 2013, 46–49).[12]

Estudiantina Centro Artístico Haydn's relationship with Orquesta Centro Artístico Haydn is reminiscent of the early years of La Paz's estudiantina tradition, when symphonic orchestras, chamber groups, choirs, and estudiantinas alternated at upper-class functions, in the style of the 1889 Sociedad Filarmónica event sketched earlier. The name of the ensemble, of course, harks back to the original Eurocentrism of Bolivian estudiantinas. That the Estudiantina Centro Artístico Haydn's repertoire in 1930 included traditional Bolivian genres, meanwhile, suggests that doing so had become common practice by this time among paceño estudiantinas, even for those of elite affiliation.

Although performing Bolivian folkloric numbers such as "Ancha Chiri" represented a recent direction in La Paz's estudiantina scene, a precedent existed in the original Spanish estudiantina tradition's inclusion of Iberian "folk" genres. Bolivian estudiantina arrangements of bailecitos, cuecas, and huayños could therefore have been seen by paceños as analogous to Estudiantina Fígaro's earlier settings of Spanish jotas and seguidillas. Given that the cueca and bailecito are Latin American variants of the Spanish jota (Chapter 1), La Paz musicians probably found it relatively straightforward to recast these two criollo-mestizo genres in particular as Bolivian estudiantina staples.

From the 1900s to 1920s, La Paz estudiantinas increasingly interpreted Bolivian-associated musical forms, at the very moment when cholo-mestizo artists started to form a major part of the estudiantina scene. That these two developments coincide suggests that the cholo-mestizo sector propelled the localization of the estudiantina repertoire, considering that Bolivian cholo-mestizos have tended to identify culturally with local "folk" genres to a greater degree than has the criollo class. Yet because paceño criollo interest in indigenista musical currents began to noticeably expand in the 1920s (Chapter 2), a more likely scenario is that elite and working-class La Paz estudiantinas became influenced by indigenismo at approximately the same time. In any event, the estudiantina movements of many Latin American countries experienced comparable processes of musical localization around the same period (see Torres 2007 for Venezuela; Ponce Valdivia 2008 for Peru; Rendón Marín 2009 for Colombia).

LIRA INCAICA AND INDIGENISMO

From its founding circa 1923 to dissolution in 1940, Lira Incaica stood at the forefront of the Bolivian estudiantina movement's growing embrace of indigenismo. Alberto

Ruiz Lavadenz directed the group, as mentioned in Chapter 2. A skilled instrumentalist and prolific composer—like his uncles Belisario Zárate and José Lavadenz Inchauste[13]—Ruiz Lavadenz disseminated his musical output through the ensembles that he organized. The name "Lira Incaica" (Incan lyre, or Incan estudiantina) reflected Bolivian indigenismo's Inca-centrism at the time.[14] It also might have taken after Compañia Lírica Incaica Ccorillacta, a Peruvian "Inca theater" troupe from Cuzco that had visited La Paz in 1917 (see Chapter 2).

Lira Incaica quickly established itself in the local scene. In the first year of the group's existence (1923), Ruiz Lavadenz secured an engagement for the ensemble at the Municipal Theater (Municipal Theater Recital Program, Dec. 1, 1923); this performance took place a month after Valcárcel's Misión Peruana de Arte Incaico had presented *Ollantay* and other Peruvian indigenista productions at the same venue (Chapter 2). Although Lira Incaica undoubtedly could stand on its own artistic merits, Ruiz Lavadenz's upper-middle-class status and family connections surely facilitated his ability to land a recital for Lira Incaica at the venerated Municipal Theater so soon after the group's formation.

Lira Incaica's repertoire at the 1923 recital encompassed an eclectic mix, as must have been customary among paceño estudiantinas at this transitional moment. In its set, the group alternated its indigenista musical numbers, such as Belisario Zárate's *Serenata Campestre—Tres Motivos Indianistas* and N. Zamudio's *Ccori Occlu* (probably a Peruvian work), with more traditional estudiantina fare, including European operetta excerpts (e.g., "Dance of the Dragonflies" by Austro-Hungarian composer Franz Lehár), and internationally fashionable non-Bolivian dances like the *maxixe*, or Brazilian tango (e.g., "Tristeza do Caboclo" [A peasant's sorrow]) (Lira Incaica Program, Dec. 1, 1923). Three years later, society figure José Salmón Ballivián (the future composer of *Suite Aymara*) gave his blessing to Ruiz Lavadenz's artistic endeavors, by awarding Lira Incaica the first-place trophy at the music contest that La Paz's Círculo de Bellas Artes (Center of Fine Arts) held in 1926 (*Hoy*, May 3, 1974).

In 1929, Ruiz Lavadenz left for Buenos Aires, where he would remain until 1934 (various documents, courtesy of Carola Cobo de Ruiz).[15] His stay in Argentina solidified his indigenista impulses (a pattern already seen with Eduardo Caba and José María Velasco Maidana; Chapter 2), as had his earlier expeditions to Peru. According to ethnologist Antonio Paredes Candia—a family member of Ruiz Lavadenz (and son of writer Rigoberto Paredes), Ruiz Lavadenz traveled to Peru on a few occasions in the 1920s, and his subsequent musical works exhibit the clear influence of Peruvian indigenismo (*Hoy*, May 3, 1974). The titles of some of Ruiz Lavadenz's compositions that date from the 1930s, especially the danza incaica "Apurímac" (named after the Peruvian departamento) and capricho "Inti Raymi," seem to confirm Paredes Candia's claim about Peruvian indigenismo's imprint on Ruiz Lavadenz's musical creations (*Hoy*, May 3, 1974).

The music scene of Buenos Aires would have been an enticing prospect for Ruiz Lavadenz. With the consolidation of the Argentine folklore movement, folkloric music artists were beginning to attract a significant audience in the national capital (Chamosa 2010). Most Buenos Aires–based folkloric musicians who were active in this period focused on expressive practices unique to, or primarily identified with, Argentina, such as the zamba, *chacarera*, and *gato*. But many of them also played the *carnavalito* (Argentine term for the huayño), yaraví, and bailecito. These Andean-associated genres animated fiestas in Argentina's northwesternmost *provincias* (equivalent to Bolivian departamentos) of Salta and Jujuy, which border southern Bolivia, and attract Bolivian migrant laborers. Many of the Andean music-dance genres that Lira Incaica performed, therefore, already had been known to folk-lore enthusiasts in Buenos Aires, as regional varieties of Argentine folkloric music, and/or as the musical traditions of the Bolivian migrants residing in the Argentine Northwest (Rios 2014, 202).

In his stay in Buenos Aires, Ruiz Lavadenz—who came to Argentina alone and organized various ad hoc ensembles there (mainly with expatriate Bolivians)—adopted performance practices that bear a striking resemblance to those of Bolivian folklore acts of the 1960s and beyond. For one, he gave his groups Andean indigenous-sounding names, not only "Lira Incaica," but also "Los Quichuas" (The Quechuas), "Los Collitas" (The Andeans, or Highland Bolivians), and "Dueto Incaico" (Incan duo).[16] Second, in promotional materials, the musicians are usually pictured in exoti-cist fashion, to match Argentine stereotypes of Bolivians, namely, the notion that "most Bolivians are Indians." A vivid example appears in a 1933 edition of the Buenos Aires newspaper *Crítica* (Aug. 20, 1933). Under the heading "Un Poco de Alma Nativa" (A touch of native soul), Ruiz Lavadenz and three bandmates, outfitted in ponchos and lluchus, pose alongside kena flutes while they partake in *chicha*, the maize-based alcoholic beverage consumed in the Andes since pre-Columbian times. In the caption accompanying the photograph, the text reads that "[i]t is necessary to have a drink of chicha before playing the kena," because doing so infuses kena melodies with "the soul of the mountain" (*Crítica*, Aug. 20, 1933).

In the area of musical interpretation, meanwhile, Ruiz Lavadenz's Argentine ver-sions of Lira Incaica—which usually had between four to six members and thus more closely resembled an Andean conjunto than his original Bolivian estudiantina—often highlighted the sonorities of typical Andean wind and stringed instruments, in a manner that again anticipated important later trends in Bolivian criollo-mestizo folkloric music. In 1933, Lira Incaica implemented this approach at the Argentine folklore festival "La Historia de Música, Canto, y Poesía Nacional" (The History of National Music, Poetry, and Song) (*La Prensa* [Buenos Aires newspaper], May 7, 1933). The ensemble, which consisted of five members on this occasion, opened its set with an introspective kena duo, the yaraví "Ckara-pampa" (Quechua-Spanish for "Barren land"). Changing the mood from contemplative to festive, the group then assumed the format of a tarka tropa, complete with accompanying caja drums, on "Cullahuas." Next up was a second meditative selection, "Canción del Llamero" (Song of the llama herder) for pinkillu and guitar. The title and instrumentation of "Canción del Llamero" strongly suggests that this number was meant to conjure up the clichéd archetype of an Andean indigenous flute player musically expressing his sorrows.[17] For their last two selections, Lira Incaica performed the *kjaluyo*[18] "Pampanjay" (Quechua for "My land") and bailecito "Estoy Chispa" (I'm shameless). The singers demonstrated their facility with interpreting texts in Andean indigenous languages, as "Pampanjay" and "Estoy Chispa" include stanzas in Aymara and Quechua, respectively.

The principal solo instruments that Andean conjuntos such as Bolivia's Los Jairas and Chile's Inti-Illimani would feature in the 1960s, namely, the kena and charango, often similarly played a starring role on the tracks that Lira Incaica recorded in the 1930s at the Buenos Aires branch of RCA-Victor. When discussing Lira Incaica's releases for the label, Argentine critics frequently mentioned the haunting kena lines present on the selections (e.g., *La Prensa*: Notas Fonográficas, Sept. 23, 1932), which Ruiz Lavadenz probably performed. He also appears to have been the group's charango soloist. In any case, on Lira Incaica's recording of the kjaluyo "Paceñita" (RCA-Victor 37022-A), the charango player alternately realizes the melody, finger-style, with *punteado* (plucked) and *rasgueado* (strummed) passages, while the guitarists provide harmonic accompaniment. This style of charango performance, which differs considerably from how rural indigenous charango musicians typically use the instrument in the Southern Andes, has long been the standard approach for criollo and mestizo *charanguistas* in Bolivia and Peru (see Turino 1984).

Lira Incaica also used conventional European stringed instruments to interpret Ruiz Lavadenz's arrangements of Andean indigenous melodies. The ensemble's RCA-Victor track "Tonada de Tarka con Cullaguas" (Tarka tune with cullaguas), for example, opens with the mandolinists and guitarists playing a pentatonic melody that has all of the features of an indigenous tarka piece, including AABBCC form; extensive borrowing of motives from section to section; standard cadences; and parallel-fifth harmony (see Example 3.1).[19] "Tonada de Tarka con Cullaguas" conceivably forms the basis of the tarka tropa number "Cullahuas" that, as discussed earlier, Lira Incaica presented in 1933 at the Argentine festival "The History of National Music, Poetry, and Song."[20]

EXAMPLE 3.1 Lira Incaica, "Tonada de Tarka con Cullaguas," mandolin melody on opening segment

In early 1934, after immersing himself in the Argentine folklore scene for five years, Ruiz Lavadenz returned to La Paz and re-established Lira Incaica as a full-sized estudiantina. It was a perfect fit for Radio Illimani. With Bolivia in the midst of the Chaco War (1932–1935), the state-operated station regularly scheduled "national music" programs to rouse patriotic sentiments among the citizenry (Chapter 2). From February to December 1934, Lira Incaica served as a house band for Radio Illimani (signed letter from Radio Illimani, Oct. 1, 1935) and thereby exposed Bolivian listeners across the country to the group's musical style and the compositional output of its director. Ruiz Lavadenz left the station's musical personnel in late 1934, to fulfill his military service. Radio Illimani continued to showcase the music of Lira Incaica, though, by broadcasting the ensemble's RCA-Victor recordings, which Ruiz Lavadenz had deposited with the station expressly for this purpose (various documents, courtesy of Carola Cobo de Ruiz).

Once the Chaco War had concluded, Ruiz Lavadenz created yet another iteration of "Lira Incaica." This group took part in a 1936 event that was tailor made for them, the 2nd Indianist Week (Chapter 2). He traveled again to Buenos Aires a few months later, this time with his estudiantina (which similarly would record numerous tracks for RCA-Victor) and his newly formed folk theater company. Ruiz Lavadenz's second period in Argentina lasted until 1939, overlapping with the Buenos Aires premiere of Bolivian composer José María Velasco Maidana's "Inca ballet" *Amerindia* (Chapter 2).

By the time Ruiz Lavadenz resettled in Bolivia in 1939, indigenismo had thoroughly penetrated La Paz's estudiantina scene, a development that must have pleased him. Unfortunately, his involvement in the Bolivian folklore movement ended soon thereafter; Ruiz Lavadenz passed away in late 1939 (*ED*, Nov. 18, 1939). Radio Illimani paid homage to his memory, with a program of poetry readings and folkloric music (undated newspaper clipping; personal collection of Carola Cobo de Ruiz). One of the highlights was the set by the vocal duo Las Hermanas Tejada, who had briefly formed part of Lira Incaica in the months prior to the estudiantina's 1936 trip to Argentina (as discussed later in the chapter). Known above all for their Andean indigenous-themed repertoire, Las Hermanas Tejada sang a few yaravís authored by Ruiz Lavadenz.

Many of Ruiz Lavadenz's compositions, especially those that Lira Incaica recorded for RCA-Victor in the 1930s, would attain the status of Bolivian folkloric classics in the following decades. Examples include "Hasta Otro Día" (Until another day; also known as "Desde Que Te Conocí" [Since I met you]), "Cacharpaya del Soldado" (A soldier's farewell), "Del Prado Vengo" (From the Prado I come), "A Los Bosques" (To the forests), "Lappa Kummu" (Aymara for "Filthy, hunchbacked man"), and "Auqui Auqui." The first full-length album of Los Jairas (released in 1966) includes a rendering of Ruiz Lavadenz's "Auqui Auqui," while for Los Jairas founder Gilbert Favre's tongue-in-cheek theme song, "El Gringo Bandolero" (recorded in 1967), the group superimposed a new text over Ruiz Lavadenz's satiric huayño "Lappa Kummu" (Chapter 7).

Lira Incaica briefly carried on after the death of its director. In February 1940, the estudiantina entered a Concurso Folklórico in La Paz, and went home with the first-place award (*ED*, Feb. 14, 1940). The prize committee bestowed the fourth-place medal to an offshoot of the group, Lira Incaica Tiwanaku. The ensemble's name referenced two pre-Columbian Andean civilizations that never had coincided temporally, an awkward attempt at combining indigenous signifiers of Cuzco and La Paz. Bolivian state-sponsored estudiantina festivals like the 1940 Concurso Folklórico, meanwhile, had recently become common in La Paz, and represented a key site where the leading criollo-mestizo indigenista musicians interacted with estudiantinas formed by cholo-mestizo artists.

1939 CONCURSO POPULAR DE ARTE FOLKLÓRICO

In September 1939, La Paz mayor Humberto Muñoz Cornejo, a founding member and then president of Los Amigos de la Ciudad (which had organized the first and second editions of the Indianist Week), informed the public that the Municipality would be staging a Concurso Popular de Arte Folklórico on October 20, the anniversary of the city's establishment. It was the Municipality's duty to "stimulate culture, especially among *las clases populares* [i.e., the working-classes]," Muñoz Cornejo declared in the summons. He also explained that the competition would be limited to plucked-string ensembles that interpreted "vernacular music." In his view, this category encompassed "autochthonous dances" (i.e., rural indigenous expressive practices) along with standard criollo-mestizo genres such as the huayño, bailecito, yaraví, and "waltzes featuring criollo motives." The types of musical practices that fell within these guidelines, the mayor stated, constituted "a manifestation of the soul of the people" (*ED*, Sept. 17, 1939).

Matching the festival's "native art" theme (*ED*, Sept. 17, 1939), the names of several of the participating estudiantinas displayed impossible-to-miss references to Andean indigenous culture. Examples include the groups Tahuantinsuyo (i.e., the Inca Empire), Kollasuyo (the Incan era designation for the La Paz region and the adjacent highland and valley regions that eventually became modern-day Bolivia), Inca Huasi (Quechua for "House of the Inca"), Inti-Karkas (Quechua for "Fortress of the sun"), and Huiñay Inti (Quechua for "Eternal sun"). The presence of the word "Inti" (Sun) in the names of the last two estudiantinas unmistakably represented an allusion to Inca cosmology, as the Cuzco-based ruling class of the Inca Empire worshiped the sun god above all other deities. The strong imprint of Peruvian indigenismo on the La Paz musical scene also explains why Quechua (a language not widely spoken in the La Paz region) rather than Aymara was the indigenous language that the members of these groups turned to when deciding what to call their estudiantinas. Also worthy of note is that none of the ensembles had adopted names that recalled the European origins of the estudiantina tradition, because doing so had fallen out of favor in urban La Paz by the late 1930s.

Adrián Patiño Carpio, Eduardo Calderón Lugones, and an unidentified representative from Los Amigos de la Ciudad formed the prize committee for the Concurso

Popular de Arte Folklórico, ensuring that ensembles of indigenista bent would fare well in the contest. As explained in Chapter 2, Patiño Carpio and Calderón Lugones were major figures in La Paz's indigenista musical scene of the 1920s. By the 1930s, Patiño Carpio, who continued to direct the Army Band and compose marches, Incan foxtrots, and other musical expressions for the brass band medium (Rojas Rojas 1989, 51–54), had become involved in various capacities with paceño estudiantinas, including Filarmónica 1° de Mayo, Estudiantina Centro Artístico Haydn, Obreros de la Cruz (Workers of the Cross), and Kollasuyo (Rivera de Stahlie 1995, 85–86). Calderón Lugones, meanwhile, still dabbled in indigenista art-classical music composition. In 1937, a recent piece of his, *La Sombra de los Llameros* (The shadow of the llama herders), obtained third place at the Gran Festival Nacional de Artes Folklóricos in the contest for musical works with "Indian motives" (*ED*, July 13 and 20, 1937). To preserve his anonymity, as the rules required, Calderón Lugones submitted *La Sombra de los Llameros* to the competition under his pseudonym "Zampoñari de Italaque" (Panpipe player from Italaque), an obvious reference to the "Sikuris de Italaque" tradition.

After finalizing their deliberations, the jury announced the winners of the Concurso Popular de Arte Folklórico. First place went to Kollasuyo. With a lineup of mandolins, guitars, charangos, kenas, and a concertina, Kollasuyo had impressed the committee with its "faithful interpretations of indigenous music," in particular the pieces "Aire Italaqueño" (Melody from Italaque) and "Pusipía" (*ED*, Nov. 4, 1939); the latter musical number was named after a type of Andean indigenous end-notched flute that resembles the kena (although pusipías are considerably larger than kenas, and have only four finger holes). Centro Artístico Illimani earned third place,[21] and special plaudits for its compositions, among which the jury singled out "Chiriguano." This selection simultaneously evoked highland and lowland "Indians"; chiriguanos (or chiriwanos) is the name of a highland panpipe-tropa genre that pays homage to the lowland chiriguano people, specifically to their bravery in fighting off Incan and Spanish attempts to subjugate them. Also pleasing the committee with its indigenous-themed repertoire was the ensemble that received the fourth-place trophy, Inti-Karkas. The group performed "Sicuri" (alternate spelling for sikuri), "Kena-Kena," and "Kaluyo Italaqueño," with an unusual estudiantina configuration in which the charango players outnumbered and as a result must have drowned out the group's mandolinists, guitarists, and kenistas (*ED*, Nov. 4, 1939).

In the verdict, the prize committee praised all of the participating groups for their nativist repertoire and instrumentation, and underscored how this trend departed from earlier Bolivian estudiantina practices:

> It is interesting and worthy of applause to note that the majority of the orquestas típicas [i.e., estudiantinas][22] who participated in this year's competition exhibited a tendency to turn to the roots of indigenous music, by using autochthonous rhythms and motives and including instruments that impart greater local flavor, such as kenas, charangos, etc.; in contrast to what occurred previously, when the estudiantinas of the working-class sector believed that it

was in good taste to assimilate music from abroad, basing their programs on pasodobles, fox-trots, and tangos, employing instruments solely of European origin (guitars, mandolins), while ignoring the vernacular. (*ED*, Nov. 4, 1939)

Of Bolivia's many locally distinctive instruments, the charango represented the most natural choice for inclusion into the estudiantina lineup, considering its close similarities in size, tessitura, and construction (e.g., double-coursed instrument) with the mandolin, bandurria, and laúd. Yet instead of replacing these estudiantina standbys, the charango filled a complementary musical function in the tradition, one that took full advantage of the sonorities afforded by the instrument's re-entrant tuning (ee-AA-eE-CC-GG is the usual setup for criollo-mestizo charangos). While the mandolinists, bandurria players, and laúdistas executed single-note passages with a plectrum, the charanguistas vigorously strummed on their instruments, with rasgueado technique, to enrichen the musical texture with tertian triad-based chords.

In Peru, charango players enacted the same role in estudiantinas in the regions of Puno, Cuzco, and Ayacucho (see Turino 1993, 126; González Ríos and González Ríos 1998; Ponce Valdivia 2008; Cornejo Díaz 2012, 381–88; Tucker 2013, 46–49). Given that many urban La Paz musicians were highly influenced by Peruvian indigenismo, it is possible that the paceño estudiantina movement's incorporation of the charango drew from the example of Peruvian ensembles. Throughout the Americas, however, estudiantinas often added regional plucked string instruments to localize their lineups in this period. Colombian estudiantinas, for instance, integrated the *bandola* and *tiple* (Rendón Marín 2009), whereas Venezuelan estudiantinas made room for the *cuatro* (Torres 2007).

The kena also entered the La Paz estudiantina format by the late 1930s, a development that again parallels the Peruvian case. Musically, the kena had a melodic function in Bolivian and Peruvian estudiantinas, similar to that of the Western transverse flute in the original tradition. Since the 1800s, Spanish estudiantinas had used the Western transverse flute, although not as a core component of the group (see Christoforidis 2017).

A month after the Concurso Popular de Arte Folklórico had taken place, Filarmónica 1° de Mayo, Kollasuyo, Inti-Karkas, Lira Andina, and various other local ensembles founded the Liga Matriz Folklórica Departamental, to coordinate estudiantina activities for the La Paz region (*ED*, Dec. 18, 1939). This entity's appearance suggests that the number of paceño estudiantinas had risen to a significant extent by late 1939. The locale chosen for the unveiling of the Liga Matriz Folklórica Departamental, the Sociedad de Obreros "El Porvenir" (Workers' Club "The Future"), reflects another important recent development in La Paz's estudiantina tradition, its increasingly strong identification with the obrero class. A mutual-aid society for blue-collar workers, the Sociedad de Obreros "El Porvenir" played an "extremely important" part in the country's "labor and socialist movements," and back in 1908, had organized Bolivia's first public May Day celebration (Lora 1977, 52, 98).

By the late 1930s, the labor movement had grown considerably in La Paz, largely as a result of the city's rising number of factories (mainly for textile production) and other manufacturing establishments that produced goods for the Bolivian market-place (see Young 2017, 117–18). Paceño musicians who derived their primary income from blue-collar occupations (most of which had affiliated unions) came to predominate in the estudiantina scene, to such an extent that by 1940, La Paz journalists were habitually using the expression *conjunto obrero*, or "worker's group," as a synonym for estudiantina (e.g., *ED*, May 4, 1940). For urban La Paz-based politicians, conveying an appreciation for, and an affinity with, the estudiantina tradition had recently become a potentially effective means for reaching out to the urban working class.

THE ORQUESTA TÍPICA LA PAZ

In December 1944, five days before Christmas, Radio Illimani commemorated the one-year anniversary of Gualberto Villarroel's ascension to the presidency, with a full day of programming devoted to the "Revolution of December 20" (*ED*, Dec. 20, 1944). RADEPA-MNR officials addressed the nation in the late evening portion of the broadcast, which began around 9:30 p.m. and ended about two hours later. Musical performances flanked each speech. A military brass band set a patriotic tone for Villarroel's lecture with a rendition of the National Anthem, while the talk that MNR chief (and future Bolivian President) Víctor Paz Estenssoro delivered was followed by Filarmónica 1° de Mayo's version of the "Danza Guerrera" (War dance) move-ment from *Suite Aymara*. Filarmónica 1° de Mayo also played the other movements of Salmón Ballivián's celebrated composition, interspersed between the ensuing three speeches. The group then offered two danceable pieces, the cueca "Raquel" (Rachel) and taquirari "Alianza" (Alliance), the second of which in all likelihood alluded to the freshly restored RADEPA-MNR alliance.[23] Another estudiantina, Los Andes, took the spotlight next, to close the transmission with an unspecified set of "native music and dance" (*ED*, Dec. 20, 1944).

Filarmónica 1° de Mayo's and Los Andes' radio performances were in accordance with the RADEPA-MNR government's overtures toward cholo-mestizo laborers. Obtaining this sector's political support was of vital importance to the administration but would prove to be a major challenge (Gotkowitz 2007, 164–232). Instead of backing the regime, much of the cholo-mestizo workforce joined the ranks of Bolivia's leading communist party, the Partido de la Izquierda Revolucionaria (Party of the Revolutionary Left; PIR). Considerably further on the left, ideologically, than the MNR and RADEPA, the PIR positioned itself as the leftist opposition to the administration (Gotkowitz 2007, 165).

Villarroel had other major problems to deal with as well. About a month before the Radio Illimani program aired, state operatives had clandestinely executed several high-ranking opposition figures—a group that included congressmen and ex-cabinet ministers—for plotting a coup against the administration. The President and his chief officers almost immediately realized that the assassinations amounted to a massive "political miscalculation" (Klein 1969, 377). Although it was far from unheard of for Bolivian political regimes to suppress dissent through violent means, these actions traditionally had targeted the cholo-mestizo sector or indigenous people, and not the uppermost socioeconomic class. The Villarroel government rashly broke from this precedent when it ordered the executions (Klein 1969, 377).

Frantically, RADEPA-MNR officials tried to portray the administration in a positive light, as the champion of the people, before the public caught wind of the regime's responsibility for the "November massacre" (Klein 1969, 377). In time for the 1944 Christmas season, President Villarroel signed off on a string of blatantly populist measures, from the establishment of a new national holiday, Day of the Miner, to the institutionalization of Christmas bonuses and paid vacations for workers employed in white- and blue-collar professions (Klein 1969, 378).

The La Paz Municipality passed a "national music" ordinance of singular breadth in Bolivian history at this exceedingly tense moment in Villarroel's presidency.[24] The decree, which applied only to the La Paz region, compelled (1) radio stations to begin and conclude broadcasts with thirty minutes of "national music," and integrate "national airs" into dance-music programs; (2) military bands and orquestas populares (e.g., estudiantinas, orquestas de jazz[25]) to start sets with three "vernacular" or "national" tunes; (3) nighttime locales with live musical entertainment (e.g., boîtes, confiterías) to offer "national" selections every half hour; (4) elite-oriented artistic events (e.g., literary readings, theater productions) to incorporate "native music by national composers" (the decree names Salmón Ballivián, Velasco Maidana, Patiño Carpio, and Simeón Roncal as examples of national composers); and (5) spectacles geared to the masses (e.g., soccer games, boxing matches) to feature "national music" acts in the proceedings.[26] Those who violated these stipulations, the decree warned, would be fined and, for a "moral sanction," undergo the indignity of having their names printed in the newspaper (ED, Dec. 20, 1944).

The extent to which paceño musicians and business operators observed the ordinance is difficult to determine, because of the current lack of available documentation. The experience of Radio Fides, though, indicates that the decree did have an effect on radio programming. Owned by the Catholic Church, the station recently had limited its musical offerings to European art-classical works. The management of Radio Fides believed that this programming was consistent with their mission of uplifting and edifying the Bolivian public (Brun 2000, 54–56). In the months following the enactment of the Municipal ordinance, none of Radio Fides's shows featured traditional Bolivian musical genres, or even Bolivian art-classical compositions. This state of affairs would have been obvious to anyone who read El Diario, given that the station advertised its broadcast schedule in the paper (e.g., ED, Jan. 10, Jan. 17, Mar. 24, and Apr. 11, 1945).

By May 1945, the Municipality had had enough of Radio Fides's intransigence. The La Paz mayor ordered the station to abide by the provisions of the decree, and ominously noted in an El Diario article that he had informed the Police department of the situation (*ED*, May 10, 1945). A compromise was soon reached. By late June, Radio Fides had added two fifteen-minute "national music" segments to its daily broadcasts: the first one opened the programming, while the second aired at approximately 6:00 p.m. (*ED*, June 23, July 14, Aug. 1, and Aug. 22, 1945).

By then, state-run Radio Municipal was complying with the decree by broadcasting the music of the Orquesta Típica La Paz, similar to how La Paz's other state-operated station, Radio Illimani, had been featuring the latest folkloric numbers of its house musicians (see the section "Música Oriental in La Paz in the Villarroel Years"). A recently created, and state-sponsored, estudiantina, Orquesta Típica La Paz exclusively played Bolivian musical works, especially indigenista compositions, a repertoire that aligned ideologically with the RADEPA-MNR government's outreach to Andean rural indigenous people (see Chapter 2).[27] And as previously noted, the ensemble's configuration as an estudiantina articulated with the regime's efforts at improving its relations with the sector then most associated with this musical tradition, the obrero class.

José Salmón Ballivián, Eduardo Calderón Lugones, and Radio Municipal director Luis Lavadenz (another relative of Alberto Ruiz Lavadenz) conceptualized the creation of the Orquesta Típica La Paz, as the "Music Committee" appointed by the Consejo Departamental de Cultura (Regional Council of Culture) (*ED*, May 3 and 11, 1945). In the upcoming Fiestas Julianas season, the same three individuals would sit on the jury for the Concurso Vernacular y Folkórico, a spectacle of Andean indigenous music and dance that President Villarroel attended (Chapter 2). Perhaps in anticipation of this festival, at an early point in its deliberations, the "Music Committee" considered having the Orquesta Típica La Paz mainly employ traditional highland indigenous wind instruments, such as the siku, kena, and pinkillu (*ED*, May 3, 1945), before ultimately settling on the estudiantina format.[28]

Potosí's Orquesta Sinfolklórica "Arte y Trabajo" (Art and labor) most likely served as a model for the Orquesta Típica La Paz. Established in the 1930s, and also known as Sociedad Arte y Trabajo (Bigenho 2002, 127–28), the Potosí group visited La Paz city in July 1945 (*ED*, July 21, 22, and 24, 1945)—the month that the Orquesta Típica La Paz debuted. Under the guidance of Dr. René Villa Gómez, the ensemble interpreted Bolivian compositions, such as Potosí musician Humberto Iporre Salinas's *Oración del Mitayo*,[29] and cueca "Tu Orgullo" (Your pride). They also performed a Peruvian piece, the classic fox incaico "Vírgenes del Sol" (*ED*, July 24, 1945). The group's lineup no doubt was eye catching. The Orquesta Sinfolklórica "Arte y Trabajo" included not only mandolins, bandurrias, guitars, charangos, and kenas, but also violins, cellos, clarinets, saxophones, trombones, flutes, piano, bandoneón, and other instruments. With over sixty musicians, Potosí's "folk-symphonic orchestra" approximated the dimensions of an actual Western symphonic orchestra, as a photograph taken at one of its recitals in La Paz attests (*ED*, July 22, 1945).

Eastern European plucked-string orchestras, which in a comparable fashion juxtapose "Western classical" and regional "folk" instruments (see Olson 2004; Buchanan 2006), might have been another source of inspiration for the Orquesta Típica La Paz. Many Bolivians were aware of these state-sponsored Socialist Bloc ensembles. Since the 1930s, La Paz radio stations had transmitted recordings of Eastern European groups of this variety, so much so that in 1939 one Radio Illimani listener who preferred to hear "national music" complained through an op-ed in El Diario that the station was devoting too much of its programming to Russian *balalaika* music (*ED*, Mar. 8, 1939).

To lead the Orquesta Típica La Paz and arrange its repertoire, the "Music Committee" appointed Erich Eisner (*ED*, July 11, 1945). A Czech-Austrian émigré, Eisner had extensive experience in Western art-classical music, and recently had taken over Velasco Maidana's former position as the conductor of the National Symphony Orchestra (Chapter 2). Given Eisner's recent arrival to the country (around 1939), it is doubtful that he was deeply knowledgeable about typical forms of Bolivian music, making him seem an odd choice for the director position with the Orquesta Típica La Paz. Yet for "Music Committee" members Salmón Ballivián and Calderón Lugones, Eisner's credentials probably represented the ideal background, in light of their own high regard for European art-classical music. It is generally true, moreover, that the Bolivian upper classes tended to view Western classical music as a "universal" musical expression, and accordingly would normally have deemed an individual as skilled in its execution as Eisner to be supremely qualified for heading any serious musical endeavor. Reflecting this Eurocentric bias, Bolivian music critics frequently characterized Eisner's interpretive approach with the Orquesta Típica La Paz—which constituted somewhat of a return to the 19th-century art-classical roots of the paceño estudiantina tradition (although not in terms of repertoire)—as "elevating" national folkloric music (e.g., *ED*, Jan. 13, Apr. 6 and 25, 1946).

The Orquesta Típica La Paz mainly performed on the live broadcasts of Radio Municipal, but from time to time the group offered concerts in public spaces. One of the earliest took place in August 1945, at an indigenista function held on Day of the Indian at the salon of the Ministry of Education, Fine Arts, and Indigenous Affairs. In a program that included recitations of the poems "Homenaje al Indio" (Homage to the Indian) and "El Poncho Rojo" (The red poncho), the Orquesta Típica La Paz interpreted Ismael Zeballos's "Chokolulu" (the name of an Andean plant), Simeón Roncal's "Kaluyo Indio No. 2" (Indian kaluyo no. 2), and Salmón Ballivián's latest composition, *Trilogía India* (Indian trilogy) (*ED*, July 31, 1945).[30] In the same spirit stylistically as *Suite Aymara*, *Trilogía India* would join the pantheon of Bolivian indigenista "classical" masterpieces, in the arrangement that Eisner crafted for the National Symphony Orchestra.[31]

By the next year, Eisner had substantially enlarged the repertoire of the Orquesta Típica La Paz, with his settings of José Lavadenz Inchauste's *Alma de la Montaña* (Soul of the mountain), Belisario Zárate's *Serenata Campestre–Tres Motivos Indianistas* and *Wara Wara*, Jorge Parra's *Escenas Incaicas* (Incan scenes), Armando Palmero's *Poema Indio* (Indian poem), and Humberto Viscarra Monje's *Canción Lejanías* (Song from far away), among other works. To lighten up its programs, the ensemble also played stylized versions of criollo-mestizo dance genres, especially the cueca (e.g., Simeón Roncal's "Huérfana Virginia" [The orphan Virginia]) (*ED*, Apr. 2 and 6; May 13, 1946).[32]

In the turbulent final months of the RADEPA-MNR government, the Orquesta Típica La Paz gave three recitals at the Municipal Theater (*ED*, Apr. 2 and 6; May 13, 1946). One was advertised as a "free concert for the workers," and thus was explicitly geared toward the obrero class (*ED*, May 13, 1946). For President Villarroel, who took the time to attend at least one of the recitals (*ED*, Apr. 6, 1946), his regime's negligible success in courting the cholo-mestizo labor force represented an ongoing source of frustration. In the end, this key sector not only was largely unmoved by his populist gestures, but also played an active role in overthrowing his administration in July 1946 (Gotkowitz 2007, 191, 233).

By late 1946 or early 1947, the Orquesta Típica La Paz had ceased to exist, in all likelihood because the Municipality severed its sponsorship of major initiatives that dated back to the RADEPA-MNR years. And perhaps because the ensemble formed part of a failed political initiative by the ousted administration, and never made recordings, paceños forgot about the Orquesta Típica La Paz relatively quickly.[33]

As for La Paz's estudiantina tradition, it entered into a long period of decline by the end of the decade. Only a handful of paceño estudiantinas that were active in the 1940s would persist into the post-1952 years; Filarmónica 1° de Mayo figures among the few examples (see *ED*, Jan. 12, 1953). Newly formed estudiantinas would be a rarity in La Paz in the 1950s and 1960s, and none would attain the recognition of their precursors. The brass band tradition, which involves a similar number of musicians, but whose capacity for volume far supercedes that of an estudiantina, appears to have gradually usurped the estudiantina's place as the ensemble format of choice for cholo-mestizo musicians in urban La Paz and the other major cities of highland Bolivia.

No Bolivian state-sponsored ensemble analogous to the Orquesta Típica La Paz would be established in the ensuing sexenio period (1946–1952). Two years after the 1952 Revolution, though, Radio Illimani debuted a new house band with an indigenista orientation. The group was named Conjunto 31 de Octubre (October 31st ensemble), a direct reference to the date in 1952 that the first Paz Estenssoro government (1952–1956) expropriated or "nationalized" the properties of the "Big Three" tin mining barons. Conjunto 31 de Octubre could be characterized as a mini-estudiantina, or proto-Andean conjunto, as its instrumentation lies somewhere in between that of a standard estudiantina and Andean conjunto (Chapter 5).

From the 1880s to 1940s, paceño estudiantinas progressively imbued their repertoire, instrumentation, and ensemble names with signifiers of indigeneity—future hallmarks of the Andean conjunto tradition—while casting aside many of the original characteristics of the Spanish plucked-string-orchestra tradition. The estudiantina scenes of many other Latin American countries underwent comparable changes over this period. Although in each setting estudiantinas incorporated regionally distinctive musical forms and oftentimes typical local instruments, these "nationalist" practices nonetheless are best understood as country- or region-specific iterations of an artistic trend that spanned the Americas. Bolivia's indigenista estudiantinas of the 1930s and 1940s thus foreshadowed Andean conjuntos of the 1960s and 1970s not only through their indigenista performance practices, but also by forming part of a widely diffused, transnational or cosmopolitan artistic movement.

The female vocal duo represented another popular ensemble format for interpreting Bolivian folkloric expressions in the 1930s and 1940s. Whereas paceños had come to strongly identify estudiantinas with obreros by the late 1930s, however, the local female duo tradition never acquired a comparable association with a socioeconomic or ethnic stratum of Bolivian society. This appears to have broadened the audience for Las Hermanas Tejada and Las Kantutas, who rose to the apex of the Bolivian folkloric music movement in the 1940s. The rest of this chapter chronicles their activities from the late 1930s to early 1950s, as another glimpse into indigenista musical currents, especially in the mass-mediated sphere (i.e., folkloric-popular music), and to document the entrance of two forms of música oriental into the national folkloric music canon.

LATIN AMERICAN FEMALE DUOS IN THE 1930S AND 1940S

In many Latin American countries, the female folkloric vocal duo experienced its golden age in the 1930s and 1940s (see Moreno Rivas 1989, 85, 93; Koegel 2002, 99, 105–6; González Rodríguez 2005, 256–61; Dent 2009; Wong 2012, 64; Santamaría-Delgado 2014, 179). Groups of this type harmonized mainly in parallel thirds and other consonant intervals (especially sixths), while occasionally inserting solos. Sisters comprised most of these ensembles, imparting a wholesome quality to the tradition, and evoking the aura of informal music making at family gatherings.

Mexico City radio station XEW (founded in 1930), whose broadcasts could be picked up as far away as South America (Pedelty 1999, 39–40), played a major role in popularizing the female duo format in Latin America. Las Hermanas Águila (the Águila Sisters) were among the earliest female folkloric duos to obtain international fame through the transmissions of XEW. From Guadalajara, the group debuted on the station's music programs in 1934, and before long became known as "The Best Duo of the Americas" (Moreno Rivas 1989, 85, 93). Many other Mexican groups of this variety performed on XEW in the late 1930s and 1940s, including the renowned Las Hermanas Padilla (Koegel 2002, 105–6).

In La Paz, male and female vocal duos received regular airplay on Radio Illimani in the Chaco War era (1932–1935); two examples were the Dueto Aymara-Illimani and Dueto Murillo-Catacora (Cárdenas 1986, 50). Newspaper reports sometimes mention the names of duos such as these, but seldom offer additional information, even the gender of the members. This omission also generally holds true for the years immediately following the Chaco War, when Dueto Nacional Luna-Tellez and Dueto de Arte Nativo performed on Radio Illimani (*ED*, Jan. 13 and 27, 1936). Dueto Las Pampitas figures among the few La Paz duos of the time whose gender identity is easy to ascertain, because the ensemble's name contains the definite article "Las" and feminine noun "Pampitas." This short-lived group made an appearance on La Paz's Radio Nacional in June 1938, to interpret a set of Bolivian *"canciones criollas"* (criollo songs) (*ED*, June 17, 1938).[34]

LAS KANTUTAS AND LAS HERMANAS TEJADA

About six months later, Radio Illimani programmed a musical extravaganza for its 1938 Christmas Eve broadcast. From 7 p.m. to midnight, Bolivian audiences, gathered in their homes for the holiday and, counting down the hours and minutes until Christmas Day, were treated to well-known and up-and-coming acts. Filarmónica 1° de Mayo, art-classical musician Jorge Parra (who conducted orchestral and choral works that evening), and pianist and indigenista composer Julio Martínez Arteaga fell into the category of established figures, while Las Hermanas Tejada, Las Kantutas, and singer Pepa Cardona represented budding artists, albeit ones who were already attracting attention in the La Paz scene (*ED*, Dec. 24, 1938).

Alberto Ruiz Lavadenz had "discovered" Las Hermanas Tejada a few years earlier, according to founding member María Luisa Tejada (personal communication). While walking past the Tejada's family home in La Paz city in 1935 or 1936, he overheard the melodious vocals of sisters María Luisa and Yolanda, accompanied by their father Zenobio's guitar strums. Impressed with the music making, Ruiz Lavadenz could not help but introduce himself and, before long, he was able to convince the Tejadas to join Lira Incaica. Their time in his estudiantina was brief, because they stayed behind in La Paz when the other members of Lira Incaica left for Buenos Aires in late 1936 (María Luisa Tejada, personal communication). Las Hermanas Tejada participated in one of the last recitals Lira Incaica gave in Bolivia before the ensemble traveled to Argentina. The program offers a rare glimpse into Lira Incaica's instrumentation. On this occasion, Ruiz Lavadenz's estudiantina consisted of four guitars, three charangos, two mandolins, two concertinas, and two kenas (Lira Incaica Recital Program, Nov. 1936).

Zenobio Tejada, who was one of Lira Incaica's guitarists at this concert, kept a close watch over his daughters' musical careers, as their artistic director and main accompanist. He made a living as a chemistry teacher, so it was in his spare time that he turned to his passion, making music. One of his favorite activities was preparing repertoire for his daughters. Zenobio Tejada's arrangements and original creations often invoked the music-dance traditions that Aymara-speaking communities practiced in the area near the Lake Titicaca town of Santiago de Huata (Omasuyos Province). Born and raised in the town, he owned hacienda lands in the province, which he regularly visited even after he had relocated to La Paz city (Elsa Tejada, personal communication).

"Kena Kena," "Waka Tokoris," "Armjjakiristta" (subtitled "huayño in classic Aymara"), and "Llakin-llakippa" are some examples of Zenobio Tejada's output as an arranger of indigenista repertoire for Las Hermanas Tejada (*ED*, Dec. 21, 1940;

Arauco 2011, 160). The sibling duo also performed standard Andean criollo-mestizo genres, such as the cueca and bailecito, and at least one of Ruiz Lavadenz's compositions with a Quechua text, his Peruvian-themed danza incaica "Apurímac" (*ED*, Feb. 10, 1941).

Zenobio Tejada's settings of Aymara musical expressions, for vocal duet with guitar accompaniment, might have drawn inspiration from Antonio González Bravo's harmonically similar works for choir, such as those found in the 1934 collection *Lírica de Warisata: 6 Canciones Aimaras* (Chapter 2). With Santiago de Huata's relatively close proximity to Warisata (32.4 kilometers, or 20 miles), Zenobio Tejada must have been familiar with Gonzalez Bravo's musical ventures at the town's pioneering ayllu-school. The two men undoubtedly crossed paths often in La Paz city. In addition to their common interests in traditional Aymara music and professional careers as educators, they had similar cultural backgrounds. Both were urban La Paz residents of rural criollo-mestizo or vecino upbringing, a combination of urban and rural life experiences they also shared with folklore artists in other Latin American countries (for the Argentine case, see Chamosa 2010).

During Germán Busch's "military socialist" administration, Las Hermanas Tejada's renditions of Aymara music caught the attention of state officials who were planning an ambitious indigenista undertaking that they termed a "Cultural Brigade" (*ED*, June 24 and 25, 1939). The endeavor reflected the Busch regime's broader objectives for rural indigenous education (see Larson 2003), as the organizers professed the "Cultural Brigade" would instill civic-patriotic virtues and so-called modern conceptions of hygiene among La Paz's rural indigenous inhabitants (*ED*, June 24 and 25, 1939). State representatives secured the Tejada sisters' participation, along with that of musicians Eduardo Calderón Lugones and Julio Martínez Arteaga. The artists toured many of the towns of the departamento of La Paz and, at each stop, taught indigenous people to sing an Aymara-language translation of the National Anthem (*ED*, June 24 and 25, 1939).

Two years later, the Tejada sisters and Calderón Lugones accepted an invitation from Enrique Peñaranda's administration to perform indigenous-themed musical selections at the salon of the Ministry of Education, for the scholars and dignitaries who would be attending the III Panamerican Assembly of Geography and History (*ED*, Apr. 25, 1941). Las Hermanas Tejada returned to the Ministry of Education the following year, this time to take part in a recital headlined by visiting Peruvian singer Yma Sumac (*ED*, June 12, 1942). As was increasingly the case, Las Hermanas Tejada alternated sets with their friendly musical rival, Las Kantutas.

Las Kantutas premiered on Radio Illimani at about the same time as Las Hermanas Tejada (about 1938). Members Irma Vásquez (first voice) and Alicia Sáenz (second voice) were seasoned musicians by then, and no strangers to Radio Illimani audiences. Prior to joining forces in Las Kantutas, Vásquez had sung as a soloist on the station's broadcasts, while Sáenz often had teamed up with her sisters Dely and Ana in El Trío Sáenz (*ED*, Jan. 13, 1936; De la Quintana and Duchén 1986, 86). Radio

Illimani's management, noticing Irma Vásquez's adeptness at interpreting melodies, and Alicia Sáenz's abilities in harmonization, believed that the two singers would make a perfect combination. In addition to persuading them to form a duo, the station's directors named the group "Las Kantutas," after the bell-shaped, red, yellow, and green-colored national flower of Bolivia (Irma Vásquez de Ronda, various personal communications). At this early stage in the ensemble's career, Radio Illimani staff pianist Jorge "Chapi" Luna was a major influence on Vásquez and Sáenz, as their usual accompanist on live radio shows, and informal artistic director. Chapi Luna's penchant for música oriental, especially the carnaval genre, played a major part in Las Kantutas' initial devotion to this repertoire (Irma Vásquez de Ronda, various personal communications).

During much of their time together in the patriotically named duo, Vásquez and Sáenz held receptionist jobs, with flexible schedules that facilitated their musical pursuits. Vásquez worked at a US firm called MacDonalds, which was conveniently located only a short walk away from the Radio Illimani studio. Sáenz's position at the Netherlands' Embassy similarly represented a socially respectable line of employment for an unmarried young criolla. It also afforded Las Kantutas opportunities to entertain foreign visitors, as local embassies often invited them to sing at their functions. To please their hosts, the versatile vocalists usually inserted a few traditional tunes from the corresponding country into their set list (Irma Vásquez de Ronda, personal communication).

Non-Bolivian musical expressions formed part of Las Kantutas' repertoire in other contexts as well. For example, in 1940 the duo sang Chilean folkloric tunes on a Radio Illimani program (*ED*, Sept. 18, 1940), and the next year interpreted the Paraguayan *guarania* "India" (Indian woman) and Uruguayan song "Margarita Punzo" in the latest ballet of Velasco Maidana, *Ritmos de América* (Rhythms of the Americas) (*ED*, Feb. 14, 1941). On occasion, Las Kantutas also performed Peruvian *marineras* and *festejos*, as well as Mexican *corridos* and *sones huastecos* (e.g., *ED*, Feb. 27, 1943; *ED*, Sept. 15, 1945). Numbers such as these distinguished Las Kantutas from Las Hermanas Tejada, who focused more exclusively on Bolivian repertoire.

Las Kantutas increasingly cultivated the look of cosmopolitan celebrities as the 1940s advanced, with their impeccably applied makeup, stylish wardrobe, and fashionable Victory Rolls hairstyles á la the Hollywood starlet Betty Grable (various documents, courtesy of Irma Vásquez de Ronda). Reinforcing this glamorous persona, newspaper articles about Las Kantutas sometimes adopted a flirtatious tone, and even played up the singers' "personal charms" (e.g., *ED*, Sept. 15, 1945). One journalist went as far as to list Irma Vásquez's body measurements, in the manner that gossip columnists often unproblematically discussed the physical attributes of internationally famous actresses (undated newspaper clipping [circa 1945]; personal collection of Irma Vásquez de Ronda). Las Hermanas Tejada, conversely, radiated a more down-to-earth, family image, and wore simple frocks and unadorned tresses in their photo shoots.

In a parallel with the Tejada sisters, Irma Vásquez was raised on an hacienda that her parents owned in the Cochabamba town of Totora (Irma Vásquez de Ronda, personal communication). Her many interactions in her childhood years with the estate's indigenous farmworkers gave her plentiful exposure to Quechua, the indigenous language widely spoken in the region. Despite Vásquez's upbringing on an hacienda, however, Las Kantutas did not specialize in Cochabamba-associated genres, or primarily perform songs with Quechua lyrics, in a manner that would have been comparable to Las Hermanas Tejadas's concentration on Aymara musical expressions of the La Paz region. The repertoire of Las Kantutas encompassed the staple Andean criollo-mestizo genres (huayño, cueca, bailecito), but the group's strong suit was música oriental, notwithstanding the *kolla* (Andean highland or valley) rather than *camba* (eastern lowland) heritage of Sáenz (a paceña) and Vásquez.

MÚSICA ORIENTAL ARRIVES IN LA PAZ: THE CARNAVAL AND TAQUIRARI

The carnaval genre of Santa Cruz, also known as the *carnaval cruceño* to distinguish it from the otherwise identically named Carnival traditions practiced elsewhere in the country, was the first form of música oriental to gain popularity outside of the eastern lowlands. Rhythmically, carnavales feature the sesquiáltera hemiola (interplay between $\frac{6}{8}$ and $\frac{3}{4}$ meters), a Spanish colonial legacy also found in cuecas and bailecitos. Whereas Bolivian cuecas and bailecitos follow AABA sectional form, though, AABB or AABBCC represent the standard setups for carnavales (as well as for huayños and many other Bolivian genres). Melodically, most carnaval tunes adhere to the major mode (in contrast, cuecas and bailecitos in the major and minor modes are both common), a characteristic that for some Bolivians lends credence to the stereotype that cruceños have a natural propensity for cheerfulness, as a consequence of their tropical habitat (e.g., see *ED*, Apr. 19, 1944).

Santa Cruz historian Hernando Sanabria maintains (1964, 12) that touring brass bands introduced the carnaval cruceño to the highland and valley regions of Bolivia. He stresses the trailblazing role of Captain César Achaval's 6th Battalion ensemble, a paceño group that apparently learned to play the genre on a 1913 visit to Santa Cruz, and afterwards popularized it in La Paz. By the mid-1920s, many highland brass bands had taken up the carnaval; the Army Band directed by Adrián Patiño Carpio is one prominent example (Sanabria 1964, 12). The genre also entered the repertoire of La Paz estudiantinas. Estudiantina Centro Artístico Haydn (discussed previously), for example, interpreted the carnavales "Vallegrandino" (Man from Vallegrande [a Santa Cruz town and province]) and "Alegre Cruceño" (Cheerful person from Santa Cruz) at the recording studios of RCA-Victor in 1930.

From the mid-1930s to early 1940s, highland musicians were most responsible for popularizing the carnaval in La Paz city, largely because few camba ensembles other than Conjunto Oriental were based there in this period.[35] The pianist and composer Chapi Luna represents one of the chief figures. From Oruro city, he joined the staff of Radio Illimani in the Chaco War years, after he had been discharged from the Army for the wartime wounds he had suffered at a battle in the Santa Cruz region

(*La Patria* [Oruro newspaper], n.d.; Rojas Rojas 1989, 15; De la Quintana 1999, 232). Even though Luna's stay in the oriente had been brief, henceforth the carnaval would figure prominently in his compositional output (see Rojas Rojas 1989, 15–16), and performances on radio shows. His artistic talents found a fan in President Busch. An amateur musician himself (Rivera de Stahlie 1995, 84), and one who identified as a camba because of his birth in Santa Cruz and childhood in Beni, Busch often requested Luna's musical services during his presidency (Rojas Rojas 1989, 15).

Of the many vocal soloists and duos that Luna persuaded to sing his compositions on Radio Illimani's programs, Las Kantutas quickly became one of his favorite acts, and that of the station. Two of Luna's most acclaimed carnavales, "Palomita del Arrozal" (Little dove of the rice fields) and "Pena Camba" (Grief of a lowlander), were signature numbers for Las Kantutas. Composed in the 1930s, with lyrics by leading Santa Cruz poet Raúl Otero Reiche—who directed Radio Illimani in the late 1930s (Terceros 2006, 343–44), these two carnavales allude to typical cruceño cultural practices and the region's geographical features, devices common in música oriental songs.[36] In "Palomita del Arrozal," Otero Reiche's text sprinkles in characteristic aspects of the local dialect (e.g., use of the *-inga* diminutive suffix, and *voseo* second-person address form), lowland indigenous words (e.g., *guapurú, ocoró* [names of tropical fruits]), and topographical references of Santa Cruz (e.g., *arrozal* = rice fields, *arenal* = sand dunes).

Carnavales such as "Palomita del Arrozal" and "Pena Camba" no doubt elicited a complex bundle of associations for highland Bolivians in the years after the Chaco War, particularly for the tens of thousands of men who, as enlisted soldiers, first had set foot in the Santa Cruz region during the brutal conflict. For many of them, the sound of a carnaval cruceño melody must have brought to mind bittersweet memories, ones that fused images of the remote tropical lands of the oriente, camaraderie of the war effort, and Bolivia's infuriating military defeat at the hands of the Paraguayan forces.[37]

Whereas the carnaval's incorporation into paceño musical life preceded the debut of Las Kantutas by over a decade, the duo's earliest performances roughly correspond with the first wave of La Paz interest in Beni's taquirari tradition—the other major form of música oriental in the national folkloric music scene of the 1940s. The taquirari is a simple-duple-meter genre, with sectional musical structure (AABB or AABBCC); tunes can be either in the major or minor mode. The rhythmic ostinato of the taquirari consists of one eighth note followed by two sixteenths, and therefore is reminiscent of the pulse of the huayño. Taquiraris stress the downbeat, though, not the offbeat as huayños do.

Beni ethnologist and musician Rogers Becerra (1990, 13–22) contends that Jesuit missionaries fostered the birth of the taquirari, as a means of converting Beni's indigenous population to Catholicism. The genre arose in the 18th or 19th century, he explains, as a culturally syncretic music-dance expression that borrowed rhythmic aspects from the lowland indigenous *takirikire* or *danza de la flecha* (arrow dance), and melodic features from Spain's *alborada gallega*. The "Spanish" musical elements eventually predominated in the taquirari, once criollo-mestizo *benianos* (Beni residents) became the genre's main cultivators (Becerra 1990, 13–22). By the 1920s, Santa Cruz criollo-mestizo musicians had adopted the genre as well, for their Carnival repertoire (Parejas 1999, 21).

Paceño curiosity in the taquirari began to develop in 1937, according to Becerra (n.d., 2), as a consequence of the Beni delegation's performance of a taquirari music-dance sketch at the Primera Olimpiada Escolar Boliviana (First Bolivian Olympics for Schoolchildren) held that year in La Paz at Hernando Siles Stadium.[38] It would not be until the mid-1940s, however, that Beni's most emblematic "folk" genre would enjoy wide dissemination in La Paz and other Andean cities as a mass-mediated folkloric expression. Las Kantutas helped to transform the taquirari into a nationally popular genre, primarily through their collaborations with another Oruro pianist and composer, Gilberto Rojas, whose predilection for the taquirari mirrored that of Chapi Luna for the carnaval (see the section "Música Oriental in La Paz in the Villarroel Years").

TO BUENOS AIRES

In June 1942, the Ministry of Education paid homage to Yma Sumac, Moisés Vivanco, and their Compañia Folklórica Peruana, by arranging a recital for them at the bureau's salon. Various local acts also performed at the concert, including an estudiantina, Huiñay Inti, that treated the audience to a "huayño paceño" played with "charangos and guitars." Las Kantutas and Las Hermanas Tejada took part as well. Reflecting their contrasting musical specializations, Las Kantutas interpreted a "beautiful carnaval from Santa Cruz," while Las Hermanas Tejada intoned a "lovely Aymara piece" (*ED*, June 12, 1942).

A few months after the recital, Las Kantutas and Las Hermanas Tejada traveled to Buenos Aires, with their chaperone Zenobio Tejada, and the plucked-string trio Los Sumac Huaynas (Quechua for "The good-looking guys").[39] The Peñaranda administration partially covered the entourage's expenses (*ED*, Oct. 25 and Dec. 12, 1942). In making their way to the Argentina, the artists followed in the footsteps not only of Yma Sumac (see Limansky 2008) and Alberto Ruiz Lavadenz, but also another Bolivian female duo. Earlier in the year, La Paz station Radio Nacional—Radio Illimani's main rival for the Bolivian market—had convinced the singers Pepa Cardona and Yola Rivero to reinvent themselves as a duo, and dispatched them to Buenos Aires to record for ODEON (*ED*, Feb. 2 and 6, 1942). While there, the Cardona-Rivero duo sang Luna-Otero Reiche's carnaval "Palomita del Arrozal," Humberto Iporre Salinas's fox incaico "Potosino Soy" (I am from Potosí), and other folkloric tunes on a live program for Radio El Mundo, then one of Argentina's top three radio stations (*ED*, Feb. 6 and 27, 1942).[40] Las Kantutas and Las Hermanas Tejada performed for the same station, and taped about seventy tracks for RCA-Victor, during their month-long stay in the Argentine capital (*ED*, Dec. 5, 1942).

Las Kantutas and Las Hermanas Tejada's time in Buenos Aires coincided with the release of a blockbuster Argentine film that engendered an upsurge in *porteño* (Buenos Aires resident) interest in the history and "folk" traditions of Argentina's mountainous northwestern region (Chamosa 2010, 164–65). Set in the province of Salta, the movie, titled *La Guerra Gaucha* (The gaucho war), re-enacts a pivotal battle in the Wars of Independence. A then little-known Argentine folkloric group called Los Hermanos Ábalos were cast as musicians in the film. They appear in an idyllic village setting, garbed in ponchos and playing a lively carnavalito or huayño with the descriptive title of "Carnavalito Quebradeño" (Carnavalito of the mountain pass) (Chamosa 2010, 164–65). On this Andean-themed tune—their first commercial hit—Los Hermanos Ábalos complement their usual ensemble format of several guitars and a bombo (or caja) drum, with the kena and charango.[41] Later generations of Argentine folkloric groups would use this lineup when they performed Andean repertoire, including such influential acts as the Paris-based Los Incas and Los Calchakis (Rios 2008). As for Los Hermanos Ábalos, their cameo in *La Guerra Gaucha* unexpectedly launched the sibling ensemble to national stardom (Chamosa 2010, 165).

Amid rising porteño fascination with the folkloric expressions of the Andes, RCA-Victor's marketing personnel unsurprisingly chose to portray Las Kantutas and Las Hermanas Tejada in ways that corresponded with Argentine stereotypes of Bolivians. The photograph of the duos that appears in a 1942 edition of the newsletter *La Voz de RCA-Victor* (The voice of RCA-Victor) illustrates this exoticist strategy. Las Kantutas look the part of *cholas paceñas* (mestiza market vendors of La Paz), as Vásquez and Sáenz are robed in full polleras (Andean multilayered skirts), with the traditional chola paceña accessories of embroidered shawls, bowler hats, and dangling earrings, and with their hair styled in long braided pigtails. The Tejada Sisters don a much simpler attire, one reminiscent of the handwoven dresses that indigenous women customarily wear in Andean villages, which contrast with the factory-made clothes of cholas paceñas. Whereas the outfits that Las Hermanas Tejada sported matched the group's musical focus, the same could not be said of the chola paceña garb that Las Kantutas modeled in the promotional piece.

This is not to say that Las Kantutas steered clear of musical practices of Andean cholo-mestizo association. Their RCA-Victor recording of the huayño "Laduyquimanta Ripusac" (Quechua for "I'm leaving your side"), for example, is a stylized interpretation of cholo or mestizo Andean music. The guitars and charango of Los Sumac Huaynas provide the accompaniment. Charanguista Gerardo "Chocni" López alternates between plucked and rapidly strummed passages on this selection, as he similarly does on Las Kantutas' recording of the *danza aymara* (actually a huayño) "Chulumañenita" (Chulumani girl) and in all likelihood on the tracks that Las Hermanas Tejada taped in their RCA-Victor sessions.[42]

Even though Las Kantutas' 1942 track "Laduyquimanta Ripusac" derives inspiration from Andean cholo-mestizo musical traditions, Vásquez and Sáenz made no attempt to emulate the sound quality of chola-mestiza vocalists, who traditionally sing at the very limit of their ranges and favor shrill timbres, in a style approximating that of Andean indigenous female singers. Las Kantutas realize their parts in a much lower tessitura, with a polished and detached-sounding delivery, one with few dynamic changes. Interestingly, Las Kantutas appear to have used virtually the same approach on every track they recorded in their career, regardless of the genre's regional, ethnic, and/or socioeconomic associations.[43] By adopting this style of vocal performance, Las Kantutas adhered to the norms of the day for mainstream Latin American popular music vocalists.

While Las Kantutas and Las Hermanas Tejada were in Buenos Aires, La Paz's leading newspapers dutifully kept the Bolivian public informed about their recent musical activities (e.g., *ED*, Nov. 21, 1942). And, after the duos returned to La Paz, reporters frequently interviewed them about their time abroad, thereby allowing the singers the chance to promote themselves to the papers' readers. These publications repeatedly emphasized the prestige that the two ensembles had garnered by performing on Buenos Aires' Radio El Mundo and recording for RCA-Victor (e.g., *La Razón*, Dec. 4, 1942; *La Noche*, Dec. 12, 1942). Without a doubt, Las Kantutas and Las Hermanas Tejada obtained a new level of prominence in Bolivia as a result of their sojourn in the Argentine capital, and were well on their way to becoming national folkloric music superstars.

MÚSICA ORIENTAL IN LA PAZ IN THE VILLARROEL YEARS

In the presidency of Villarroel (1943–1946), Radio Illimani branded itself as "The Voice of Bolivia" and functioned as an official state propaganda vehicle (Coronel Quisbert 2013, 190). The station's directors therefore had to keep in mind RADEPA-MNR ideology when they planned the musical programming for the December 1944 show commemorating Villarroel's first year in office. This obligation surely explains why Filarmónica 1° de Mayo's *Suite Aymara* performance occupied such a prominent place in the broadcast, as previously noted in this chapter. Yet maintaining ideological consistency was not the sole consideration the station's management had to weigh when they finalized the musical acts. Since it could not be guaranteed that a large audience would even tune in that day to the transmission, the artistic directors of Radio Illimani needed to take into account the Bolivian public's musical preferences—even if these preferences did not comfortably align with the political priorities of the RADEPA-MNR regime.

Tellingly, it was música oriental, not indigenista numbers, that predominated in Radio Illimani's broadcast in the three hours leading up to the President's address (i.e., from around 6:00 p.m. to 9:00 p.m). Various female vocalists, all of non-oriente heritage, interpreted carnavales and taquiraris in this key portion of the program (*ED*, Dec. 20, 1944). Irma Vásquez and Alicia Sáenz performed, but not as Las Kantutas, because they briefly had put the group on hiatus.[44] Vásquez was pursuing a solo career, while Sáenz had joined forces with singer Maruja Lavadenz in a new duo,

Las Kjenayitas (The little kenas) (*ED*, May 28, July 27, and Oct. 10, 1944). Accompanied on the piano by Gilberto Rojas, Las Kjenayitas opened their set with one of Rojas's rare indigenista-themed songs, "La Danza Incaica Es Así" (That's how Incan dance is), before the duo moved on to música oriental numbers, with Rojas's carnaval "Qué Lindos Ojos" (What beautiful eyes; lyrics by Ricardo Cabrera), and Román Sandoval's taquirari "Espina de Cristal" (Crystal thorn). Vásquez, with Chapi Luna on the piano, sang three waltzes, two of which fell into the música oriental category, Luna-Otero Reiche's "Alma Cruceña" (Santa Cruz soul), and Rojas's "Bajo el Cielo de Vallegrande" (Under the Vallegrande sky) (*ED*, Dec. 20, 1944).

The popularity of música oriental reached new heights in La Paz during the Villarroel era.[45] At a time of widespread opposition to the RADEPA-MNR government—which escalated in the wake of 1944's "November massacre" and other controversial state actions such as the regime's outreach to Andean indigenous people and hosting of 1945's Indigenous Congress (Chapter 2)—música oriental appears to have served as an escapist type of national folkloric music for many paceños. Performing or listening to a carnaval or taquirari in the La Paz setting would have conjured up images of Santa Cruz or Beni, tropical locales far removed from the political strife and interethnic tensions that highland residents were experiencing. In the case of the taquirari, for paceños the relative novelty of the genre (compared to most other Bolivian criollo-mestizo folkloric genres, including the carnaval) contributed as well, and perhaps even more substantially, to its allure in the mid-1940s.

More than anyone else, Gilberto Rojas vaulted the taquirari from a regionally circumscribed to nationally popular genre. Beni music authority Rogers Becerra acknowledged as much in 1946, in an *El Diario* article titled "El Taquirari" (*ED*, Apr. 28, 1946). Like Chapi Luna, Rojas was a native son of the nearby highland city of Oruro who began his professional musical career on Radio Illimani. Prior to securing this position on the station around 1940 (*ED*, July 28, 1940), he lived for a few years in the Santa Cruz region, in the late 1930s. It was in this period that Rojas became enamored of the taquirari and composed his earliest songs (Rojas Foppiano 1991, 35–39).

By 1944, Rojas had gained considerable fame as a tunesmith in La Paz. Accordingly, his taquiraris and carnavales were well represented in Radio Illimani's December 1944 tribute to the RADEPA-MNR regime (*ED*, Dec. 20, 1944). He scored one of his biggest hits the next month, with the taquirari "Negrita" (Dark-complected woman) (*ED*, Jan. 25, 1945; Rojas Foppiano 1991, 55–56, 71–73). Inspired by Rojas's first love, a cruceña whose identity he guarded, "Negrita" earned first place at a 1945 Carnival season contest in La Paz. The song had clearly moved Antonio González Bravo (Rojas's former music teacher), Eduardo Calderón Lugones, and the rest of the prize committee (Rojas Foppiano 1991, 55–56). By the end of the year, many paceño ensembles were playing the taquirari, from Adrián Patiño Carpio's Army Band (*ED*, May 13, 1945), to Fermín Barrionuevo's in-demand orquesta de jazz (*ED*, Dec. 16, 1945).

"Negrita" figures among the first batch of Rojas's compositions whose recording he oversaw; this group of songs also includes the taquiraris "Sentimiento Camba"

(Sentiments of a lowlander), "Flor Benianita" (Flower of Beni), "Los Indios Latinos" (The Latin Indians, the eponymous duo's theme song), and nonsensically titled "Tiquiminiqui" (*ED*, July 16, 1946). Released under the ODEON label in 1946, these tracks showcase the vocal harmonies of Los Indios Latinos. A popular La Paz duo formed by Jorge Landívar (first voice) and Hugo Claure (second voice), in 1944 they had united with Rojas, who at that point became their director and piano accompanist (*ED*, Aug. 23, Sept. 14, Oct. 1, and Nov. 4, 1944). The tuxedo-clad "Latin Indians" mainly sang Rojas's taquiraris and carnavales from this moment onward. In 1945, Los Indios Latinos and Rojas toured Bolivia, with concerts in each departamento except for Pando, before making their way to Buenos Aires and the studios of ODEON (Rojas Foppiano 1991, 57–75)—a route that Rojas would revisit the next year with Las Kantutas.

Rojas and Las Kantutas began performing together on Radio Illimani in the Villarroel years, in 1944 or 1945. The station's musical workforce at the time also included Las Hermanas Tejada (Elsa had replaced her sister Yolanda in the ensemble by then), Chapi Luna (who was the director of musical programming), Los Sumac Huaynas, and the recently established Voces del Oriente (Voices of the orient).

A male vocal duo accompanied by three guitarists (i.e., a quintet), Voces del Oriente—one of the era's few La Paz-based folklore groups that consisted mainly of eastern lowland musicians—emerged on the paceño scene in 1944 (*ED*, Aug. 25, 1944).[46] The ensemble had a breakthrough run of performances that year at Boîte Embassy, an upscale venue adjacent to Sucre Palace Hotel (*ED*, Oct. 20, 1944). The following year, Voces del Oriente, along with Las Kantutas, Los Sumac Huaynas, and La Paz singer Chela Rea Nogales aka Kory Chuyma (Aymara for "heart of gold"), presented a series of concerts in Potosí's mining towns of Llallagua, Catavi, and Siglo XX—strongholds of the Bolivian labor movement—as part of an artistic delegation that Radio Illimani coordinated with the Dirección General de Propaganda (Propaganda Department). Without a doubt, a major purpose of this state-sponsored folkloric musical spectacle was to spread goodwill about the RADEPA-MNR regime among the mine workers in this important region (personal collection, Irma Vásquez de Ronda).

Radio Illimani's music shows and occasional folkloric delegations conferred música oriental interpreters a prominent place in the years of Villarroel's presidency, even though the national dissemination of eastern lowland genres articulated minimally with RADEPA-MNR projects and ideology. The oriente, from the regime's perspective, represented a distant and sparsely inhabited region. Consequently, the administration allocated relatively few resources to developing alliances with camba leaders and communities, compared to the sustained efforts that RADEPA-MNR officials made in the Andean highlands and valleys. For similar reasons, the regime's public statements and writings concerning the ideal regional foundation for Bolivian "national culture" granted much greater importance to the peoples and cultural traditions of the country's Andean zone than to their counterparts in the eastern lowlands (see Gotkowitz 2007, 164–91).

It is ironic, then, that the song that came to be most associated with Villarroel and the MNR, "Siempre" (Always), is a taquirari. Mario Velasco Otero, the precocious fourteen-year-old son of MNR founder Gastón Velasco, composed it, with which he received the top prize at a Fiestas Julianas music contest staged in the final week of Villarroel's presidency (*ED*, July 16, 1946). "Siempre," which opens with the line "Viva el movimiento, gloria a Villarroel" (Long live the movement, glory to Villarroel), rapidly became the MNR theme song when the party went underground in the sexenio (Paredes 1949, 150; Peñaloza 1963, 140). At this critical juncture for the *movimientistas*, when they desperately sought to win over the hearts and minds of the masses, that they turned to a catchy taquirari to diffuse their message further corroborates música oriental's popularity at the time in La Paz and elsewhere in the country.

LAS KANTUTAS AND LAS HERMANAS TEJADA IN THE SEXENIO

Soon after the violent ouster of the RADEPA-MNR government, the newly installed regime unleashed a persecution campaign against those it suspected of being movimientistas or *villarroelistas*. This move had negative repercussions for many former state employees. The folkloric singer Pepa Cardona, whose duties for Radio Illimani had included reading the RADEPA-MNR administration's propagandistic news reports (Coronel Quisbert 2013, 70), found herself charged by the sexenio authorities with being a "spy for the deposed regime" (*La Noche*, Aug. 10, 1946). Las Kantutas and Las Hermanas Tejada, meanwhile, appear to have abruptly lost their positions at Radio Illimani. A cloud of suspicion might have hung over Las Kantutas because of the MNR affiliation of Alicia Sáenz's brother Carlos Sáenz. One-half of the cross-dressing comedic act Las Dos Comadres, which parodied the mannerisms of cholas paceñas, he was placed under arrest in 1946 for his membership in the MNR, as was his sidekick in Las Dos Comadres, Julio Rodríguez (Peñaloza 1963, 102).

Perhaps sensing that it was the right moment to spend some time away from their home base, Las Kantutas and Gilberto Rojas left La Paz a few weeks after the July 1946 coup, for a tour of the country, with concert engagements in Oruro, Cochabamba, Potosí, Chuquisaca, Tarija, Santa Cruz, and Beni—reprising many of the stops from Rojas and Los Indios Latinos's 1945 tour. In what would become a signature look for Las Kantutas, their new outfit for the trip entailed matching striped gowns with white cotton embroidered "peasant" blouses, topped with overcoats, and with a corsage of kantuta flowers adorning their lapels. The women's trendy hairstyles and makeup complemented their polished stage attire. Rojas's sartorial choice was a vest that was made out of the same striped material used for Las Kantutas' dresses, along with a tassel that hung at his waist. The overall visual effect of their performance attire was one of fashionable folksiness that did not call to mind a specific Bolivian region.

The taquirari unquestionably represented the preferred musical genre of Las Kantutas and Gilberto Rojas at this moment in their careers, and accordingly it figured prominently in their programs throughout the tour. At the recitals they gave in Cochabamba, Tarija, and Potosí, for instance, taquiraris made up about half of the musical offerings, and more often than not, a taquirari number, usually one of Rojas's compositions, closed the show. The preponderance of taquiraris in their repertoire was even higher at Las Kantutas and Rojas's concert in the capital of Beni, Trinidad. Eleven of the fifteen songs that they interpreted at this engagement fell into the música oriental category, with nine of these selections being taquiraris (various concert programs, courtesy of Irma Vásquez de Ronda).

After completing the Bolivian leg of the tour in early 1947, Rojas and Las Kantutas continued onward to Buenos Aires, where they recorded about twenty-one tracks for ODEON (*ED*, Apr. 7 and Sept. 8, 1947). To the accompaniment of an Argentine orquesta de jazz, or alternately a pianist (probably Rojas), one or two guitarists, and a harp player, Las Kantutas taped carnavales (e.g., "Pena Camba"), cuecas (e.g., "A Bolivia," or "Viva Mi Patria Bolivia"),[47] huayños, and waltzes, but as would have been expected, taquiraris predominated among these recordings (e.g., Rojas's "La Tarasca," Becerra-Rojas's "Nostalgia," Barrientos-Ortíz's "Cunumicita"). One of their hits was Rojas's light-hearted, and musically novel, carnaval-taquirari "Coctelito" (A little cocktail), which shifts back and forth between the two genres.

Despite their focus on música oriental, Las Kantutas and Rojas often performed in Buenos Aires as "Los Ruiseñores del Altiplano" (The nightingales of the high plain). This stage name of course referenced Bolivia's highlands rather than eastern lowlands, and thus tallied with the primary image that most Argentines had of Bolivia. The musicians also might have renamed the group because they suspected that few porteños would know that the kantuta was the national flower of Bolivia. In any case, as Los Ruiseñores del Altiplano, in February and March 1947, Rojas, Vásquez, and Sáenz appeared on Radio Belgrano's weekly show Ritmo de Quena y Maraca (Rhythm of the kena and maraca). A Brazilian singer, Lupe Cortés, and her band supplied the "maraca" portion of the program (*Democracia* [Buenos Aires newsletter], Feb. 28 and Mar. 1, 1947). The rationale behind the station's placement of Bolivian and Brazilian musical acts in the same slot apparently was that both represented a form of musical exoticism to the Argentine public.

Bolivians who wished to make a living as musicians in Buenos Aires often ended up conforming to Argentine preconceptions about Bolivians (e.g., Alberto Ruiz Lavadenz). For Las Kantutas and Rojas, this strategy did not have a major impact on their subsequent careers, because their stay in Argentina was brief. Ex–Voces del Oriente guitarist Tito Véliz, in contrast, made Buenos Aires his home around this time. Rather than maintaining his former profile as a música oriental artist, he reinvented himself as an Andean music expert and charanguista. Véliz crossed paths with Las Kantutas and Rojas in 1947, as did fellow expatriate Mauro Núñez.

Soon after participating in the Indianist Week of 1931–1932 (Chapter 2), Núñez, a charango soloist from Chuquisaca, embarked with the La Paz folkloric theater troupe Tiwanaku on a three-year tour that took him to Peru, Ecuador, and Colombia. He parted ways with the company in 1934 and settled in Lima, where he lived for eight years. It was in this period that he met Yma Sumac and Moisés Vivanco, and joined their Compañia Folklórica Peruana. In 1942, Núñez traveled with the troupe to Buenos Aires. Once the company had fulfilled its artistic engagements in the Argentine capital, he made the decision to make Buenos Aires his new home base (Torres 2006, 59, 186).

Alongside Mauro Núñez and Tito Véliz, Las Kantutas and Gilberto Rojas performed various selections at the studios of Buenos Aires' Radio Splendid in August 1947, for a broadcast commemorating Bolivian Independence Day (*Radiolandia*, Aug. 16, 1947). One of Núñez's charango students, a nine-year-old Argentine of partial Bolivian ancestry by the name of Jaime Torres—who in the mid-1960s would be hailed as Argentina's top charanguista and record an Andean folkloric music album with kena soloist Mariano Uña Ramos that attained bestseller status in the Bolivian market (Chapter 6)—displayed his charango skills in the live program, despite his tender age (*Radiolandia*, Aug. 16, 1947).

Las Hermanas Tejada seem to have remained in La Paz for the duration of the sexenio. After a period of inactivity, they resurfaced in late 1947, when they participated in a Municipal Theater concert featuring a mix of local and foreign musicians (*ED*, Dec. 27, 1947). Las Kantutas had returned to La Paz by then and were back on the airwaves, through the transmissions of Radio Bolívar (*La Noche*, Oct. 30, 1947). The next year, Las Hermanas Tejada and Las Kantutas rekindled their friendly musical rivalry from their days on Radio Illimani, as the two duos entertained the spectators at a Municipal Theater event in which former station regulars Los Sumac Huaynas and Pepa Cardona also took part (*ED*, July 13, 1948). If sexenio officials had previously viewed any of these artists as somewhat politically suspect because of their associations with the state-operated station in the years of the Villarroel presidency, it was no longer an obstacle. President Mamerto Urriolagoitia apparently had no problem with Las Kantutas during his term in office (1949–1951). In 1949 and 1950, he posed with them for the *El Diario* photographer in the Fiestas Julianas season, on both occasions after the usually dour-faced head of state and charismatic duo had attended the elite society luncheon that Los Amigos de la Ciudad hosted at the Club de La Paz (*ED*, July 18, 1949; July 19, 1950).

By 1948, Zenobio Tejada also was clearly in the good graces of sexenio officials. He had the honor of serving on the jury for the "música criolla" composition contest that formed part of La Paz's remembrance of the city's 400-year anniversary. Bandurria virtuoso Federico Otero de la Peña (formerly of Estudiantina Verdi) and art-classical musician Jorge Parra joined him on the committee. Considering the "La Paz theme" of the IV Centenary celebration, surely none of them expected to find many taquiraris and carnavales among the submissions, and yet they did. One of these entries, Alfonso Pardo Uzeda of Sucre's taquirari "16 de Julio," at least referenced La Paz in the title of the song (July 16 = Fiestas Julianas, or La Paz Day), and in all likelihood also through the lyrics. Opting for a different approach, Santa Cruz musician and music educator Susano Azogue Rivero—a prolific composer of música oriental (Terceros 2006, 67–68)—placed oriente imagery front and center in "Quiéreme Cunumisinga."[48] The song so captivated the jury that they were about to award Azogue Rivero the third-place trophy. Before finalizing their rankings, however, they withdrew his tune from consideration. The reason the committee offered for their sudden change of mind? Música oriental, they emphasized, "does not bear even the slightest resemblance to highland music" (*ED*, Nov. 24, 1948).

As Chapter 2 explains, La Paz's IV Centenary commemoration offers clear evidence that by 1948 influential paceño society figures had come to imagine Andean indigenous music-dance traditions as La Paz identity emblems, by virtue of the fact that the Concurso Folklórico Indígena del Departamento—a large-scale exhibition of indigenous tropa styles such as Los Sikuris de Italaque and Kantus de Charazani—represented a showpiece event at the festivities. Indigenismo was not the sole folkloric music trend in 1948 La Paz city, however, as the proceedings in the "criollo music" contest underscore. Música oriental continued to experience widespread local popularity, rivaling the appeal of mass-mediated folkloric music with Andean-flavored indigenista characteristics. For Las Hermanas Tejada and Las Kantutas, these contrasting currents in the scene enabled them to carve out artistic personas that were distinct but that equally found favor among paceños.

Of the two duos, though, Las Kantutas maintained the higher profile in the waning years of the sexenio. In July 1950, for example, only a few days after they had performed for President Urriolagoitia and other members of the elite at the Club de La Paz luncheon, Las Kantutas sang to the masses at the Teatro al Aire Libre (Open Air Theater). Organized by the Municipality, this event inaugurated a free-to-the-public concert series that would take place weekly at the spacious locale, which seated about 12,000 (*ED*, July 23, 1950). Las Kantutas also participated in the Open Air Theater series' 1951 season, which featured an even wider array of musical offerings, including orchestral renderings of Salmón Ballivián's *Suite Aymara* and *Trilogía India*, brass band performances of the morenada genre, Andean indigenous panpipe music played by a Sikuris de Italaque tropa, and boleros crooned by La Paz's Trío Panamérica Antawara (Pan-American sunset trio), Colombia's Trío Atlántico, and Mexico's internationally famed Trío Los Panchos (*ED*, various, 1951). Estudiantinas were absent from the 1950 and 1951 editions of the series, a reflection of the tradition's decline in the La Paz music scene.

At the conclusion of the 1951 Open Air Theater season, municipal officials announced that Las Kantutas represented one of the most "distinguished" musical acts or artists who had graced the stage that year (*ED*, Nov. 18, 1951). Gilberto Rojas, Adrian Patiño Carpio, Eduardo Caba, and "folk ballet" director Graciela "Chela" Urquidi (profiled in Chapter 4) received this honor as well. The specializations of this exclusive group of artists once again highlights the contrasting directions in urban La Paz's folkloric music scene. After all, whereas Las Kantutas privileged música oriental songs in their repertoire and Rojas cemented his reputation as a composer through his taquiraris, Patiño Carpio's best known musical creations by this time were his Incan foxtrots, and Caba's magnum opus indisputably was the six-movement *Aires Indios*.

After the 1952 Revolution, Las Kantutas and Las Hermanas Tejada would per-form from time to time in La Paz (e.g., 1953 Concurso de Arte Nativo; Chapter 4), and record for the recently established Bolivian label Discos Méndez (Chapter 5). Yet as the decade advanced, their musical engagements lessened and eventually stopped, because the members of the group shifted their attention to traditional domestic matters. A new cohort of La Paz–based female duos had made names for themselves as folklore interpreters by then; the standouts were Las Imillas (Quechua for "The girls"), Las Hermanas Espinoza, and Las Hermanas Arteaga (Chapters 4 and 5). These all-sibling ensembles looked up to the pioneering Las Kantutas and Las Hermanas Tejada, as did most Bolivian female as well as male criollo-mestizo folkloric musi-cians who began their careers in the 1940s or early 1950s and dreamed of one day becoming superstar artists at the national level.

La Paz's música oriental vogue of the 1940s left various legacies. In the eastern lowlands, highland interest in the carnaval and taquirari prompted local artists to follow suit, especially in Santa Cruz, where a regionalist folkloric music movement took shape in the 1940s and reached consolidation in the 1950s (see Terceros 2006). Faced with competition from artists who were actually from the oriente (e.g., singer Gladys Moreno), highland Bolivian musicians would no longer specialize in lowland genres. Indeed, the 1940s marks the last time that kolla musicians such as Gilberto Rojas, Chapi Luna, and Las Kantutas would figure among the leading composers and/ or performers of música oriental.

Yet from this decade onward, most paceño folkloric musical acts—from urban pan-pipe tropas such as Los Cebollitas (Chapter 5), to Andean conjuntos like Los Jairas (Chapter 7)—would include carnavales and taquiraris in their sets, in part to demon-strate the national scope of their otherwise Andean-centered repertoire. In the com-ing decades, Bolivia's Andean conjuntos would successfully incorporate many other non-paceño-associated genres into the national folklore canon (e.g., Chuquisaca's chuntunqui, Potosí's tinku, Amazonian region's tobas; see Chapter 8: Postlude). This important characteristic of the Bolivian variant of the transnational Andean con-junto tradition thus built on the La Paz folkloric music movement's earlier assimila-tion of música oriental.

The estudiantina's declining popularity in La Paz in the late 1940s, meanwhile, prompted some members of this once-vibrant artistic movement to bid farewell to their bandmates, and try their luck with other folkloric ensemble formats. Western transverse flutist Esteban del Río and charango player Nicolás "K'auquita" García, who were both long-standing members of the estudiantina Huiñay Inti, chose this course of action.[49] In 1954, del Río took on the role of musical director and wind soloist in Radio Illimani's latest house band, Conjunto 31 de Octubre, while later in the decade, K'auquita García teamed up with kenista Jaime Medinaceli in Conjunto Kollasuyo/ Bolivia (which was apparently unrelated to Estudiantina Kollasuyo). Through their participation in these two ensembles, Esteban del Río and K'auquita García directly link paceño indigenista estudiantinas of the 1940s with the La Paz scene's proto-Andean conjuntos of the 1950s (Chapter 5).

As Chapters 2 and 3 have shown, the Bolivian folkloric music movement made major strides in the early-to-mid-20th century, often with the support of state officials or state-affiliated entities. Largely because of the lack of continuity at the highest levels of government, combined with Bolivia's frequent shifts between left-leaning and conservative-reactionary administrations, however, state-sponsored initiatives involving musical practices had relatively limited impact on artistic trends in the pre-1952 period. It is worth underscoring that Peñaranda's presidency, which lasted less than three years (thirty-three months), represents the lengthiest term in office for a Bolivian head of state from the Chaco War era to the 1952 Revolution. Villarroel, for instance, was President for only two and a half years. Peru's Augusto Leguía (term in office: 1919–1930), Brazil's Getúlio Vargas (term in office: 1930–1945), and Argentina's Juan Domingo Perón (term in office: 1946–1955) remained in power over much longer periods. Consequently, their populist regimes were able to influence local folklore movements and related artistic currents to a far greater degree than could their Bolivian contemporaries (see Raphael 1990; Turino 1993, 2003; Chamosa 2010). In the twelve-year period following the 1952 Revolution, Bolivian government-affiliated bureaus and individuals would have a comparable opportunity to shape the direction of the country's folkloric music scene.

NOTES

1. Scholars of Bolivian music often mention the estudiantina tradition's local popularity in the early-to-mid-20th century (e.g., Céspedes 1984, 218; Cárdenas 1986, 39–40; Sánchez C., 1994, 6; Rossells 1996, 107–8; Bigenho 2002, 126–28; Bigenho 2012, 37–39). Prior to my work on Bolivian estudiantinas, though, the tradition's emergence and stylistic transformation in the La Paz context had not been the subject of detailed historical research.

2. In overviews of the history of Bolivian mass-mediated folkloric music, Las Kantutas and Las Hermanas Tejada are usually acknowledged as early figures. However, these writings seldom offer information about the duos, beyond the members' names (e.g., Cárdenas 1986, 66; Sánchez C., 1995, 80; Pekkola 1996, 62; Rossells 1997a, 10; Arauco 2011, 160). The trajectories of these two superstar groups consequently remain poorly understood.

3. Studies of Bolivian música oriental invariably focus on the eastern lowland context (e.g., Becerra 1959; Sanabria 1964; Becerra 1990; Becerra 1998; Parejas 1999; Terceros 2006), not on the performance and reception of música oriental in the highlands, as I do here. Interestingly, Las Kantutas' identification with música oriental in their glory decade of the 1940s has long slipped from popular memory. Bolivian music scholars, meanwhile, often assume that because the members of Las Kantutas hailed from the departamentos of La Paz and Cochabamba, the duo specialized in Andean-themed musical repertoire.

4. That musicologist María Eugenia Soux mentions a local estudiantina only once in her detailed publications on the musical life of La Paz city from 1845 to 1885 (Soux 1992, 169) indicates that the estudiantina tradition had yet to take hold in urban La Paz by this period.

5. In Sucre and Cochabamba, the earliest estudiantinas were associated with schools. In the case of Sucre, by 1897 the medical school of the Universidad de San Francisco Xavier

de Chuquisaca had an affiliated estudiantina (Rossells 1996, 181–82). In Cochabamba, the Colegio de San Alberto formed a group by 1899 (Sánchez C. 1994, 6).

6. The banjo player was Mr. W. Olphert, who might have been a US expatriate.

7. Led by Juan Barragán, Estudiantina Verdi (founded around 1903) counted three of Bolivia's most acclaimed plucked-string players in its ranks: bandurria virtuoso Federico Otero de la Peña (who also played laúd and piano), and guitar soloists Nataniel Bravo and Federico Arancibia (*EI*, Aug. 9, 1904; Alejo 1925, 361; González Bravo 1961b, 94; Rossells n.d.). In the 1910s, approximately forty musicians made up Estudiantina Verdi (Rossells n.d., 6). The group disbanded at some point in the late 1910s or early 1920s.

8. Prior to Hernando Siles Reyes's term in office, Bautista Saavedra's Republican regime (1921–1925) had made important concessions to organized labor. Faced with opposition to his rule not only from the ousted Liberals, but also from powerful figures in his party (which splintered into three rival factions), Saavedra turned to labor leaders for support, then a novel strategy in Bolivian national politics (Klein 1969, 64–70). To build this alliance, Saavedra officials granted some of the demands of the labor movement, such as the right to an eight-hour workday, and ability to coordinate strikes (Klein 1969, 71–72).

9. In the nearby city of Oruro, a group bearing the same name of Filarmónica 1° de Mayo actively participated in labor-union-led festivities in the 1910s (Smale 2010, 61).

10. For the names and genres of the tracks Filarmónica 1° de Mayo recorded for RCA-Victor in 1928, see the website for Discography of American Historical Recordings: https://adp.library.ucsb.edu.

11. The website for Discography of American Historical Recordings also lists the recordings that Estudiantina Centro Artístico Haydn made for the RCA-Victor label.

12. Estudiantina Centro Artístico Haydn's 1930 track "Ancha Chiri" is the sole recording of Bolivian estudiantina music from this period that I have been able to access.

13. A mandolinist and prolific composer from Potosí, José Lavadenz Inchauste teamed up with guitarists Telmo Solares and Belisario Zárate in Trío Lavadenz-Solares-Zárate (Cárdenas 1986, 86–88). This ensemble performed at the 1st Indianist Week (*La Razón*, Jan. 5, 1932). Lavadenz Inchauste led various estudiantinas as well, including a new iteration of La Paz's 6 de Agosto circa 1920 (Rossells 1996, 191–92).

14. In Bolivia and other countries, "lira" was a common alternate name for estudiantina.

15. Ruiz Lavadenz's time in Buenos Aires coincided with Felipe V. Rivera's stay there. From Potosí, Rivera recorded Bolivian folkloric music for the Argentine branch of RCA-Victor with the ensembles that he led. For a biography of Felipe V. Rivera, see R. Sánchez Patzy 2014.

16. When performing at Argentine folklore festivals, Ruiz Lavadenz sometimes obscured his Bolivian identity and that of his bandmates by designating the group as "Conjunto Tipico Norteño" (Typical Northern [Argentine] ensemble). Other Bolivian musicians employed similar strategies in Buenos Aires (Rios 2014, 211).

17. In Chapter 7, I discuss the stereotype of the melancholy Andean Indian kena player, in relation to Los Jairas's 1966 hit recording of the yaraví "El Llanto de Mi Madre."

18. An offshoot of the huayño, the kjaluyo (also spelled kaluyo) is usually played at a slower tempo.

19. Lira Incaica's RCA-Victor track "Tonada de Tarka con Cullaguas" appears on the 1958 Ethnic Folkways album *The Dances of the World's Peoples, Vol. 3: Caribbean and South America* (but listed a Peruvian piece titled "Collaguas"), and the 1990s release *Secret Museum of Mankind, Vol. 4, Ethnic Music Classics 1925–1948* (Yazoo 7010).

20. The "Danza de Cullawas" that Lira Incaica played at the 2nd Indianist Week (Chapter 2) also might have featured the opening melody of "Tonada de Tarka con Cullaguas."

21. The second-place prize went to Conjunto de Cuerdas Arteaga (Arteaga String Band). The *El Diario* article that details the judges' decision provides little information on the ensemble, although it notes the members could read music scores (*ED*, Nov. 4, 1939).

22. Bolivians also used the compound term "orquesta típica" for Argentine tango groups in the 1930s and 1940s (e.g., *ED*, Aug. 22, 1942), as well as later. The context usually clarifies which ensemble type the term is referencing. "Orquesta típica" operated as a synonym for estudiantina in Venezuela as well (Torres 2007, 43).

23. In the Radio Illimani broadcast marking the one-year anniversary of Villarroel's presidency, Filarmónica 1° de Mayo played the taquirari "Alianza" (Alliance) in the slot before MNR founder Hernán Siles Zuaso's address (*ED*, Dec. 20, 1944). Nine months earlier, RADEPA had expelled MNR members from the cabinet and other state positions, as a result of US pressure. The MNR rejoined the administration in December 1944 (Klein 1969, 372–77), in time for Radio Illimani's commemorative transmission.

24. The La Paz Municipality's "national music" decree of December 1944 might have been modeled after the similar measures that Argentina's military-led government had implemented the previous year (see Chamosa 2010, 161–66 for the Argentine case).

25. In 1940s La Paz, the compound term "orquesta de jazz" referred to ensembles that emulated the format, and to varying degrees the repertoire, of US swing bands.

26. Nowhere in the 1944 Municipal decree were the terms "national," "vernacular," or "folkloric" defined. Musicians could apparently comply with the ordinance by performing any music that could be construed as a national folkloric expression.

27. Although technically it was the La Paz Municipality rather than Bolivian state that funded the Orquesta Típica La Paz and operated Radio Municipal, the RADEPA-MNR regime controlled local municipalities, no doubt especially in La Paz.

28. The Orquesta Típica La Paz in all likelihood represented a modified estudiantina format that included several Western art-classical instruments. Among the written sources I was able to consult, none offer detailed information on the group's instrumentation or membership. That the Orquesta Típica La Paz never recorded for a commercial label has further complicated my attempts to reconstruct its usual lineup.

29. The term "mitayo" refers to an indigenous person whom the Spanish colonial authorities conscripted to provide labor for the state, usually as a mine worker.

30. Salmón Ballivián's *Trilogía India* consists of three movements: "Plegaria Copacabana" (Copacabana prayer), "Sikuri Thokoñani" (Aymara for "Panpipe dance"), and "Marcha Militar Indio" (Indigenous military march).

31. Eisner often arranged similar repertoire for the Orquesta Típica La Paz and National Symphony Orchestra (for the latter group, see *ED*, May 24, 1946, and July 18, 1949).

32. Simeón Roncal, who was born in Sucre but raised in Potosí, had been acclaimed as Bolivia's foremost composer of the cueca since the 1920s (Cárdenas 1986, 81–83).

33. In the 1980s, Rolando Encinas founded the La Paz group Música de Maestros (Music of the masters), whose repertoire and performance style bears a striking resemblance to that of the Orquesta Típica La Paz. His primary model for Música de Maestros, though, was Potosí's Orquesta Sinfolklórica "Arte y Trabajo" (Bigenho 2002, 127–29). Despite his avid interest in the history of Bolivian estudiantinas, Encinas apparently was unaware of the Orquesta Típica La Paz.

34. By the 1940s most La Paz–based duos had dropped the designation "dueto" and were going by their group name instead. Examples include Las Hermanas Mejía (*ED*, Mar. 2, 1941; Apr. 25, 1942), Las Hermanas Travesí (*ED*, Jan. 3, 1941), Las Paceñitas (*ED*, Sept. 11, 1943; June 10, 1944; Mar. 24, 1945), Las Indiecitas (*ED*, Dec. 20, 1944), Las Ñustas (*ED*, Apr. 23, 1945), and Las Collitas (*ED*, Sept. 3, 1946). Most of these groups were short lived, and none attained the celebrity of Las Hermanas Tejada and Las Kantutas.

35. A quartet led by Medardo Cuellar (who would later join Voces del Oriente), Conjunto Oriental regularly performed on Radio Illimani from the late 1930s until the group disbanded in mid-1942 (*ED*, Oct. 27, 1939; May 16, 1942). The next year, Conjunto Oriental had a brief comeback in La Paz, and triggered a bidding war among Radio Illimani, Radio Los Andes, and Radio La Paz (*ED*, Apr. 20, 1943).

36. The waltz "Alma Cruceña" (Soul of Santa Cruz) and "Poema Beniano" (A Beni poem) represent additional examples of Chapi Luna's collaborations with poet Raúl Otero Reiche (Rojas Rojas 1989, 15–16). Luna teamed up with other Santa Cruz poets as well.

37. In the early-to-mid-20th century, paceños might have associated the carnaval genre with the racialized discourses of whiteness and Spanish heritage that Santa Cruz writers had constructed to differentiate their region's inhabitants from the ostensibly more "indigenous" residents of the highlands (see Soruco, Plata, and Madeiros 2008; Pruden, 2012). However, I have not uncovered evidence that La Paz residents attached these meanings to carnaval music during the period covered in this chapter.

38. The Santa Cruz music-dance contingent that participated in the Primera Olimpiada Escolar Boliviana similarly presented a taquirari music-dance sketch (*ED*, Aug. 13, 1937).

39. Gerardo "Chocni" López and Antonio Cáceres founded Los Sumac Huaynas (or Los Sumac Waynas) as an instrumental duo around 1940 (*ED*, Feb. 10 and Apr. 4, 1941). By the time the group traveled to Buenos Aires in 1942, former Estudiantina La Paz guitarist Alfredo del Río had become a member (*ED*, July 8, 1942). Henceforth the ensemble would also be known as the Conjunto López-Cáceres-Del Río (e.g., *ED*, Aug. 4, 1944). Los Sumac Huaynas' default configuration was that of a guitar trio. When they played Andean-themed repertory, however, López often switched over to the charango. His nickname, "Chocni," is a local term that refers to the sleep in one's eyes.

40. Two years later, Yola Rivero joined Yma Sumac and Moisés Vivanco's troupe (*ED*, June 8, 1944), with which she would perform under the pseudonym of Cholita Rivero.

41. Even though Los Hermanos Ábalos' first hit was "Carnavalito Quebradeño," the group would become best known in Argentina and internationally for the zambas and chacareras that they popularized (e.g., "Zamba de Mi Pago," "Chacarera del Rancho").

42. Unfortunately, I have not been able to obtain Las Hermanas Tejada's recordings.

43. I wish to thank Irma Vásquez de Ronda's son, Juan Ronda, for dubbing several Las Kantutas tracks for me from their RCA-Victor, ODEON, and Discos Méndez records.

44. Vásquez and Sáenz reformed Las Kantutas the next month (*ED*, Jan. 10, 1945).

45. The growing presence of carnavales and taquiraris in the orquesta de jazz repertoire of La Paz bands represents one clear indicator of música oriental's popularity in the Villarroel era (see *ED*, Sept. 23 and Dec. 20, 1945; Rojas Foppiano 1991, 71–73).

46. Voces del Oriente was formed in 1942 by the lead singers Luis Eugenio Velasco (first voice) and Ángel Camacho (second voice), and the guitarists Medardo Cuellar, Jorge Brown, and Tito Véliz (*ED*, Aug. 25, 1944; Terceros 2006, 83, 321–22). Véliz, originally from Cochabamba, was the sole non-camba member of this música oriental ensemble.

47. Las Kantutas made the earliest recording of the cueca "A Bolivia" (To Bolivia), a tune more commonly known as "Viva Mi Patria Bolivia" (Long live my homeland Bolivia). Composed by Apolinar Camacho (with lyrics by Ricardo Cabrera), this cueca would gain popularity during the 1963 South American Soccer Cup (which Bolivia hosted and won), and henceforth serve as an unofficial national anthem. When Las Kantutas recorded it for ODEON in 1947, though, few Bolivians knew the song.

48. The word "cunumisinga" is camba slang for "country girl." "Quiéreme Cunumisinga" thus can be translated as "Love me, country girl of the eastern lowlands."

49. Huiñay Inti appeared in La Paz in 1936, and became known as a top estudiantina within a few years (*ED*, Nov. 6, 1939; July 11, 1940; July 21, 1941; Feb. 21, 1942). The nickname of Nicólas García, K'auquita, takes after a traditional type of Bolivian bread.

II

Musical Folklorization in the Era of
Revolutionary Nationalism (1952–1964)

4

STATE-SPONSORED FOLKLORIZATION OF MUSIC-DANCE

TRADITIONS IN THE MNR ERA

ON APRIL 9, 1952, the Movimiento Nacionalista Revolucionario set into motion a coup d'état against the military junta led by President General Hugo Ballivián. The insurgents accomplished one early objective shortly after midnight, when they seized control of Radio Illimani. At ten o'clock the next morning, with the station now a mouthpiece for the MNR, Radio Illimani's operatives proclaimed to the nation that "the revolution" had succeeded, although prematurely, as the fighting between the military and insurrectionists would continue until the latter emerged victorious on Good Friday, April 11 (Knudsen 1986, 158). Over those momentous three days, Radio Illimani interspersed MNR propaganda with recordings of the National Anthem and Bolivian folkloric music (Knudsen 1986, 157; Coronel Quisbert 1997, 55–56), to paint the movimientistas as patriots who would represent the genuine interests of the masses once the party gained power.

Víctor Paz Estenssoro triumphantly returned to La Paz from his six-year exile in Argentina on April 15, 1952 to assume the presidency that most Bolivians believed rightfully belonged to him; the MNR chief had won the 1951 presidential election that the military invalidated to install General Ballivián as head of state instead (Klein 1969, 399–400). When Paz Estenssoro disembarked from his plane at the La Paz airport, an enthusiastic crowd greeted him, waving posters with movimientista slogans such as "Villarroel Martyr—Estenssoro Savior" and "The MNR is El Pueblo"

Panpipes & Ponchos. Fernando Rios, Oxford University Press (2020). © Oxford University Press.
DOI: 10.1093/oso/9780190692278.001.0001.

(Dunkerley 1984, 41–42). The party faithful honored their beloved leader by loudly intoning the strains of the MNR's unofficial theme song, the taquirari "Siempre" (Fellman Velarde 1954, 18–19):

Viva el Movimiento	Long live the Movement
Gloria a Villarroel	Glory to Villarroel
el Paz Estenssoro	Paz Estenssoro
ya está en el poder.	already is in power.
(First stanza of "Siempre")	

A few months into Paz Estenssoro's presidency, on the six-year anniversary of the murder of Villarroel (i.e., July 21, 1952), the MNR regime promulgated universal suffrage, by eliminating the discriminatory criteria that had denied women and the vast majority of non-elite men (especially rural indigenous people) the right to vote and hold public office. It represented the first of three groundbreaking pieces of legislation the administration would pass.[1] The second one, the state's expropriation of the "Big Three" tin mining companies, was decreed three months later, on October 31. Paz Estenssoro signed into law the third historic MNR measure, the Agrarian Reform, the next year on Day of the Indian (August 2, 1953). A milestone for Bolivian state-indigenous relations, the Agrarian Reform granted legal status to the Andean indigenous population's increasingly bold confiscations of hacienda properties. In the months after the 1952 Revolution, indigenous people in multiple areas of the rural Andes had forcefully asserted their ownership of the lands that they had long worked on, and at times inflicted violence on the hacendados who had been exploiting their labor. These actions by the indigenous sector incited such terror in criollo-mestizo society that historian Herbert Klein likens it to the "Great Fear" that the French upper class had experienced at the onset of the French Revolution (1992, 234; see also Gotkowitz 2007, 269–71).[2]

Of these three landmark rulings, the Paz Estenssoro government wholeheartedly supported only the ratification of universal suffrage. The capitalist-minded regime expressed far less enthusiasm for nationalizing the core of the Bolivian mining industry. That it nonetheless implemented this state expropriation was largely the result of pressure from the militantly leftist Central Obrera Boliviana (Bolivian Workers' Center; COB). The MNR was compelled to acknowledge the COB as its partner in governance, in an arrangement termed *co-gobierno* that fell apart soon after Paz Estenssoro's first term as head of state (which ended in 1956). As for the Agrarian Reform, most MNR leaders initially had opposed this type of measure. By 1953, though, they realized that the MNR administration's only viable response to the indigenous sector's land grabs would be to try to co-opt them. Tellingly, movimientista officials designed the Agrarian Reform on the capitalist conception of private property, and not on the communal land-ownership principles that rural indigenous communities traditionally practiced in the highlands (see Platt 1982). An overriding MNR goal was Bolivia's "modernization," which the party leadership regarded as synonymous with state-directed capitalist development.

Like many other Latin American political regimes of the early-to-mid-20th century that placed their faith in state-directed capitalism and nation building, the MNR governments of the "revolutionary nationalist" period (1952–1964) championed mestizaje (ethnic-cultural fusion) as the primary "cultural" means for modernizing the masses and fashioning national unity across the nonindigenous-indigenous divide.[3] From the MNR perspective, the Andean cholo-mestizo population represented the "best hope for a formative middle class" (Albro 1998, 100). Cholo-mestizos appeared to fully embrace so-called modern capitalist entrepreneurism and individualism, whereas indigenous ayllu members instead prioritized "traditional" egalitarianism and communitarianism. And what is more, cholo-mestizos, as a result of their intermediate status in the social hierarchy, blended indigenous and criollo cultural practices in ways that the MNR imagined could serve as the cultural nexus for criollos, mestizos, and indigenous people. But standing in the way of the MNR dream of a predominantly mestizo nation was that most Bolivians belonged to the rural indigenous sector (Toranzo 2008, 36). Faced with this reality, the first MNR government decreed that *indios* (Indians) no longer existed in Bolivia and henceforth would be called *campesinos* (peasants).[4] The party leadership believed this terminological change—from an ethnicized and racialized classification, to a socioeconomic and occupational designation—would make it easier for indigenous people to culturally pass into the mestizo or cholo category, and thereby eventually foster the rise of a largely mestizo Bolivian population.

The MNR's stance on the nation-building merits of mestizaje began to take shape in the years of the Villarroel-MNR coalition government (i.e., 1943–1946; see Gotkowitz 2007, 164–191). Prior to the 1940s, most La Paz political figures and intellectuals had characterized mestizaje and cholo-mestizos in explicitly negative terms, largely because the elite feared that an expanded cholo-mestizo sector might challenge the status quo (Larson 2011). Interestingly, the MNR's pro-mestizaje rhetoric drew much of its early ideas from regionalist (rather than nationalist) Cochabamba writers, who extolled mestizaje to highlight their departamento's cultural distinctiveness vis-à-vis the La Paz region (e.g., Spanish-Quechua bilingualism had long been commonplace in Cochabamba, even among the urban elite) (Gotkowitz 2007, 171). Cochabamba is not the birthplace of political ideologies that celebrate mestizaje, though. That honor falls to Mexico, where the ruling Partido Revolucionario Institucional (Institutional Revolutionary Party) exalted the patriotic virtues of mestizaje in the decades after the 1910–1920 Mexican Revolution.[5] Like the case with indigenismo, therefore, Bolivians borrowed the nationalist discourse and ideology of mestizaje from a foreign source and adapted it to fit local conditions.

Bolivia's "revolutionary nationalism" epoch saw a remarkable upsurge in the number, scope, and variety of state-sponsored folkloric music-dance events involving criollo-mestizo, cholo-mestizo, and indigenous performers. It was also in the years of MNR rule that Bolivia obtained a state-funded folkloric ballet company and fully operational Department of Folklore. The 1952–1964 MNR era thus represents not only a time of momentous political, social, and economic change for Bolivia, but also a critical juncture for the national folklore movement. This chapter analyzes the major musical folklorization initiatives that state-affiliated entities launched in La Paz city from 1952 to 1964, with special attention given to their connections with MNR projects and agendas, in particular the party's panacea of cultural mestizaje. As this chapter demonstrates, MNR-sponsored musical folklorization initiatives at times contradicted party ideology, and in some instances articulated to a greater extent with indigenismo than with mestizaje.[6]

MUNICIPALITY-SPONSORED FESTIVALS OF INDIGENOUS MUSIC-DANCE TRADITIONS IN LA PAZ CITY, 1953–1956

In July 1953, about two weeks before the Agrarian Reform would become the law of the land, the Municipality of La Paz's Council of Culture (Consejo Municipal de Cultura) coordinated an "autochthonous" music-dance competition for Andean rural indigenous tropas (traditional wind consorts) of the La Paz region. Named the Gran Concurso de Música y Danza Autóctona, it took place at Hernando Siles Stadium in the Fiestas Julianas season, the traditional time of year in La Paz city for folklore festivals prepared by the Municipality. President Paz Estenssoro donated additional funding, as did the Ministry of Peasant Affairs and the Ministry of Education.[7] To maximize participation in the event, the Council of Culture sent invitations "via the telegraph, [to] all the folkloric groups, from the most isolated places" (ED, July 8, 1953), and vowed that it would cover the ensembles' trip costs (ED, May 24, 1953). And in an unprecedented move, the Bolivian state allocated monies to transport two of the music-dance groups to La Paz city by airplane (ED, July 19, 1953). About thirty Andean tropas, ranging in size from twelve to seventy-four members, made their way to Hernando Siles Stadium to vie for the trophies and cash prizes on hand at the Gran Concurso de Música y Danza Autóctona (ED, Apr. 7, 1954). The number of indigenous wind ensembles that competed in the 1953 festival therefore exceeded by almost double the quantity that had taken part in either 1945's Concurso Vernacular y Folklórico, or 1948's Concurso Folklórico Indígena del Departamento (see Chapter 2).

The 2nd Gran Concurso de Música y Danza Autóctona took place the following year during Fiestas Julianas, with an even greater number of participants, approximately seventy-five tropas (ED, July 12, 1954). Although the subsequent iteration of the series—which the Municipality rebranded the III Festival de Música y Danza Nativa—represented a decline in the sum total of contestants, because only about fifty-six groups competed in the festival (ED, July 19, 1955), ninety tropas registered for the final edition, the IV Festival de Música y Danza Nativa (ED, Aug. 4, 1956). The 1956 event thus set a new high for indigenous tropa participation at a Bolivian state-funded folklore festival.

The La Paz Municipality's "autochthonous/native" music-dance festival series of 1953–1956 has long been the most-remembered MNR government-sponsored initiative involving music making, a testament to the strong impression that the series made on the public. For the MNR, these spectacles of indigenous "folklore" were politically useful, because they functioned as public enactments of the party's burgeoning alliance with the Andean rural indigenous population. The movimientistas would increasingly rely on this coalition at election time (see Mitchell 1977; Gordillo 2000). Notably, state officials postponed 1956's IV Festival de Música y Danza Nativa from its original date of mid-July, to August 5, to make the event coincide with the festivities surrounding Hernán Siles Zuaso's inauguration as president (*ED*, July 15, Aug. 4 and Aug. 12, 1956).

With 83% of the popular vote, Siles Zuaso—who had served as Paz Estenssoro's Vice President from 1952 to 1956—obtained a landslide win in 1956 in Bolivia's first presidential election under the conditions of universal suffrage (Mitchell 1977, 57). This large margin of victory owed much to the overwhelming support that Andean rural indigenous people gave to his candidacy, to ensure the government would keep intact the Agrarian Reform (see Gordillo 2000). In metropolitan centers, where criollos and mestizos rather than indigenous people represented the majority, however, Siles Zuaso earned a far lower percentage of the vote, approximately 58%; most of the remainder went to the candidate of the right-wing Falange Socialista Boliviana (Mitchell 1977, 57, 63).

The opposition party's strong showing in the 1956 election in major cities such as Cochabamba, Sucre, and Oruro worried the movimientistas. The MNR knew full well, given their frustrated experience in 1951, that the losing side of a presidential election often attempted to overturn the results through forceful means. By re-scheduling the IV Festival de Música y Danza Nativa so that hundreds of traditionally dressed Andean indigenous musicians-dancers formed the backdrop to the swearing in of Siles Zuaso, the MNR intended to send a vivid signal to the Falange Socialista Boliviana and other opposition groups that the indigenous masses fully supported the ruling party. Four years later, MNR officials organized a similar spectacle involving Andean indigenous music-dance ensembles in the run-up to the 1960 presidential election (won by Paz Estenssoro). Held at La Paz's recently erected Coliseo Cerrado (Indoor Coliseum), this event featured performances by indigenous tropas from nine La Paz provinces (*ED*, Apr. 21, 1960).

The IV Festival de Música y Danza Nativa of 1956 and the 1960 folklore exhibition at the Coliseo Cerrado no doubt stirred up elite and middle-class anxiety about the highland indigenous sector's supposed savagery and long-repressed desire to annihilate the criollo-mestizo population (see Chapters 1 and 2). The Siles Zuaso administration knowingly conjured up this enduring stereotype of "the belligerent Indian" for political purposes, by deploying MNR-affiliated Andean indigenous militias to urban areas, a tactic that the regime began to implement in the late 1950s (Mitchell 1977, 70–71). Seen in this light, 1956's IV Festival de Música y Danza Nativa represents a harbinger of a disturbing strategy that the Siles Zuaso administration was about to unveil, and that the ensuing MNR government of Paz Estenssoro would make recourse to as well in the early 1960s to intimidate its opponents (e.g., see Field 2014, 22).

Antonio González Bravo (profiled in Chapter 2), who was still Bolivia's foremost scholar of Andean indigenous music, served as one of the organizers of, and sat on the prize committees for, the 1953–1956 editions of the Municipality's "autochtho-nous/native" folklore contests.[8] His involvement surely explains why the format of the festivals resembled that of the sexenio's Concurso Folklórico Indígena del Departamento of 1948. As explained in Chapter 2, González Bravo played the chief role in coordinating the 1948 Concurso, in which indigenous tropas competed in one of four musical instrument categories: siku (open to all forms of the panpipe), pinkillu (i.e., duct flutes of any type), kena (i.e., end-notched flutes), and flauta traversa. The Council of Culture used the same instrument groupings at 1953's Gran Concurso de Música y Danza Autóctona and its three ensuing iterations.

Over the course of the series, Sikuris de Italaque and Kantus de Charazani ensem-bles earned the most accolades. This pattern began with the 2nd Gran Concurso de Música y Danza Autóctona.[9] Italaque's Sikuris de Taypi Chiñaya won first place in the panpipe contest, while the runner-up prize went to an unspecified kantus con-sort from Charazani (ED, Aug. 5, 1954).[10] Six years earlier, Italaque and Charazani panpipe tropas had achieved the same ranking from the judges at the Concurso Folklórico Indígena del Departamento of 1948 (Chapter 2), another parallel between pre- and post-1952 Bolivian folklore spectacles showcasing Andean indigenous ensembles.

At the III and IV editions of the Festival de Música y Danza Nativa (i.e., 1955 and 1956 editions), Sikuris de Italaque and Kantus de Charazani groups came out on top again, not only in their instrument grouping, but also in the overall category for "music"—the best-remunerated contest. Italaque's Sikuris de Taypi Chiñaya (for the second time) and Sikuris de Taypi Jancohuma shared the honors at III Festival de Música y Danza Nativa, along with a kantus tropa from the town of Niño Korin (ED, Nov. 5, 1955). The fourth and final version of the contest saw plenty of familiar faces among the winners. Sikuris de Taypi Chiñaya, Sikuris de Taypi Jancohuma, and Kantus de Niño Korin were jointly awarded the top prize in the "siku" and "music" classifications, beside a new-comer to the competition, Italaque's Sikuris de Taypi Ayka (ED, Aug. 12, 1956).

González Bravo's admiration for the Sikuris de Italaque tradition in all likelihood swayed the judgments of the other committee members, as surely had been the case at the Concurso Folklórico Indígena del Departamento. The second major competi-tive advantage that Italaque siku tropas benefited from at MNR-era folklore festi-vals, their greater experience performing for criollo-mestizo audiences in the urban La Paz setting, without a doubt had also represented an important factor at the 1948 event.

Since the early 20th century, Bolivian criollo-mestizo indigenistas had viewed Los Sikuris de Italaque as the country's most notable indigenous tropa tradition. It was not until the "revolutionary nationalist" era, however, that the broader criollo-mestizo public (i.e., those outside of the indigenista camp) learned that Italaque was home to a much-admired siku consort style, by attending an edition of the Gran Concurso de Música y Danza Autóctona or Festival de Música y Danza Nativa, browsing the contest results in the paper, and/or reading editorials that exalted the authenticity of Italaque's sikuris (e.g., *ED*, Aug. 5, 1955). The indigenous music-dance festivals that the Municipality coordinated annually from 1953 to 1956 therefore considerably expanded the Sikuris de Italaque tradition's name recognition in urban criollo-mestizo circles.[11]

The Kantus de Charazani tradition—distinguished sonically from other indigenous Bolivian panpipe styles by its prominent parallel fifth and fourth harmonies (Chapter 2)—experienced an even more dramatic rise in its regional and national profile in the MNR years, because Charazani panpipe groups previously had not taken part in folklore exhibitions staged in La Paz city, other than 1948's Concurso Folklórico Indígena del Departamento. But from the mid-1950s onward, Kantus de Charazani tropas (primarily ensembles from the town of Niño Korin) would regularly earn plaudits at state-sponsored folklore festivals. This musical tradition thus quickly acquired a reputation in Bolivian criollo-mestizo society as a premier panpipe tropa style, on a par with Los Sikuris de Italaque (e.g., see *ED*, Aug. 5, 1955).[12]

The writings of Charazani-born ethnologist and lawyer Enrique Oblitas Poblete on the history and traditions of his home province contributed to the criollo-mestizo public's newfound appreciation of kantus music. Although his publications mainly explore the spiritual practices of Kallawaya healers, he documented local music-dance practices through articles such as "Report on Bautista Saavedra Province: Folkloric, Ethnographic, and Archeological Aspects." This essay appears in a 1954 edition of *Khana*, the MNR government's "cultural" magazine. Oblitas Poblete's later book, *Cultura Callawaya* (1963), discusses the indigenous music-dance traditions of the Charazani Valley; Antonio González Bravo's transcriptions of 136 Charazani tropa melodies appear in the appendix (Oblitas Poblete 1963, 327–465). Oblitas Poblete's earliest collaboration with González Bravo might have occurred in the 1953 Fiesta Julianas season, around the same time as the 1st Gran Concurso de Música y Danza Autóctona. At La Casa de Murillo (home of the patriot-martyr honored at Fiestas Julianas, Pedro Domingo Murillo), Oblitas Poblete and González Bravo put together a Charazani-themed "folklore" exposition that included a display of the varieties of panpipes that indigenous musicians used in the region (Alcaldia Municipal La Paz 1953).

On an ideological level, the 1953–1956 municipal festival series fit uneasily with the MNR's championing of mestizaje. Indeed, the guidelines for these contests explicitly encouraged indigenous musicians and dancers to preserve—rather than instead abandon, hybridize, or "modernize"—their traditional expressive practices. The summons for the 1953 and 1954 festivals, moreover, unambiguously stated that if an ensemble wanted to be seriously considered for the top prizes, mestizo-associated musical repertoire was off limits:

> The music of the ensembles should be authentically native and, as much as possible, [feature] the most ancient tunes that are remembered, avoiding those of mestizo origin or otherwise contaminated by harmonies foreign to vernacular art. (*ED*, May 24, 1953; reprinted in *ED*, May 21, 1954)[13]

The competition guidelines bear the imprint of González Bravo's negative appraisal of cultural mestizaje. In his publications and lectures he often proclaimed that Andean indigenous musical expressions ought to remain as pure as possible, by which he meant that indigenous musicians should refrain not only from borrowing melodies from criollo-mestizos, but also from adopting criollo- or mestizo-associated ensemble formats. Obeying this logic, the brass band—strongly identified locally with mestizos yet part of indigenous community life—was absent from the Council of Culture's itemization of appropriate ensemble types. The rising popularity of brass bands in highland indigenous La Paz communities rankled González Bravo's purist instincts (see *ED*, Nov. 7, 1955), particularly because these groups often replaced flauta traversa (transverse flute) tropas as the performance medium for genres such as the *llamerada* (llama herders' dance) and cullawas (González Bravo 1938, 170–72; 1948, 421; Bedregal de Conitzer and González Bravo 1956, 26–27). Apparently to revive the older practice in rural areas, the festival committee's summons consistently list the cullawas and llamerada under the "flauta traversa" heading (*ED*, May, 24, 1953; May 21, 1954; June 12, 1955; June 13, 1956).

Interestingly, the morenada genre, or "dance of the blacks," also appears in the flauta traversa category in the advertisements for the 1st and 2nd Gran Concurso de Música y Danza Autóctona. The morenada was a signature item for brass bands at the time, although earlier in the century, the genre had been a flauta traversa mainstay in the small towns of greater La Paz (see *ED*, Jan. 1, 1905; Paredes Candia 1966, 25; Valeriano Thola 2004, 30–31, 48; Cuba and Cuba, 38–39). By the mid-1950s, the Charazani Valley seems to have represented one of the few sites in the departamento where morenada dancers still paraded to the music of flauta traversa tropas, which would explain why Charazani's morenada-flauta traversa tradition is the sole example of this practice mentioned in the summons for the 1953 and 1954 festivals (*ED*, May, 24, 1953; May 21, 1954).[14]

Like most Bolivian folklore scholars (e.g., Paredes 1913, 180–81), González Bravo categorized the morenada as a mestizo expression, rather than an "authentic" indigenous tradition (e.g., González Bravo 1948, 421; Bedregal de Conitzer and González Bravo 1956, 26). This classification stemmed from the genre's overt allusions to Afro-Bolivians, which clearly signal that the morenada originated in Spanish colonial times and not the pre-Columbian age (in contrast, the cullawas and llamerada traditions exhibit an air of greater antiquity, because the dancers mimic the traditional indigenous practices of weaving and llama herding, respectively). What must have made Charazani's morenada–flauta traversa tradition nonetheless acceptable to González Bravo and the rest of the committee was that indigenous musicians had resisted the temptation to adopt the "mestizo" brass band in place of the more "indigenous" flauta traversa tropa. As for the flauta traversa itself, González Bravo recognized its Spanish origin, but often stressed that highland indigenous people had integrated the instrument into their cultural life so long ago that they viewed it as their own tradition (González Bravo 1938, 171; 1948, 418).

A more recent musical trend in Andean indigenous communities, one involving misti sikuris, or "mestizo siku tropas," disturbed González Bravo to a far greater extent than the indigenous brass band phenomenon. Originally associated with vecinos (rural criollo-mestizos), the misti sikuri tradition arose in provincial La Paz in the late 1800s. Over time, it became characterized by the ensembles' brass band-style percussion section, the members' lavish dance outfits, and other distinguishing features of the tradition (see Chapter 5). By the late 1940s, indigenous communities in the provinces of Camacho, Larecaja, and other parts of the departamento of La Paz had adopted the misti sikuri format and its main genre (González Bravo 1948, 411–12; Taborga 1948a, 217; Taborga 1948b, 384; Rios 2012, 18–19).[15] As a case in point, in 1948 a misti sikuri tropa from the La Paz village of Sapaqui figured among the indigenous panpipe groups that competed in the Concurso Folklórico Indígena del Departamento (*ED*, Nov. 24, 1948).[16]

González Bravo had presided on the jury for the 1948 Concurso, and his writings from the late 1940s briefly describe misti sikuri practices of rural La Paz (González Bravo 1948, 411–12; 1949, 97, 100), so he certainly knew about the misti sikuri tradition's existence when the committee drafted the call for participants for the 1953–1956 festival series. Yet nowhere in the summons does the name "misti sikuris" appear. This omission represented a deliberate move, when one considers that the committee tried to be comprehensive in its itemization of genres for each instrument category (i.e., siku, kena, pinkillu, flauta traversa). Under the "siku" heading, for instance, the summons lists the following genres: sikuris, kantus, ayarachis, chiriguanos, loco palla pallas, *jula-julas, lakitas, mimulas, taquiris*, and *tuaillos*.

Unquestionably, the very name "misti sikuri," with its conspicuous reference to mestizos, made the tradition an awkward fit for the Municipality's "autochthonous" folklore spectacles. The organizers could have used a similar rationale, however, to exclude from the proceedings the morenada, flauta traversa, and other local genres or musical instruments of obvious post–Spanish Conquest origin that indigenous musicians nonetheless were not only allowed but also encouraged to perform at the festivals (additional examples include the *tinti-caballos* and waka-tokoris genres). Whether or not a locally practiced music and dance tradition appeared to exhibit "authentic indigenous roots" thus did not represent the sole criterion the committee weighed when writing up the contest summons.

González Bravo's strongly negative assessment of the misti sikuri tradition is what most likely explains its exclusion from the festival series. In 1948 he observed, with palpable anxiety, "Misti Sicuris . . . to the great detriment of indigenous art, are propagating themselves among the Indians, erasing the traces of the true indigenous dances" (González Bravo 1948, 411). In his publications he habitually took on a dismissive tone when discussing misti sikuris, including the tradition's eclectic repertoire (which features criollo-mestizo and non-Bolivian genres), the musicians' creativity (he characterizes it as "weak"), the ensembles' extravagant attire, and even the members' claim that devotion to God and the Virgin Mary had inspired the birth of La Paz's earliest misti sikuri groups (González Bravo 1936, 256; 1948, 411–12; 1949, 97).[17]

What seems to have most irritated González Bravo about the misti sikuri tradition is how it so effectively blurred the boundary between indigenous and mestizo cultural practices. After all, whereas it would have been unnecessary for him to point out to his predominantly criollo-mestizo readers that indigenous brass bands modeled themselves after mestizo-criollo ensembles, it is unlikely that many urban Bolivians were conscious of the rural mestizo or vecino sector's central role in the trajectory of the misti sikuri tradition.

Overall, the Municipality's 1953–1956 music-dance series championed indigenous expressive practice that displayed minimal mestizo influence. The festivals thus were openly at odds with the MNR's pro-mestizaje message, and more in line with conservative strands within pre-1952 indigenismo. González Bravo's purism regarding indigenous music, a view then commonly shared among folklore scholars worldwide, in all likelihood played a major part in the festivals' anti-mestizaje and anti-modernization stance. His opposition to new developments in indigenous music making did not extent to the performance context, however. The folklore festival format radically departed from Andean indigenous fiesta norms (e.g., inter-ayllu versus intra-ayllu scope; criollo-mestizo juries rather than indigenous community members designating the "best ensembles"; see Chapter 2), as González Bravo would have been aware. This deviation clearly did not bother him too much, though, given his involvement in organizing the festivals and choosing the winning groups.

The number of participating ensembles, meanwhile, notably increased over the course of the series, in tandem with the MNR's growing reliance on the political support of Andean indigenous people. Yet the IV Festival de Música y Danza Nativa would have no sequel. A few months after the 1956 contest, the Siles Zuaso administration slashed government expenditures, including much of the budget for folklore spectacles. These cuts were in accordance with International Monetary Fund (IMF) stipulations, with which the MNR regime complied to receive vast sums of US aid. In the years of movimientista rule, the US government provided more financial assistance to Bolivia than it did to any other Latin American country, in a concerted, Cold War–era attempt to restrain the direction of Bolivia's "revolution" without having to make recourse to a CIA-coordinated coup à la Iran (1953) and Guatemala (1954) (Lehman 1999; Siekmeier 2011). The La Paz Municipality's annual indigenous music-dance competition figures among the state-funded initiatives and programs that fell by the wayside in Bolivia's post-1956 economic climate of IMF-recommended austerity measures. The criollo-mestizo musical events that the Subsecretary of Press, Information and Culture had been offering in the first MNR term met the same fate.

THE SUBSECRETARY OF PRESS, INFORMATION, AND CULTURE'S CRIOLLO-MESTIZO MUSIC EVENTS, 1953–1956

Movimientista stalwart José Fellman Velarde directed the propaganda arm of the first MNR government, the Subsecretaría de Prensa, Información y Cultura (SPIC), which he modeled after the Peronist Argentine bureau of the same name (Coronel Quisbert 1997, 64–88). The SPIC oversaw various agencies, including the Instituto

Cinematográfico Boliviano (Bolivian Cinematographic Institute). Led by Paz Estenssoro's brother-in-law, Waldo Cerruto, the Bolivian Cinematographic Institute coordinated the SPIC's first large-scale musical undertaking, 1953's Concurso de Arte Nativo. Despite its name, the festival represented an entirely mestizo and criollo musical affair. SPIC-sponsored festivals and recitals generally were closed to rural indigenous musicians, a segregationist policy that ran counter to the MNR's pledge to dismantle ethnicized socioeconomic divisions.

Over four days in the setting of the Municipal Theater, the Concurso de Arte Nativo showcased the talents of La Paz favorites such as Las Kantutas, Las Hermanas Tejada, Los Sumac Huaynas (and its charango soloist Chocni López), Huiñay Inti, and Filarmónica 1° de Mayo. Recently formed groups also took part. This cohort included the vocal duos Las Hermanas Viscarra Cordero and Las Hermanas Alberty; bolero trios Los Carlos and Los Indios; orquesta de jazz Ritmo y Melodía; mestizo siku tropa Los Cebollitas (The little onions; profiled in Chapter 5); and various solo vocalists. To see such a mix of established and rising artists, and juxtaposition of "folkloric" and "cosmopolitan" ensemble formats, would be the norm at SPIC-funded festivals. At the conclusion of the Concurso de Arte Nativo, the jury rewarded the contestants whom it deemed best embodied the event's indigenista theme. The seasoned Las Hermanas Tejada captured first place, while Los Cebollitas' siku tropa rendition of "Caminito del Indio" (Little pathway of the Indian) earned them the runner-up award (*ED*, Jan. 12 and 16, 1953).[18]

The SPIC launched its most ambitious musical endeavor the following year, a weekly concert series held at the spacious Open Air Theater.[19] Offered on Sundays and free to the public, it lasted through at least eleven iterations. The SPIC dedicated one of the concerts to the "Labor Delegates" who had come to La Paz city for the "First Workers' Congress" (*ED*, Nov. 7, 1954). On other occasions, the advertisements brandished nationalist slogans such as "hacer arte es hacer patria" (to make art is to make the nation), and "arte en servicio del pueblo" (art in the service of the people) (e.g., *ED*, Sept. 25, 1954; Oct. 10, 1954). During the sexenio regimes of Urriolagoitia and Ballivián, the Open Air Theater similarly had presented weekly folkloric music shows for the masses (as noted briefly at the end of Chapter 3), but these concerts had been devoid of such blatantly populist propaganda. In most other respects, including the musical programming, however, the 1954 Open Air Theater season resembled its sexenio predecessors from 1950 and 1951.

A typical program in the 1954 series presented a range of criollo-mestizo musical acts and styles, interspersed with dance sketches and comedy routines. Folklore stars who had made their names well before the 1952 Revolution performed in these events (e.g., Las Hermanas Tejada, Los Sumac Huaynas, Gilberto Rojas), along with up-and-coming artists such as Las Hermanas Castillo, Las Hermanas Aliaga de la Barra, Las Hermanas Espinoza, and Las Hermanas Arteaga (*ED*, Sept. 5, 12, and 25; Oct. 10; Nov. 7; Dec. 12, 1954). The latter two duos, whose members incidentally hailed from the same La Paz village of Sorata (Larecaja Province), were on their way to becoming acclaimed artists. The previous year, Las Hermanas Espinoza had won first place in the Radio La Paz contest "En Busca de Una Estrella" (In search of a star) after collecting the most votes from the studio audience (Grimanesca and Josefina Espinoza, personal communications). The runner-up, Las Hermanas Arteaga, earned the top honor at the next year's iteration of the competition on Radio La Paz (Irma and Elsa Arteaga, personal communications).

Orquestas de jazz (US swing-band style ensembles) and bolero trios often served as the main attractions at the 1954 Open Air Theater season. At the inaugural concert, La Paz bandleader Fermín Barrionuevo's orquesta de jazz Los Reyes del Mambo (The mambo kings) filled the headliner role (*ED*, Sept. 5, 1954), while at the tenth edition, bolero singer Raúl Shaw of Oruro (profiled in Chapter 5) had star billing (*ED*, Oct. 24, 1954). Oscar Loayza y Su Orquesta de Jazz, Trío Ritmo Tropical, and Trío Los Reyes also performed in the 1954 series (*ED*, Sept. 5; Oct. 10 and 24, 1954). Programming bolero trios and orquestas de jazz represented a sure-fire way for the SPIC to obtain a mass turnout at its spectacles, because these ensemble formats enjoyed high levels of popularity in Bolivia's major cities in the MNR years.

The SPIC ceased scheduling free admission shows at the Open Air Theater by early December 1954, and instead began to offer ticketed recitals in the intimate setting of the Municipal Theater. These concerts sometimes featured non-Bolivian artists; examples from 1954 include the Argentine folklore company Los Arrieros de Yaví (The muleteers from Yaví) (*ED*, Dec. 5, 1954), and Peruvian-Cuzco troupe Ccanchis (*ED*, Apr. 10, 1955). More commonly, though, these Municipal Theater events presented an assortment of Bolivian musical acts (e.g., *ED*, Jan. 16, Feb. 6, and July 6, 1955)—the same variety-show format that the SPIC had used in the 1954 Open Air Theater series.

In January 1957, the Siles Zuaso regime abolished the Subsecretary of Press, Information and Culture, one of many measures the administration enacted to reduce state spending and thereby procure continued US financial assistance. The SPIC was re-founded the next year, but with more limited duties (Coronel Quisbert 1997, 85–87). And no longer would it organize musical activities. As a result, the number and scope of state-funded criollo-mestizo music events dramatically declined in the second MNR term (1956–1960). Those that did occur usually were arranged by the Municipality, or Ministry of Education and Fine Arts, for the Fiestas Julianas season (e.g., *ED*, July 18, 1957; July 13, 1958).

From 1953 to 1956, SPIC-coordinated musical performances for criollo-mestizo artists happened on a far more regular basis in the city of La Paz than the Municipality's contemporaneous offerings for indigenous musicians (which consisted solely of annual festivals in the first MNR term), especially in 1954, when the SPIC staged its musical events weekly. However, the SPIC's musical spectacles did not substantially influence paceño artistic currents, other than reinforce preexisting trends, perhaps because they seldom took the form of competitions (1953's Concurso de Arte Nativo represents one of the few music contests the SPIC coordinated in this period). Nor did these events foster the canonization of particular genres or ensemble formats, unlike the Municipal series' effect on the Sikuris de Italaque and especially Kantus de Charazani panpipe traditions.

In another difference, SPIC-run musical performances exhibited considerable leeway in terms of the permitted ensemble types, so much so that even bolero trios and orquestas de jazz were allowed to participate—a striking contrast to the Municipal Council of Culture's strict policing of the varieties of appropriate Andean indigenous ensemble configurations. The SPIC's flexibility matched the MNR leadership's viewpoint that mestizos and criollos were more modern than indigenous people, even if pragmatism more than political ideology appears to have motivated this SPIC policy. A commonality between the SPIC and Municipality's musical offerings in the first MNR term is that their respective foci implicitly upheld rather than challenged Bolivia's ethnicized sociocultural divisions. The Primera Semana Folklórica Boliviana, discussed next, constitutes a rare instance in which criollo-mestizo *and* rural indigenous ensembles took part in the same Bolivian state-funded music-dance event in the MNR period.

THE PRIMERA SEMANA FOLKLÓRICA BOLIVIANA

In 1961, President Paz Estenssoro appointed ex-SPIC director José Fellman Velarde to head the Consejo Nacional de Arte (National Council of Art). Under the dominion of the Ministry of Education and Fine Arts, the new agency assumed the La Paz Municipality's traditional role of programming "cultural" events for Fiestas Julianas (Ministerio de Educación y Bellas Artes 1961a, 141–44). The 1961 season saw a major increase in these types of activities. The offerings included a music contest for art-classical works "based on autochthonous motives" (Gustavo Navarre won first place), along with competitions for visual artists (painting, sculpture), writers (novels, essays, short stories, poems, theater works), photographers, and architects (*ED*, July 1, 1961; Ministerio de Educación y Bellas Artes 1961b, 171–78).

The National Council of Art's showcase event for 1961 was the Primera Semana Folklórica Boliviana (First Bolivian Folkloric Week). In the opening ceremony held at Hernando Siles Stadium, an Incan-style *chasqui* (foot messenger) delivered sacred fire from the ruins of Tiwanaku to President Paz Estenssoro, as the sound of *pututus* (Andean horns) echoed through the arena and added a local touch to a scene otherwise reminiscent of the Olympic games (*ED*, Apr. 8 and 9, 1961). A succession of music-dance acts followed, beginning with two Oruro dance groups and affiliated brass bands that performed the tobas (an Amazonian-inspired genre) and morenada. Next, seven indigenous tropas, beginning with Los Sikuris de Italaque and then Kantus de Charazani, entertained the spectators. Performances by K'ashuiris de Challapata, Laquitas de Ambaná, Jachasicus de Tiwanaku, Ujusiris de Laja, and Jachamakolulu-Ussipias de Chúa rounded out the indigenous music portion of the program (*ED*, Apr. 8 and 9, 1961).

A fashion show followed. Representing their departamentos, nine young women paraded around the stadium, in the hopes of being crowned by the judges as the "native beauty of the nation" (*ED*, Apr. 8 and 9, 1961). The Diablada Ferroviaria de Oruro (Oruro Railway Workers' Diablada Troupe)—a 150-member dance group and its accompanying brass band—concluded the entertainment, fittingly, given the diablada's surging popularity lately (discussed later in this section). Also as part of the Primera Semana Folklórica Boliviana, the Ballet Folklórico Oficial and National Symphony Orchestra offered recitals at the Municipal Theater; Radio Illimani broadcast the theater work *Pachamama* (Quechua for "Mother Earth"); the Municipal Library featured readings of nativist poems; and the Casa de la Cultura exhibited film screenings, art showings, and a display of the spectacular masks that diablada and morenada dancers typically wear in processions (*ED*, Apr. 8 and 9, 1961).

Despite carrying the descriptor "First," the Primera Semana Folklórica Boliviana bore more than a passing resemblance to the two editions of the Semana Indianista that the elite civic association Los Amigos de la Ciudad had convened in the 1930s (Chapter 2). This likeness led one observer to contend that to be more accurate, the Primera Semana Folklórica Boliviana should be relabeled the "Tercera," or third, "Semana" (*ED*, Mar. 26, 1961). Unlike the Indianist Weeks of the 1930s, though, the Primera Semana Folklórica Boliviana represented an exclusively state-sponsored venture. The 1961 event also more fully incorporated music-dance performances by actual Andean indigenous tropas.

The Primera Semana Folklórica Boliviana had two official goals. The first, to "awaken the collective spirit towards the cultivation and admiration of all that is eminently Bolivian" (*ED*, Apr. 4, 1961), recalled Los Amigos de la Ciudad's justification for the 2nd Indianist Week (*ED*, Jan. 14, 1936). The second, "to maintain and increase the interest of the studious and of the foreign tourists whose visits will economically benefit the State" (*ED*, Apr. 4, 1961), on the other hand, reflected a new concern.

In 1961 alone, the MNR government passed six Supreme Decrees to stimulate the growth of the local tourism industry, particularly Tiwanaku's transformation into an international attraction (Téllez 1998, 12–13). The same year in Peru, a month before the Primera Semana Folklórica Boliviana, the residents of Cuzco had marked the fiftieth anniversary of US explorer Hiram Bingham's so-called discovery of the Macchu Picchu ruins, with a celebration featuring Andean music that was attended by foreign tourists (De la Cadena 2000, 281). It must have been on the radar of the MNR officials who dreamed up the Primera Semana Folklórica Boliviana, given its close timing. In any case, as the 1960s progressed, non-Bolivian tourists visiting the Andes would increasingly add the city of La Paz to their stopovers, a development that occurred in tandem with Cuzco's establishment as a major tourist destination (Chapters 6 and 7).

The First Bolivian Folkloric Week had a politically partisan purpose too, one that would have been obvious to paceños, because the National Council of Art scheduled the Semana Folklórica Boliviana to coincide with the nine-year passing of the 1952 Revolution. In another attempt to link the Nationalist Revolutionary Movement to local music-dance practices, in 1962 party officials programmed a "festival of native dances" for the same time of year, and also for the same locale, as an "homage to the tenth anniversary of the National Revolution" (*ED*, Apr. 5, 1962). Thirty ensembles performed at this follow-up event, in which a diablada troupe from Oruro filled the coveted role of headliner.

The diablada, or "devil's dance," characterized by the extravagant outfits and horned masks worn by the dancers, and musically accompanied by brass bands, traditionally formed part of Carnival and other major seasonal fiestas in Oruro city and Potosí's mining centers. By the early 1960s, though, the popularity of this mestizo-associated genre had expanded far beyond these geographic confines, to include much of the Bolivian Andes, in urban and rural areas. Indigenous musicians and dancers increasingly adopted the diablada as their own tradition in the MNR years (see Vellard and Merino 1954, 108–10; Beltrán 1956; Fortún 1961, 1–2, 96–100; Beltrán 1962, 42–54). And they did so with such enthusiasm that Department of Folklore director Julia Fortún describes this trend as "something of a fad among indigenous people" in her 1961 book on the genre, *La Danza de los Diablos* (Fortún 1961, 2).

Featuring diablada troupes at the ninth and tenth commemorations of the 1952 Revolution made ideological sense for MNR-affiliated agencies. Bolivians identified the genre with mestizos or cholos (and especially mine workers), while the indigenous sector's assimilation of the genre qualified as a clear instance of cultural mestizaje. Yet in all likelihood the organizers programmed diablada groups chiefly to attract a large audience, in a manner akin to the SPIC's showcasing of bolero trios, orquestas de jazz, and foreign musical acts at the Open Air and Municipal Theaters. As a general rule, MNR officials tried to co-opt expressive practices that already were popular with the public, whether or not they corresponded with the party's pro-mestizaje rhetoric.

The Primera Semana Folklórica Boliviana of 1961, coupled with the expanded range of "cultural" activities that the National Council of Art had offered in the city of La Paz earlier in the year for Fiestas Julianas, must have reminded paceños of the abundance of state-sponsored music-dance spectacles that they had witnessed during Paz Estenssoro's first presidency (1952–1956), and led them to expect that the third MNR government soon would be presenting many more of these types of folkloric events. However, for reasons that are unclear, the Primera Semana Folklórica Boliviana ended up being a one-off event, and state bureaus would coordinate exceedingly few music festivals in the next three years. The Department of Folklore, though, would continue to function with state support for the remainder of the third movimientista government.

THE DEPARTMENT OF FOLKLORE AND JULIA FORTÚN

Since the 1940s, Bolivian state-funded folklore departments had operated in La Paz (Chapter 2), but it was not until the MNR period that local folklore agencies would devote significant attention to music-dance traditions. Julia Elena Fortún de Ponce was the driving force behind this new development. In 1954, she re-founded the Departamento de Folklore and, within a few years, oversaw the Dirección General de Cultura (after 1956) and Dirección Nacional de Antropología (after 1961) (Gildner 2012, 413–24, 438–40). Fortún's academic credentials made her the clear choice for these positions. Whereas Antonio González Bravo, Enrique Oblitas Poblete, Antonio Paredes Candia, Rogers Becerra, and Bolivia's other leading folklore researchers were largely self-taught, Fortún had studied ethnomusicology and folklore in the 1940s under the renowned Argentine scholar Carlos Vega at Buenos Aires' Instituto Nacional de Musicología. Moreover, in 1952 she had earned a PhD in "primitive history" from Spain's Universidad de Madrid, with a dissertation on the Christmastime music and dance traditions of Bolivia (*ED*, Jan. 16, 1953).

Soon after accepting the directorship of the Department of Folklore, Fortún left for Mexico City to take two years of postdoctoral coursework in anthropology at one of Latin America's most prestigious centers of learning, the Universidad Nacional Autónoma de México or UNAM (Gildner 2012, 414–19). She returned to La Paz in 1956, at which point the Department of Folklore went forward with her project of creating a traditional music archive that would contain field recordings and transcriptions, along with concise descriptions of the context within which musicians typically performed the genre. Unsurprisingly, Italaque figured among the early sites that the agency selected to collect "ethnological data" for the archive (*ED*, May 29, 1958).

The department's staff consisted only of Fortún, González Bravo, Paredes Candia, and archaeologist Maks Portugal (Gildner 2012, 421). Recruiting untrained volunteers to assist the bureau in its endeavors therefore was essential. With this necessity in mind, Fortún wrote the *Manual para la Recolección de Material Folklórico* (Manual for the collection of folkloric materials). In this 100-page book, which the agency published in 1957, Fortún guides aspiring folklore collectors by laying out her criteria for authentic folk music: traditional, anonymous, functional, collectively shared, and orally transmitted (Fortún 1957, 87–92). This limited definition of a folkloric expression—one that folklore scholars later would problematize (e.g., Bauman 1992)—reflects how folklore researchers around the world tended to conceptualize their object of study in the 1950s.

Nationalism typically represents a core doctrine for folklore departments. Accordingly, in the *Manual para la Recolección de Material Folklórico* Fortún observes as a matter of fact that the "folk tunes" placed in the agency's traditional music archive henceforth would constitute Bolivian national—rather than individual or community—property. To entice folklore collectors to help build the repository, though, she also points out that those who registered the "folkloric materials" with the department "likewise" would enjoy "property rights" over them (Fortún 1957, 87–92). And in an unmistakable plea to Bolivian art-classical musicians to craft compositions featuring these "folkloric materials" as motives, Fortún explains that the tunes would be "at the disposal of those interested in elevating these samples of our shared artistic heritage to the level of grand works" (Fortún 1957, 88). She also maintains that art-classical music compositions of this type would receive wide diffusion on state-run radio programs, and moreover be performed by the National Symphony

Orchestra and other government-funded ensembles. Fortún additionally asserts that the original melodies would be incorporated into the music curricula of primary and secondary schools (Fortún 1957, 88–89).

It is currently unclear if MNR era musicians used the Department of Folklore's collection of traditional tunes in the manner that Fortún envisions in the *Manual*. In the art-classical music scene, for instance, few if any composers seem to have made recourse to this stockpile of melodies. "Nationalist" compositional styles were of little interest to most Bolivian art-classical music composers active in the MNR era. They preferred to follow the experimental or avant-garde artistic trends emanating from Europe instead, much to the dismay of the Bolivian public (Auza León 1985, 133–34). When the National Symphony Orchestra dedicated concerts to "national" repertoire, the programs mainly featured indigenista classics from pre-Revolution times, such as José Salmón Ballivián's *Trilogía India*, Belisario Zárate's *Serenata Campestre—Tres Motivos Indianistas*, and Humberto Iporre Salinas' *Oración del Mitayo* (e.g., *ED*, Nov. 11, 1956).

Yet even if no Bolivian musician took advantage of the archive, the very existence of a Bolivian state-owned folkloric music repository lent credence to the premise that local expressive practices of this variety represented valuable facets of national culture and warranted preservation. These ideas, although not new ones, obtained further legitimacy through Fortún's regular statements in newspapers and other forums in which she reiterated the bureau's mission of safeguarding rural traditions.

Four years after the Department of Folklore's publication of *Manual para la Recolección de Material Folklórico*—whose front cover features the image of a diablada dancer marching in a Carnival procession (presumably Oruro's)—the Ministry of Education and Fine Arts issued Fortún's next major book, *La Danza de los Diablos* (1961). It was meant to be the first in a series of monographs that the bureau would publish on traditional music-dance genres (Fortún 1967, preface). This initiative never came to fruition in the MNR years, in much the same way that the National Council of Art failed to follow up the 1961 Primera Semana Folklórica Boliviana.

Fortún unmistakably drew on the teachings of her mentor Carlos Vega when she wrote *La Danza de los Diablos*. As is often noted in overviews of South American ethnomusicology and folklore studies (e.g., Béhague 1991; Romero 2016), Vega focused much of his research on uncovering the origins of Latin American (especially Argentine) music-dance expressions, and illuminating how present-day traditions represented "survivals" from the distant past—an evolutionist concept he borrowed from anthropologist Edward Tylor. To aid him in these projects, Vega developed a classificatory system for "folk tunes," made up of *cancioneros* (song families based on melodic characteristics), and a "method for the structural analysis of musical phrases" that he termed *fraseología* (phraseology) (Romero 2016, 84). In *La Danza de los Diablos*, Fortún applies fraseología analysis, to categorize the three main varieties of diablada tunes into Vega's *cancionero europeo* (European cancionero), *cancionero incaico hibridizado* (hybridized Incan cancionero), and *cancionero criollo occidental* (Western criollo-mestizo cancionero) (Fortún 1961, 75–83, 105). And in various places in the book, she discusses the roots of the diablada tradition practiced in highland Bolivia.

The Bolivian diablada, Fortún contends, is derived from Iberian expressive practices such as Catalonia's *ball des diables*, and over time integrated numerous aspects of Andean indigenous and mestizo traditions (e.g., see Fortún 1961, 105). In Bolivia and other Latin American countries, folklore scholars have usually classified cultural forms exhibiting these general characteristics as "mestizo" (e.g., González Bravo 1948, 421).

By devoting a book to the diablada and presenting ample evidence that the genre's trajectory embodies cultural mixture, Fortún and the Department of Folklore were in accordance, ideologically, with the MNR's valorization of mestizaje. Fortún would have been cognizant of the ideological implications of her research on the genre. She moved in movimientista circles, and then was married to a prominent party member, archaeologist Carlos Ponce Sanginés—who in the early 1960s headed the Ministry of Peasant Affairs (Dunkerley 1984, 113). She also had lived for two years in Mexico, where nationalist politicians and intellectuals had long extolled mestizaje. Given that her 1952 dissertation draws comparable conclusions about Bolivia's Christmastime music-dance traditions, and that she completed the volume before the MNR's position on mestizaje had become well known, however, Fortún's findings on the diablada in all likelihood were not the product of her strict adherence to party orthodoxy, but primarily stemmed from her use of the investigative techniques that she had learned from Carlos Vega.

Interestingly, Fortún implies in the preface to *La Danza de los Diablos* that the Department of Folklore's mission of cultural preservation is at variance with MNR priorities, when she remarks that the "new political-social reforms" are "changing the mentality" of indigenous people and leading them to "abandon their age-old customs and traditions" (quoted in Gildner 2012, 383). Her statement alludes to the movimientista regime's attempts to instill "modern" values in the rural indigenous population. This modernist-capitalist agenda actually constituted the raison d'être of another bureau, the Department of Anthropology. As historian Matthew Gildner explains (2012, 394–404), the Department of Anthropology launched a series of "applied" programs in rural areas in the MNR years, with the aim of "modernizing" or "acculturating" indigenous people. For these initiatives to succeed, the indigenous population would have to abandon many of the cultural expressions that the Department of Folklore sought to preserve. In other words, two contemporaneous Bolivian state agencies that regarded "indigenous culture" as their principal object of study were directly in conflict on the issue of whether indigenous people should either maintain or "modernize" their cultural traditions.

Fortún also observes in *La Danza de los Diablos* that Andean indigenous musicians and dancers had increasingly been replacing their own "authentic" genres with the diablada (e.g., Fortún 1961, 1). The tradition's dissemination to highland indigenous communities thus shares some parallels with the spread of misti sikuris to the same populations. Whereas the latter development impelled González Bravo to disparage misti sikuris, however, Fortún's observations about the pan-regional popularization of the diablada are devoid of negative criticism. And by penning a book on the "devil's dance," she willfully played a part in the genre's consolidation in the Bolivian folklore canon—thereby complementing the efforts of MNR-funded folkloric ballet productions such as *Fantasía Boliviana* (discussed later in this chapter), something that is hard to imagine González Bravo doing for the misti sikuri tradition or any other mestizo-associated musical practice that recently had found favor in Andean indigenous communities.

In the MNR period, the state agencies that Fortún led spearheaded initiatives (e.g., traditional music archive) and issued publications that helped to locally enshrine the nationalist concept that "folkloric musical expressions" represent a pillar of the nation's cultural patrimony and identity. Yet for Fortún, she arguably had the greatest impact on the Bolivian folkloric music scene in the first year of the post-MNR era, 1965, when the Bolivian music-dance delegation that she organized for the inaugural Festival Latinoamericano de Folklore (held in Salta, Argentina) so impressed the panel of judges that they awarded the contingent the most first-place trophies (Chapter 6). Ernesto Cavour, the future charango virtuoso of Los Jairas, was among the artists for whom the 1965 "triumph at Salta" would shape his subsequent career. In selecting Cavour and the other members of the delegation, Fortún and the rest of the committee had weighed various factors, from showmanship (Cavour's forte), to "authenticity" (which prompted her to invite the indigenous tropa Los Chajes de Colquencha). As detailed in Chapter 6, the Bolivian contingent interpreted highland indigenous traditions more than other varieties of cultural expression, an approach that by then had become the standard for Bolivian folklore extravaganzas. Folkloric ballet productions played an important role in establishing this convention.

CHOREOGRAPHING FOLKLORE: CHELA URQUIDI AND THE ACADEMIA DE DANZAS

Prior to the MNR era, the field of Bolivian folkloric ballet was in its infancy, and no local dance company of this type had received regular state funding. Graciela "Chela" Urquidi de Ascarrunz represents the country's first folkloric dance troupe director to secure consistent state support. Born in Potosí and raised in La Paz city, she left a lasting legacy in Bolivia as a choreographer of the country's criollo-mestizo and indigenous music-dance traditions. Her early background in dance interpretation, though, was in European classical ballet, which she studied in the 1930s, when still a young girl, with the La Paz–based Russian instructor Valentina Romanoff. In 1940, another expatriate European ballet teacher, the Austrian Klary Kleiner, thought so highly of Urquidi's artistic abilities that she added her to the dance corps for the Bolivian premiere of Velasco Maidana's *Amerindia* (*ED*, May, 26, 1940; Rivera de Stahlie 2003, 183–84, 192). Later in the decade, Urquidi and her family moved to Buenos Aires, where it is possible that they crossed paths with Julia Fortún (who was enrolled at Carlos Vega's Instituto Nacional de Musicología around this time). In any event, Urquidi continued her dance studies, in the "modern-contemporary" and "Spanish" styles, during her extended stay in the Argentine capital (Chela Urquidi, personal communication).

The Urquidi family resettled in La Paz around 1948, and it was not long before Chela, full of ideas and energy, established her own dance troupe. In the final two years of the sexenio, the yet unnamed company presented her stylized versions of the huayño, cueca, and other local genres at the Municipal Theater and Open Air Theater (e.g., *ED*, July 14 and 15, and Aug. 13, 1950; Nov. 18, 1951). The troupe's performances at the latter venue represented one of the standouts of the 1951 season, according to the Municipal officials who listed Urquidi among the most "distinguished" artists of the series, alongside Las Kantutas, Gilberto Rojas, Adrian Patiño Carpio, and Eduardo Caba (Chapter 3). Also in 1951, Urquidi's group debuted her most ambitious production to date, *El Poema de la Kena* (The poem of the kena), a work set to the music of Eduardo Caba's eponymous orchestral composition. As Velasco Maidana previously had done with *Amerindia*, Urquidi used the descriptor "Inca ballet" for *El Poema de la Kena* (*ED*, Oct. 22, 1951).

When the MNR seized power in April 1952, Urquidi was La Paz's most highly regarded folkloric ballet director-choreographer and thus ideally placed to take advantage of the new regime's soon-to-be unveiled expanded commitment to offering state-sponsored folklore spectacles. An early opportunity for Urquidi to impress the movimientista leadership presented itself five months after the 1952 Revolution. At the Municipal Theater, the Ministry of Education put together a Fiesta Indianista, which the agency dedicated to First Lady Carmela Cerruto de Paz Estenssoro. This gesture formed part of the MNR campaign to persuade the public that the party leaders, and in this case even their wives, sincerely identified with the plight of el pueblo. In the program, actress Matilde Garvía (who was married to the MNR figure and prolific author Augusto Céspedes) regaled the audience with Aymará "vernacular poetry," party member Reynaldo López Vidaurre played piano pieces, bolero group Trío Panamérica Antawara (Pan-American sunset trio) crooned "national" tunes, and as the grand finale, Urquidi's troupe interpreted an assortment of folkloric dance sketches (*ED*, Sept. 6, 1952).

A childhood friend of Urquidi's, Waldo Cerruto—the brother-in-law of Paz Estenssoro (as previously noted)—approached her the next year with the enticing offer of leading a folkloric ballet company whose main expenses (i.e., studio rental fees, students' tuition, Urquidi's salary) would be covered by the SPIC agency that he oversaw, the Bolivian Cinematographic Institute. Urquidi gladly accepted Cerruto's proposal that she direct the troupe, which became known as the Academia de Danzas (Waldo Cerruto and Chela Urquidi, personal communications). Its first major production, 1954's *Viajando por Nuestra Tierra* (Traveling through our land), recycled the name of a Bolivian Cinematographic Institute newsreel segment starring the actor and comic Celso Peñaranda (Waldo Cerruto, personal communication). The Academia de Danzas' version of *Viajando por Nuestra Tierra* incorporated the panpipe music of

Los Cebollitas (*ED*, Oct. 11, 1954). This was the cholo-mestizo siku tropa that, in 1953, had won second place at the Concurso de Arte Nativo staged by the Bolivian Cinematographic Institute.

Bolivian state funding for ballet companies had previously been reserved for troupes that specialized in European classics such as *The Nutcracker*. This policy had been in effect since 1948, when the Hertzog government's Ministry of Education authorized the creation of Bolivia's first state-supported ballet troupe, the similarly named Academia Nacional de Danzas (Rivera de Stahlie 2003, 145, 191). It retained its state-subsidized status after the 1952 Revolution, but was renamed the "Ballet Oficial" (Official ballet), and as such, continued to present European ballets. In keeping with the times, though, by 1954 the Ballet Oficial had added a few nativist productions to its repertoire, including *El Indio y Su Esperanza* (The Indian and his aspirations) and *Despertar del Indio* (The awakening of the Indian) (Rivera de Stahlie 2003 177, 187). For Urquidi's Academia de Danzas, the situation was the reverse. Although the troupe occasionally performed European ballets, as well as Spanish "folk" dance skits (e.g., *ED*, Feb. 13, 1953), Urquidi's recreations of Bolivian expressive practices constituted the company's signature repertoire.

A COUNTRY OF INDIANS? *FANTASÍA BOLIVIANA*, FROM LA PAZ TO THE WORLD

In 1955, the Academia de Danzas premiered *Fantasía Boliviana* (Bolivian fantasy). Of the many folklore productions the company presented in the MNR years, this work unquestionably received the most publicity.[20] It would also have the greatest influence on subsequent Bolivian folkloric ballet revues, as well as other domains of folkloric expression (e.g., peña shows; Chapter 7). Considering the name of the production and Urquidi's reputation as a choreographer, the audience that attended the 1955 debut of *Fantasía Boliviana* at the Municipal Theater must have expected that the work would depict regionally distinctive Bolivian traditions in a series of music-dance sketches.

This was indeed the case. In the skit "Amor Chapaco" (Chapaco love), two dancers playfully engaged in the *contrapunto*, a song-dueling courtship genre practiced in rural areas of the southernmost departamento, Tarija (Rivera de Stahlie 2003, 219–20). Four sketches later, in "En Las Playas del Beni" (On the beaches of Beni), the company artistically transported the spectators to a place that most if not all of them had only read about, the riverbank of the Mamoré in the Amazonian jungles of Beni, through a rendering of the *machetero* (hatchet dance)—which the program notes describe in exoticist fashion as a "tribal ritual dance" (Rivera de Stahlie 2003, 222). The eastern lowlands represented the imagined backdrop as well for "Romance Oriental," in the more familiar setting of Santa Cruz. Dressed as rural cambas, troupe members intoned música oriental songs to guitar accompaniment in this number (Rivera de Stahlie 2003, 222).

Notwithstanding Urquidi's inclusion of these non-Andean-themed sketches, the overwhelming majority of the skits in *Fantasía Boliviana*—fifteen of the eighteen numbers—depicted scenes from the Bolivian Andes. Several of them showcased Andean music folklorists. For example, the siku tropa stylings of Los Cebollitas animated "Matrimonio en el Altiplano" (Highland wedding) and "Aguayos y Zampoñas" (Textiles and panpipes) (Rivera de Stahlie 2003, 222), while the solo kena music and impassioned singing of Fabián Humberto Flores, aka Tito Yupanqui, was the center of attention in "Plegaria de la Puna" (Mountain prayer) and "Cantar Indio" (Song of the Indian). Yupanqui—who the next year would establish the duo Los Wara Wara with singer Pepa Cardona (Chapter 5)—acted out his usual artistic persona, a "highland Indian," in his skits (K. Cerruto 1996, 118; Rivera de Stahlie 2003, 215, 220). For the finale, the entire troupe danced the diablada, with several members wearing the horned devil's masks, embroidered capes, and tunics associated with the genre (Rivera de Stahlie 2003, 213–27).

The countrywide scope of *Fantasía Boliviana* reflected the movimientista-nationalist vision of Waldo Cerruto (see K. Cerruto 1996, 116–21). It also set the production apart from the earlier Academia de Danzas work *Viajando por Nuestra Tierra*, which had exclusively portrayed the traditions of Potosí (*ED*, Feb. 2, 1955). *Fantasía Boliviana*'s focus on indigenous and criollo-mestizo music-dance expressions then practiced in Bolivia, meanwhile, differentiated the work from Urquidi-Caba's *El Poema de la Kena* and Velasco Maidana's *Amerindia*. These "Inca ballets," after all, had conjured up the age of the Inca Empire, rather than present-day Bolivia.

Fantasía Boliviana was not entirely novel, however. In 1945, the paceño folklore company Copacabana had presented a similarly themed production, *Estampas de Bolivia* (Vignettes of Bolivia), more than twenty times at the Municipal Theater (*ED*, Aug. 21, 1945). Three years later, the troupe enjoyed another successful run at the venue with the work (*ED*, Feb. 18 and 21, Mar. 11, 1948). Like *Fantasía Boliviana*, *Estampas de Bolivia* is composed of an array of folkloric music-dance sketches (e.g., "La Diablada," "Estampas Cruceñas"). Both productions, notably, featured the same lead actors, Tito Landa and Lucho Espinoza (*ED*, Aug. 6, 12, and 21, 1945; Feb. 18, 1948). For *Estampas de Bolivia* director Francisco Álvarez García, the parallels were so striking that in a 1957 *Khana* article he accused the creators of *Fantasía Boliviana* of "nationalizing" his "original idea" without his permission.[21]

After offering forty-two shows in La Paz and various engagements in Cochabamba and Oruro (*ED*, Mar. 3 and 28, 1955), and earning rave reviews from critics (e.g., *ED*, Jan. 24, Feb. 6 and 19, 1955), in November 1955 the *Fantasía Boliviana* company embarked on an international tour with stops in the capitals of Argentina, Paraguay, and Uruguay (K. Cerruto 1996, 73–158). To cover some of its expenses, President Paz Estenssoro authorized a government loan (*ED*, July 2, 1955). This tour, which lasted until January 1956, represents an exceptional enterprise in the history of Bolivian state-supported folklore spectacles, as never before had the Bolivian government provided funding for a music-dance revue of comparable scale and international trajectory.

Urquidi made several modifications to the *Fantasía Boliviana* program. "Canto al Sol" (Song for the sun), which was one of the new skits, evoked the Incas' worship of the sun. Los Cebollitas played the tarka, in tropa style, on "Canto al Sol," illustrating their growing versatility as performers of Andean indigenous wind instruments. Since Tito Yupanqui apparently did not join the excursion, Los Cebollitas took over his role as the musical lead on "Plegaria de la Puna," this time with their customary panpipe music. Yupanqui's other solo number in the original production, "Cantar Indio," now starred the vocal duo Las Imillas (see K. Cerruto 1996, 92–93, 152; Rivera de Stahlie 2003, 264–69).

Formed by the sisters Norah and María Luisa Camacho, Las Imillas (Quechua for "The girls") no doubt sang in Quechua on "Cantar Indio." The members of the duo were fluent in the language, which they had learned in their childhood in the Cochabamba town of Arani, where the Camacho family owned hacienda lands prior to the 1952 Revolution (Norah and María Luisa Camacho, personal communications). Their father, Max Camacho, often accompanied Las Imillas' singing with his guitar—in an arrangement highly reminiscent of Zenobio Tejada's usual role with Las Hermanas Tejada (Chapter 3). Besides "Cantar Indio," Las Imillas served as the featured vocalists on "Serenata Campestre" (Serenade of the countryside) (Rivera de Stahlie 2003, 269). This sketch in all likelihood was inspired by, and perhaps also used the music of, Belisario Zárate's indigenista classic *Serenata Campestre—Tres Motivos Indianistas*.

About a month after Urquidi's troupe had returned to La Paz, it presented her newest production at the Municipal Theater, *Bolivia en Colores* (The many colors of Bolivia). Chinese government officials attended the show, and soon afterwards unexpectedly offered Urquidi the opportunity to take her company to China, Czechoslovakia, and the USSR (*ED*, Feb. 16, 1959; *Presencia*, July 13, 1959). The well-connected Urquidi immediately sought the advice of President Siles Zuaso, who was a longtime friend of her husband, Hugo Ascarrunz. In the meeting, Siles Zuaso told Urquidi that if her company undertook the tour, he would be concerned that it might arouse the displeasure of US officials (Chela Urquidi, personal communication). Siles Zuaso's caution is understandable, when one takes into account that for much of the MNR period, the Bolivian government had relied heavily on US aid (see Lehman 1999; Siekmeier 2011).

Yet Siles Zuaso eventually gave his blessing to Urquidi to accept the invitation. Facing a sudden decline in US financial support, the MNR administration had tentatively begun to cultivate alliances with China and other socialist countries, in the hope that this strategy would prompt the United States to renew its former monetary commitment to the MNR government, as indeed it did. Consistent with this bargaining tactic, the Siles Zuaso regime sanctioned various cultural exchanges with the Socialist Bloc in 1959 and 1960 (Lehman 1999, 133–34). It was in this period that the poet and novelist Yolanda Bedregal de Conitzer went to the USSR and China as part of a "delegation of Bolivian ladies concerned with cultural activities" (*ED*, Mar. 9, 1960), and folkloric singers Luis Gutiérrez and María Luisa Tirado presented concerts in the USSR and Cuba (Luis Gutiérrez, personal communication; Fernández Coca 1994, 82).

Urquidi revived the name *Fantasía Boliviana* for the 1959 tour, which lasted over three months and was the most publicized of Bolivia's cultural exchanges in this period with socialist countries. Further changes were made to the production and musical cast. Las Hermanas Espinoza replaced Las Imillas (Grimanesca and Josefina Espinoza, personal archive), while Conjunto Kollasuyo was added to the troupe, under the band's alternate name of Conjunto Bolivia. Led by kena soloist Jaime Medinaceli, Conjunto Kollasuyo/Bolivia stood out in the La Paz folklore scene, as one of the very few groups in the mold of an Andean conjunto (see Chapter 5).

The *Fantasía Boliviana* company's exploits overseas did not escape the attention of the Bolivian press (e.g., *La Nación*, Oct. 26, 1959), as tended to happen whenever Bolivian artists experienced acclaim abroad (e.g., *Fantasía Boliviana*'s 1955 tour of the Southern Cone; see K. Cerruto 1996). These unfailingly positive reports generated considerable interest for performances of Urquidi's production when the troupe returned to La Paz. But perhaps because the *Fantasía Boliviana* cast was suffering from exhaustion, the company did not offer recitals in the weeks following its reappearance in late 1959.

Sensing an opportunity, rival director José Ibáñez Estrada chose this moment to debut his own "Fantasía Boliviana" at the Municipal Theater. Named *Fantasía Boliviana 1959* and billed as "The Unforgettable Spectacle Solicited by the Entire World," it incorporated some sketches from his 1957 work *Bolivia Indiana* (Indian Bolivia), such as a *tundiqui* number ostensibly based on Afro-Bolivian traditions (*ED*, Nov. 26, 1959, Dec. 10, and Dec. 19, 1959). Ibáñez Estrada largely based *Fantasía Boliviana 1959* on Urquidi's *Fantasía Boliviana*, though. He even hired members from the original 1955 cast who had not taken part in the 1959 tour, including the duo Las Imillas and actors Tito Landa and Lucho Espinoza. Taking over the role of Los Cebollitas in *Fantasía Boliviana 1959*, meanwhile, was another paceño mestizo siku tropa with ample experience performing in folklore shows, Los Choclos (profiled in Chapter 5).

Ibáñez Estrada's *Fantasía Boliviana 1959* elicited negative criticism from some reviewers, who ranked Urquidi's version as the superior one. It compelled Ibáñez Estrada to issue a defense of his opus. In a message printed in *El Diario*, he called for a "competent jury" to judge for themselves the quality of his ballet vis-à-vis that of "any company that boasts of having traveled to China" (*ED*, Dec. 4, 1959). And if anyone had any doubt about which troupe he was referring to, Ibáñez Estrada spelled it out the next day, when he "cordially invited to *a mano a mano* the group of Chela Urquidi that is said to have triumphed on European stages" (*ED*, Dec. 5, 1959). Whether Urquidi accepted the challenge has yet to be documented, although the next month the two companies performed in the same program at the Indoor Coliseum of La Paz (*ED*, Jan. 30, 1960). At any rate, the rivalry created even more publicity for *Fantasía Boliviana*, in each of its variations. It also spurred Urquidi to develop yet another version, *Fantasía Boliviana 1960*. Her troupe presented it in Cali, Colombia as part of 1961's IV Feria de la Caña de Azúcar (Sugar Cane Festival) (*Occidente* [Colombian newspaper], Dec. 28, 1961).[22]

All in all, *Fantasía Boliviana* captured the imaginations of the Bolivian public to an extraordinary extent in the mid-to-late 1950s, especially Urquidi's iterations of the work. Staying true to Cerruto's nationalist vision, her *Fantasía Boliviana* productions creatively portrayed an array of criollo-mestizo and indigenous music-dance traditions from the country's highland, valley, and lowland regions. Most of the sketches, however, drew their inspiration from Andean expressive practices, particularly those of rural indigenous association. In doing so, Urquidi's *Fantasía Boliviana* often conflated "Bolivian culture" with "Andean indigenous culture." Foreign audiences tended to respond positively to this practice (see K. Cerruto 1996, 130–31, 153–54), unsurprisingly, as it corresponded with how non-Bolivians usually imagined the cultural heritage of Bolivians. Urquidi must have had this widespread perception in mind when she originally designed *Fantasía Boliviana* in 1955. Her first major role as a dancer, after all, had been in *Amerindia*, whose positive reception in Argentine and German elite circles had much to do with Velasco Maidana's use of long-standing exoticist tropes about the Andean region and Incan Empire. But conforming to outsiders' stereotypes surely was not the sole reason why Urquidi's *Fantasía Boliviana* emphasized Andean indigenous cultural expressions. The typical music-dance traditions of Bolivia's highland indigenous communities represent locally distinctive expressive practices, musically and visually, making them ideal for a production meant to showcase uniquely Bolivian "folk" customs.

For Luis Alberto Alipaz, the editor of the official MNR newspaper, *La Nación* (The nation), Urquidi's original *Fantasía Boliviana* was admirable not only for its artistry, but also for the ways in which it could transform Bolivian national identity:

> Throughout the long years of our history we had been distancing ourselves from the wisdom that gave origin to this nation. Contempt increasingly marked our attitude toward anything that reminded us of our Indian origin, . . . But, with the passage of time, . . . a new type of consciousness arose: our Indian roots no longer were something to repudiate, nor something to be embarrassed of. Instead [the Indian] constituted the very foundation upon which Bolivians could be proud of their nation. . . . Returned to his [the Indian's] dignified place in the Bolivian community, all of his cultural manifestations entered the forefront, and his art, the fruit of his restlessness, took its place in national life. . . . And thus was born the endeavor of transporting Indian art, Bolivian art, to the countries of the Americas, under the name of "Fantasía Boliviana." . . . As a result, today we have begun to appreciate ourselves for who we are, for what Bolivia is, without the fear of our ambivalences; with the pride instead, from this point forward, of acknowledging ourselves as a "country of Indians." (*La Nación*, Dec. 5, 1955; quoted in K. Cerruto 1996, 155–57)

A "country of Indians" was not of course what the MNR leadership pictured as a desirable future for Bolivia, but rather a country of mestizos, or at least a country with a mestizo majority in which the individualist and so-called modern values of capitalism superseded the egalitarianism and communitarianism traditionally favored in many Andean indigenous communities. To be sure, in any political party or movement the degree of adherence to party ideology varies from individual to individual, often tremendously. That a movimientista would espouse views contrary to the party line thus is not surprising. Yet that such a prominent public face of the regime as the editor of *La Nación* would do so in the very newspaper that the party used to disseminate its propaganda nonetheless is worthy of note. It also reflects the wide range of positions that existed in the MNR ranks with regard to the proper role that traditional Andean indigenous expressive practices—and stylized criollo-mestizo folkloric renderings of these traditions—should play in the process of constructing the cultural foundations of a modern Bolivian nation-state.

THE BALLET FOLKLÓRICO OFICIAL

In early 1961, the National Council of Art renamed Urquidi's Academia de Danzas as the "Ballet Folklórico Oficial" (Ministerio de Educación y Bellas Artes 1961a, 1961b), in all likelihood heeding the example of Mexico's Ballet Folklórico—which by the late 1950s had gained international fame (see Hutchinson 2009, 215). April 1961 offered La Paz residents an early opportunity to see the revamped troupe. The company performed at the Municipal Theater that month, as part of the Primera Semana Folklórica Boliviana (as previously noted). Almost exactly one year later, in "homage to the Tenth Anniversary of the National Revolution," the Ballet Folklórico Oficial returned to the venue to present Urquidi's *Mercados de Bolivia* (Markets of Bolivia). Choreographed to the music of Sucre's Simeón Roncal, *Mercados de Bolivia* trod similar ground as *Fantasía Boliviana*, as it consisted of regional sketches, in this case "La Paz," "Cochabamba," and "Potosí" (Rivera de Stahlie 2003, 198). Over the next two years, the Ballet Folklórico Oficial would expand its repertoire to include classic European ballets and "modern" dance productions, which Urquidi programmed alongside her trademark Bolivian folkloric works. This juxtaposition perhaps implied to the spectator that classical, modern, and nativist works were on a par with one another, an idea that folklore artists often hope to instill in the public.

The Ballet Folklórico Oficial displayed the full range of its new repertoire in September 1964 at the Municipal Theater, to an audience that included President Paz Estenssoro (*ED*, Sept. 22, 1964). Compositions by Tchaikovsky, Saint Saëns, and other European art-classical musicians of international renown formed the backdrop for the first segment, the "ballet clasico" *Invitación a la Danza* (Invitation to the Dance). Then the company interpreted the "modern ballet" *La Gran Ciudad* (The big city). Urquidi set it in an unidentified locale, to the jazzy music of Gershwin. The next work in the program was blatantly partisan. Titled *Los Tres Movimientos* (The three movements), it paid tribute to the 1952 Revolution, with the acts "Oración y Esperanza" (Prayer and hope), "Revolución," and "Triunfo" (Triumph). For its closing number, the Ballet Folklórico Oficial presented *El Minero*, which given its subject matter in all likelihood also praised the accomplishments of the MNR (*ED*, Sept. 22, 1964; Rivera de Stahlie 2003, 195–204).

Although the MNR period was in its final months by then, Urquidi would retain her position with the Ballet Folklórico Oficial and standing as Bolivia's premier "folk dance" choreographer for many decades to come and thereby continue to influence the Bolivian folklore movement. Her dance troupes would also function as a training ground for folkloric musicians, including charango soloist Ernesto Cavour and singer-bombo player Percy Bellido—who would team up in 1966 in an early version of Los Jairas named Conjunto de la Peña Naira (Chapter 7). Urquidi even played a part in the Andean conjunto's incipient canonization as a nationally representative folkloric ensemble format on the international stage—a subject that Chapter 5 more fully addresses—when she added Conjunto Kollasuyo/Bolivia to the *Fantasía Boliviana* cast for the company's 1959 tour of the USSR, China, and Czechoslovakia. Urquidi's MNR-era folkloric ballet productions had a major impact as well on the cholo-mestizo panpipe tropa scene of La Paz city, as a consequence of the Academia de Danzas and Ballet Folklórico Oficial's frequent use of Los Cebollitas for "indigenous" musical numbers. The remarkable trajectories of Los Cebollitas and rival group Los Choclos receive detailed attention in Chapter 5, along with another topic that this book has only touched on so far, the bolero trio boom that urban La Paz and Bolivia's other major cities experienced throughout much of the 1950s.

NOTES

1. My overview of the first MNR regime's three historic decrees draws from the work of political scientists and historians (e.g., Malloy 1970; Malloy 1971; Mitchell 1977; Antezana and Zavaleta Mercado 1983; Dunkerley 1984; Zavaleta Mercado 1986; Klein 1992; Grindle and Domingo 2003; Gildner 2012). For an insightful discussion of the historiography on the 1952 Revolution and MNR period, see Dunkerley 2013.

2. Prior to the Paz Estenssoro regime's 1953 enactment of the Agrarian Reform, "6 percent of landowners . . . owned 1,000 hectares or more of land and controlled fully 92 percent of all cultivated land in the republic" (Klein 1992, 228). The Agrarian Reform also abolished the highly exploitative hacienda institutions of pongueaje and mitanaje.

3. Recent publications that examine MNR mestizaje projects and discourses in relation to nation-state construction include Sanjinés 2004, Gotkowitz 2007, and Gildner 2012. For scholarship on the politics of mestizaje in other Latin American contexts, see Stutzman 1981, Smith 1996, Gould 1998, De la Cadena 2000, and Mendoza 2008.

4. The 1955 Education Reform institutionalized the use of the term "peasant" as a substitute for "Indian" in classroom settings. Consistent with the MNR's mestizaje agenda, the Education Reform prioritized Spanish-language acquisition skills in rural schools and excluded indigenous languages from the curriculum (Contreras 2003).

5. Bolivia's Movimiento Nacionalista Revolucionario was similar ideologically to Mexico's Partido Revolucionario Institucional (Knight 2003), and accordingly the party often looked to the revolutionary process of Mexico as an inspiration (Knudsen 1986, 331–40).

6. The state-sponsored musical initiatives of the MNR period have received relatively little attention from Bolivianist scholars (exceptions include Bigenho 2006, and Gildner 2012).

7. The previous year, Paz Estenssoro had attended the indigenous tropa performances held at the Open Air Theater on the first Día del Indio of the MNR period (*ED*, Aug. 3, 1952).

8. Society figures served on the prize committees for the Municipal Council of Culture's indigenous music-dance festival series of 1953–1956. At the 1954 edition, for example, the jury consisted of Antonio González Bravo, poets-novelists Yolanda Bedregal de Conitzer and Guillermo Viscarra Fabre, art historian José de Mesa, dance specialist Luis Soria Lens, editor Jacobo Liberman (who founded the MNR's "cultural" magazine *Khana*), and filmmaker Alberto Perrín Pando (*ED*, Aug. 5, 1954).

9. For some reason, panpipe groups from the Italaque and Charazani regions did not participate in the first Gran Concurso de Música y Danza Autóctona.

10. While Italaque's Sikuris de Taypi Chiñaya were in La Paz city for the 2nd Gran Concurso de Música y Danza Autóctona, the group recorded several tracks for Discos Méndez (*ED*, July 9 and 18, 1954). These may be among the earliest recordings of Bolivian indigenous siku tropa music made for a commercial label. By 1960, Discos Méndez's catalogue also included examples of Charazani's kantus and *tuaillo* panpipe genres, as played by a "Conjunto Charazani" (*ED*, Oct. 16, 1960). In 1955, a member of the United States Foreign Service, Eduardo Medina, taped some of the performances at the III Festival de Música y Danza Nativa. This live recording includes five selections by the kantus tropa from Niño Korin that won top honors (*Bolivian Folk Music Festival, La Paz, Bolivia, 1955*; AFC 1961/010). On these tracks, the group's harmonic framework exhibits the parallel fourth and fifth harmonies that, as of 2020, characterize Kantus de Charazani music. The tropa also uses the "bouncing ball" drum pattern that kantus ensembles currently employ as the stock introduction for their musical selections.

11. In a nod to the Italaque region's status as a bastion for Andean indigenous music, in 1955 Instituto Indigenal Boliviano director Felix Eguino argued that it represented the ideal site for a state-funded "Indigenous Music School" (*ED*, Nov. 7, 1955). The endeavor never came to fruition, though (Cejudo Velázquez 1966, 65; Costa Ardúz 1996, 94–95).

12. It appears that no other indigenous tropa tradition enjoyed a comparable increase in its profile as a consequence of local musicians' participation in MNR-era folklore festivals.

13. In his travels in rural La Paz, González Bravo must have heard Andean indigenous tropas perform tunes that he deemed to be "mestizo" or "nonindigenous," which would explain why the festival summons discouraged indigenous musicians from playing this type of repertoire. Indigenous tropas often adapt criollo-mestizo melodies, as many scholars have documented (e.g., Paredes 1913, 158; Solomon 1997, 546–52; Bigenho 2002, 37; Stobart 2006, 179–84).

14. Despite being invited, Charazani flauta traversa tropas did not participate in the 1st or 2nd Gran Concurso de Música y Danza Autóctona. Perhaps because the committee thought their efforts once again would be in vain, they did not list Charazani's morenada-flauta traversa tradition in the summons for the third and fourth editions of the festival series.

15. Outside of the La Paz region, Andean indigenous communities in the departamentos of Potosí, Chuquisaca, and Cochabamba also eventually adopted the misti sikuri tradition, and often resignified it as a traditional indigenous expression (see Rios 2021, 18–19).

16. The misti sikuris that played in 1948's Concurso Folklórico Indígena del Departmento is listed as "mozo sikuris," an alternate term for the tradition (Chapter 5).

17. Antonio González Bravo's distress over the misti sikuri's spread to Andean indigenous communities dates back to at least the 1920s (see Wahren 2014, 73, 83).

18. I am unsure if Los Cebollitas' panpipe piece "Caminito del Indio" was inspired by Argentine folkloric musician Atahualpa Yupanqui's famed song of the same name.

19. Prior to launching the 1954 Open Air Theater series, MNR agencies occasionally had used the venue for free-admission events. Las Kantutas and an Oruro diablada troupe performed at one of these concerts in June 1952 (*ED*, June 2, 1952).

20. In "Embodied Matters: Bolivian Fantasy and Indigenismo" (2006), anthropologist Michelle Bigenho examines the 1955 *Fantasía Boliviana* production. The article does not delve into the post-1956 trajectory of the work and its variants, however, or discuss the *Fantasía Boliviana* company's 1959 tour of the USSR, China, and Czechoslovakia.

21. In a reprinted version, Francisco Álvarez García's 1957 *Khana* article "Medio Siglo de Teatro Boliviano" appears in the 2011 volume *500 Años de Teatro en Bolivia: Testimonios y Reflexiones desde el Siglo XVI al XX*, edited by Carlos Cordero Carraffa.

22. Some of the additions to Urquidi's *Fantasía Boliviana 1960* include solo charango numbers by K'auquita García (formerly of estudiantina Huiñay Inti), sketches depicting the *chutillo* genre of Potosí, and a rendering of the tobas tradition.

5

BOLERO TRIOS, URBAN MESTIZO PANPIPE GROUPS, AND

EARLY INCARNATIONS OF THE ANDEAN CONJUNTO

OVER A DECADE prior to the birth of Los Jairas, Conjunto 31 de Octubre appeared on the scene in La Paz. The group existed for only two years (1954–1956), when it served as the house band for Radio Illimani. Conjunto 31 de Octubre's interpretive approach, especially on instrumental pieces (e.g., "Sicuris"), highlighted the wind soloist and secondarily the string players, in a manner that anticipated the musical practices that Andean conjuntos like Los Jairas would adopt in the next decade. The early repertoire of Los Jairas, in fact, would include Andean indigenous-themed numbers that they had learned from the Radio Illimani ensemble's recordings. In this chapter, the first part examines the career, repertoire, and legacy of Conjunto 31 de Octubre, and also briefly discusses Conjunto Kollasuyo and a few other MNR-era groups that constitute early incarnations of what would become Bolivia's Andean conjunto tradition. By the late 1950s, these proto-Andean conjuntos were beginning to operate as Bolivia's unofficial musical ambassadors abroad, even though ensembles of this variety remained few and far between in the country.

It was also in the MNR years that panpipe tropa music increasingly became an integral part of the cultural life of La Paz city. The second part of this chapter illuminates this development through a close look at the two groups at its forefront, Los Cebollitas and Los Choclos, and the wind band tradition they performed, which was originally termed as "misti sikuris." By the end of the MNR era, the misti sikuri

Panpipes & Ponchos. Fernando Rios, Oxford University Press (2020). © Oxford University Press.
DOI: 10.1093/oso/9780190692278.001.0001.

tradition no longer was usually referred to as such in La Paz city, because paceños had come to regard it as an "authentic" form of Andean indigenous music. The tradition's resignification from "mestizo" to "indigenous," which Los Cebollitas and Los Choclos fostered through their performances (especially those that took place in state-sponsored folkloric productions), would facilitate the post-1960s assimilation of the misti sikuri tradition's signature genre—known variously as *sikuris, sikureada* (*sicureada* and *sicureada* represent alternate spellings), and *zampoñada*—into the repertoire of criollo-mestizo folkloric musical acts.

The final part of this chapter explores Bolivia's adoption and localization of the bolero trio or trío romántico format in the MNR period, through the trajectory of Oruro-born singer Raúl Shaw and his backing bands, from his time in Mexico's celebrated Trío Los Panchos, to his later activities with La Paz's Los Peregrinos (originally called Trío Los Indios).[1] Besides interpreting the bolero, an internationally fashionable ballad form of Caribbean derivation and cosmopolitan association, Shaw and Los Peregrinos were known to creatively render, in the polished trío romántico style, local criollo-mestizo genres such as the huayño, oftentimes while one band member strummed on the charango. These selections unquestionably represented Bolivia's most popular type of national folkloric music in the "revolutionary nationalist" era. Shaw and Los Peregrinos' stylistic approach on national repertoire, furthermore, functioned as a model for a generation of Bolivian criollo-mestizo musicians, a cohort that included soon-to-be leading figures in the Andean conjunto scene.

This chapter serves as a counterpart to Chapter 4's discussion of MNR government-funded music-dance folklorization, by providing detailed studies of MNR–era Bolivian musical acts that developed new directions in national music that would influence major trends of the late 1960s and beyond. To highly varying degrees, the three stylistic currents discussed in the pages that follow articulated with the ideologies and discourses of indigenismo, mestizaje, and modernization. MNR-affiliated agencies and individuals, as well as movimientista economic policies, played a part, sometimes inadvertently, in encouraging the musical developments that this chapter analyzes. But of the musical acts that this chapter profiles, only Conjunto 31 de Octubre was born through the deliberate efforts of a high-ranking MNR functionary.

A NEW HOUSE BAND FOR RADIO ILLIMANI: CONJUNTO 31 DE OCTUBRE

In 1954, Carlos Montaño Daza, a movimientista figure with substantial propaganda experience (Coronel Quisbert 2013, 71, 78, 80), took the helm at Radio Illimani. The station, known as "The Official Voice of the Revolution" in the years of MNR rule (Coronel Quisbert 1997, 67–69), had recently moved to the same building that housed the office of the Subsecretary of Press, Information, and Culture or SPIC, an arrangement that eased coordination among propaganda staff working in various mediums. Another benefit of Radio Illimani's new setting is that the building contained a large auditorium that seated 250 people (Coronel Quisbert 1997, 67–69). Contracting a house band that could take advantage of these facilities was on Montaño Daza's agenda when he began his tenure as station director. He was more or less compelled to do so, as a consequence of the MNR regime's passage earlier in the year of Supreme Decree 3653. A nationalist measure, it obligated the country's radio stations to devote at least 25% of their regular musical programming to live acts, and fill 60% of this slot with Bolivian artists (Coronel Quisbert 1997, 67, 76).

Montaño Daza came up with the name for Radio Illimani's new house ensemble, "Conjunto 31 de Octubre," which obviously paid tribute to the MNR government's expropriation of the "Big Three" tin mining companies on October 31, 1952. Montaño Daza imagined the band as a "superstar folkloric group," and accordingly he carefully selected its members (band member José Aramayo Martínez, personal communication).

Esteban del Río signed on as the group's main soloist by mid-1954. A Western transverse-flute player, he was an ex-member of the estudiantina Huiñay Inti (Chapter 3), and of late had played an entirely different repertoire in Fermín Barrionuevo's orquesta de jazz (e.g., *ED*, Sept. 4, 1953). Del Río had recently figured among the accompanists for Las Kantutas' 1953 Discos Méndez recording of Gilberto Rojas's taquirari "Viborita Chis-Chis-Chis" (Méndez 182-A), whose humorous title can be translated as "little snake that makes the sound chis-chis-chis." The guitar stylings of the trio Los Provincianos (The provincials) also appear on this Las Kantutas track. Formed by Sergio Suárez Figueroa (from Uruguay), Hugo Sevillano, and Roberto "Cacho" Córdoba, Los Provincianos had been making music together since the late 1940s (*Última Hora*, June 17, 1949). The trio was integrated into Conjunto 31 de Octubre, a move that immediately gave the new ensemble a solid foundation.

Montaño Daza probably had been acquainted with Los Provincianos' lead guitarist Suárez Figueroa well before he joined Conjunto 31 de Octubre, because the Uruguayan musician had been working as an editor for the SPIC since 1953 (Castro Riveros 2016, 116). It is also likely that Montaño Daza had previously crossed paths with another core member of Conjunto 31 de Octubre, Jorge Zegarra. A charango player and guitarist from Cochabamba, Zegarra had spent a month in La Paz city in 1953 with his former band Los Inti Huasi (Quechua for "The house of the sun"), to fulfill a contract at El Gallo de Oro (The golden rooster), then a popular gathering place for the MNR leadership (Fernández Coca 1994, 52–53, 63–64). It was at this movimientista hangout that Montaño Daza may have first become aware of Zegarra's abilities as a musician.

José Aramayo Martínez rounded out the lineup of the Radio Illimani band. Its sole percussionist, he played the bombo, specifically, the Argentine *bombo legüero*. First popularized internationally by Argentine folklore bands such as Los Chalchaleros and Los Fronterizos in the 1950s, and slightly later becoming an obligatory component in the Andean conjunto lineup, the bombo legüero differs in its construction from the types of bombos that Andean indigenous tropas traditionally employ in rural Bolivia. For example, the bombo legüero has a raised rim, which the player hits with the mallets, in alternation with striking the head of the drum. Indigenous musicians generally do not perform the bombo in this manner, because indigenous models of the instrument in most cases lack the raised rim characteristic of the bombo legüero.

Rather than pointing out the distinguishing facets of the bombo legüero, though, Radio Illimani's deejays gave listeners the impression that Aramayo Martínez played a genuine Andean indigenous drum, by referring to his professionally made, Argentine bombo legüero as a "bombo indio" (Indian bombo) when they introduced the members of Conjunto 31 de Octubre on the air (José Aramayo Martínez, personal communication). Newspaper advertisements for the band's engagements at venues such as the Open Air Theater also used the descriptor "bombo indio" for Aramayo Martínez's instrument of choice (e.g., *ED*, Sept. 12, 1954).[2]

It is entirely plausible that the Radio Illimani staff and El Diario's journalists were not up to speed on bombo construction techniques and therefore could not distinguish a bombo legüero from indigenous versions of the instrument. But this explanation does not account for why, in a similar vein, Radio Illimani's announcers frequently misidentified del Río's Western transverse flute as a kena (José Aramayo Martínez, personal communication), because they could easily see which instrument del Río actually played in the studio.[3] In all likelihod, the deejays wanted the public to believe that Conjunto 31 de Octubre's lineup included wind and percussion instruments of Andean indigenous origin, to bestow greater authenticity to the ensemble's folkloric interpretations.

Most of the time, Conjunto 31 de Octubre's instrumentation consisted of a flute, charango, bombo legüero, and three guitars, and thus fell somewhere in between that of an estudiantina and an Andean conjunto. The group prioritized its wind soloist (though a Western transverse flutist rather than kenista), and included the soon-to-be signature string and percussion instruments of the Andean conjunto tradition (charango, bombo legüero). In a nod to the estudiantina format, however, Conjunto 31 de Octubre used a relatively large number of guitarists, one of whom, Suárez Figueroa, alternated the lead soloist role with the flutist. Few La Paz ensembles seem to have employed this ensemble configuration during Conjunto 31 de Octubre's period of activity (i.e., 1954 to 1956).[4]

Of the instruments in the band's lineup, the bombo legüero represented the main novelty in La Paz's criollo-mestizo folklore scene. With the exception of paceño misti sikuri tropas such as Los Choclos, urban La Paz ensembles of nonindigenous affiliation generally shied away from using folkloric and indigenous versions of the bombo, as well as other percussion instruments of Andean indigenous derivation or association (e.g., wankara, caja). It was in Argentina, while he had been enrolled at the Universidad de La Plata (around 1949–1953), that José Aramayo Martínez learned to play the bombo legüero, to make music with his brothers and fellow students Gerardo (first kena, or charango) and Fernando (lead vocals and guitar, or second kena) in the aptly named group Los Hermanos Aramayo Martínez (José Aramayo Martínez, personal communication).

An Andean conjunto—with three members instead of the customary four to six— Los Hermanos Aramayo Martínez had largely restricted their activities to the campus of the Universidad de La Plata, though from time to time they performed in urban La Paz during extended breaks in the university calendar such as summer vacation (José Aramayo Martínez, personal communication). After José Aramayo Martínez joined Conjunto 31 de Octubre in 1954, the sibling trio occasionally resurfaced in their home city. In 1955, for example, Los Hermanos Aramayo Martínez took part in an SPIC-organized Municipal Theater recital (*La Nación*, Feb. 6, 1955). It was also in the 1950s that the group recorded for Discos Méndez (José Aramayo Martínez, personal communication), and in doing so became one of Bolivia's earliest Andean conjuntos to make commercial releases. The highlight of the ensemble's career, however, was its appearance on the soundtrack of the 1953 film *Vuelve Sebastiana* (Return, Sebastiana). A critically acclaimed Bolivian documentary featuring untrained Andean indigenous actors, *Vuelve Sebastiana* explores the hardships of the Chipaya people of Oruro.[5] By contributing musical passages to a film with this subject matter, Los Hermanos Aramayo Martínez foreshadowed how, from 1960s onward, Andean conjuntos often would misrepresent their folkloric numbers as faithful renderings of rural indigenous music.

A visiting Argentine solo guitarist and kena player, Arsenio Aguirre, was an intermittent member of Conjunto 31 de Octubre in 1954 (e.g., *ED*, July 10 and Sept. 12, 1954), and it was on the occasions that he played the kena with them that the band most approximated an Andean conjunto.[6] According to his daughter, Perla Aguirre (personal communication), Arsenio Aguirre had been amazed to discover that kena soloists then were so scarce in La Paz city (a result of the estudiantina tradition's decline) and, moreover, that he, an Argentine, could fill the kenista role in a prominent Bolivian folklore group—a scenario akin to the one that Los Jairas' Swiss kena player Gilbert Favre would encounter twelve years later in La Paz (Chapter 7). Prior to his stay in Bolivia, Aguirre had acquired substantial experience performing Andean-themed Argentine carnavalitos, bailecitos, and cuecas, as a member of the backing band for Argentine folkloric singer Margarita Palacios, Los Coyas (coyas is an alternate spelling for kollas) (Portorrico 2004, 36). He was thus no stranger to interpreting Andean folkloric repertoire when he set foot in La Paz in 1954. Besides Aguirre, guitarist Alfredo del Río (of Los Sumac Huaynas, and cousin of Esteban del Río) occasionally joined the ranks of Conjunto 31 de Octubre, as did lead singer Luis Santalla (e.g., *ED*, Oct. 17, 1954), who was known primarily in the La Paz music scene as a tango vocalist (José Aramayo Martínez, personal communication).

Until the group dissolved in 1956, Conjunto 31 de Octubre occupied a regular slot on Radio Illimani, as Montaño Daza had intended. The ensemble also performed at a few MNR-sponsored concerts and festivals, particularly in 1954, when criollo-mestizo musicians had the most opportunities to participate in these events (Chapter 4). In September 1954, Conjunto 31 de Octubre was among the forty acts that took part in a "Fiesta de Arte" at the Municipal Theater (*ED*, Sept. 23, 1954), while four weeks later, the group played a set in the SPIC's Open Air Theater series alongside another Argentine folklore act that concentrated on Andean repertoire, María Luisa Buchino y Los Llameros (*ED*, Oct. 17, 1954). Outside of La Paz, Conjunto 31 de Octubre gave concerts in Cochabamba and Tarija, but not Oruro or the mining towns of Potosí, surprisingly, as the group's name would have assured them a positive reception in these centers of the Bolivian mining industry and labor movement (José Aramayo Martínez, personal communication).

In the pre-1952 era, Las Kantutas and the Orquesta Típica La Paz had similarly been created to serve as the house bands for Bolivian state-owned radio stations (Chapter 3), although neither musical act used a politically partisan name in the vein of "Conjunto 31 de Octubre." Of these two precursors, the Orquesta Típica La Paz—an estudiantina from the years of the Villarroel presidency and RADEPA-MNR coalition government—shares the most in common with Conjunto 31 de Octubre, because whereas only some of Las Kantutas' repertoire qualifies as indigenista, Orquesta Típica La Paz mainly performed works of this variety. As the next section shows, Conjunto 31 de Octubre's musical arrangements and recordings of Andean indigenous tropa pieces not only exhibit stylistic commonalities with La Paz estudiantina practices of the 1940s, but also anticipate how Andean conjuntos of the 1960s and beyond would folklorize highland indigenous musical expressions.

THE RECORDINGS OF CONJUNTO 31 DE OCTUBRE

Discos Méndez had been in business for about five years when Conjunto 31 de Octubre debuted. Bolivia's first record company, and the sole one in operation until the 1960s, it was founded in 1949 by Gastón Méndez (an amateur violinist) and his brother Alberto in the upper middle-class La Paz neighborhood of Sopocachi (Rossells 1997a, 37–40, 56). On every disc that the company released, the patriotic caption "El Alma de Bolivia en Su Música" (The soul of Bolivia in its music) appears on the disc cover, along with an artistic representation of La Paz city and image of the snow-peaked Illimani mountain.

The members of Conjunto 31 de Octubre had recorded for the label with their former groups, as noted earlier. With experienced studio musicians in its lineup, the ensemble found itself in demand as the session accompanist for vocal acts, a request they obliged for pillars of the folklore movement, including Las Kantutas, and more recently formed groups such as Dúo Larrea-Teran and the bolero trio Los Indios (Gobierno Municipal de la Ciudad de La Paz Oficialia Mayor de Cultura 1993, 67, 69). It was the instrumental selections of Conjunto 31 de Octubre, though, that would have the most impact on later generations of musicians in Bolivia and abroad.

The version of "Sicuris" that Conjunto 31 de Octubre taped for Discos Méndez around 1955, for example, would make its way into the repertoire of Los Jairas (Chapter 7), and also be recorded by the Argentine-led, and Paris-based, group Los Incas (Rios 2008, 159). Esteban del Río arranged this generically titled instrumental. Labeled on the original Discos Méndez EP as a "danza autóctona" (Méndez 186-A), "Sicuris" is in simple-duple meter and follows AABBCC sectional form (after a brief, unaccompanied flute solo played by del Río), which are common features of siku tropa tunes. The A section has five measures and ends with a standard cadence in the Andean mestizo-associated panpipe tropa style known as misti sikuris (discussed later in this chapter). In the rest of "Sicuris," new melodic material appears only in the first measure of the B; measures 2–4 of this section are identical to measures 3–5 from the A, while the C section recapitulates the final three measures of the A and B (see Example 5.1). Andean tropa tunes often exhibit such extensive borrowing of melodic passages from section to section, to facilitate a high degree of musical participation (see Turino 1993; Stobart 2006).

Del Río executes the melody with his flute on the first pass of the "Sicuris" tune, as the charango player (Zegarra) and two of the guitarists (probably Sevillano and Córdoba) strum chords and Aramayo Martínez maintains a steady beat on the bombo legüero.[7] Del Río drops out on the repeat, at which point two of the guitarists (Suárez Figueroa and Sevillano or Córdoba) pluck out the melodic material in parallel-third harmony while the other ensemble members accompany them. On the remaining three iterations of the principal melody, the flutist and two guitarists continue to alternate the lead role. The band quickens the tempo on the final rendition, as is customary in many Andean criollo-mestizo and indigenous genres. Yet by constantly highlighting instrumental soloists, the musical practices of Conjunto 31 de Octubre clearly differ from the far less individualistic style of estudiantinas, vocal duos, brass bands, and other typical paceño criollo-mestizo ensemble traditions. They also contrast, and even more substantially, with the pronounced egalitarianism of siku tropa performance practices.

Conjunto 31 de Octubre uses a similar interpretive approach on the selection found on the B side of this two-track EP, "Auqui Auqui" (e.g., the flute soloist and two guitarists take turns realizing the melody) (Méndez 186-B). It is another instrumental that Los Jairas' founding members would record in the mid-1960s (in the initial

EXAMPLE 5.1 Conjunto 31 de Octubre, "Sicuris," Western transverse-flute melody

incarnation of Los Jairas, Conjunto de la Peña Naira). Listed on the disc as a "danza indígena" (indigenous dance) and credited to Alberto Ruiz Lavadenz (of the estudiantina Lira Incaica) (Méndez 186-B), this piece is named after the auqui auqui genre. In this Andean tradition, indigenous flauta traversa tropas animate the mischievous and often hilarious antics of costumed dancers who impersonate elderly men ("auqui auqui" means "old men" in Aymara). Ruiz Lavadenz's "Auqui Auqui" incorporates stock phrases, cadences, and other melodic and rhythmic hallmarks of the original genre, as is true of del Río's "Sicuris." However, "Auqui Auqui" encompasses two tunes, and accordingly exhibits greater melodic variety.

As a folklorist and Western transverse flutist, del Río was naturally drawn to Bolivia's flauta traversa tropa traditions. Examples of del Río's other settings of flauta traversa melodies include "Llamerada" (which Los Jairas would also record), "Kullaguas" (alternate spelling for the cullawas genre), and "Hirpastay."[8] On Conjunto 31 de Octubre's Discos Méndez recordings of the latter two pieces, they introduce the melody at a slow to moderate tempo, before dramatically speeding up the pace to that of a brisk huayño for the next major section of the piece (i.e., the second rendition of the melody in "Hirpastay"; the group introduces a new tune at this point in "Llamerada"). The band employs this major shift in tempo at other key moments as well in "Hirpastay" and "Llamerada."

To construct "presentational" versions of "participatory" musical expressions (Turino 2008a), artists around the world often incorporate the types of modifications that Del Río, Ruiz Lavandez, and Conjunto 31 de Octubre did when they arranged, composed, and/or recorded "Sicuris," "Auqui Auqui," "Llamerada," and "Hirpastay" (i.e., tempo shifts, medley format, alternation of soloists, transparent musical texture). As Turino illuminates in *Music as Social Life* (Turino 2008a), these changes enable musicians to maintain audience interest in presentational contexts, that is, in situations where there is a clear line of separation between the artists and spectators, and the latter is not expected to participate in the music making. Given that Conjunto 31 de Octubre almost exclusively performed in presentational settings (i.e., Radio Illimani broadcasts, MNR-sponsored festivals and recitals), it is entirely fitting that the ensemble's musical practices fall on the presentational side of the participatory-presentational music continuum. Presentational performance practices similarly would characterize the Andean conjunto tradition.

Besides tropa tunes, Conjunto 31 de Octubre's repertoire included criollo-mestizo genres, from the cueca and bailecito, to the eastern-lowland carnaval and taquirari— yet another way in which the ensemble's musical practices foreshadow those of Andean conjuntos. When interpreting these Bolivian criollo-mestizo mainstays, the guitarists use an accompaniment style that is far more complex, harmonically and rhythmically, than their customary approach on tropa-derived numbers. For instance, whereas on the carnaval "Milongueros" the guitar section weaves almost continuous countermelodies to the Western transverse-flute part, primarily in the middle register of their instruments, the guitarists simply strum chords to accompany del Río's flute solos on "Sicuris," "Auqui Auqui," "Llamerada," and "Hirpastay"

(Méndez 203-B).[9] By employing such contrasting practices for their "indigenous" and "criollo-mestizo" repertoire, Conjunto 31 de Octubre underscored these ethnicized distinctions, in a manner comparable to that of Andean folkloric musical acts of the 1960s such as the Potosí band Los Chasquis (Chapter 6).

In 1956, Conjunto 31 de Octubre disappeared from the Bolivian music scene, when the band members (though without bombista Jóse Aramayo Martínez) joined forces with Tito Yupanqui and Pepa Cardona for a tour of the Americas. In an unplanned turn of events, most of the group settled down at the first major stop, Caracas, Venezuela (Tito Yupanqui, personal communication). Undeterred, the recently married Yupanqui and Cardona continued the journey on their own, as the duo Los Wara Wara, and made it all the way to Mexico and the United States (see the next section). Suárez Figueroa and Zegarra eventually returned to La Paz, but never reformed Conjunto 31 de Octubre (see Castro Riveros 2016, 116–17).

Three years after Conjunto 31 de Octubre's departure from La Paz, four of their Discos Méndez tracks resurfaced on the Folkways album *Folk Songs and Dances of Bolivia*: "Sicuris," "Llamerada," "Hirpastay," and a taquirari mislabeled on the credits as the *tonada* "Amor Chapaco" (FW 6871). This 1959 LP, which also includes selections by Las Kantutas, seems to entirely consist of previously released Bolivian recordings featuring criollo-mestizo folklorists. However, the liner notes do not mention the names of any of the musicians or ensembles. Folkways Records apparently wanted its potential customers to believe that *Folk Songs and Dances of Bolivia* contained "anonymous" folk tunes that had been collected in remote villages. This strategy would also explain why photographs of traditionally dressed Andean indigenous musicians and dancers decorate the LP cover and text inside the jacket, rather than images of the criollo-mestizo artists whose performances are actually heard on the album.[10]

Folkways Records' misrepresentation of the contents of *Folk Songs and Dances of Bolivia* thus gave listeners the impression that the musical practices of Conjunto 31 de Octubre and the LP's other artists were typical of Andean indigenous music making, in much the same way that, from the 1960s to recent times, European-based labels would often market Andean conjunto music to cosmopolitan audiences (Rios 2008, 165).[11] For Paris's Los Incas and Los Calchakis, then, *Folk Songs and Dances of Bolivia* must have seemed an ideal source for "authentic" repertoire. Within a few years of the album's release, both groups recorded "Sicuris," "Llamerada," and "Hirpastay," in versions that clearly are based on the arrangements of Conjunto 31 de Octubre (Rios 2008, 159). It was through Los Incas and Los Calchakis' recordings in France that these tropa-inspired pieces would become staples of the Andean conjunto repertoire in the European scene.

BOLIVIAN ANDEAN CONJUNTOS, LATE 1950S TO EARLY 1960S

Around the time that Conjunto 31 de Octubre disbanded, a new folklore act with a similar stylistic orientation began to make a name for itself in La Paz city, Conjunto

Kollasuyo. The group's configuration varied, but usually took the form of an Andean conjunto. Jaime Medinaceli directed Conjunto Kollasuyo.[12] A classically trained musician, he began his musical career as a Western transverse flutist, and spent an extended period of time in Peru, where he worked as a brass band conductor and chamber musician (Rojas Rojas 1989, 73). By the mid-1950s, Medinaceli had become a kena soloist, which was his primary instrumental role in Conjunto Kollasuyo. A composer as well, he authored the huayño "El Minero" (The miner), with which the Andean conjunto Savia Andina would score one of their biggest hits in 1980 (see Chapter 8: Postlude).[13] Medinaceli's compositions also include "Al MNR" (To the MNR) (Rojas Rojas 1989, 75), the subject matter of which suggests that he was a committed MNR member.

Conjunto Kollasuyo undertook its first trip overseas in 1957, after winning the contest that La Paz radio station Emisoras Unidas (United Broadcasters) had organized to select the musicians who would travel to Moscow to represent Bolivia at the VI World Festival of Youth and Students for Peace and Friendship. Besides Medinaceli, the ensemble's lineup at the audition consisted of singer Lola Molina, guitarist Godofredo Núñez Chávez, and multi-instrumentalist José René Moreno Kreidler (*ED*, June 18 and July 16, 1957). For some reason, Molina stayed behind in La Paz when the group journeyed to the USSR. Now a trio, Conjunto Kollasuyo took part in the Moscow festival, under the name of "Conjunto Bolivia" (Terceros and Parada 1989, 95–97). Medinaceli returned to the USSR two years later, heading another "Conjunto Bolivia," as part of the 1959 *Fantasía Boliviana* delegation that also toured Czechoslovakia and China (Chapter 4). He formed this version of the ensemble, a quartet, with ex–Conjunto 31 de Octubre charango/guitar player Jorge Zegarra, charanguista K'auquita García (of estudiantina Huiñay Inti), and paceño musician Tito Melgar (*Presencia*, July 13, 1959). On two occasions in the late 1950s, then, Conjunto Kollasuyo/Bolivia musically represented "Bolivia" on the international stage with an ensemble format—the Andean conjunto—that was far from typical in Bolivia, as only a few groups used this instrumental configuration at the time.

In 1960, *Fantasía Boliviana* director Chela Urquidi once again put together a folkloric music-dance contingent, this time to compete in the Festival Panamericana de Danzas Folklóricas that would be held in January of the next year in Buenos Aires (*ED*, Sept. 17, 1960). K'auquita García and Jorge Zegarra reprised their roles in the entourage's Andean conjunto, "Conjunto Musical Bolivia." They were joined by guitarists Armando Valdéz (of Trío Panamérica Antawara) and Miguel Butrón (of another popular bolero group, Arturo Sobénes y Los Cambas); and bombo player and kenista José Aramayo Martínez (formerly of Conjunto 31 de Octubre) (*ED*, Oct. 1, 1960).[14]

In the end, the Bolivian delegation never made it to Argentina, apparently because of financial reasons (*La Nación*, Jan. 3, 1961). When Urquidi was in the process of selecting the delegation for the Festival Panamericana de Danzas Folklóricas, three key members of the soon-to-be finalized "Conjunto Musical Bolivia"—José Aramayo Martínez, Armando Valdéz, and Miguel Butrón—had recently laid down the tracks for the album *Pinceladas de Bolivia* under the group name of "Armando Valdéz y su Conjunto Andino" (Armando Valdéz and his Andean Conjunto) (*ED*, Sept. 25, 1960).

This LP in all likelihood offers a window into the interpretive approach of Conjunto Musical Bolivia, and perhaps earlier versions of the ensemble.

Pinceladas de Bolivia (Bolivian brushstrokes) is an instrumental album in which Andean criollo-mestizo genres predominate on the selections (huayño, cueca, bailecito), although the LP includes two música oriental numbers (AUZA LPX 1001). On almost every track, the kena player (Aramayo Martínez) executes the first rendering of the tune, and then alternates the lead melodic role with one guitarist (probably Valdéz). The rest of the band, which is composed of guitarists Miguel Butrón and Juan Melazzini (both formerly of the bolero act Arturo Sobénes y Los Cambas), charanguista Pepe Camacho, and "bombo indio" player Carlos Varela, mainly accompanies the soloists.

If this album is representative of Armando Valdéz y su Conjunto Andino's performance style, it closely resembles the approach used by Conjunto 31 de Octubre, with the caveat that Armando Valdéz y su Conjunto Andino features a kenista rather than a Western transverse flutist. The preponderance of guitarists, meanwhile, constitutes a similarity between the two groups, as does the major role that the ensembles afford to their respective first guitarists, legacies of the Bolivian estudiantina tradition that most Bolivian Andean conjuntos would discard by the late 1960s.

Armando Valdéz y su Conjunto Andino's treatment of eastern lowland genres, however, looks forward to imminent developments in Andean conjunto practices. On the música oriental track "Tranquilízate" (Calm down), a taquirari by Gilberto Rojas, Armando Valdéz y su Conjunto Andino uses the same "Andean" instrumentation and performance style that the members adopt when they play highland genres. Bolivia's Andean conjuntos of the 1960s usually would perform eastern lowland tunes in this manner, thereby Andeanizing musical expressions of non-Andean origin or derivation.

In the late 1950s, the Andean conjunto (and early incarnations of the tradition) was starting to function as an emblematic Bolivian folkloric ensemble type, tentatively, and mainly outside of the country. The Andean conjunto's prominent use of musical instruments of highland indigenous association conformed with non-Bolivian preconceptions of "authentic Bolivian folk music," while the range of genres that these ensembles interpreted offered a sampling of Bolivia's musical diversity—although in stylized renderings that minimized the level of diversity. Semiotically, the performance practices of these early Bolivian Andean conjuntos therefore articulated with indigenismo (by foregrounding Andean indigenous-associated instruments and repertoire) and mestizaje (mainly through their assimilation of genres from disparate populations or regions—e.g., criollo-mestizo and indigenous; highland and lowland)—among the factors that would facilitate the Andean conjunto's eventual canonization as the preeminent ensemble format for performing música folklórica nacional.

LOS WARA WARA

The early recordings of Los Wara Wara (Tito Yupanqui and Pepa Cardona) also presage future directions in Bolivian folkloric musical practices. As previously noted, in 1956 the duo commenced a tour of the Americas that would take them to Mexico and the United States. Cardona, a singer who in the MNR years performed as "La Khosinaira" (Aymara for "The girl with green eyes"), had emerged on the La Paz music scene in the late 1930s, as a contemporary of Las Kantutas and Las Hermanas Tejada (Chapter 3). Yupanqui's trajectory as a folklorist began in Argentina, where he studied plastic arts at Buenos Aires' Academia Superior de Bellas Artes "Ernesto de la Carcova" from 1946 to 1953 (Tito Yupanqui, personal communication). To make ends meet, he often performed at the city's "folk music" venues (e.g., peñas), but rather than using his birth name of Fabián Humberto Flores Espinoza, he adopted the Incan pseudonym "Tito Yupanqui" (Tito Yupanqui, personal communication). He apparently chose it in imitation of Argentine singer-guitarist Héctor Chavero's alias "Atahualpa Yupanqui."[15] The name that Tito Yupanqui and Cardona selected for their duo, Los Wara Wara (Aymara for "the stars"), was hardly original, either. It recalled Velasco Maidana's 1930 film *Wara Wara* (Chapter 2), and Belisario Zárate's indigenista musical composition of the same name (Chapter 3).

While in Mexico City circa 1959, Los Wara Wara recorded two LPs that would circulate widely in the Americas and Europe: *Dioses y Demonios de Bolivia* (Gods and demons of Bolivia; Vanguard 70.280), and *Folklore Boliviano* (Dimsa 8155). Yupanqui and Cardona interpret a range of genres, with various instrumental formats, on these albums. At the time, criollo-mestizo rather than indigenous musical repertoire constituted their forte. The record labels' on-site managers, though, were most intrigued by Los Wara Wara's indigenous-themed numbers, so much so that they insisted that Yupanqui and Cardona record "autochthonous" tracks (Tito Yupanqui, personal communication).

The yaravís "Thaya" (Aymara for "Wind") and "Vicuñita" (My little or dear vicuña) on *Dioses y Demonios de Bolivia* no doubt satisfied the company's misinformed desire for authentic Andean indigenous music. "Thaya" also appears on *Folklore Boliviano*, with the subtitle *"lamento indígena"* (indigenous lament). In both versions, Yupanqui sings the melody in a melodramatic style, rather like wailing—probably similarly to how he interpreted "Cantar Indio" (Song of the Indian) and "Plegaria de la Puna" (Mountain prayer) in the 1955 *Fantasía Boliviana* production (Chapter 4). Without question, Yupanqui enacts the stereotype of the "anguished Indian" on these recordings of "Thaya." Notably, he plays the instrument most identified with this trope, the kena, a formula that Los Jairas would revisit in 1966 on their first hit, the yaraví "El Llanto de Mi Madre" (Chapter 7).

At a time when urban Bolivian folkloric musicians expressed little interest in taking up the Andean panpipe, with the exception of those of exceedingly low socioeconomic standing (e.g., Los Choclos, Los Cebollitas), Yupanqui highlights the instrument on two selections on *Dioses y Demonios de Bolivia*: "Italaqueñita" (From Italaque, or Girl from Italaque), and "Sicureada." A pair of siku players realize the melody in hocket on "Sicureada," while a guitarist and bombista accompany them. On "Italaqueñita," in contrast, Yupanqui uses the panpipe exclusively as a solo instrument, despite his obvious technical limitations as a zampoñista.

"Italaqueñita" portends the solo panpipe's eventual centrality in the Andean conjunto tradition, a development that would not occur until the 1970s (Chapter 8: Postlude). Eight years after the release of *Dioses y Demonios de Bolivia*, Paris's Los Calchakis reprised the spirit of Yupanqui's solo panpipe performance of "Italaqueñita" on the 1967 blockbuster album *La Flûte Indienne* (The Indian flute). The Argentine-led group recorded it under a different title, though, "Quiaqueñita," which refers to the northwestern Argentine town of La Quiaca, Jujuy. Los Calchakis' version fascinated French pop duo Marianne Mille and Maurice Dulac, as well as Greek singer Nana Mouskouri. Both musical acts would score hit singles in France in 1970 with their vocal arrangements of this siku tune (Chapter 7).

In Bolivia, it was urban mestizo siku tropas who played the critical, early role in incorporating the Andean panpipe into the nonindigenous music scenes of La Paz city and other metropolitan centers such as Oruro and Cochabamba. They were well positioned for this undertaking. The siku tradition that these groups specialized in, originally known as misti sikuris, tended to aesthetically appeal to mainstream criollo-mestizo audiences to a greater extent than was true of more typical indigenous panpipe tropa expressions, a state of affairs that owed much to the mestizo sector's central role in the emergence and stylistic development of the misti sikuri tradition.

THE MISTI SIKURI TRADITION IN RURAL LA PAZ, 1900S TO 1940S

By the turn of the 20th century, the rural provinces of La Paz were home to a panpipe tropa style called misti sikuris that, as its name indicates (misti is a synonym for mestizo), differed from other siku traditions of the Bolivian Andes in its identification with mestizos rather than indigenous people. In the 1913 article "El Arte en la Altiplanicie" (Art in the altiplano) (Paredes 1913, 176, 182), ethnologist Rigoberto Paredes asserts that La Paz's misti sikuri tradition departed from local indigenous practice. He provides few details, though, other than pointing out that the misti sikuri dance was a choreographed one involving lines of paired musicians who exhibited athletic moves, and that the performers' attire consisted of embroidered jackets, beribboned hats, and colorful socks that peeked below short pants (Paredes 1913, 176, 182). By the 1940s, Antonio González Bravo notes (1948, 412), misti sikuri outfits had become "extremely luxurious," being made of "expensive, multicolored cloth, embroidered with gold and silver thread, with precious stones." In carnivalesque style, the musicians often masqueraded as "(Spanish) bullfighters, (U.S.) boy scouts, turks, etc.," alongside dancers who depicted equally colorful characters, such as "old men, bears, monkeys, cats, lions, angels, devils, and whatever else they dream up" (González Bravo 1948, 412).

Conspicuously absent from this cast of characters were "Andean Indians," given the misti sikuri tradition's eventual transformation into a folkloric representation of highland indigenous music. Prior to the 1950s, however, misti sikuri artists maintained a clear line of separation between their panpipe tradition and that of indigenous musicians. It thus would have made little sense for them to visually obscure this distinction by wearing ponchos, lluchus, or other attire inspired by the regalia of indigenous ensembles. Instead, misti sikuri groups of this period donned expensive costumes that flaunted the members' access to economic resources that were unavailable to most indigenous people, implementing a well-worn mestizo strategy for differentiating members of this sector from those whom they often disparaged as "Indians." Notably, "mozo sikuris" served as an alternate designation for misti sikuris in the 1940s (*ED*, Nov. 24, 1948; González Bravo 1948, 411–12; 1949, 71). The Spanish term for unmarried, male youths, "mozo" has traditionally referred to adolescent males of the vecino class in the rural La Paz context.

Misti sikuris also set themselves apart from indigenous tropas, and underscored their mestizo identity, through their characteristic use of a brass band-style rhythm section. By the 1940s, the rhythm section of misti sikuri ensembles comprised a snare drum, bombo (or military bass drum), and various cymbals and triangles (González Bravo 1948, 411).[16] Indigenous siku bands of the La Paz region, in contrast, normally employed only one kind of drum (e.g., bombo, wankara), and these ensembles seldom used a separate rhythm section, because a few of the wind players usually doubled as the percussionists (see González Bravo 1948, 406–11).[17] The manner in which instrument makers fabricated misti sikuri panpipes, specifically the second row of tubes (which in both traditions act as a resonator for the first row), might have further differentiated misti sikuris from indigenous sikuris (see Izikowitz 1935, 394, 398–99), perhaps in a way comparable to the role of the *tablasiku* (which differs visually from indigenous sikus) in the closely related Peruvian mestizo panpipe tropa style known as *sikumoreno* or *pusamoreno* (see Valencia 1983; Acevedo Raymundo 2003; and Macedo Juárez 2006).

The misti sikuri repertoire centered on the huayño, although it also included the cueca, bailecito, and assorted non-Bolivian genres, such as the tango, habanera, and waltz (González Bravo 1948, 411). That misti sikuris of this period interpreted such a range of genres, even ones in contrasting tempos and meters (e.g., $\frac{2}{4}$, $\frac{3}{4}$, $\frac{6}{8}$), brings to mind the practices of estudiantinas, vocal duos, brass bands, and other contemporaneous Bolivian criollo-mestizo ensemble formats. It moreover reveals a further point of separation between mestizo and indigenous siku traditions of the region, because indigenous siku tropas then usually played only a single genre per festive occasion (see González Bravo 1948, 406–23).

In the Peruvian departamento of Puno, La Paz's misti sikuri style generated an offshoot, the previously mentioned sikumoreno or pusamoreno tradition. According to Peruvian music scholar Américo Valencia (1983, 68), Puno's earliest sikumoreno tropas date from the 1890s and modeled themselves after misti sikuris from the La Paz town of Sicasica.[18] Bolivian misti sikuris and Peruvian sikumorenos appear to have maintained regular contact with, and mutually influenced, one another from this point onward (see Valencia 1983, 95; Macedo Juárez 2006, 28–29; Rios 2012, 19). It would explain why the trajectories of the two traditions bear a striking resemblance, from the predominantly mestizo membership of the groups, to the ensembles' use of brass band rhythm sections and lavish attire (see Valencia 1983, 63–90; Acevedo Raymundo 2003; Ichuta Ichuta 2003; Macedo Juárez 2006; Sánchez Huaringa 2013). Moreover, since at least the 1950s Bolivian misti sikuri and Peruvian sikumoreno groups have performed similar cadential figures when playing huayños (spelled without the tilde in Peru, i.e., huayno or wayno). These passages involve rapid hocketing between the *ira* (leader) and *arca* (follower) sikus, usually in octaves, or octaves and fourths. A common iteration of this cadence appears in Conjunto 31 de Octubre's 1955 recording of "Sicuris" (see Example 5.1).

In another parallel between Bolivia's misti sikuri and Peru's sikumoreno traditions, these mestizo-associated panpipe ensemble styles took hold in the early-to-mid-20th century in many indigenous communities of the La Paz and Puno regions, respectively, where they often replaced more traditional indigenous panpipe tropa formats (Rios 2012, 18–19). In rural La Paz, this development gradually blurred the lines separating highland indigenous and mestizo music-dance forms, and as a result, it articulated with the MNR leadership's modernist-nationalist ideal of cultural mestizaje.

Yet when the Municipality of La Paz organized "autochthonous" or "native" music-dance festivals at Hernando Siles Stadium from 1953 to 1956, the guidelines precluded misti sikuris from taking part in these spectacles, illustrating how MNR-funded folklorization initiatives sometimes ran counter to official movimientista goals (Chapter 4). Nevertheless, for the urban La Paz–based misti sikuris Los Choclos and Los Cebollitas, the MNR years represented a time of unparalleled opportunity to perform at state-funded folkloric events, and thereby expose urban La Paz criollo-mestizo audiences to siku tropa music on a far more regular basis than had been the case in recent memory.

LOS CHOCLOS, LOS CEBOLLITAS, AND THE MISTI SIKURI TRADITION IN LA PAZ CITY

In 1926, the shoeshiners of urban La Paz established a union (Reyes Zárate 2017, 106), and it was around this time that a contingent of them founded the misti sikuri tropa Los Choclos. Henceforth the ensemble would be strongly affiliated with those who polished shoes for a living, a highly stigmatized occupation that afforded a meager income and consigned its practitioners to the bottom of the city's socioeconomic hierarchy.[19]

From the early years of the group's existence, Los Choclos paraded in the Fiesta del Señor del Gran Poder (The fiesta of the all-powerful Father), the main patron saint celebration for Ch'ijini (Albó and Preiswerk 1986, 111; Ichuta Ichuta 2003, 131). A working-class neighborhood located just outside the city limits (the border was redrawn later) and on the site of a former hacienda, Ch'ijini in the 1920s was developing into an important commercial district for the urban La Paz area (Guss 2006). The residents of Ch'ijini variously identified as mestizo, cholo, or indigenous, depending on the context (Sierra 2013). Expressive practices, including the misti sikuri tradition, constituted one of the means through which the neighborhood's inhabitants negotiated their ethnicized social identities at festive events (Albó and Preiswerk 1986; Guss 2006; Sierra 2013).[20]

Participation in a misti sikuri group enabled Los Choclos' members to musically represent how they envisioned themselves, as mestizos. They would have needed to frequently assert this claim, given their low social status, and because criollo-mestizos habitually denigrated them as social inferior, uncouth indios. As Chapter 3 explains, the estudiantina and brass band represented the principal musical mechanisms for working-class mestizos to construct their place in urban La Paz society in the early-to-mid-20th century. For the members of Los Choclos, however, forming an estudiantina or brass band was beyond their means. At a considerable monetary disadvantage compared to most of their fellow mestizos, but desirous of expressing their religious devotion through music in the patron-saint fiestas of Ch'ijini and the Lake Titicaca port town of Copacabana, the shoeshiners of La Paz chose a mestizo-associated ensemble tradition that centered on an instrument they could afford, the siku, an entire set of which could be purchased for less than the cost of one brass instrument, mandolin, or guitar. Their performance outfits, meanwhile, took inspiration from those of rural misti sikuris, although for obvious reasons were not as opulent.

Los Choclos seem to have been the only urban La Paz–based misti sikuri tropa that was continuously active from the 1920s to 1950s. After the 1952 Revolution, it separated into two groups, along generational lines. The newer ensemble, at first called Club Juventud Los Choclos (Los Choclos Youth Club), became known simply as Los Choclos as the older group faded away (Jorge Miranda and Arturo Gutiérrez, personal communication). Numerous times in the MNR years, the younger group performed at the revered Municipal Theater, either playing the part of a rural indigenous tropa in state-funded folkloric theater productions such as *Bolivia Indiana* (see the next section, "From Mestizo to Indigenous"), or as one of the acts in the musical extravaganzas that MNR agencies coordinated (e.g., *ED*, July 10, Aug. 18, Aug. 26, and Sept. 23, 1954).

One of the latter events took place in the 1954 Fiestas Julianas season (*ED*, July 10, 1954). The participants ranged from veteran folklore artists Las Hermanas Tejada, Gilberto Rojas, and Los Sumac Huaynas, to newer talents such as Conjunto Folklórico Armonía (a modified version of Conjunto 31 de Octubre), Las Imillas, Las Hermanas Arteaga, and Las Hermanas Espinoza. The orquesta de jazz tradition also was well represented at the concert (e.g., Orquesta "Tropical Boys," Orquesta Loayza, Fermín Barrionuevo's Los Reyes del Mambo, Castro Mérida's Gran Orquesta de Jazz). Bolivia's most popular musician, bolerista Raúl Shaw, performed too, accompanied by Trío Los Indios.

Considering this impressive list of musical acts, it is remarkable that the name and image of Los Choclos appears most prominently in the concert advertisement (*ED*, July 10, 1954). And even more remarkable, the ad credits Los Choclos as the organizer of the event, although the low socioeconomic standing of the ensemble members made this scenario an unlikely one. As propaganda, however, the flyers aligned with MNR's populist message that the state acted in partnership with the downtrodden.

Los Choclos' main competitor in the MNR years was the other vegetable-named siku tropa of La Paz city, Los Cebollitas.[21] Its debut occurred in 1950, at Ch'ijini's fiesta for La Virgen del Rosario (The Virgin of the Rosary). Members of the newspaper deliverers' trade union established the ensemble, which by the mid-1950s organized itself like a union, with elected officers who included secretaries of culture, relations, propaganda, and sports (El Arte de los Sindicatos 1956, 11–14). In 1954, Los Cebollitas headlined a Municipal Theater concert that, like the one that Los Choclos also took part in that year, featured leading criollo-mestizo musicians in the rest of the show, in this instance Las Kantutas, Las Hermanas Tejada, and Conjunto 31 de Octubre (Municipal Theater Program, 1954).

A friendly rivalry characterized relations between Los Cebollitas and Los Choclos. They often squared off in informal musical duels in public parks (Manuel Cruz of Los Cebollitas, personal communication), perhaps consciously taking after the competitive style of indigenous tropa performances in ayllu fiestas. The members of Los Cebollitas and Los Choclos surely bonded over their analogous socio-economic standing, and the unfortunate experience of having criollo-mestizos regularly belittle them as "boys" (regardless of their actual age), simply for carrying out their professions as shoeshiners and newspaper deliverers. It was not unusual for individuals to occasionally combine these low-paying occupations (Reyes Zárate 2017, 126), or switch from one to the other. Musicians accordingly passed between the tropas associated with these lines of work. In the early 1950s, Antonio Valdivia and a Mr. Centeno left Los Choclos for Los Cebollitas, which the two men led for the rest of the decade (Manuel Cruz, personal communication). Unsurprisingly, then, Los Cebollitas "emulated Los Choclos" in this period (Manuel Cruz, personal communication).

Once Los Cebollitas had joined the cast of Fantasía Boliviana in 1955, though, its status in the folklore movement began to surpass that of Los Choclos. Los Cebollitas' greater international trajectory over the next few years would consolidate the group's reputation. By the time the MNR era concluded, Los Cebollitas had brought their musical stylings to Argentina, Paraguay, and Uruguay in 1955; China, Czechoslovakia, and the USSR in 1959; and Colombia in 1961 (Chapter 4). On home ground, in 1964 the tropa acted as unofficial Bolivian cultural ambassadors for Libertad Lamarque's visit to La Paz. When the popular Argentine singer and movie star disembarked at the city's airport, Los Cebollitas serenaded her with their panpipe tropa music (ED, Sept. 11, 1964).

Los Choclos performed abroad, too; the first occasion occurred at Mexico's Pablo Casals Festival. As part of the Ballet Folklórico Boliviano, the group participated in the event's 1960 edition, which took place in Acapulco (Jorge Miranda, personal communication; Rivera de Stahlie 2003, 191, 237).[22] A couple of weeks later, the company fulfilled concert engagements in Mexico City (*ED*, Dec. 31, 1960), where they might have crossed paths with Raúl Shaw and Los Peregrinos, who had been living there since 1958 (discussed later in the chapter). And in October 1964, Los Choclos traveled with Tito Yupanqui (who recently had returned to Bolivia) and other La Paz artists to Termas de Río Hondo, Argentina, to compete in the Third Festival Internacional de Folklore against delegations from Paraguay, Chile, Brazil, Spain, and an unspecified African country (*ED*, Oct. 17, 1964). As the MNR period was nearing its end, Los Choclos and Los Cebollitas both had seized the opportunity to play the part of Bolivia's musical representatives outside of the country.

In keeping with the eclecticism of the misti sikuri tradition, the repertoire of Los Choclos and Los Cebollitas spanned from Andean criollo-mestizo genres and música oriental, to non-Bolivian genres popular internationally. Los Choclos were known to play the tango, especially the La Paz–themed favorite "Tango Illimani" (by paceño composer Néstor Portocarrero), and also the Colombian *cumbia* (Arturo Gutiérrez of Los Choclos, personal communication). Not to be outdone, Los Cebollitas juxtaposed Andean indigenous-sounding pentatonic melodies with Cuban-inspired rhythms in their take on the "mambo dance," as visiting French ethnologist Louis Girault discovered in 1954 (for his transcription of this piece, see d'Harcourt and d'Harcourt 1959, 98–99).

An MNR favorite, the taquirari "Siempre," figured among Los Cebollitas' música oriental numbers by 1955. They recorded it that year in Argentina, during a break in their activities with the *Fantasía Boliviana* troupe (TK-10082).[23] "Indiecito de la Puna" (Little Indian from the mountains) appears on the other side of the disc. A huayño by Los Cebollitas member Paulino Quispe, its patronizing title recalls that of "Caminito del Indio" (Little pathway of the Indian), the instrumental selection with which the group had earned second place in 1953 at the SPIC-coordinated Concurso de Arte Nativo (Chapter 4).

By 1956, Los Cebollitas had "recorded a considerable number of records of national music" for Discos Méndez (El Arte de los Sindicatos 1956, 13). "Ese Vaso de Cerveza" (That glass of beer; by group member Dionisio Cusicanqui) is one of these tracks, and likely reflects the ensemble's performance practices at the time (Méndez 450-B). A lively huayño with stock misti sikuri cadences, it is in sectional form (AABB). The differences between the two sections are limited to the opening notes of the B section (see Example 5.2), as also holds true for Conjunto 31 de Octubre's recording of "Sicuris." Los Cebollitas generate a smooth sound quality on their panpipes that contrasts, strikingly, with the more strident timbre typical of Andean indigenous panpipe music. That the sikus the ensemble uses on "Ese Vaso de Cerveza" lack the wide tuning variance characteristic of indigenous tropa instruments partially explains this sonic difference.[24] Making the track even more accessible to mainstream elite and middle-class audiences, the members of the criollo-mestizo band Los Pregoneros (The town criers) sing along with the panpipe melody at a number of points in the selection, and they do so in Spanish rather than Quechua or Aymara.

EXAMPLE 5.2 Los Cebollitas, "Ese Vaso de Cerveza," panpipe melody

On the flip side of the EP, Los Cebollitas interpret the huayño "Corocoreña" (Girl from Corocoro; by Francisco Cabrera). Once again, Los Pregoneros supply the vocals, and in Spanish, but Los Cebollitas now realize the melody in parallel fifths with a tarka tropa (Méndez 450-A). Although the siku continued to be the ensemble's signature instrument, the members no longer limited themselves to the panpipe. In addition to the tarka, Los Cebollitas also learned to play the kena-kena. Los Choclos likewise became proficient at performing on the tarka and kena-kena, in the traditional tropa format, and used these instruments in folkloric theater productions (e.g., *ED*, June 12, 1957).

Additional misti sikuri groups emerged on the urban La Paz scene by the late 1950s, no doubt inspired by Los Choclos and Los Cebollitas. These new groups similarly drew their core membership from the lower socioeconomic levels: those who made their living as manual laborers, or by selling goods and services on the street. Many of these ensembles seem to have been attached to trade unions, akin to La Paz city's cholo-mestizo estudiantinas of the 1930s and 1940s (Chapter 3). The expanded unionization that the Bolivian laborforce experienced in the MNR years apparently played a part in the rise of urban panpipe groups whose core personnel hailed from a single blue-collar profession.[25]

Manuel Cruz, who joined Los Cebollitas in the 1950s, remembers (personal communication) paceño sikuris of the MNR period such as Los Clavelitos (The little carnations), whose members sold flowers; Los Pastelitos (The little pastries), who peddled pastries; and Los Cigarritos (The little cigarettes), who washed cars and "smoked too much." The window factory also had its own siku tropa. In 1958, visiting US jazz musician Woody Herman jammed over "some huayños" with the poncho-clad ensemble at their place of employment, in a clearly staged photo op (*ED*, Sept. 6, 1958). Los Caballeros del Campo represented another urban panpipe tropa from this period. Its name, "The country gentlemen," alluded to the misti sikuri tradition's original association in rural areas with vecinos. The members of Los Caballeros del Campo belonged to the urban working class, however; Girault characterized them as "workers of La Paz" (d'Harcourt and d'Harcourt 1959, 84–87). In 1954, the French ethnologist witnessed the group perform several huayños, including "Copacabana" and

"Viva la Fiesta," as well as a classic Bolivian Incan foxtrot that dates from the years of the Chaco War, "Boquerón Abandonado" (Abandoned [Fort] Boquerón) (d'Harcourt and d'Harcourt 1959, 84–87).

Los Choclos were directly responsible for disseminating the misti sikuri tradition to peers in their line of work in Oruro city. In 1953, 1954, and 1955, the group participated in Oruro's carnival festivities, to honor La Virgen del Socavón (The Virgin of the mineshaft) (Beltrán 1956, 26). While in town, Los Choclos established a close relationship with local shoeshiners and taught some of them how to play the siku. By 1954, Los Choclos' oruneño counterparts had created their own panpipe tropa, Los Hijos del Pagador (Alfredo Solíz of Los Hijos del Pagador, personal communication; various documents from his collection). The name "Los Hijos del Pagador" (The sons of Pagador) referenced the Pagador mountain, an emblem for Oruro analogous to the Illimani's status for La Paz. The similarly named group that shoeshiners founded in Cochabamba city, Los Hijos del Tunari (after the Tunari mountain of Cochabamba), was another non-paceño urban siku tropa established in imitation of Los Choclos (Alberto Orosco of Los Choclos, personal communication).[26] When Víctor Paz Estenssoro hosted Charles de Gaulle in the city of Cochabamba in 1964, Los Hijos del Tunari in all likelihood was the ensemble that entertained the French President with a panpipe tropa version of "La Marseillaise" (see Trigo O'Connor d'Arlach 1999, 157).

Despite the rising number of mestizo siku tropas based in urban La Paz and Bolivia's other major Andean cities in the MNR years, forming ensembles of this type continued to hold little appeal for urban musicians outside of the lower rungs of the working class. Indeed, the siku tropa remained strictly a "cholo" phenomenon in urban centers, seemingly in large part because of the tradition's identification with shoeshiners and newspaper deliverers. Only in the late 1960s, after the MNR had fallen from power, would urban Bolivian musicians of elite and middle-class backgrounds establish their own siku consorts (Chapter 7). The directors of one of the earliest of these groups related to me their fears at the time about being mistaken for shoeshiners. To avoid being identified as such, the group consciously projected a "classy" image, by wearing suits and ties when they arrived at venues (they changed to ponchos at the locale), and after having bathed and applied deodorant (personal communications, anonymous).[27] Using the discourse of modern hygiene to construct middle- and upper-class identities has long been common in the Andean region (Stephenson 1999; Weismantel 2001) and elsewhere. This disturbing example reveals the extent to which criollo-mestizos viewed the urban siku tropa's class associations as undesirable, a state of affairs that, prior to the late 1960s, generally discouraged elite and middle-class musicians from seriously considering the idea of specializing in the siku.

Los Choclos' and Los Cebollitas' extensive musical activities in the MNR era inadvertently prompted a shift in the misti sikuri tradition's associations in La Paz city and other urban centers, from "vecino" (high-class, rural mestizo) to "cholo" (working-class, urban mestizo). It was not the only major change to the original meanings of the misti sikuri style and its main genre that can be traced to Los Choclos and Los Cebollitas, though.

FROM MESTIZO TO INDIGENOUS

Both ensembles were also at the forefront of the misti sikuri tradition's transformation into a folkloric representation of indigenous siku music. Tellingly, the designation "misti sikuris" fell into disuse in the MNR years (although some rural La Paz communities preserved the tradition's original name; see d'Harcourt and d'Harcourt 1959, 87–88). From then on, urban-based Bolivian panpipe groups would simply be called "sikuris" (i.e., dropping the "misti" prefix), or drawing from the Spanish word for the panpipe, zampoñaris or zampoñeros. The upbeat huayños they performed, meanwhile, would be known as sikureadas (also spelled sicureada, or sicuriada), zampoñadas, and sikuris. None of these descriptors underscored the key distinctions between indigenous and mestizo siku tropa styles that misti sikuri artists previously had so carefully maintained in rural La Paz. When taking part in folkloric theater works, Los Cebollitas accentuated their "Andean Indian" image by using the name "Los Sikuris del Altiplano" (The panpipes of the highlands), which had more of an autochthonous ring to it than The Little Onions.

Adding a visual component to these changes, after 1952 Los Cebollitas and Los Choclos adopted a new attire that consisted of matching ponchos, lluchus, and rubber-soled ojota sandals. It was quite a departure from traditional misti sikuri outfits. Perhaps for this reason, Los Choclos and their Oruro spin-off, Los Hijos del Pagador, only gradually set aside their former outfits. Well into the late 1950s, the two groups still were dressing up as Musketeers, Afro-Cuban dancers, Arabs, and other non-Andean characters when they peformed in carnival processions in their home cities (Alfredo Solíz of Los Hijos del Pagador, personal communication; various documents from his personal archive).

Los Choclos and Los Cebollitas' participation in MNR-funded folkloric theater productions played a decisive role in the misti sikuri tradition's reframing as a folkloric rendering of indigenous music making. Of the various cholo-mestizo siku consorts active in La Paz city, Los Choclos and Los Cebollitas were the only ones to obtain stable employment (albeit part time) in these state-sponsored productions. Initially, they most likely presented misti sikuri–style huayños à la Los Cebollitas' "Ese Vaso de Cerveza" when playing the part of Andean indigenous community musicians, and almost no one in the audience would have been the wiser. As time passed, however, Los Choclos and Los Cebollitas learned to perform more representative rural indigenous sikuri music. One place where they collected these tunes was Copacabana, then a pilgrimage site for indigenous musicians from rural La Paz and neighboring provinces in Peru's Puno region (Arturo Gutiérrez, personal communication).

To acquire additional indigenous repertoire, Los Choclos and Los Cebollitas appear to have attended the "autochthonous" music-dance contests that the Municipality organized in the first MNR term. At the 1956 edition of the series, a Kantus de Charazani tropa from the town of Chulina presented "Surimana"—described in the program notes as "the music of a beautiful Quechua epic" (*ED*, Aug. 4, 1956). The next year, Los Choclos interpreted the same piece in José Ibañez Estrada's theater work *Bolivia Indiana*, as Antonio González Bravo observed in his review (*ED*, June 12, 1957).[28] He approved of Los Choclos' repertoire in the sketch, although could not help pointing out that the "misti sikuri" consort they used was inappropriate, because it was tuned solely to unison and octaves and therefore lacked the characteristic parallel fifths and fourths of kantus tropas (*ED*, June 12, 1957).[29] Evidently, Los Choclos (and in all likelihood also Los Cebollitas) played their customary misti sikuri pan-pipes when performing traditional indigenous sikuri genres such as the kantus.

Given the MNR's pro-mestizaje stance, it is ironic that Los Choclos' and Los Cebollitas' involvement in state-funded cultural productions steered them to downplay the mestizo affiliation of the misti sikuri tradition and instead highlight indigenous signifiers. In other, contemporaneous Latin American contexts, local "folk" music-dance traditions more commonly underwent the opposite resignification, to make them better align with the prevailing nationalist ideology. In Mexico, the *mariachi* musical ensemble style largely lost its earlier identification with indigenous peasants, while the *son jarocho* genre's Afro-Mexican roots were conveniently overlooked, at the moment when Mexican artists, producers, and writers constructed these traditions as expressions of the nation's mestizo identity (Jáureguí 2007; González 2010). And in Venezuela, ethnomusicologist Isabel Aretz (a student of Carlos Vega, and classmate of Julia Fortún) rebranded the *son de negros* or *baile de negros* as the *tamunanque*, an ethnically ambiguous appellation that made it easier for her to portray it as the embodiment of Venezuela's tri-ethnic mestizaje of African diasporic, indigenous, and European cultures (Guss 2000, 133–72).

This is not to say that nationalist proponents of mestizaje in Mexico, Venezuela, and other Latin American countries completely excluded non-mestizo (or non-mestizo-associated) music-dance practices from state-sponsored folklore exhibitions. These events often incorporated at least a few indigenous numbers, to underscore the nation's cultural diversity. In Mexico and Venezuela, respectively, the P'urhépecha *danza de los viejitos* (dance of the old men) and Warao *nahanamu* dance have long fulfilled this tokenistic function (Briggs 1996; Hellier-Tinoco 2011). The misti sikuri tradition diverges notably from these two examples (and many other comparable Latin American cases), however, because whereas practitioners of the danza de los viejito and nahanamu associated their traditions with indigenous identity long before the moment of nationalist canonization, the misti sikuri style lacked such meanings in Bolivia until the MNR years.

The Sikuris de Italaque tradition in this respect is more comparable to Mexico's danza de los viejitos and Venezuela's nahanamu genre. If Italaque had been located near urban La Paz, siku groups of the region might have participated regularly in the city's folklore scene throughout the MNR era, rather than largely restricting their appearances there to the Fiestas Julianas contests that the Municipality staged annually from 1953 to 1956, and the Primera Semana Folklórica Boliviana held in 1961. But the journey from Italaque to La Paz city then was arduous, uncomfortable, and exhausting—the near five-hour bus ride today would have easily translated into double the time back then—on unpaved dirt roads that zigzagged through mountainous terrain, with few amenities available along the way. As for the Charazani Valley, home of the Kantus de Charazani tradition (the only other Andean rural indigenous musical ensemble style that enjoyed a comparable level of esteem in paceño criollo-mestizo circles in the MNR years), it is located about forty miles north of Italaque and thus is even more remote in relation to La Paz city.[30]

Los Choclos and Los Cebollitas were far from being inaccessible to MNR officials stationed in urban La Paz. Not only did the musicians live in or close to the city, but many spent a considerable amount of time at Plaza Murillo, to sell newspapers to, or shine the shoes of, state employees working at the Presidential Palace or nearby offices. Whenever Waldo Cerruto of the Bolivian Cinematographic Institute—who along with Chela Urquidi formed part of the "honorary directory" of Los Cebollitas in the mid-1950s (El Arte de los Sindicatos 1956, 14)—needed to contract the services of a panpipe group, all he had to do was walk over to the newspaper stand that a core member of Los Cebollitas operated at Plaza Murillo (Waldo Cerruto, personal communication).

As an additional advantage, Los Cebollitas and Los Choclos were founded *before* the 1952 Revolution, unlike the other mestizo siku tropas active in 1950s La Paz city. Consequently they had little competition to contend with in the early years of the "revolutionary nationalist" period when MNR-funded folkloric theater companies began looking for locally based ensembles who could interpret typical Andean indigenous musical expressions, a situation that allowed the two groups to secure a musical niche in the first MNR term.

By the time the MNR era concluded, Los Choclos and Los Cebollitas had amassed a wealth of experience as "indigenous music" performers in state-sponsored folkloric events geared to criollo-mestizo audiences. It would stand them in good stead for the next phase of the folklore movement, in which the venue Peña Naira would figure prominently. Under the direction of Gilbert Favre of Los Jairas, from 1966 to 1969 the programs of Peña Naira would consistently feature siku tropa music, and most times, the ensemble was Los Choclos. Los Jairas would also collaborate with Los Choclos on recordings, even on some of Los Jairas' most popular singles, such as the Charazani-themed huayño "Agüita de Phutina" (Chapter 7). As for Los Cebollitas, near the onset of the post-MNR years it would split into two groups, one of which would permanently take on the name Los Sikuris del Altiplano (Manuel Cruz, personal communication). Both ensembles, along with Los Choclos, would avidly participate in La Paz's burgeoning peña scene throughout the mid-to-late 1960s. Their sikureadas or zampoñadas were ideal for this setting. Criollo-mestizo audiences tended to find these numbers more aesthetically pleasing than traditional forms of indigenous panpipe tropa music, while at the same time, they classified this mestizo style of siku ensemble music as "indigenous."

The misti sikuri tradition's folklorization in the MNR years occurred in the heyday of the Latin American trío romántico, whose signature repertoire consisted of boleros with lyrics that explored "themes of bittersweet, unrequited, betrayed, or eternal love" (Torres 2002, 161). Considering the non-Bolivian origin of the bolero genre and trío romántico lineup, that these musical expressions attained such popularity in "revolutionary nationalist" Bolivia may seem curious. Beyond question, listening to local cover versions of international bolero hits enabled many Bolivians to temporarily escape the turbulent political, economic, and social changes that they were living through. But escapism was not the sole reason many of them found Bolivian bolero trios so appealing. The sound of crooning lead singers and rich vocal and instrumental harmonies also could conjure up national sentiment, particularly when Bolivian groups played local criollo-mestizo genres in the trío romántico style, a practice they localized even further when one guitarist switched to the charango. As unlikely as it may appear, Bolivia's bolero trio vogue articulated meaningfully with the folklore movement. And it was bolero trio-esque takes on traditional Bolivian criollo-mestizo musical forms—rather than the indigenous-themed music of Los Choclos, Los Cebollitas, or Conjunto 31 de Octubre—that represented Bolivia's most popular variety of "national music" in the MNR period.

THE BOLERO GENRE AND TRÍO ROMÁNTICO IN THE AMERICAS

A moderate-tempo vocal genre in duple meter, the Latin American bolero (unrelated to the triple-meter Spanish bolero) emerged in eastern Cuba in the late 1800s as a regional offshoot of the *contradanza* (also called habanera) and *danzón*, which in turn had developed from the European country dance. The bolero soon made its way to Mexico, first to the Yucatán peninsula, where it was taken up by songwriters Ricardo Palmerín and Augusto "Guty" Cárdenas. Mexico City musicians added the bolero to their repertoire slightly later, in the aftermath of the 1910–1920 Mexican Revolution (Torres 2002, 152–57). Agustín Lara was one of these artists. A pianist and prolific composer, he scored his first bolero hit in 1928 with "Imposible" (Impossible), and would go on to author about five hundred boleros, including the classics "Solamente una Vez" (Only once) and "Mujer" (Woman) (see Wood 2014). He also transformed the genre's rhythmic feel. Dispensing with the tradition's $\frac{2}{4}$ meter and "Cuban-influenced *cinquillo* rhythm" ($\frac{2}{4}$ time: eighth-note-sixteenth-eighth-sixteenth-eighth), Lara's boleros have "a smoother $\frac{4}{4}$ meter that stressed accents on beats one, three and four" (Torres 2002, 158). In the 1930s and 1940s, the powerful broadcasts of Mexico City's Radio XEW—which in the same period played a major role in canonizing the female duo as a mass-mediated folkloric tradition in much of Latin America (Chapter 3)—disseminated the less syncopated, Mexican bolero variant, which became the version most popular internationally (Pedelty 1999, 39–40).

A new way of interpreting the bolero, the trío romántico (an ensemble format and musical style), became fashionable in Latin America in the mid-to-late

1940s, largely because of the influence of Mexican artists, radio stations, and films. Trío Los Panchos represented the gold standard for this ensemble tradition. Founded in 1944 in New York City by Chucho Navarro and Alfredo Gil of Mexico and Hernando Avilés of Puerto Rico, Trío Los Panchos spent the next three years on tour before relocating to the Mexican capital. Their ensemble sound centers on carefully blended, three-part vocal harmonies, made up of three independent lines. Imparting a "modern" sensibility to the music and enriching the texture, the vocal harmonies occasionally incorporate non-triadic notes (i.e., dissonances). Countertenor parts provide additional musical interest. The group's instrumentation, meanwhile, consists of two acoustic guitars (lightly strummed, arpeggiated, and/or plucked), a *requinto* (a tenor guitar, tuned a fourth above the standard or "Spanish" guitar, it is used mainly to render ornamented lines in the introductions and bridge sections), and percussion instruments of Cuban origin or association (e.g., maracas, *timbales, bongós*). Trío Los Panchos' international fame was much enhanced by their appearances in Mexican films, which often were named after the boleros they sang in these productions. Associated with cosmopolitan sophistication and romantic love, Trío Los Panchos spawned imitators in every Latin American country, and many other sites around the world (see Dueñas 1993; Torres 2002, 158–71; Ortíz 2004).

TRÍO LOS PANCHOS IN BOLIVIA!

In the year that Trío Los Panchos debuted in New York (1944), Las Kantutas briefly disbanded, so Irma Vásquez could pursue a career as a solo vocalist in La Paz (Chapter 3). She focused on internationally fashionable Latin American ballad forms, and accordingly her repertoire featured the bolero (personal collection of Irma Vásquez de Ronda). Within a few years of Vásquez's brief time away from Las Kantutas, trío romántico renderings of the bolero had become part of La Paz's music scene. The Oruro-born Shaw Boutier brothers, Raúl, Alex, and Víctor, were early exponents of this trend. By the late 1940s, Víctor Shaw was singing at paceño nightspots with his friends Enrique Larrea and Mario Barrios in Trío Shaw-Larrea-Barrios, who sometimes wore Mexican *sombreros* at their gigs (*ED*, July 4 and July 13, 1947). Alex Shaw created another popular La Paz group of this type, Trío Los Indios (Alex Shaw, personal communication). As for Raúl Shaw, who early into his bolerista trajectory was being characterized by La Paz critics as "the tenor of the Americas" (*ED*, June 15, 1945; Sept. 3, 1946; July 4, 1947), he sang in various tríos románticos in the 1940s. He formed one of them, Trío Los Altiplánicos (The highlanders), with Jorge Sáenz (the brother of Las Kantutas' Alicia Sáenz) and Cacho Córdoba (a future member of Conjunto 31 de Octubre). In 1946, Raúl Shaw embarked on his first international tour as a performing musician, when Trío Los Altiplánicos played at various locales in Peru, Ecuador, and Colombia (Shaw 2007, 45). After they returned to La Paz, Raúl Shaw teamed up with Jorge and Armando Valdéz in Trío Panamérica Antawara (Pan-American sunset trio), a cover band that concentrated on the music of Trío Los Panchos (Raúl Shaw, personal communication).

About six months before the 1952 revolution, paceños had the chance to see and hear the real Trío Los Panchos, because the group's tour of South America included a stopover of a few weeks in La Paz (*ED*, Oct. 1 and 15, 1951). Their concerts not surprisingly drew large crowds and frenzied receptions. To coincide with the ensemble's visit, a consortium of La Paz movie theaters, the Empresa Boliviana de Cines, prepared a "Grand Competition for Melodic Trios in the Style of Los Panchos" (*ED*, Oct. 4, 1951). Raúl Shaw participated in the contest with Trío Panamerica Antawara (*ED*, Oct. 14, 1951), not realizing how it would impact his life. His mellifluous vocals, and ample experience performing the repertoire of Trío Los Panchos, caught the attention of Navarro and Gil, who asked Shaw to join their ensemble in replacement of Avilés, with whom they were feuding. Of course Shaw could not turn down this amazing offer. There was one unusual condition. Navarro and Gil asked him to change at least one of his European-sounding last names, because their foreign ring clashed with the Mexican image of Trío Los Panchos. Borrowing Navarro's maternal surname, Raúl Shaw Boutier adopted the artistic name "Raúl Shaw Moreno," and as such, took on the role of lead tenor in Trío Los Panchos in November 1951 (Raúl Shaw, personal communication).

This dream gig lasted only until September 1952 (when Julito Rodríguez of Puerto Rico took the place of Raúl Shaw), apparently because Shaw's powerful singing overshadowed that of his bandmates, who preferred a more seamless balance of voices (Ortíz 2004, 158–59, 165–66; Fernández Coca 2005, 50). In Shaw's ten-month stay in Trío Los Panchos, they toured Argentina, Ecuador, Venezuela, Peru, and Brazil, and recorded thirty-one tracks, including Shaw's composition "Lágrimas de Amor" (Tears of love), and other hits such as Agustín Lara's "Solamente una Vez," Consuelo Velázquez's "Bésame Mucho" (Give me many kisses), and Alberto Domínguez's "Perfidia" (Treachery) (Ortíz 2004, 162–67, 380–81; Fernández 2005, 49–54).

For the first time, Bolivia had produced an internationally recognized superstar musician. While Alberto Ruiz Lavadenz, Gilberto Rojas, Las Kantutas, and other Bolivian artists or musical acts had spent extended periods outside of the country in the pre-1952 era, none of them could be accurately characterized as luminaries on the world stage. Without a doubt, Raúl Shaw's international visibility in his time in Trío Los Panchos far exceeded that of any other Bolivian musician up to this point. In the remainder of the decade, Shaw would add to his pedigree through his activities with Los Peregrinos, and represent one of the primary models for Bolivian criollo-mestizo popular musicians as well as folkloric artists.

RAÚL SHAW MORENO AND LOS PEREGRINOS

After leaving Trío Los Panchos in late 1952, Shaw relocated to Santiago, Chile, where he formed Trío Los Peregrinos (The wanderers), with Chilean artists Fernando

Rossi and Pepe González. The group recorded Shaw's "Magaly" and other boleros for ODEON-Chile the next year, and also accompanied Chilean singer Luis "Lucho" Gatica on six albums. Gatica, who in a few years would become one of Latin America's most admired bolero performers (see Party 2012), netted his earliest hits in 1953 with "Contigo en la Distancia" (With you from afar), and "Sinceridad" (Sincerity); Trío Los Peregrinos supplied the vocal harmonies and stringed accompaniment on both selections (González Rodríguez, Ohlsen, and Rolle 2009, 531).

Shaw brought Trío Los Peregrinos to La Paz city soon after ODEON released these recordings. The group's local debut took place at a movie theater, Cine Ebro, alongside a screening of the Mexican romantic film "Peregrina." The film's title referenced a well-known bolero by Ricardo Palmerín, and conveniently was also almost identical to the name of Shaw's ensemble. In newspaper advertisements for Trío Los Peregrinos' shows at Cine Ebro, the musicians appear in elegant tuxedos and bowties, the customary attire for bolero trios. Curiously, given that two of the band members were Chilean, the ad describes the group as "the youthful trio who with Raúl Shaw have elevated the name of the country" (ED, May 19 and June 2, 1953).

Rossi and González returned to Chile the next year, prompting Raúl Shaw to join forces with his brother Alex's group, Trío Los Indios (Shaw 2007, 217). Recently, Trío Los Indios had been a fixture at confiterías (establishments serving coffee, tea, and sweets), hotels, and other privately owned La Paz venues (e.g., ED, May, 31, 1953; Apr. 27, 1954). The group even had played at MNR government-sponsored folklore festivals, such as 1953's Concurso de Arte Nativo (Chapter 4). Illustrating the bolero genre and trío romántico style's surging popularity in La Paz city, in 1954 Trío Los Indios was one of six bolero trios that performed at an Open Air Theater event organized by the Subsecretary of Press, Information, and Culture (the other groups were: Trío Azul, Trío Libertad, Trío Tradicional, Ritmo Tropical, and Ritmo y Melodia). Urquidi's Academia de Danzas, and Los Cebollitas, also took part, along with various other acts (ED, Mar. 27, 1954).

With the addition of Raúl Shaw, the ensemble, called Raúl Shaw Moreno y Trío Los Indios, played at a similar range of locales in La Paz as Alex's former group had done, from the Open Air Theater to the intimate Confitería Los Manzanos (e.g., ED, Aug. 5 and Oct. 10, 1954). The group's format, meanwhile, duplicated that of Lucho Gatica's collaborations with Trío Los Peregrinos, that is, one lead singer with an accompanying vocal and instrumental trio. This expanded trío romántico lineup, an international trend in the 1950s, placed far more emphasis on the first voice—compared to the style of Trío Los Panchos—and for this reason represented an ideal platform for Raúl Shaw's powerful singing.

In late 1954, Raúl Shaw traveled to Chile with Trío Los Indios, which he rebranded as Los Peregrinos, to capitalize on the reputation that the original Trío Los Peregrinos enjoyed in the Chilean music scene (ED, Dec. 22, 1954). Logically, they dropped the "Trío" prefix, as the group, now known as Raúl Shaw Moreno y Los Peregrinos, had five members: Raúl Shaw (first voice), Hugo Encinas (second voice and guitar), Mario Barrios (third voice and first guitar), Alex Shaw (countertenor voice and guitar), and

Lucho Otero (second guitar or charango).[31] The ensemble recorded for ODEON-Chile and, as would be expected, most of the tracks were boleros. Several became major hits in Chile and elsewhere in the Americas, most of all "Cuando Tú Me Quieras" (When you will love me). Co-authored by Raúl Shaw and Mario Barrios, it reached the number-one spot on Chile's music single charts in 1955 (González Rodríguez, Ohlsen, and Rolle 2009, 531–32).

"Cuando Tú Me Quieras" is the first selection on Raúl Shaw Moreno y Los Peregrinos' debut album, *Boleros-Música del Altiplano* (LDC-3013). Released in 1955 under the ODEON-Chile label, the LP features boleros on the "A" side, while the other half of the album presents folkloric repertoire mainly, but not exclusively, of altiplano or highland association. The "B" side includes a huayño-bailecito medley ("Acuarela Boliviana"; Bolivian watercolors), two huayños ("Naranjitay" [My dear orange], "Rie Corazón" [Laugh, my heart]), and an Argentine carnavalito ("El Humahuaqueño"),[32] all of which fit the theme of "music of the highlands." Also appearing on this part of the album, though, is a música oriental track, the *polca beniana* "Palmeras" (Palm trees).

Shaw and his band recorded Gilbero Rojas's arrangement of "Palmeras," which is largely based on a traditional polca tune from Beni (Rojas Foppiano 1991, 91). Unrelated to the European polka, the polca beniana genre exhibits the sesquiáltera hemiola, a characteristic it shares with the Paraguayan polca. "Palmeras" represented a major hit for Raúl Shaw Moreno y Los Peregrinos (Raúl Shaw, personal communication), and in anticipation of this reception, it opens the B side of *Boleros-Música del Altiplano*. The track "Naranjitay," a traditional huayño credited here to Tito Véliz, also figured among the LP's most popular selections (Raúl Shaw, personal communication).

When interpreting Bolivian criollo-mestizo genres on this album, Raúl Shaw Moreno y Los Peregrinos' singing style largely adheres to their standard approach on boleros. Shaw's solo tenor, full of vibrato on long notes, alternates with the vocals of Los Peregrinos, who often repeat Shaw's previous phrase in three- or four-part harmony. The instrumentalists' practices vary, though, on the tunes set in Andean genres (i.e., huayño, bailecito, carnavalito), as the band's usual second guitarist, Lucho Otero, changes over to the charango. His technique on the instrument mainly consists of medium-tempo strums and is somewhat rudimentary—compared to the virtuosic rasgueos of Los Sumac Huaynas' Chocni López (briefly discussed in Chapter 3)—apparently because Otero had only recently begun to devote time to mastering the charango. In any case, by incorporating this Andean stringed instrument into their lineup, Raúl Shaw Moreno y Los Peregrinos followed in the path of La Paz estudiantinas of earlier decades such as Lira Incaica (Chapter 3). The charango's tessitura, meanwhile, closely approximated that of the requinto that Trío Los Panchos had instituted as a core component of the trío romántico.

Using bolero-trio-style vocals to interpret non-Caribbean genres was not an innovation of Raúl Shaw Moreno y Los Peregrinos. In Shaw's brief time with Trío Los Panchos, the acclaimed group had recorded Peruvian *valse criollos* (criollo waltzes), and Mexico's *son huasteco* and *ranchera* genres (Ortíz 2004, 380–81). From the 1940s onward, in part to differentiate themselves from their competitors, many Latin American bolero acts rounded out their repertoire with bolerista versions of the "national" genres of their respective countries, such as the Argentine tango, Ecuadorian *pasillo*, Chilean *tonada*, and Brazilian *samba-canção* (see Araujo 1999; González Rodríguez, Ohlsen, and Rolle 2009, 515–16, 530, 534; Wong 2012, 87, 106). This practice juxtaposed musical signifiers of "modernity" and "tradition," because in Latin America the bolero genre and trío romántico format then generally were identified with "modernity" (Pedelty 1999), and "national" genres with "tradition." In Bolivia, attaching "modern" meanings to the bolero genre and trío romántico format adhered to a long-standing local predilection, that of equating international trends in the sphere of popular music with modernity or sophistication.

For Raúl Shaw, recording "national" genres enabled him to deflect a persistent accusation that many Bolivians leveled against him, that he had denied or downplayed his national identity while in Trío Los Panchos. Early into his post–Trío Los Panchos career, around the time he was performing at Cine Ebro with the "first" Trío Los Peregrinos in 1953, MNR functionaries summoned Shaw to the office of the Subsecretary of Press, Information and Culture, so that he could respond to these allegations (*ED*, June 13, 1953). Seen in this light, Shaw's subsequent addition of "national" numbers to his repertoire might have been motivated by his need to assuage the anger of nationalist Bolivians who questioned his patriotism.[33]

By mid-1955, not long after the release of their ODEON-Chile records, Shaw and his band were back in La Paz. MNR agencies had scaled down their folklore spectacles (e.g., the SPIC discontinued the Open Air Theater series; Chapter 4), but the group had the option of performing at upscale confiterías and boîtes. At Confitería Los Manzanos and Boîte-Grill Maracaibo, they often alternated sets with orquestas de jazz, whose signature mambos made a nice contrast to boleros best suited for slow dancing. Shaw and Los Peregrinos also rotated with orquestas típicas, the designation used in this period for tango bands (rather than estudiantinas, as had been the case in prior decades). Non-Bolivian genres constituted the mainstay at confiterías and boîtes, but Shaw's group nonetheless pulled out their national folkloric repertoire. An advertisement for Confitería Los Manzanos announced that Raúl Shaw Moreno y Los Peregrinos would perform "the songs of Bolivia and the Americas in one embrace" (*ED*, July 29, 1955), while Boîte-Grill Maracaibo promoted them as a "folkloric group" who would wow the audience with "the new huayño-sikuri rhythm" (*ED*, Aug. 4, 1955), by which the person who wrote the flyer most likely meant the sikuris genre (also known as zampoñada, sikureada, and sicureada) that Los Choclos and Los Cebollitas performed.

It was only through a bolero group's highly stylized renderings that paceños might occasionally hear a sikuri tune at a boîte or confitería in the MNR years. These locales were off limits to mestizo and indigenous panpipe tropas, as well as to other indigenous-associated musical traditions, just as they had been before the 1952 Revolution. This enduring segregationism reveals the limits of the MNR regime's dismantling of the discriminatory tactics that elite-oriented venues traditionally practiced.[34]

In November 1955, Raúl Shaw Moreno y Los Peregrinos offered their last performance in Bolivia before going on a tour that would take them all around Latin America. The anticipated farewell concert took place at the familiar Boîte-Grill Maracaibo and was broadcast on Radio Altiplano (*ED*, Nov. 12, 1955). The musicians left soon afterwards for Santiago. While the group was in the Chilean capital, their recordings outsold those of homegrown bolero star Lucho Gatica, according to a local newspaper report that also described how the Bolivian artists incited crazed enthusiasm among their Chilean fans, to such a degree that it seems to have resembled Elvis mania in the United States:

> In every place where they perform there is screaming, fainting, fights, basically the whole range of a scandal . . . they have broken all the records for LP sales . . . Raúl Shaw now has had to contract the services of a professional bodyguard and four well-built male secretaries, under the pretext that their job is to carry the guitars, to protect him from feminine aggressions. (Chilean newspaper article, quoted in *ED*, Feb. 27, 1956)

Concerts and recording sessions followed in Peru, Argentina, and Brazil, before the group finally ended up in Mexico, where they remained from 1958 until disbanding around 1960. The Bolivian press eagerly chronicled the international adventures of Raúl Shaw Moreno y Los Peregrinos, most of all their time in Mexico City (e.g., *ED*, June 29, Aug. 9, Oct. 26, and Oct. 27, 1958). The Latin American bolerista dream was to triumph in the Mexican capital, as the highest concentration of bolero figures lived there. Gatica, for one, had relocated to Mexico City in 1955 and flourished as an artist (González Rodríguez, Ohlsen, and Rolle 2009, 514–17; Party 2012). In their new base of operation, Shaw and his band performed on Radio WEW, offered shows at the prestigious Astoria night club and Iris theater (*ED*, Oct. 26, 1958), and snagged cameo roles in the films *Mi Mujer Necesita Marido* (My wife needs a husband) and *Jazz* (*ED*, Oct. 27, 1958). Of the two movies, *Mi Mujer Necesita Marido* gave the most exposure to Raúl Shaw Moreno y Los Peregrinos, because it featured their bolero hit "Cuando Tú Me Quieras."

The perfectly coiffed, clean-cut looks of Raúl Shaw, always seen in a suit and tie or tuxedo when he was on stage, by then had attracted a legion of female admirers in Bolivia, leading some to join the all-female fan club that Radio Altiplano created in time for the first La Paz screening of *Mi Mujer Necesita Marido* (*ED*, Apr. 5, 1960). With his then-modern sound, Raúl Shaw was without question the favorite Bolivian musician among criollo-mestizo audiences. His appeal could rival even that of bolerista heartthrobs from abroad, as revealed by Shaw's showing in Radio Altiplano's call-in program "Yo Soy el Público y Yo Soy el Juez de la Música Popular" (I am the public and I am the popular music judge; *ED*, July 1, 1958). Despite facing stiff competition from Chile's Lucho Gatica, Ecuador's Julio Jaramillo, and Mexico's

Miguel Aceves Mejía, nonetheless Shaw earned first place in the contest (*ED*, July 1, 1958).

Bolivian access to imported records was at its highest point so far, which generally steered paceños to prefer foreign artist's over Bolivian ones and thus made Raúl Shaw's level of local popularity truly extraordinary. The MNR government had recently made foreign records more affordable to Bolivian consumers, by eliminating record sale taxes in mid-1958 (see *ED*, Nov. 9, 1962). This piece of so-called free trade legislation, which predictably favored US companies, took effect at a critical moment in the US recording industry's expansion into Latin American markets. As historian Eric Zolov explains in his analysis of the Mexican case (1999, 20–26), record sales represented a key revenue source for US technology corporations for the first time in the mid-to-late 1950s. Similarly to what Zolov documents for Mexico City, La Paz was rapidly inundated with foreign-made recordings, overtaking the limited output of Discos Méndez.

The latest offerings of US vocalists such as Elvis Presley and Nat King Cole; US-promoted "Latin" dance bands, including Xavier Cugat's orchestra; and bolero superstars from many Latin American countries suddenly were available to Bolivian consumers as never before. This massive influx of imported records prompted many paceños to construct "modern" social identities through their consumption of, and professed cultural affinity with, internationally trendy musical styles. In a creative manifestation of this development, La Paz criollo-mestizo youths began to hold neighborhood parties called *Fiestas de Animación* at which the hosts and their guests improvised percussion parts to accompany their favorite albums (various personal communications).

The proliferation of foreign recordings in the Bolivian marketplace took place when MNR government sponsorship of folklore festivals and related activities had been severely curtailed to satisfy the IMF's austerity demands (Chapter 4). US–approved economic policies therefore brought the MNR into conflict with the party's populist rhetoric and nation-building project (see Dunkerley 1984, 83–84). It also stunted the local recording industry's development, lessening the chance that Bolivian entrepreneurs would try to create and maintain a profitable countrywide market for mass-mediated versions of locally distinctive, traditional musical styles. Yet because the MNR's laissez-faire policies toward imported records also made the international releases of Raúl Shaw Moreno y Los Peregrinos readily available at home, the group's commercial successes abroad evoked national pride for Bolivians who were well aware of their country's lack of presence on the world stage. In La Paz newspaper columns, for example, writers thanked the traveled bolero stars for serving as "great artistic ambassadors" (*ED*, Feb. 27, 1956), being "one of the few of our compatriots who has acquired international prestige" (*ED*, June 29, 1958), and even personifying "high patriotic spirit" (*ED*, Oct. 26, 1958).

That Raúl Shaw Moreno y Los Peregrinos' recordings consistently feature Bolivian genres also explains why local audiences attached national meanings to the ensemble's international activities. This type of repertoire is the focus of one of the group's most popular LPs from this period, the English-titled *Music of Bolivia* (Capitol T-10088), which Capitol Records released in 1957 (*ED*, Oct. 27, 1957). Shaw and his band reprised five compositions that they previously had taped for ODEON, including the polca "Palmeras," and huayño "Naranjitay." "Pollerita" (Layered skirt) represents another standout track on *Music of Bolivia*. A light-hearted huayño composed by Raúl Shaw, "Pollerita" features a stanza in Quechua, and at various points in the lyrics, the text mentions the charango. According to Bolivian bolerista Víctor Córdova of Trío Los Danubios (founded in 1959), Raúl Shaw Moreno y Los Peregrinos' recording of "Pollerita" was so popular in Bolivia that it "caused a frenzy" (Víctor Córdova, personal communication).

For the front cover of *Music of Bolivia*, Capitol Records placed a touristic photograph, credited to Pan-American World Airways, in which four women wear polleras, bowler hats, aguayo shawls, and other attire that Bolivian market vendors or cholas traditionally don. The label's marketing personnel must have thought that this "typical" Andean image—combined with the album's English title and the many references to traditional Andean culture that can be seen on the back cover—would maximize sales of the recording outside of Bolivia, among the kind of consumer who in later decades would be drawn to "world music" releases. Capitol Records' marketing strategy with the 1957 LP *Music of Bolivia* thus resembles that of Folkways with the 1959 album *Folk Songs and Dances of Bolivia* (which, as explained previously in this chapter, features the music of criollo-mestizo artists such as Las Kantutas and Conjunto 31 de Octubre).[35]

Although no contemporaneous Bolivian bolero group rivaled the popularity of Raúl Shaw Moreno y Los Peregrinos, several local ensembles took after them stylistically and counted a large number of devoted fans. Most of these groups similarly consisted of a lead singer and backing vocal trio, and interspersed boleros with Bolivian criollo-mestizo genres. Raúl Shaw's former band, Trío Panamérica Antawara, reborn in the late 1950s as Jorge Valdéz y Trío Panamérica, released a 1959 album that, in addition to boleros, Cuban *guarachas*, and other Caribbean genres, includes a cueca, a carnaval, and two huayños (*ED*, July 6, 1959). Arturo Sobénes y Los Cambas dedicated entire LPs to Bolivian folkloric repertoire, as did Quique Mercado y Los Pregoneros, and other bolero acts from this period (*ED*, May 12, 1959; June 23, 1960).

The title of Arturo Sobénes y Los Cambas' 1959 album, *Bolivia y Su Música* (Bolivia and its music), is reminiscent of Raúl Shaw Moreno y Los Peregrinos' *Music of Bolivia*. Another similarity between these releases is that the cover images do not reflect the musical content. On *Bolivia y Su Música*, a photograph of a diablada dancer appears on the front of the album, even though the genre is absent from the recording. As a São Paulo–based label produced the album, the artwork probably reflects the company's opinion that the diablada ranked among the few Bolivian genres that Brazil's record-buying public might have heard of. This choice of image also reflects the diablada tradition's rising prominence, nationally and internationally, among Bolivian folkloric expressions (Chapter 4).

The charanguista that performs on Arturo Sobénes y Los Cambas' *Bolivia y Su Música*, Lucho Otero, represents another commonality between this album and

Raúl Shaw Moreno y Los Peregrinos' earlier release *Music of Bolivia*. Despite his far-from-stellar charango skills, Otero, who recently had returned to Bolivia and joined Sobénes's ensemble, was the country's best-known charango performer at the time, as a result of his association with Raúl Shaw's band. Otero's charango playing on the recordings of Arturo Sobénes y Los Cambas, and especially on the releases of Raúl Shaw Moreno y Los Peregrinos, motivated a number of Bolivian bolero guitarists to try their hand at playing the charango and integrating it into the format of their ensembles.

Jaime Lafuente was among the first to emulate this aspect of the performance practices of Raúl Shaw Moreno y Los Peregrinos (Jaime Lafuente, personal communication). Primarily a guitarist, around 1956 he founded the bolero group Los Dandys with three neighborhood friends: Arturo Gutiérrez (the lead singer; he performed as "Tito Morlán"), Hugo Solares, and Zenon Ibañez. Eleven years later, Los Dandys would become Los Laickas (Aymara for "The sorcerors"), one of the earliest La Paz bands to adopt the Andean conjunto format in direct imitation of Los Jairas (Chapter 7). In their bolerista days, when the band's name purposefully evoked the image of an elegant "dandy," their musical repertoire was very similar to that of Raúl Shaw Moreno y Los Peregrinos (Jaime Lafuente, personal communication). At one point, Los Dandys had a regular gig at a former haunt of their more famous countrymen, Confitería Los Manzanos. In a 1960 newspaper ad for the exclusive locale, Los Dandys is described as "four voices, three guitars, and one charango" (*ED*, Jan. 16, 1960).[36]

As a reflection of growing paceño interest in the charango, by the late 1950s advertisements for method books began to appear in the city's major newspapers, perhaps for the first time (e.g., *ED*, Dec. 4, 1958; *La Nación*, Jan. 7, 1960). Charango soloists also started to become more common in urban La Paz. Some came from other parts of the country, such as Chuquisaca's Mauro Núñez (*ED*, July 18, 1957), and Potosí's Modesto Gómez (personal communication; *ED*, Jan. 16, 1959) and Toribio Oros Alba (*La Nación*, Jan. 7, 1960).[37] To be sure, charango players long had formed part of the paceño music scene (though few charango soloists). However, Bolivian bolero groups that included a charanguista unquestionably raised the instrument's standing as a marker of national identity, a crucial step in the charango's eventual canonization as Bolivia's most representative type of stringed instrument.

On one occasion, Raúl Shaw and his band made use of a kena player on a recording. The kena soloist, who was probably an Argentine studio musician, executes pentatonic passages on the track "Huayra Huayra" (Quechua for "Powerful wind"). Raúl Shaw composed this indigenista-themed selection, which shifts back and forth between a yaraví and huayño. Needless to say, "Huayra Huayra" has almost nothing in common on a musical level with Andean tropa music, unlike, say, Conjunto 31 de Octubre's "Sicuris," which at least follows the melodic conventions of Andean panpipe genres.

"Huayra Huayra" appears to represent the sole number in the repertoire of Raúl Shaw Moreno y Los Peregrinos that is unambiguously indigenista. The group's minimal interest in performing this type of music differentiated them from more overtly folkloric acts such as Conjunto 31 de Octubre, Los Choclos, and Los Cebollitas. Bolivian listeners consequently would not have associated Raúl Shaw Moreno y Los Peregrinos' "national numbers" with Andean indigenous culture. In elite and middle-class Bolivian circles, where many expressed dismay over the MNR's alliance with the Andean rural indigenous population (Chapter 4), the music of Raúl Shaw's ensemble could thus elicit national sentiment without necessarily calling to mind the traditions of highland indigenous people.

Perhaps Shaw and his accompanists believed that if they had devoted a large portion of their sets to Andean indigenous-themed numbers, it would have conflicted too starkly with their modern or cosmopolitan artistic image. As previously noted, Raúl Shaw Moreno y Los Peregrinos musically juxtaposed signifiers of "tradition" and "modernity," but of the two, they most emphasized the second. In light of the MNR leadership's discourses about modernization and nationalism, the group's boleroesque renderings of local genres therefore could have been seen by Bolivians as a musical realization of the ruling party's nationalist vision. Yet although the Siles Zuaso administration's post-1958 taxation policies on imported records fostered (unintentionally) the blossoming of Bolivia's bolero trio vogue, it is unlikely that many people identified the band's musical output with the MNR, because the regime's officials did not try to establish this connection. In sum, this urbane form of Bolivian national music enjoyed wide popularity in criollo-mestizo society in the "revolutionary nationalist" period, not in spite of its cosmopolitan aura, but because of it.

THE DECLINE AND LEGACY OF BOLIVIA'S BOLERO TRIO BOOM

Bolivia's bolero trio boom began to fade in the early 1960s. By then, Raúl Shaw Moreno y Los Peregrinos had ceased to exist as a musical act.[38] No other Bolivian bolero ensemble would come close to reaching their renown, either at home or abroad. The moment of glory for the trío romántico format had passed, in much of Latin America (see Torres 2002, 167). The expansion of Bolivia's recording industry played an important part in the declining number of local bolero artists. In 1962, the MNR government reinstituted taxes on sales of imported records (*ED*, Nov. 9, 1962), to stimulate Bolivian capitalist entrepreneurship, one of the MNR's goals all along. Unlike in the 1950s, though, protectionist Bolivian state policies now had US backing. In the wake of the Bay of Pigs fiasco and Cuban missile crisis, the Kennedy administration had begun to support local capitalist development initiatives in Latin America such as Import Substitution Industrialization, as a way of preventing the spread of socialism (Lehman 1999). In this more protectionist economic climate, new Bolivian record labels emerged that focused on exploiting the national market, by marketing local genres to the record-buying public.

This capitalist strategy helped to usher in the Bolivian folklore boom, because it persuaded a number of criollo-mestizo musicians to concentrate on "national" expressions. Many Bolivian boleristas gradually pushed their favorite ballad form aside and reinvented themselves as fully committed folklore artists (Chapter 6). At first glance, this might seem like an abrupt change, but as this chapter has shown, by the late 1950s Bolivian bolero bands normally reserved a place in their repertoire for local criollo-mestizo genres such as the huayño and taquirari, a practice that Raúl Shaw Moreno y Los Peregrinos played a major role in popularizing. The trademark vocal style of the trío romántico (three- or four-part harmonies with occasional countertenor lines, soloists with wide vibrato), meanwhile, would be used from this period onward by many of Bolivia's most popular criollo-mestizo folkloric musicians, with little questioning of its national origins.

The future lead singer of Los Jairas, Edgar "Yayo" Joffré, figures among the cohort of paceño musicians who got their start as boleristas. In 1964, two years before he would team up with Ernesto Cavour, Gilbert Favre, and Julio Godoy in Los Jairas, Joffré and his bolero band Cuarteto de Oro (Golden quartet) collaborated with Cavour on a Bolivian folkloric-themed album. Around the same time, Hery Cortéz, who would become a founding member of the "autochthonous" folklore act Los Rhupay in 1968 (Chapter 7), played guitar and sang harmony in another La Paz quartet known mainly for its boleros, Elsita Navarro y Los Melódicos (Hery Cortéz, personal communication). And as previously noted, the Andean conjunto Los Laickas drew most of its members from the bolero group Los Dandys. Los Laickas' first full-length album (released in 1968) includes one composition that dates from their bolerista period, Raúl Shaw's yaraví-huayño "Huayra Huayra" (Discolandia-Lyra 13065). For a number of criollo-mestizo musicians who emerged on the scene in the MNR period and would later become known primarily as national folklore interpreters, performing in a bolero group unexpectedly served as a foundational experience for their long-term musical careers.

THE END OF THE MNR ERA

Seven weeks into his third presidency, Paz Estenssoro caught a show by the Ballet Folklórico Oficial at the Municipal Theater (*ED*, Sept. 22, 1964). The blatantly partisan *Los Tres Movimientos* ("Oración y Esperanza," "Revolución," and "Triunfo") formed part of the September 1964 program, along with the production *El Minero* (as noted in Chapter 4). Given that *Los Tres Movimientos* looked back to the euphoric early days of the post-1952 era, while *El Minero* recalled the first Paz Estenssoro regime's most admired action—its expropriation of the "Big Three" tin mining companies—the concert must have provided the President with a welcome, nostalgic distraction from his duties as head of state. It also surely reminded him, though, of the magnitude to which his popularity and that of the movimientista party had eroded since the early 1950s.

In the August 1964 presidential election, Paz Estenssoro had won 97.9% of the popular vote. This overwhelming victory did not accurately reflect how most Bolivians viewed him, however. The election, for one, was riddled with fraud (Whitehead 2003,

50). Second, much of the citizenry, and principal opposition figures, had abstained, as a vote of no confidence in the regime's oversight of the electoral process (Field 2014, 152). The MNR chief had faced intense animosity in his campaign for a constitutionally unsound third term, and not only from the right-wing Falange Socialista Boliviana. Paz Estenssoro's recently concluded second administration (1960–1964) had greatly angered many Bolivians of leftist sympathies—including movimientista-affiliated groups such as La Juventud del MNR (Youths of the MNR). The government's escalating persecution of communist and labor-union leaders, severance of its relations with Cuba, and entrance into the US-led Alliance for Progress had so incensed those on the left that many joined forces with the right, in an "awkward embrace" of former political enemies (Field 2014, 131). Even Paz Estenssoro's former Vice Presidents, Hernán Siles Zuaso and Juan Lechín, openly plotted against his candidacy in the 1964 election (Dunkerley 1984, 117–18).

The shocking level of violence that the MNR regimes had inflicted on the opposition in the previous twelve years also motivated the public's antagonism toward the party (the Andean indigenous sector, which largely remained allied with the MNR, represents the main exception to this trend). By the early 1960s, MNR officials had dispatched a multitude of political prisoners to concentration camps, where they often suffered brutal torture. The evil mastermind behind this state-sanctioned violence was the director of the Control Político (Political police, or Secret police), Claudio San Román, who borrowed interrogation methods from the Nazis (Field 2014, 167–168, 189).

Anti-government protests erupted regularly in La Paz and elsewhere in Bolivia in the three months following the August 1964 election (Mitchell 1977, 96; Lehman 1999, 142; Field 2014, 159–188). In response, the Paz Estenssoro administration deployed "constant police action to keep control" (Dunkerley 1984, 118), and granted San Román's feared Control Político carte blanche to deal with the situation (Fields 2014, 167). For Vice President General René Barrientos and fellow conspirator General Alfredo Ovando, the chaotic political climate indicated that it was a propitious moment for them to launch a coup d'état, which they successfully executed in November 1964. The MNR era thus abruptly ended, and a long period of military-led governments was just beginning for Bolivia. Rather than portraying the new political order as a radical break from the years of MNR rule, however, Co-Presidents Barrientos and Ovando promised to "restore the Revolution." They accordingly made recourse to the populist tactics of the deposed movimientistas, including those involving traditional music-dance expressions.

NOTES

1. Of the artists and ensembles this chapter discusses, only Raúl Shaw has been written about in more than a few pages. In 2007, his brother, Víctor Shaw Boutier, authored a biography on the singer's career (Shaw 2007). Featuring many photographs, summaries of newspaper clippings, and lists of recordings, it is geared to fans rather than scholars.

2. Initially, Argentine folklore artists and fans also had used the descriptor "bombo indio" for this type of drum, although "bombo legüero" became the favored designation as the 1950s advanced (Pérez Bugallo 1993, 39). The word "legüero" can be translated as "league." It refers here to the instrument's capability of being heard from a long distance.

3. When Radio Illimani broadcast the music of Conjunto 31 de Octubre, most listeners probably would not have been able to tell that Esteban del Río played a Western transverse flute rather than a kena, because local radios generally had low-quality speakers.

4. In May 1954, an unidentified La Paz ensemble comprising a flutist, a charanguista, five guitarists, and a maraca player interpreted a "Peruvian Dance" for French ethnologist Louis Girault (d'Harcourt and d'Harcourt 1959, 94–95). This instrumentation suggests that the group might have been an early version of Conjunto 31 de Octubre.

5. The film *Vuelve Sebastiana* earned the top honor in the "ethnographic-folkloric" category at 1956's II Festival Internacional de Cine Documental y Experimental del S.O.D.R.E. (II International Festival of Documentary and Experimental Film), which took place in Montevideo, Uruguay (SODRE 1956, 68, 189). It was the first time that a Bolivian film won an award at a prestigious international competition (Susz 1997, 10, 27). Besides Los Hermanos Aramayo Martínez, the soundtrack of *Vuelve Sebastiana* features the music of charango player K'auquita García and guitarist Jorge Eduardo.

6. During Arsenio Aguirre's time in Conjunto 31 de Octubre, the group briefly served as the house band for La Paz station Radio Armonia. For this reason, they sometimes performed as "Conjunto Folklórico Armonia" (e.g., *ED*, July 10 and Sept. 12, 1954).

7. The sound quality is poor on Conjunto 31 de Octubre's recording of "Sicuris," which makes it difficult to hear the accompanying guitar, charango, and bombo legüero parts.

8. Conjunto 31 de Octubre's recording of "Kullaguas" appears on a Discos Méndez EP; the B side contains "Morenada" (Gobierno Municipal de la Ciudad de La Paz Oficialia Mayor de Cultura 1993, 67). The group's renditions of "Llamerada" and "Hirpastay," meanwhile, can be found on the 1959 Folkways LP *Songs and Dances of Bolivia*. As Chapter 2 mentions, Filarmónica 1° de Mayo played an estudiantina arrangement of "Hirpastay" at the 1st Indianist Week in 1931.

9. The title of the Bolivian carnaval "Milongueros" probably refers to the Argentine *milonga* genre, or milonga dancers (who are known as milongueros).

10. In 1961, the music of Conjunto 31 de Octubre appeared on another Folkways release, the fifth edition in the series *Music of the World's Peoples*; US composer Henry Cowell produced it (FW04508). Conjunto 31 de Octubre's contribution, and the sole Bolivian track in the series, is the bailecito "El Cholito." This time, the liner notes correctly attribute the selection to "31 de Octubre." Perhaps to lend the ensemble's professionally sounding performance an air of rustic indigeneity, however, Cowell inaccurately claims that "two Indian kenas" realize the melody. This statement recalls how Radio Illimani's deejays often said that Conjunto 31 de Octubre's wind soloist, Esteban del Río, was a kenista, even though he actually played the Western transverse flute.

11. The Andean conjunto format predominates on another Folkways Records album that was released around the same time as 1959's *Folk Songs and Dances of Bolivia*, the similarly named 1958 LP *Folk Dances and Dance Songs of Argentina*. Kena soloists (and future stars of the Andean music scene in Europe) Mariano Uña Ramos of Jujuy and Facio Santillán of Santiago de Estero perform on this album, as members of the Argentine band Segundo Castro y Los Trovadores de Angaco (FW 8841).

12. Jaime Medinaceli of Conjunto Kollasuyo might have been related to acclaimed writer Carlos Medinaceli, who also was from Sucre and moved to La Paz. Carlos Medinaceli's most

celebrated work is the novel *La Chaskañawi* (Quechua for "Beautiful eyes"). First published in 1947, it champions mestizaje, at a time when few Bolivian writers adopted this position (Sanjinés 2004, 96, 134).

13. The duo Las Hermanas Espinoza played an important role in popularizing Medinaceli's huayño "El Minero" in the MNR years (*Combate*, Mar. 19, 1955).

14. José Aramayo Martínez, formerly the bombo player of Conjunto 31 de Octubre, had become a kena soloist by the time Armando Valdez y su Conjunto Andino recorded the 1960 album *Pinceladas de Bolivia*.

15. Fabián Humberto Flores Espinoza's pseudonym "Tito Yupanqui" also takes after the name of the 16th-century sculptor Francisco Tito Yupanqui, who lived near the La Paz town of Copacabana (Salles-Reese 1997, 18–29), where Flores Espinoza was born.

16. Paredes's 1913 essay does not mention the percussion instruments that misti sikuri groups played at the time (176, 182), whereas González Bravo only remarks in an 1948 article that misti sikuris of yesteryear used "an indigenous wankara" (411). Misti sikuris probably began to employ brass-band-style percussion in the early-to-mid-20th century.

17. In the La Paz region, indigenous-associated siku traditions did not incorporate the snare drum or other brass band percussion in this period, but indigenous musicians had integrated these instruments into a few non-siku traditions, such as the pallapalla genre (which parodies the military), and tarka music (see González Bravo 1948).

18. The La Paz town of Sicasica is known to Andeanist historians as "the cradle of Indian rebels and successive uprisings" in highland Bolivia from the 1780s to the 1890s (Larson 2004, 232). Further research is required to ascertain if Sicasica's misti sikuri tradition developed in relation to indigenous political developments of the town and nearby areas.

19. Siku musician Jorge Miranda, who joined Los Choclos in the early 1950s and soon afterwards became its director, stated to me that the ensemble was founded around 1925. In Peru, two roughly contemporaneous sikumoreno groups of Puno performed under a similar name, Los Choclos of Juli, and Los Choclitos—4 de Diciembre of Illave (Valencia 1983, 70).

20. In the 1925 article "The Pentatonic Mode in National Music," González Bravo decries the misti sikuri tradition's recent spread "to the outskirts of the cities" (quoted in Wahren 2014, 73). The sites that he was referring to most likely included Ch'ijini.

21. The ensemble name Los Cebollitas might have been a humorous reference to the musicians' ability to bring audiences to tears (see Reyes Zárate 2017, 116).

22. For this 1960 trip to Mexico, Melba Zárate led the Ballet Folklórico Boliviano (Rivera de Stahlie 2003, 191, 237). The next year, Chela Urquidi replaced her as the director of the troupe, which was renamed the Ballet Folklórico Oficial (Chapter 4).

23. Los Cebollitas' alternate name, Los Sikuris del Altiplano, appears on this 1955 disc (TK-10082). According to *Fantasía Boliviana* member Fausto López (see Bigenho 2006, 282), Los Cebollitas often played mambos and the tango "La Cumparsita" to pass the time between engagements in their 1955–1956 tour.

24. Louis Girault, who heard Los Cebollitas perform in 1954, praised the group for its "excellent" performance style and for being much more "in tune" than the indigenous tropas that he had encountered in his visit to Bolivia (d'Harcourt and d'Harcourt 1959, 98). In 1959, while on tour in Czechoslovakia with the *Fantasia Boliviana* troupe, Los Cebollitas recorded two instrumental pieces for the 1959 album *Bolivian Folk Songs*, a release that mainly showcases the vocal duo Las Hermanas Espinoza (Supraphon SUL 32133). Los Cebollitas' siku playing on these two selections exhibits a highly polished sound quality, similar to that which the group produced on the earlier tracks they made for Discos Méndez circa 1955.

25. Many of Peru's early sikumoreno groups were likewise affiliated with trade unions (see Valencia 1983, 68–71; Turino 1993, 146–47; Acevedo Raymundo 2003, 133–40).

26. Los Hijos del Illimani was another paceño siku tropa of the MNR era. From time to time, this group provided musical accompaniment for folkloric theater shows at the Municipal Theater, such as *Serenata Potosina* (e.g., *ED*, Apr. 16, 1958; Sept. 3, 1960). Given the name "Los Hijos del Illimani," the ensemble might have had some connection to Oruro's Los Hijos del Pagador. In Potosí city, meanwhile, Crecencio Durán and his son, Jorge, established a siku tropa by 1958 (Torres 2006, 212). I am uncertain if it was a working-class mestizo ensemble and thus comparable in its membership to Los Choclos and Los Cebollitas.

27. I have withheld the names of these particular musicians for reasons of discretion.

28. About one month after Los Choclos performed "Surimana" in 1957's *Bolivia Indiana*, Enrique Oblitas Poblete's dramatization of the Surimana epic appeared in the MNR magazine *Khana*. This publication includes a transcription of the "Surimana" tune, and describes the Surimana epic as a "Callawaya legend" (Oblitas Poblete 1957).

29. González Bravo also chastised Los Choclos for playing the auquiauqui genre with their usual siku tropa, instead of switching to flautas traversas (*ED*, June 12, 1957).

30. Writing in the 1970s, anthropologist Joseph Bastien notes that the trip from La Paz city to Charazani "takes anywhere from twenty hours during the dry season to several days in the rainy season when the roads become muddy and impassable" (1978, 2).

31. The requinto might have been employed by one of the members of Los Peregrinos.

32. Edmundo Zaldívar of Argentina composed the carnavalito "El Humahuaqueño" (The man from Humahuaca). Its lyrics evoke an Andean fiesta in the northwestern Argentine town of Humahuaca, Jujuy. Stylistically and thematically, "El Humahuaqueño" strongly resembles "Carnavalito Quebradeño"—the first hit for Argentina's Los Hermanos Ábalos (Chapter 3). Around the time that Raúl Shaw Moreno y Los Peregrinos recorded "El Humahuaqueño," many other Latin American as well as European artists were performing this carnavalito (see Rios 2008, 152–53).

33. When I interviewed him, Raúl Shaw mentioned these accusations, and offered as proof of his patriotism his many recordings of traditional Bolivian genres.

34. From time to time, MNR officials publicly reprimanded elite-oriented establishments for barring the entry of "cholos" and indigenous people (e.g., *ED*, Aug. 14, 1954).

35. In a similar vein, the front cover of Bolivian bolero-rock group Los Pepes' album *Folklore de Bolivia* (recorded in 1958 in Argentina, for the Columbia label) displays an indigenous kena player, standing next to a llama, with Lake Titicaca in the backdrop.

36. An early performance by Los Dandys took place in mid-1957 (*ED*, June 12, 1957). A few months later, in September 1957, an identically named Mexican trío romántico debuted in Mexico City (see García Corona 2015, 106–111). That the two groups have the same name appears to be a coincidence, as it is highly unlikely the Mexican Los Dandys had been aware of the prior existence of the Bolivian ensemble.

37. While in La Paz this year (1957), Mauro Núñez recorded a Discos Méndez album (*ED*, July 18, 1957), in which he showcases his compositions for solo charango (e.g., "El Arriero"; The muleteer), and formidable musicianship (see Torres 2006).

38. Following the breakup of Los Peregrinos around 1960, Raúl Shaw performed as a soloist with various non-Bolivian bolero acts, first in Mexico City, and then in Buenos Aires, where he lived until his passing in 2003 (see Shaw 2007).

The Folklore Boom and Its Legacies

III

The Folklore Boom and Its Legacies

6

1965

The Onset of the Folkloric Music Boom

IN MAY 1965, President General Réne Barrientos witnessed an unusual rendition of the National Anthem at the Palace of the Government's luxuriously decorated, crimson and gold meeting space, the Salón Rojo (Red salon). A group of Andean indigenous musicians from the La Paz town of Colquencha (Aroma Province), dressed in their fiesta regalia of striped ponchos and towering rhea-feathered hats, played the patriotic tune for him with their panpipes and wankara drums. Not one to miss a photo opportunity that exhibited his connection with the folk, Barrientos posed with the Colquencha ensemble, and entire contingent of Bolivian musicians and dancers who had won accolades the month before at the Primer Festival Latinoamericano de Folklore in Salta, Argentina. The director of Bolivia's folklore delegation, and head of the Dirección Nacional de Antropología, Julia Fortún (who founded the Departamento de Folklore; Chapter 4), brought along their trophies and medals, to show them to Barrientos. She also offered the President a memento from the trip, a *poncho salteño* (Salta-style poncho) of the kind worn by internationally popular Argentine folklore bands like Los Chalchaleros and Los Fronterizos. For his part, Barrientos gifted the delegation a cash prize, congratulated them for stoking national pride through their "triumph" on Argentine soil, and expressed his ardent belief that "our folklore" conveyed the essence of Bolivian culture (*ED*, May 14, 1965).

Panpipes & Ponchos. Fernando Rios, Oxford University Press (2020). © Oxford University Press.
DOI: 10.1093/oso/9780190692278.001.0001.

For a sitting Bolivian president to avow his admiration for the nation's folkloric music and dance traditions was nothing new, of course. Nor was it out of the ordinary for a high-ranking politician, as well as journalists and the public, to grant exaggerated significance to, and use the phrase "national triumph" to characterize, the achievements that Bolivian artists had obtained abroad. These continuities notwithstanding, the Bolivian contingent's exploits at the Primer Festival Latinoamericano de Folklore represented a remarkable feat. It was the first time that Bolivian folklore performers had been awarded a gold medal at a major international competition. That the festival took place in the city of Salta—the capital of the region that Bolivians most associated with the esteemed Argentine folkloric music movement—made this accomplishment even more meaningful from the Bolivian perspective.

In the months after the reception at the Palace of the Government, Bolivian state-affiliated agencies coordinated four high-profile spectacles devoted to rural indigenous music-dance expressions: the Primer Festival Folklórico Nacional, Primer Concurso Regional de Danzas Autóctonas en Compi, Primer Festival Cívico Folklórico del Niño Campesino, and a Fiestas Julianas concert at Hernando Siles Stadium. This flurry of state-sponsored indigenous folklore festivals surpassed the offerings that prior administrations had staged in a comparable time frame, and aligned with the Barrientos-Ovando regime's ostensible pro-Indian stance and rising investment in tourism initiatives. Bolivia's recording industry, meanwhile, experienced dramatic growth in 1965, and started to play a far greater role in fostering the mass popularity of criollo-mestizo folkloric music.

By narrowing the focus to the major events and happenings involving Bolivian musical folklorization that occurred in 1965, this chapter sheds light on the intertwined local and translocal factors that made this year in particular such a pivotal conjuncture for the country's folkloric music movement. This chapter also reveals that by 1965 the conditions were strongly favorable in La Paz city and other Bolivian metropolitan centers (especially Cochabamba) for the rise to stardom of a locally based criollo-mestizo folklore band whose performance practices foregrounded signifiers of Andean indigeneity, a niche that Los Jairas would fill the following year (Chapter 7).

"THE RESTORATION OF THE REVOLUTION"

For the inaugural Fiesta Julianas season of the Barrientos-Ovando years, the La Paz Municipality organized a "Festival of the Culture of La Paz" that was reminiscent of the first MNR government's exhibitions of regional and national culture in the 1953–1956 period. The Ballet Folklórico Oficial (still headed by Chela Urquidi) and National Symphony Orchestra gave recitals at the Municipal Theater on the evening of July 17, 1965, while at nearby Hernando Siles Stadium, indigenous tropas and a diablada group performed in the afternoon and next morning (*ED*, July 16 and 18, 1965). Of the twelve indigenous ensembles taking part in the stadium events, the audience would have been most familiar with the musical style of the Italaque panpipe groups, Sikuris de Ticata and Sikuris de Taypi Ayka, the second of which had distinguished itself nine years earlier at the IV Festival de Música y Danza Nativa. To close the show at Hernando Siles Stadium, La Fraternidad Artística y Cultural la Diablada de Oruro presented various numbers, following the precedent established in the MNR years of having the music and pageantry of Oruro's diablada tradition serve as the finale at Bolivian national folklore expositions.

Two weeks later, on Day of the Indian, hundreds if not thousands of primary and secondary school students from various indigenous communities gathered in the early morning at La Paz's Prado boulevard, for the Primer Festival Cívico Folklórico del Niño Campesino (First Civic Folkloric Festival for Peasant Children). In this out-door space, the schoolchildren sang criollo-mestizo indigenista compositions and the National Anthem, and at one point, an unidentified "peasant boy" recited an Aymará poem (Ministerio de Asuntos Campesinos 1965). All in all, the program recalled what the students of the Warisata ayllu-school had performed almost three decades ear-lier in La Paz city to mark the first Day of the Indian, when another military man governed Bolivia, the "military socialist" leader Germán Busch (Chapter 2). On both occasions, the student choirs interpreted "Marcha de los Cóndores" from Antonio González Bravo's compilation *Lírica de Warisata: 6 Canciones Aimaras*. And in a further parallel, once again government agencies were responsible for managing the pro-ceedings. But whereas the Ministry of Education had organized the 1937 recital held at the Municipal Theater, the Ministry of Peasant Affairs was the entity tasked with staging the far more ambitious 1965 festival.

Indigenous music-dance performances represented the principal attraction of the Primer Festival Cívico Folklórico del Niño Campesino, together with the "indigenous beauty contest" for young women that also took place at the stadium (Ministerio de Asuntos Campesinos 1965). In the MNR period, the La Paz Municipality's "indig-enous" folklore festivals had been limited to tropas from the La Paz region. The Primer Festival Cívico Folklórico del Niño Campesino, in contrast, had a national scope, and accordingly the event featured a considerably greater variety of indig-enous expressive practices. Ensembles from most of the country's major regions participated in the festival, some of whom visited the offices of *El Diario*, including at least three groups that had traveled to La Paz from the Chuquisaca region (*ED*, Aug. 3, 1965).

The turnout of indigenous musicians and dancers, which the Ministry of Peasant Affairs spokesperson estimated reached 17,000, pleased Co-Presidents René Barrientos and Alfredo Ovando.[1] Barrientos, who was always eager to give the public the impres-sion that indigenous people constituted the bedrock of his popular support, described the festival as the "largest concentration of peasants in the [history of the] capital of the Republic" (Ministerio de Asuntos Campesinos 1965, 5, 11). To distinguish this highly orchestrated mobilization of "Indians" from those that the MNR regimes had coordinated, an official from the Ministry of Peasant Affairs pronounced,

For the first time in thirteen years, the Agrarian Reform and Day of the Indian were remembered without any mention of politics, and without converting these celebrations into instruments of propaganda or political demagoguery. (Ministerio de Asuntos Campesinos 1965, 1)

Barrientos and Ovando often declared that their administration epitomized the authentic nationalism of fellow military-populists Busch and Villarroel and thus represented a major improvement over the MNR governments, even though their policies seldom deviated significantly from those of the movimientistas. This continuity owed much to Barrientos's history in the MNR. Back in 1946, in the immediate aftermath of the Villarroel-MNR coalition government's fall from power, he had pledged his loyalty to the Movimiento Nacionalista Revolucionario. He volunteered his skills as an aviator to support the MNR cause, and in the days after the 1952 Revolution, had piloted the airplane that returned Paz Estenssoro to Bolivia from his exile in Argentina. Barrientos subsequently proved his worth as a mediator between the MNR leadership and the Andean indigenous sector, especially in his home region of Cochabamba. Although Paz Estenssoro did not think highly of Barrientos, regarding him with "little more than intellectual disdain" (Field 2014, 148), the party chief felt compelled to nominate the politically ambitious military man for the vice-president position in the 1964 general election.[2]

In his term as president, Barrientos kept intact the Agrarian Reform and other groundbreaking MNR legislation. And he repeatedly made the case, in the long-winded, illogical but forcefully delivered speeches he was known to give, that "the restoration of the [MNR] revolution" represented the prime objective of his regime (Brill 1967, 50; also see Ventocilla 1969; Peña Bravo 1971, 123–27; Dunkerley 2007, 190–91). The indigenous ensemble performances held at Hernando Siles Stadium in the 1965 Fiestas Julianas season reinforced Barrientos's message about "restoring the revolution," because they took place at the same venue and time of year as the Municipality's "autochthonous" or "native" festivals of the first Paz Estenssoro presidency. The Primer Festival Cívico Folklórico del Niño Campesino was a slightly different kind of event, given that it involved schoolchildren, but nonetheless it also harked back to the MNR state-funded festivals of the 1950s. For Barrientos—the key player in the creation of 1964's Pacto Militar-Campesino, or Military-Peasant Pact (Gordillo 2000, 143)—associating himself with indigenous folklore spectacles had the additional benefit of fortifying his image as a populist with an affinity for the peasantry. Aided by his fluency in Quechua and ebullient personality—the latter represented a striking contrast to the reserved character of Paz Estenssoro, Siles Zuaso, and Ovando—the self-styled "General del Pueblo" (The People's General) developed far greater rapport with the Andean indigenous population than had his predecessors in their years as Bolivian head of state, barring only Villarroel.

Another strategy, characterized by intimidation and violence, unfortunately served as Barrientos and Ovando's default approach in their dealings with urban working-class labor organizations, above all in the mining centers of northern Potosí, where military forces massacred striking workers in 1965 and 1967 (Dunkerley 1984, 122–25, 148–49). Barrientos's hostility toward the Andean obrero class did not spell indiffer-ence regarding the musical expressions traditionally identified with mestizos, how-ever. Far from it, Barrientos was renowned for his enthusiasm for this variety of "folklore," something he enjoyed demonstrating by showing off his ability at dancing genres such as the cueca (various, personal communications). He also formed close ties with two of Bolivia's most popular criollo-mestizo folklore performers of the day, Oruro singer Zulma Yugar (see *ED*, Dec. 18, 1966; Fernández Coca 1994, 238–39) and Cochabamba trio Los Brillantes.

Los Brillantes, then formed by Rúben López (first voice and guitar), Jaime Barrios (second voice and charango), and Oscar Rojas Caballero (piano accordion), were a particular favorite of Barrientos. Member Jaime Barrios discovered as much in August 1965 when the President's personal assistant–bodyguard, or *edecán* (*aide-de-camp* in French), showed up at his home in Cochabamba, with no advance notice, to invite the group to travel to La Paz for a series of engagements at Monje Campero Theater (Fernández Coca 1994, 124–25). It was a win-win situation for both parties. Los Brillantes secured lucrative performances and ample publicity in La Paz, while Barrientos bolstered his populist image through an action he could easily portray as sincere because of his Cochabamba roots. Over two weeks, Los Brillantes had a gig at Monje Campero Theater, with several shows dedicated to "the Presidents of the Military Junta" (e.g., *ED*, Sept. 6, 1965). The trio also performed at the Presidential Palace, as documented in the photographs printed in the Cochabamba newspaper *Prensa Libre* (Sept. 18 and 26, 1965). Barrientos even summoned the group to visit him at the presidential residence in San Jorge neighborhood, a request they of course accepted (Fernández Coca 1994, 124–25). Soon thereafter, Los Brillantes journeyed to Paraguay in a capacity akin to that of Bolivian cultural ambassadors, as part of the entourage accompanying Barrientos and Ovando for their meeting with the President of Paraguay, General Alfredo Stroessner (*Prensa Libre*, Sept. 18 and 26, 1965).[3]

CULTURAL TOURISM AND INDIGENOUS MUSIC-DANCE

Before flying to Paraguay in September 1965, Barrientos and Ovando spent a few days in Cochabamba, to attend the Primer Festival Folklórico Nacional. Like the Primer Festival Cívico Folklórico del Niño Campesino held the previous month, the Primer Festival Folklórico Nacional exhibited "authentically indigenous" music-dance styles from every departamento except for remote Pando (*Prensa Libre*, Sept. 12, 1965). On the opening day, the spectators listened to the pinkillu musical traditions of rural La Paz's Los Chajes de Colquencha (profiled later in the chapter), observed a dance troupe from Tarija re-enact the *rueda chapaca* (a circle dance), and heard Andean pan-pipe music as played by a jula-jula tropa from provincial Cochabamba and an ayara-chi group from the Chuquisaca town of Tarabuco, along with many other numbers (*Prensa Libre*, Sept. 12, 1965).[4]

The Primer Festival Folklórico Nacional commenced with the entrance of a chasqui to the stadium, in the style of the Primera Semana Folklórica Boliviana of 1961 (Chapter 4). This time the foot messenger had walked a much longer distance to arrive at the festival, from La Paz's Tiwanaku ruins to Cochabamba city, and delivered "a message from the highland peasants to the peoples of the valley and to the visitors from the oriental region of the country" (*ED*, Sept. 13, 1965). The Dirección Nacional de Turismo (National Tourism Board) organized the Primer Festival Folklórico Nacional. Enticing tourists therefore represented a major goal of the event (*Prensa Libre*, Sept. 14, 1965)—another parallel with the Primera Semana Folklórica Boliviana of 1961.

The National Tourism Board also promoted Compi's Primer Concurso Regional de Danzas Autóctonas, which similarly had its first edition in 1965. With the astonishing blue-green waters of Lake Titicaca as its backdrop, the Compi festival took place in the La Paz village of the same name located in Manco Kapac Province. Unlike the Primer Festival Folklórico Nacional, then, the Primer Concurso Regional de Danzas Autóctonas sought to lure spectators to a small town in the altiplano, rather than the capital of a departamento. In the *El Diario* advertisements for the Compi festival (e.g., *ED*, May 30, 1965), the Andean panpipe, end-notched flute, and pinkillu tropa styles traditionally practiced in the region are described as "exotic" and "native," but nevertheless "ours," a nationalist message that the National Tourism Board aimed at Bolivian tourists.

Of the foreign contingent who showed up for the Primer Concurso Regional de Danzas Autóctonas, the majority consisted of representatives from the Confederación de Organizaciones Turísticas de America Latina (Latin American Confederation of Tourism Organizations) or COTAL, along with local embassy personnel. Founded in Mexico in 1957, COTAL was holding a meeting in the city of La Paz that week. After observing the music and dance traditions on display at Compi, COTAL's Secretary-General, Héctor Tesoni of Argentina, characterized the Concurso Regional de Danzas Autóctonas as "a magnificent fiesta" with "enormous" promise as a tourist destination (*ED*, June 5, 1965).[5]

The Barrientos-Ovando regime had recently passed a pro-tourism Supreme Decree (see Cárdenas Tabares and Valencia Caro 1972, 15–16), and in a further sign that the administration gave its blessing to the Compi festival, the two heads of state made personal appearances at the event (*ED*, June 5, 1965). The next year, the National Tourism Board and Compi community members instituted the Concurso Regional de Danzas Autóctonas as an annual undertaking (Buechler 1980, 330–37).[6] An "abundance of tourists, especially North Americans and Europeans" figured prominently among the spectators at the 1966 edition, which included a boat race on Andean *totora* reed ships coordinated by the Yacht Club Boliviano (*ED*, May 29, 1966). Over 600 miles away, in Tarija, the municipal authorities became intrigued with the "possibilities of [similarly] converting Tarija into an important tourist center, in order to strengthen its weakened economy" (*ED*, June 3, 1966). Inspired by the Compi event, in June 1966 Tarija's Municipality put on the Primer Festival Folklórico del Sur (First Folkloric Festival of the South). Its main attraction was "authentically autochthonous" ensembles from greater Tarija and the adjacent southern provinces in the neighboring departamentos of Chuquisaca and Potosí (*ED*, June 13, 1966).

The third edition of Compi's Concurso Regional de Danzas Autóctonas (1967) featured two new contests: a bicycle race for young women, and "Potato Queen" beauty pageant (*ED*, May 24, 1967). The organizers also opened the music-dance competition to ensembles from any La Paz province, at the behest of the National Tourism Board (Buechler 1980, 332). Taking advantage of this opportunity, the pinkillu tropa Chino-Chino de Colquencha made the trek from Aroma Province to the 1967 festival, and returned home as the grand prize winner (*ED*, May 29, 1967). The Concurso reverted to its original intra-province focus in 1969 (*ED*, May 18, 1969), apparently to guarantee that Compi groups would monopolize the trophies and cash awards (Buechler 1980, 332–33).

Anthropologist Hans Buechler, who conducted extensive fieldwork in Compi and neighboring indigenous communities in the 1960s, has observed that the Concurso Regional de Danzas Autóctonas sparked a "renaissance of types of traditional music" that had been on the verge of disappearing in the region (1980, 334), such as the mimula and lakita panpipe tropa styles (Buechler 1980, 339; Buechler and Buechler 1971, 69). As ethnomusicologists, historians, and anthropologists have shown for numerous sites, from Bali to Mexico to the Caribbean, "cultural tourism" generates heightened local and foreign awareness and appreciation, and often also spurs revivals, of locally distinctive musical expressions, and tends to reframe certain traditions as regionally or nationally emblematic folkloric customs (see Picard 1990; Hagedorn 2001; Hellier-Tinoco 2011; Rommen and Neely 2014). Even though it is often thought that "folklore" represents the antithesis of capitalism or modernization, an indisputably capitalist enterprise such as the tourism industry frequently can foster musical folklorization processes (see Hafstein 2018).

Compi's Concurso Regional de Danzas Autóctonas and Cochabamba's Primer Festival Folklórico Nacional formed part of a broader regional pattern. In much of Latin America, the 1960s saw the proliferation of folklore festivals whose organizers sought to capitalize on the national and international tourist markets. In Cosquín, Argentina, for instance, in 1961 the Comisión Municipal de Cultura y Turismo spearheaded the establishment of the Festival Nacional de Folklore en Cosquín, which within a few years became Argentina's major annual gathering for folkloric music artists (see Giordano and Mareco 2010). In the neighboring Argentine province of Santiago del Estero, the city of Termas de Río Hondo hosted its first Festival Internacional de Folklore in 1962, while three years later, in one of the strongholds of Argentina's folkloric-popular music movement, Salta prepared its own event, the Festival Latinoamericano de Folklore.

BOLIVIA TRIUMPHS IN SALTA!

Fresh from the vivid experience of witnessing Oruro's Carnival celebration, in March 1965 the Salta lawyer and ex–Los Chalchaleros member José Antonio Saravia Toledo stopped in La Paz city to meet with the head of the National Bureau of Anthropology, Julia Fortún. On behalf of the organizing committee for Salta's upcoming Festival Latinoamericano de Folklore, he informed her that if Bolivia sent a folkloric music-dance delegation to the event, the local authorities would cover its travel and lodging expenses (*ED*, Mar. 9, 1965). Fortún and her associates accepted the invitation and began planning the contest that would select the artists traveling to Salta. The guidelines the Dirección Nacional de Antropología posted in *El Diario* underscored that to maximize one's chances of earning a spot in the contingent, performers should wear "typical dress" and interpret melodies that were "legitimately folkloric, that is, from the anonymous patrimony of the nation" (*ED*, Mar. 14, 1965).

The possibility of fulfilling the role of Bolivian folklore ambassador at the festival represented an exciting prospect for many artists. So was the once-in-a-lifetime opportunity of being on the same stage as such luminaries of Argentina's folklore movement as Los Fronterizos, Los Cantores de Quilla Huasi, Los de Salta, Horacio Guarany (Heráclito Rodríguez Cereijo), Jaime Torres, and Eduardo Falú, who would be taking part in the proceedings as invited guests rather than competitors. Bolivian musicians and audiences much appreciated the music of Argentine folklore artists, especially those who sang poetic zambas in two- or three-part harmony, accompanied at a leisurely tempo by guitars and the bombo legüero—a performance style that generated a similar following in many other Latin American countries in the 1960s (for the Mexican case, see Arana 1988; for Chile, see González Rodríguez, Ohlsen, and Rolle 2009). In La Paz, the cover bands Los Huanchaqueños (founded in 1959) and Los Inti Huasi (established around 1960) made names for themselves in the music scene through their note-for-note renditions of the hits of Los Chalchaleros and Los Cantores de Quilla Huasi, respectively (see Rios 2014, 213–14).[7]

To satisfy the National Bureau of Anthropology's criteria for the auditions, Los Inti Huasi focused on traditional Bolivian criollo-mestizo genres instead of their usual Argentine zamba numbers. The La Paz bolero trio Los Caminantes (The travelers) transformed itself, too. Formed by singers-guitarists Pepe Murillo, Oscar Moncada, and Emilio Guachalla, the group impressed the committee with their lively musical style and newfound national repertoire. The jury was especially taken with the quality of Murillo's singing, so much so that they asked him to join the delegation, but not his bandmates. In like fashion, the adjudicators chose only one member of Los Inti Huasi, its lead vocalist, Carlos Palenque.[8] Then the committee announced that Murillo and Palenque would be performing together as a duo at Salta, to the surprise of the two musicians, because the jury had reached this decision without even bothering to consult them about the matter (Pepe Murillo, personal communication). The female duo Las Imillas—veterans of the *Fantasía Boliviana* company's 1955 tour of Argentina, Uruguay, and Paraguay—and baritone Víctor Montaño rounded out the vocalists who were selected for Bolivia's delegation (*ED*, Apr. 15, 1965).

Versatile instrumentalist and future Los Jairas member Ernesto Cavour also landed a spot. Since 1962, he had been on the salaried roster of the Ballet Folklórico Oficial, with which he had become an accomplished dancer and honed his musicianship on his principal instrument, the charango, as well as on the guitar, kena, and harp. His solo charango sets in the company's productions invariably displayed his formidable punteados and rasgueos, and to maintain audience interest, humorous stunts such as playing the instrument behind his back, and abruptly switching the position of the charango and the roles of his left and right hands in the middle of a number (Ernesto Cavour, various personal communications). One year before the Festival Latinoamericano de Folklore, Cavour had traveled to Argentine city of San Miguel de Tucumán with the Ballet Folklórico Oficial for the Primer Festival Nacional Estudiantil de Folklore (First National Folkloric Student Festival), where he earned plaudits for his virtuosic and "ambidextrous" charango skills (personal collection of newspaper clippings, Ernesto Cavour). Music educator and pianist Justino Jaldín directed the Ballet Folklórico Oficial at the event and thus saw firsthand how Cavour's showmanship electrified Argentine audiences. The next year, Jaldín sat on the jury that picked Bolivia's delegation for the Salta festival (*ED*, Mar. 14, 1965), which all but guaranteed Cavour would make the cut.

Fortún persuaded an Andean indigenous tropa to join the folklore delegation, adding diversity to its otherwise entirely criollo-mestizo cast. Under the leadership of guía Marcelino Fernández and mainly comprising his relatives, the ensemble hailed from the La Paz town of Colquencha (Aroma Province). The National Bureau of Anthropology had recently filmed a documentary about the village, and it was through this endeavor that Fortún had deepened her knowledge of the community's indigenous traditions (Marcelino Fernández, personal communication). Her initial exposure to Colquencha's most emblematic music-dance practice, which centers on the chajes, or *khajchas*, probably had occurred in 1956, when a tropa of this type competed in the IV Festival de Música y Danza Nativa and ranked among the "best ensembles" (*ED*, Aug. 12, 1956).[9]

The chajes is a large-sized variant of the pinkillu that is constructed out of tree branches. The instrument therefore differs greatly from the bamboo-made, and considerably smaller, pinkillus that indigenous musicians generally use in the La Paz region. Bolivian pinkillus of the chajes type are most extensively used in northern Potosí, where the instrument is known by such names as the flauta, *rollano*, and *lawato* (Cavour 1994, 101–2, 135–42).[10] In the early twentieth century, Colquencha musicians who had visited Potosí incorporated the chajes into their community's fiesta practices (Marcelino Fernández, personal communication), no doubt in light of the instrument's sonic and visual distinctiveness in the La Paz context. The chajes tradition in all likelihood caught Fortún's attention for similar reasons. Folklore scholars, after all, tend to be drawn to regionally unique cultural expressions.

Consistent as well with her academic training, Fortún was invested in the notion of cultural authenticity, which influenced her decision to seek out a rural indigenous ensemble for the delegation. She could have far more easily turned to a cholo-mestizo tropa based in La Paz city, such as Los Choclos or Los Cebollitas, and tasked them with simulating the part of an indigenous tropa, as the *Fantasía Boliviana* company had done for its international sojourns in the 1950s (Chapters 4 and 5). By opting for the Colquencha ensemble, Fortún broke from this precedent, as she was well aware (Julia Fortún, personal communication). So was the *El Diario* writer who observed, before the delegation left for Argentina, that "this is the first time that an authentically indigenous ensemble" would fill the role of Bolivian cultural ambassador outside of the country (*ED*, Apr. 10, 1965). Under the dubious impression that Andean indigenous people would never alter their performance practices to make their music more palatable to criollo and mestizo audiences, the journalist confidently asserted that the Colquencha group would present "native folklore" abroad without subjecting it to "stylizations of any kind" (*ED*, Apr. 10, 1965).

Another advantage the Colquencha ensemble had over Los Choclos and Los Cebollitas was the greater range of indigenous wind instruments that the members could play, a flexibility that they demonstrated at the Bolivian delegation's open rehearsal at the Casa de Cultura (*ED*, Apr. 15, 1965). Besides the chaje, the Colquencha musicians performed on the *waka-pinkillu* (a type of three-hole pinkillu), pusipía (four-hole kena), tarka, and two types of panpipe, *j'acha siku* (literally "big siku") and mimula. On each of their numbers, they used the tropa format and wore traditional attire. When playing the waka-pinkillu, for example, the members dressed as the *kusillo*, the clown-masked jokester character whose antics enliven fiestas in the highlands.

Indigenous imagery also infused most of the selections that the delegation's criollo-mestizo artists presented at the dry run. Cavour, for instance, highlighted the indigenous (rather than mestizo or cholo) associations of the charango, by executing his solos on the instrument while donning the characteristic poncho and other fiesta regalia of an ayllu member from Yamparáez, complete with the Spanish conquistador-style *montonero* helmet that indigenous musicians and dancers are known to sport at celebrations in this province of Chuquisaca. Cavour's Yamparáez-inspired wardrobe signaled an emergent folkloric trend in La Paz. To expand their "indigenous" repertoire beyond rural La Paz–associated traditions, paceño criollo-mestizo folklore artists had been increasingly looking to the expressive practices of Chuquisaca's Yamparáez Province, whose customs they termed *tarabuqueño* after the name of the provincial capital, Tarabuco. Soprano María Luisa Camacho folklorized the music of Yamparáez as well, by opening her set with a tune from the area with a Quechua text, "Tarukitaswan," which recounts the life of a deer. Her next number was a song from Calcha, Potosí, "Mamalita" (Quechua for "Little mother"). She interpreted it without changing out of her tarabuqueña garb, though, as also held true for Cavour and the rest of her backing ensemble (*ED*, Apr. 15, 1965). Later in the show, María Luisa Camacho teamed up with her sister, Norah, as the duo Las Imillas. They performed selections with Quechua lyrics, including "Chiri Wayra" (Quechua for "Cold wind") and the self-referential "Taqui Imilla" (Quechua for "Girl's dance"), while outfitted either as kallawaya or cullawa dancers.

The other vocal duo, Pepe Murillo and Carlos Palenque's, offered a música oriental set in which Cavour accompanied them on the harp.[11] It opened with a song in

Guaraní (a lowland indigenous language), "Yorebabasté Ignasiano," which they followed up with a *chovena* (a genre from Santa Cruz's Chiquitania Province), before concluding with a carnaval (*ED*, Apr. 15, 1965). Andean criollo-mestizo genres also formed part of the delegation's repertoire at the Casa de la Cultura, especially the cueca. Through a succession of sketches, the dancers in the contingent interpreted the regional variants of the cueca practiced in La Paz, Cochabamba, Chuquisaca, and Tarija. The closely related bailecito tradition was the subject of a dance sketch as well, along with the morenada (the troupe's opening number), and *carnaval cochabambino*.

Their preparations complete, the Bolivian folklore delegation left for Argentina the following week. Soon after arriving in Salta city, known for its Spanish colonial architecture, pleasant climate, and internationally acclaimed folklore artists, they became acquainted with the competition. Peru, Chile, Paraguay, Brazil, and Uruguay had dispatched their own contingents, as had the nine provinces of Argentina (¡América Canta en Salta! 1965). The repertoire and instrumentation of the Peruvian and Jujuy troupes most closely resembled that of the Bolivians. The Jujuy ensemble included two charanguistas and two kena players, a combination that imparted a strong Andean flavor to their carnavalitos, bailecitos, and cuecas (¡América Canta en Salta! 1965, 52–53). The Peruvian delegation offered two sets. The first, "a sampling of the folklore of Lima," in all likelihood centered on the valse criollo, marinera, and festejo. Moving from the coast to the highlands, the second half of Peru's presentation focused on the traditions of Cuzco (¡América Canta en Salta! 1965, 15). The Paraguayan delegation, meanwhile, featured a harp virtuoso (Cristino Báez Monges), and performed songs with Guaraní lyrics (¡América Canta en Salta! 1965, 14)—a repertoire that exhibited some similarities with the Bolivians' música oriental sketches.

After eight days of performances, the contestants eagerly awaited the final decision of the committee. The directors of the contingents from Bolivia (Julia Fortún), Chile (Alejandro Gamuzo Harriet), Paraguay (Mauricio Cardozo Ocampo), Peru (Rosa Elvira Figueroa), Uruguay (Mauricio Maidanik), and Jujuy Province (Justiniano Torres Aparicio), along with a chief organizer of the more famous Cosquín festival, Reynaldo Wisner, constituted the jury. After completing their deliberations, the committee announced their decision: Bolivia and Peru would share the most prestigious award, the trophy for Best Delegation. The panel also bestowed the prize of Best Dance Troupe to the two countries. In the other competitions, Ernesto Cavour earned the top prize in the category of Best Instrumental Soloist (a distinction he shared with Paraguayan harpist Cristino Báez Monges, Argentine guitarist Amable Flores of La Rioja Province, and Argentine violinist Alejandro Grillo of Tucumán Province), while Las Imillas were designated as the Best Vocal Duo. The Colquencha group's "peasant dance" sketches obtained an "honorable mention" (¡América Canta en Salta! 1965, 20–22).

The Bolivian delegation's focus on Andean indigenous-associated traditions had proved to be a masterstroke. Argentine folklore festival committees and audiences then generally were highly receptive to this type of repertoire. Three months earlier, Mercedes Sosa had learned as much at the fifth Cosquín festival—the first edition in which the trophies feature the imaginary pre-Columbian indigenous figure called Camín Cosquín (Molina 1986, 105). Sosa was a little-known Argentine singer at the time, to the extent that her name did not even appear on the program. Yet she made such an impression at the 1965 Cosquín festival with her voice and caja rendition of "Canción del Derrumbe Indio" (Song of the downfall of the Indian) that "within a year, it was already legendary" (Karush 2017, 155). Set to a pentatonic melody, the lyrics of "Canción del Derrumbe Indio" (by Argentine author Fernando Figueredo Iramain) echo tropes of South American indigenismo: the Andean Indian's ongoing sadness over the Inca Empire's conquest by "the white man," and compulsion to channel this anguish by playing a traditional Andean musical instrument, in this instance the charango. As historian Matt Karush details (2017), Sosa's emergence as an Argentine folklore star owed a great deal to the indigenous artistic persona she recently had adopted, which borrowed from Argentine precedents like Atahualpa Yupanqui, and transnational models of indigeneity. One of the main coordinators for the Cosquín festival, Reynaldo Wisner, witnessed Sosa's breakthrough with "Canción del Derrumbe Indio" (Giordano and Mareco 2010, 44), only a few months before he would assume his duties as president of the jury at Salta's First Latin American Folklore Festival.

To their amazement, Bolivia's representatives at the Primer Festival Latinoamericano de Folklore made national history, as never before had Bolivian folkloric musicians and dancers achieved a comparable showing at an international competition of this prestige. Back in Bolivia, the major newspapers ran numerous stories detailing the delegation's "triumphs" (e.g., *ED*, Apr. 27 and May 6, 1965; *Presencia* Apr. 28 and May 2, 1965; *Última Hora*, May 14, 1965). As a result of this glowing publicity, when the contingent returned to La Paz in early May, the members were treated as national heroes (Norah Camacho of Las Imillas, personal communication).

President Barrientos welcomed the troupe home with a reception at the Palace of the Government, as noted in the opening page of this chapter. Barrientos's gesture, seemingly arranged with little advance planning, marks the start of a new Bolivian populist tradition, that of presidents using the Palacio de Gobierno to host folklore performances and publicizing these events to demonstrate the administration's patriotism. The next folklore show held at this exalted space happened one month later. The Ballet Folkórico Oficial and its affiliated musicians, which then included Ernesto Cavour, Víctor Montaño, and Los Sikuris del Altiplano (i.e., Los Cebollitas), entertained Barrientos, Ovando, and other state officials with selections from the program that the company soon would be presenting in Ecuador and Peru (*ED*, June 16, 1965).

For Cavour, the 1965 Salta festival signified a defining event. Besides his activities with the Ballet Folklórico Oficial, up to this juncture he had dabbled in various non-Bolivian musical expressions, from Paraguayan genres such as the *guarania*[12] in his time as the harpist for the La Paz group Alto Guaraní, to flamenco as a solo acoustic guitarist, to rock music as the lead electric guitarist in a short-lived local band with Pepe Murillo (Ernesto Cavour, personal communication; Arauco 2011, 16–19). Winning at Salta gave Cavour the impetus to focus his energies as a musician on the charango and typical Bolivian genres from this point forward (Ernesto Cavour, personal communication).

Pepe Murillo and Carlos Palenque's artistic lives also experienced a dramatic change. Although the two musicians had not been known as Bolivian folklore specialists before 1965, in the aftermath of the Salta festival they rose to the summit of the "national music" scene, as the duo Los Caminantes (Pepe Murillo, personal communication).[13] Las Imillas, in contrast, had established their reputation as folklorists over a decade before the Latin American Folklore Festival. Nonetheless, their successful showing at Salta had a positive impact on their trajectory, because it opened the door for them to reach a new generation of fans (Norah Camacho, personal communication). Over the next year, the duo would put out recordings such as *Las Imillas: Las Triunfadores Hermanas Camacho* (Las Imillas: The triumphant Camacho sisters; BOLIART RTE 12030), and sing their characteristic Quechua-language duets at various La Paz venues, including Peña Naira at its debut show in March 1966 (Chapter 7).

The Colquencha ensemble had its moment in the national spotlight in the months after the Primer Festival Latinoamericana de Folklore. During 1965's Fiestas Julianas, Los Kusillos de Colquencha were among the twelve indigenous tropas that performed at Hernando Siles Stadium (*ED*, July 16 and 18, 1965), while in September, Los Chajes de Colquencha took part in Cochabamba's Primer Festival Folklórico Nacional (Sept. 12, 1965). It was also in the mid-1960s that Colquencha ensembles made the earliest commercial recordings of their community's indigenous musical styles for a Bolivian label.[14] These recordings consist of one Discos Méndez EP (Marcelino Fernández, personal communication), and the sole chaje piece that appears on a 1966 Lauro Records LP that is devoted to the winning Bolivian acts for the second edition of the Salta festival, *Ganadores del Segundo Festival Latinoamericano de Folklore en Salta* (LRGP-730).

The inclusion of a Los Chajes de Colquencha number on the latter album merits an explanation, because no Colquencha ensemble had actually participated in the second Salta festival. The owner of the Cochabamba label that issued the album, Laureano Rojas (profiled in the next section), knew that Los Chajes de Colquencha enjoyed some name recognition in criollo-mestizo circles—the intended market for the release—and must have surmised that adding the group to the LP thus would boost sales. This prediction also probably explains why although the recording contains three indigenous music tracks, only in the case of the Colquencha piece does the name of the musical expression's regional provenance appear on the cover and LP itself.

Despite their brush with national fame in the mid-1960s, Los Chajes de Colquencha disappeared from view soon afterwards, or so it must have seemed to criollo-mestizo folklorists and enthusiasts. Around 1967, the Colquencha musicians chose to restrict their activities to rural events (e.g., Compi festivals). It appears they opted for this course of action because the ensemble members had tended to become uncomfortable when they spent extended time in urban criollo-mestizo spaces, partly as a consequence of their limited Spanish skills.[15]

For Salta's second edition of the Festival Latinoamericano de Folklore, Bolivia sent a new group of musicians and dancers (although Murillo and Palenque kept their places). Once again, the troupe ran away with the most prizes, something the Bolivians would repeat at the third and final edition of the competition in 1967 (Chapter 7). By then, a considerable number of Bolivian folklore artists had "triumphed at Salta" and benefited from an immediate upsurge in their profile and popularity at home, developments that persuaded many other Bolivian musicians to focus on "national" (rather than "foreign") musical expressions. The recent growth of the Bolivian recording industry constituted another important factor that motivated local artists to specialize in música folklórica nacional.

THE RISE OF LAURO RECORDS OF COCHABAMBA

By 1965, Discos Méndez's monopoly over the Bolivian record market was a thing of the past. Four additional La Paz record labels were in operation (*ED*, Nov. 21 and Dec. 19, 1965), and of these, Discolandia represented Discos Méndez's main competition. Miguel Dueri, a businessman and National Symphony violinist, founded Discolandia in 1958, as a record store specializing in imports. In 1962, he added a recording studio, and at that point Discolandia began issuing original releases, with one of the earliest featuring the music of Fermín Barrionuevo's orquesta de jazz. The company initially lacked the equipment to press vinyl albums, so Dueri sent his label's master tracks for processing to São Paulo—then a prime destination for Bolivian musicians who wished to record abroad (as Buenos Aires previously had been). For Discolandia, this inconvenient step no longer was necessary after December 1963, when the La Paz company acquired the technology and expertise necessary to produce EPs and LPs (Discolandia Brochure 1999).

Outside of La Paz, the sole Bolivian label of note in 1965 was Cochabamba's Lauro Records. Its proprietor, Laureano Rojas, originally established himself as a producer-distributor with the 1960 hit LP *Fiesta en Bolivia* (*ED*, Aug. 3, 1960; Fernández Coca 1994, 8–9, 14, 18–20, 22–23). Recorded in São Paulo, with the musical accompaniment provided by a Brazilian jazz orchestra, the album stars paceño singer Luis Gutiérrez, whose smooth and rounded baritone voice calls to mind the bolerista style of Raúl Shaw Moreno. The bolero was, in fact, one of the genres that Gutiérrez most often had performed, along with the tango and Peruvian valse criollo. At the insistence of Laureano Rojas, for the *Fiesta en Bolivia* album Gutiérrez diverged from his usual repertoire, and instead interpreted Bolivian criollo-mestizo folkloric numbers such as the cueca "Orgullo de Kochala" (Cochabamba pride) (Luis Gutiérrez, personal communication).

Fiesta en Bolivia followed in the path of two other popular São Paulo–made releases devoted to Bolivian folkloric music, Arturo Sobénes y Los Cambas' bolero-inflected 1958 LP *Bolivia y Su Música* (Chapter 5), and Santa Cruz singer Gladys Moreno's 1959 album *La Voz del Oriente Boliviano* (The voice of the Bolivian orient) (*ED*, Apr. 26, 1960; Rossells 1997b, 25). *Fiesta en Bolivia* even went so far as to mimic the title of Gladys Moreno's *La Voz del Oriente Boliviano*, by placing the line "La Voz del Ande Boliviano" (The Voice of the Bolivian Andes) under Gutiérrez's name on the front cover.

The commercial success of *Fiesta en Bolivia* convinced Laureano Rojas that he was on the right track. A savvy businessman, he persuaded the director of Radio Cultura of Cochabamba to arrange a national folkloric music competition named Los Barrios Cantan (The neighborhoods sing) whose winners would have the chance to record in São Paulo. Tempted by this opportunity, about fifty-four criollo-mestizo soloists and ensembles registered for the contest, which ran from March to July 1961. For many of these artists, performing typical Bolivian genres had not previously been their forte.

This much was true of two of the prizewinners, vocalist Ketty Gudmundssen, whose artistic pseudonym "La Morocha del Tango" (The brunette tango singer) reflected her favored genre, and Los Latinos, a voice and guitar trio known for their renderings of the bolero, Ecuadorian pasillo, and Paraguayan guarania. Los Latinos changed not only their repertoire for the contest, but also their name, to Los Amautas (Quechua for "The wise ones"). They also cast off their bolerista attire of suits and ties and instead wore Andean ponchos. On the musical side, the charango strums of invited Cochabamba artist Remberto Herbas accompanied the tracks that Los Amautas and several of the other musical acts recorded in Brazil in 1961 (Fernández Coca 1994, 9, 37, 41–45, 57, 67–72).

Following the completion and distribution of this set of releases, Rojas scored additional hits in 1962, with the São Paulo–produced albums of Las Hermanas Arteaga, and the recordings of another bolero trio turned folklore act, Oruro's Los Ases Andinos (The Andean aces) (Fernández Coca 1994, 104–5, 109–111). Selling foreign-made albums was no longer as profitable for Bolivian labels after 1962, though, as an outcome of the third MNR government's restoration of tariffs on sales of imported music recordings (Chapter 5). Motivated to develop another business strategy, Rojas started the process of forming his own record company, an endeavor that he accomplished by establishing Lauro Records in Cochabamba in May 1964 (Fernández Coca 1994, 14).

The new label gained countrywide publicity in September 1965 by organizing another contest for aspiring criollo-mestizo folklorists, the Festival Lauro de la Canción Boliviana (Lauro Festival of Bolivian Song)—which would become an annual occasion and launch the careers of many artists over the following decades (see Fernández Coca 1994). Serving as the co-sponsor for the first Festival Lauro de la Canción Boliviana was the Cámara Boliviana de Discos (Chamber of Commerce for Bolivian Recordings); the very existence of this bureau signals that Bolivia's record-buying public had grown considerably by the mid-1960s (*Prensa Libre*, Sept. 8, 1965). By scheduling the Lauro Festival of Bolivian Song for September 1965, meanwhile, Rojas's record company benefited from the soaring interest in "national music" that recently had been generated by the Bolivian delegation's success at Salta's First Latin American Folklore Festival.

Much like the Primer Festival Folklórico Nacional held the same month in Cochabamba (but for rural indigenous ensembles), the 1965 Lauro Festival of Bolivian

Song was a national competition with contingents from each Bolivian departamento. After wrapping up their deliberations, the jury conferred the first- and second-place trophies, respectively, to the Potosí and Oruro delegations. Lauro Records personnel announced soon thereafter that the label's upcoming releases would feature the contest's standout artists: the Potosí ensemble Los Chasquis and its charango soloist Willy Loredo, and the Oruro vocalist Zulma Yugar (*ED*, Sept. 19, 1965; *Prensa Libre*, Oct. 2, 1965).

The Lauro festival marked a pivotal moment for Zulma Yugar. Henceforth she would concentrate on traditional Bolivian criollo-mestizo genres—and eventually earn the unofficial title of Queen of Bolivian Folklore—while she would largely abandon her once favored repertoire of Peruvian valse criollos and Paraguayan guaranias (Zulma Yugar, personal communication). Yugar's debut LP *Paisajes Orureños* (Scenes from Oruro) and her other 1965 releases for Lauro thus introduced Bolivians to a future folklore star (*Prensa Libre*, Oct. 2, 1965). But these recordings offered little novelty in a stylistic sense. The same could be said of almost the entirety of the Cochabamba company's musical catalog up to this point. One exception was *Folklore con Los Chasquis*.

FOLKLORE CON LOS CHASQUIS

Los Chasquis members Willy Loredo, Jorge Arana, Ismael Guzmán, and Juan Velasco Forest began playing music together in Potosí city in the late 1950s. It was as a tongue-in-cheek reference to their full-time jobs as telegraph workers, or "modern chasqui messengers," that they had elected their ensemble name (Willy Loredo, personal communication). Their first full-length album, 1965's LP *Folklore con Los Chasquis* (Lauro LPLR 1082), presented a new repertoire to Bolivia's mass-mediated folkloric music scene, criollo-mestizo adaptations of the indigenous musical traditions from northern Potosí.[16]

Listed as *tonadas regionales* (regional tunes) on *Folklore con Los Chasquis*, the tracks "Casarasun" (Quechua for "We're getting married"), "Kqan Raiku" (Quechua for "Because of you"), and "Sueray Wañupusqa" (Quechua for "My mother-in-law has passed"), exemplify how Los Chasquis folklorized indigenous northern Potosí musical expressions. On these selections, Loredo plays the melody on the kena while the other members accompany him on the charango, guitar, and caja (i.e., Andean conjunto performance style), or alternately, the entire group sings in unison, to lyrics in Quechua. In the latter case, the musicians often sprinkle in the vocables "lo, lo, lo" or "ni, ni, ni," or sometimes whistle the melody, in the style (purportedly) of indigenous musicians (Willy Loredo, personal communication). The individual sections in these three numbers are extremely short, imparting a sense of musical simplicity. In the case of "Casarasun," the whole piece consists of one section. When Los Chasquis interpret standard Bolivian criollo-mestizo genres on the album, in contrast, these tracks have much lengthier sections, and richer harmonies (e.g., cueca "Linda Cholita," or "Beautiful Cholita"). The ensemble thus stylistically differentiated its "indigenous" and "criollo-mestizo" repertoire, paralleling the interpretive approach of Conjunto 31 de Octubre (Chapter 5).

Two future staples of the Andean conjunto canon, the yaraví-huayño "Manchay Puito" and Argentine carnavalito "El Humahuaqueño," also appear on *Folklore con Los Chasquis*. The group employs its customary Andean conjunto musical style on these selections, foreshadowing how a multitude of Latin American– and Europe-based ensembles would perform these two tunes in the ensuing decades. Apparently to assert the Bolivian provenance of "Manchay Puito"—perhaps in light of its incorporation into the Argentine folkloric repertory (see Rios 2014, 205–6)—this piece is classified as a "tonada regional" on *Folklore con Los Chasquis*.

Laureano Rojas had a specific market in mind for *Folklore con Los Chasquis*, as the dedication "to our tourist guests" that appears on the back cover reveals (Lauro LPLR 1082).[17] The recent efforts of the National Tourism Board (e.g., Cochabamba's Primer Festival Folklórico Nacional) clearly had led Rojas to ponder which Lauro Records releases would appeal to foreign tourists. He concluded that they would enjoy hearing folklore artists who performed "authentic" Andean indigenous music, and that for this audience, Los Chasquis' blend of standard Andean conjunto numbers and indigenous Potosí-themed pieces best approximated this ideal. Rojas's instincts were sound. Non-Bolivians would make up the bulk of Los Chasquis' fan base from the release of *Folklore con Los Chasquis* in 1965, to the group's dissolution circa 1970 (Willy Loredo, personal communication). For similar reasons, Los Chasquis would be selected for the Bolivian folklore delegation that earned accolades at the second Salta festival (1966), and in 1969, serve as one of the main musical acts in the Bolivia Andina troupe that would tour Europe (Chapter 7).

VIRTUOSISMO EN CHARANGO

Around the same time as the release of *Folklore con Los Chasquis* (late 1965), group member Willy Loredo recorded three solo charango EPs for the Lauro label: *El Príncipe del Charango* (The prince of the charango), *El Príncipe del Charango Vol. II*, and *Polkas del Paraguay en Charango* (CDLR 5304; CDLR 5304; CDLR 5061). Loredo's punteados and rapid-fire rasgueos on Volumes I and II of *El Príncipe del Charango* bear a close resemblance to those of Los Sumac Huaynas' Chocni López, whose style of charango performance greatly influenced his own (Willy Loredo, personal communication).[18] On *Polkas del Paraguay en Charango*, meanwhile, Loredo mimics the bravura of Paraguayan harpists, by executing elaborate arpeggios, glissandos, and other techniques. The solo charango EPs that Loredo recorded for Lauro in 1965 hit the Bolivian market at an opportune time. Cavour's first-place finish in the instrumental soloist category at the inaugural Salta festival had recently stoked Bolivian criollo-mestizo interest in the charango.

So had Jaime Torres's album *Virtuosismo en Charango* (Virtuosity on the charango). An Argentine musician of partial Bolivian heritage, Jaime Torres had learned to play the charango in Buenos Aires, under the guidance of Mauro Núñez (Chapter 3). It was not until the release of the 1965 album *Misa Criolla* (Creole/mestizo mass), though, that many Bolivians heard of Torres. Featuring the compositions and arrangements of Argentine folklorist Ariel Ramírez, and the charango strums of Torres on three of the movements, *Misa Criolla* rapidly became a bestseller in many Latin American countries, including Bolivia. Later in the same year, Torres's *Virtuosismo en Charango* (released in Argentina in 1964, but not widely available in Bolivia until 1965) rose to the top of the Bolivian charts as well, no doubt in part because musical selections and genres of Bolivian origin or association comprise the majority of the tracks (see Rios 2014, 203).

Laureano Rojas probably had wanted his label's 1965 catalogue to include something analogous to *Virtuosismo en Charango*. Bolivian record companies habitually created spin-offs of commercially successful Argentine albums. In response to the popularity of *Misa Criolla*, for instance, in July 1965 Discolandia produced a "Bolivian folk mass," *Misa Incaica en Quechua* (Incan mass in Quechua) (Orlando Rojas of Discolandia, personal communication; *ED*, July 11, 1965). Yet regardless of whether Rojas had planned it, Loredo's charango EPs reached Bolivian consumers at the very moment when sales of Torres's *Virtuosismo en Charango* were beginning to skyrocket in the country's urban centers (see *ED*, Nov. 7, 21, and 28, 1965).

Despite the album's title, *Virtuosismo en Charango* does not exclusively consist of solo charango numbers. The kena playing of Mariano Uña Ramos—who in the 1970s would leave Argentina for France to join Los Incas (Rios 2008, 165)—appears on several tracks, such as the cueca "La Tarijeña" (The woman from Tarija). Uña Ramos takes up the melody on the kena on this selection, after Torres's charango passages had introduced the A section. On some of the LP's other tracks, including the taqui-rari "Negrita" (by Gilberto Rojas), Uña Ramos' musical contribution is even more significant, because the solo kena and charango parts have equal prominence. Overall, *Virtuosismo en Charango* features many of the folkloric musical conventions that soon would characterize Andean conjunto performance practices in Bolivia and elsewhere.

Given the high sales of *Virtuosismo en Charango*, it is evident that by early 1966 Bolivian consumer demand had grown considerably for Andean folkloric music recordings that showcased the sounds of the kena and charango, even if, up to this point, no La Paz–based ensemble had benefited much from this state of affairs.[19] The paceño folklore scene thus was ripe for a local folklore act in the style of Los Jairas when the band debuted in mid-1966.

NOTES

1. On the day of the November 1964 coup, Barrientos and Ovando announced they would share the head of state position in a *co-presidencia*. Ovando stepped down the next day, but was reinstalled alongside Barrientos in May 1965. The two military men ruled together until the end of the year, at which point Barrientos relinquished the office so that he could legally

run for president in the 1966 election (Ovando occupied the presidency on his own in this brief period). Victorious at the polls, Barrientos served as (the sole) President from August 1966 until April 1969 (Dunkerley 1984, 120–21).

2. My synthesis of Barrientos' political career draws from the accounts presented in Mitchell 1977; Dunkerley 1984, 2007; Malloy and Gamarra 1988; and Field 2014.

3. Los Brillantes' Rúben López and Jaime Barrios initially focused on non-Bolivian genres. Their first band was a bolero trio, Los Indiecitos (The little Indians), which they formed in the 1950s in the Potosí mining town of Uncía. The group's name took after Alex Shaw's Trío Los Indios, who were a major influence on López and Barrios. Another bolero trio, Mexico's Los Tres Diamantes (The three diamonds), meanwhile, was the inspiration behind the name Los Brillantes (The bright or shining ones). By 1965, Los Brillantes largely had shed their bolero repertoire, to focus instead on danceable renditions of local criollo-mestizo genres, which they sang in vocal duo style, accompanied by guitar, charango, and piano accordion (Jaime Barrios and Rúben López, personal communications).

4. About a month after Cochabamba's Primer Festival Folklórico Nacional, Oruro hosted the II Festival Nacional de Belleza Campesina y Conjuntos Folklóricos de Bolivia (II National Festival of Peasant Beauty and Folkloric Ensembles of Bolivia). Indigenous music-dance tropas, mainly ones from the Oruro region, competed in the event (*ED*, Oct. 4, 1965).

5. The next year (1966), the Barrientos regime obtained financial and logistical support from UNESCO to develop the touristic potential of Tiwanaku. The organization had recently granted similar assistance to the Peruvian tourism industry's efforts in Cuzco. As a UNESCO representative explained in 1966, "[w]e hope to be able to do in Bolivia what is being planned for Peru . . . so that when a tourist goes to Lima or La Paz, he will be able to go easily from one country to the other" (*New York Times*, June 19, 1966).

6. As of 2019, Compi has continued to host an annual Andean indigenous folklore festival.

7. A zamba that Los Chalchaleros had recorded, "La Huanchaqueña," represented the source of the ensemble name for La Paz's Los Huanchaqueños. For rival La Paz band Los Inti Huasi (Quechua for "House of the sun"), their name appears to have taken after Argentina's Los Cantores de Quilla Huasi (Quechua for "The singers of the house of the moon") (Rios 2014, 214). The 1960s version of Los Inti Huasi is unrelated to the identically named Cochabamba group that is briefly mentioned in Chapter 5.

8. For a discussion of Carlos Palenque's later career as a TV personality, politician, and presidential candidate, see Himpele 2008.

9. Also in 1956, French ethnologist Louis Girault visited Colquencha, where he recorded several performances of the chajes genre (d'Harcourt and d'Harcourt 1959, 59–63).

10. Similar types of pinkillus also are used in highland Peru (see Turino 2008b, 40).

11. Santa Cruz is among the few regions of Bolivia where musicians have traditionally used the harp to interpret local genres (Cavour 1994, 293–94).

12. Guaranias are typically performed at a slow tempo, in the style of a folkloric ballad. The genre features sesquiáltera cross-rhythms, as do most forms of Paraguayan folkloric music and dance, such as the *polca paraguaya, polca canción*, and *galopa*.

13. Murillo and Palenque were able to use the name "Los Caminantes" for their duo because the "original Los Caminantes" (i.e., Murillo's former bolero trio) had disbanded by then (Pepe Murillo, personal communication).

14. An earlier recording of Colquencha's chajes genre, albeit not a commercial release, appears as the opening track on the "live" recordings that United States Foreign Service

member Eduardo Medina taped at 1955's III Festival de Música y Danza Nativa (*Bolivian Folk Music Festival, La Paz, Bolivia, 1955;* AFC 1961/010).

15. When I interviewed Los Chajes de Colquencha guia Marcelino Fernández, he repeatedly mentioned the musicians' lack of Spanish-language skills. He also stressed that it put them at a major disadvantage in securing engagements in La Paz city, compared to tropas whose members were fluent in Spanish, such as Los de Umala (a group discussed in Chapter 7).

16. For a detailed discussions of indigenous northern Potosí music, see Solomon 1997, and Stobart 2006. Since the 1980s, Bolivian folklore artists and fans have viewed northern Potosí as a primary site where "authentic" Andean indigenous musical traditions still exist in Bolivia. Chuquisaca's Yamparáez Province has long had a similar reputation. In the 1980s, Bolivian folkorists created new *entrada* (folkloric parade) genres that reference the indigenous expressive practices that criollo-mestizo most identified with northern Potosí and Yamparáez (or Tarabuco), respectively: the tinku (briefly mentioned in Chapter 8: Postlude), and *pujllay* (Martinez 2010, 144).

17. Another Lauro Records album that the label planned to market to foreign tourists was in the works in 1965, although it never came to fruition. The proposed LP, simply titled *Bolivia*, was to feature the music of indigenous ensembles from the highland, valley, and lowland regions (*Prensa Libre*, Oct. 2, 1965). In all probability, Laureano Rojas had hoped to hire groups who had come to the city of Cochabamba for the Primer Festival Folklórico Nacional.

18. Reflecting this influence, Willy Loredo's solo charango numbers on the 1966 Lauro album *Ganadores del Segundo Festival Latinoamericano de Salta* include the huayño "Chulumañenita" (LRGP-730). In the 1940s, Chocni López's group Los Sumac Huaynas had recorded the same tune with Las Kantutas for RCA-Victor (Chapter 3).

19. After recording *Folklore con Los Chasquis*, Los Chasquis remained based in Potosí, which limited the group's impact on the "national" folklore scene centered in La Paz city.

7

LOS JAIRAS, PEÑA NAIRA, AND THE FOLKLORE BOOM

SATURDAY EVENINGS IN mid-to-late 1960s La Paz city buzzed with the sounds of deejay Micky Jiménez's popular Radio Méndez program "El Show de los Sábados" (The Saturday show). The broadcast for February 12, 1966 stands out in hindsight. It kicked off with Jiménez in the company of Miss Bolivia hopefuls, who practiced their interview skills with the magnetic host. Next, the announcers paid tribute to the Bolivian delegation's victories at Salta's inaugural Latin American Folklore Festival, with an awards ceremony. The rest of the show offered listeners a cavalcade of musical acts, ranging from the boleristas Los Genios (The geniuses), visiting Argentine folklore group Los Trovadores del Norte (The troubadours of the north), various local rock bands affiliated with the trendy Club de la Juventud (The Youth Club), and solo numbers in which singers and instrumentalists performed to the accompaniment of the station's ensemble (*Presencia*, Feb. 12, 1966).

Ernesto Cavour served in a double capacity that evening on "El Show de los Sábados," as a member of Bolivia's 1965 Salta contingent, and as the charango player in the Radio Méndez house band (which also included guitarist Julio Godoy). One of Cavour's tasks in the broadcast was to accompany the guest musician listed in the program, mysteriously, as "el afuerino y su kena" (the outsider or foreigner and his kena) (*Presencia*, Feb. 12, 1966). "He's an artist of international renown . . . Gilbert Favre," exclaimed Micky Jiménez, in his usual, animated style (Favre 1981, 90).[1] Despite the glowing introduction, Favre's performance did not go smoothly. Cavour had dragged him to the venue with little advance notice, and ultimately a lack of sufficient rehearsal, coupled with

Panpipes & Ponchos. Fernando Rios, Oxford University Press (2020). © Oxford University Press.
DOI: 10.1093/oso/9780190692278.001.0001.

stage fright, got the best of Favre. Nevertheless, to his surprise the studio audience responded enthusiastically to his halting kena solo, even demanding an encore from him (Favre 1981, 89–90). The lanky Swiss artist with an easy smile had won them over, by performing Andean folkloric music on the kena, no less.

In a few months, Favre, Cavour, and Julio Godoy would team up with singer-bombo legüero player Edgar "Yayo" Joffré to form one of Bolivia's most influential folkloric-popular music bands, Los Jairas. The group's characteristic performance practices (i.e., interpretive approach, repertoire, instrumentation) did not represent a radically new direction for the Bolivian folklore scene at the time, though, because they bore a close resemblance to those of various criollo-mestizo ensembles from earlier periods, such as Lira Incaica (Chapter 3), Conjunto 31 de Octubre, Conjunto Kollasuyo/ Bolivia, and Armando Valdéz y su Conjunto Andino (Chapter 5). Los Jairas' main contribution to the field of Bolivian national music would be their mass popularization of preexisting musical folklorization practices, rather than their occasional innovations. This is not to downplay Los Jairas' indisputably crucial role in the canonization of the Andean conjunto as Bolivia's preeminent ensemble format for interpreting música folklórica nacional, but rather to underscore that the musical style of Los Jairas shared important continuities with, and built on the foundations of, the folklorization approaches that criollo-mestizo musicians had developed in La Paz city and other sites in the early-to-mid-20th century.

The 1966–1969 conjuncture within which Los Jairas' career unfolded in Bolivia, however, presented the group with a wealth of opportunities that had not previously been available to local artists. Through a detailed look at the trajectory of Los Jairas, this chapter illuminates how the band members successfully navigated these opportunities, and in the process launched their ensemble to national stardom and established the Andean conjunto tradition as a paramount expression of Bolivian folkloric-popular music.[2] This chapter also discusses numerous additional facets of the folklore boom, including the emergence and expansion of the peña scene and its significant impact on contemporaneous and future trends in música folklórica nacional.

The story of Los Jairas is inseparable from that of the creation and initial years of Bolivia's first folkloric music peña, Peña Naira. Favre was the driving force behind the founding of this pioneering locale, which he envisioned as a Bolivian version of Chile's La Peña de los Parra. Prior to the mid-1960s, there had been few direct links between the folklore movements of Bolivia and Chile. Favre's close relationship with the influential Parra family would change this state of affairs at a critical moment in the history of the Bolivian folkloric music movement.

GILBERT FAVRE AND THE PARRA FAMILY, 1960 TO 1965

Favre, fascinated with South America, made his first trip to the continent in 1960. On a whim, he decided to join a Swiss archeological expedition to Chile's Atacama

Desert, to serve as the Spanish interpreter for the group. At some point, he parted ways with the team, and journeyed to the capital city for another adventure. It was in Santiago that he met, and became romantically involved with, Violeta Parra, whose musically talented son, Ángel, and daughter Isabel he also befriended (Favre 1981, 3–5, 27–40; Sáez 1999, 119–26). By 1963, the four of them had relocated to Europe, where they would remain until 1965. The Parra family settled in Paris, while Favre shuttled back and forth between the French capital and his Geneva apartment (Oviedo 1990, 89–97; Sáez 1999, 127–42). Violeta Parra was no stranger to Paris, as she had lived there for several months in the mid-1950s (Sáez 1999, 77–87). It was in that period that Violeta Parra apparently had first encountered Andean music, albeit as interpreted by folklore artists from Argentina (Rios 2008).

Wishing to participate in the Parra clan's music making with a bonafide Latin American instrument, Favre took up the kena in the early 1960s. The clarinet had previously been his instrument of choice, with which he had dabbled in the New Orleans musical style called Dixieland or trad jazz. His first kena, of Argentine manufacture, was a gift from a friend who recently had visited South America. Once he felt confident enough to perform on the instrument in front of an audience, Favre secured his first paid experience as a kenista, at the Geneva restaurant Le Péruvien (Favre 1981, 11, 205–6). By 1965, he had made great strides as a kena soloist, as his assured performances demonstrate on the "live" album *Violeta Parra en Ginebra* (Violeta Parra in Geneva) (Warner Music 857380702-2).

Favre invariably ended up at L'Escale (The Stopover) and La Candelaria (Candlemas) on the many occasions that he traveled to Paris to visit the Parra family from 1963 to 1965. These intimate venues, located in the Quartier Latine neighborhood of the Left Bank, then were the places to go to hear Latin American folkloric music in the French capital (Rios 2008). At the time, Violeta Parra rented a room in the building that housed La Candelaria, and had a steady gig as a singer-guitarist at L'Escale (Sáez 1999, 119–26). Los Incas and Los Calchakis often performed at both venues, and as a result, Favre regularly crossed paths with them. The manner in which they interpreted Andean folkloric tunes greatly influenced Favre at this early moment in his career as a kenista.

Most of the spectators at L'Escale and La Candelaria probably assumed that the members of the Andean folklore acts that played at these nightspots were Peruvian, Bolivian, or Ecuadorian. If so, they would have been mistaken. Argentine musicians (most of whom were from Buenos Aires) virtually monopolized Paris's Andean music niche in the 1960s; Los Incas' Carlos Ben-Pott, Ricardo Galeazzi, and Jorge Milchberg; Los Calchakis' Héctor Miranda; and freelance kenista Alfredo de Robertis represented the major figures. Guillaume de la Rocque, a kena player with the Latin American–sounding pseudonym of "Guillermo de la Roca" (William of the Rock), is a partial exception to this pattern, because of his French nationality. In any case, Bolivian, Ecuadorian, and Peruvian folklore artists were absent from the Paris scene in the early-to-mid 1960s (Rios 2008).

The Andean music ensembles active in the French capital primarily modeled their approaches after those of Argentine-based folklore bands. The recordings of

Los Hermanos Ábalos functioned as an early reference point for Los Incas and Los Calchakis.[3] Relatively easy to obtain in Paris, these releases mainly feature Argentine "folk" genres of non-Andean association (e.g., zamba, chacarera), but the carnavalito, bailecito, cueca, and yaraví often appear on them as well; Los Hermanos Ábalos usually performed these numbers in Andean conjunto style (Chapter 3). Los Incas and Los Calchakis also mined the output of Folkways for repertoire (Rios 2008, 158–59). The US label's 1959 LP *Folk Songs and Dances of Bolivia*, for instance, introduced them to Conjunto 31 de Octubre's arrangements of "Sicuris" and "Llamerada" (discussed in Chapter 5), which Los Incas and Los Calchakis learned to perform and also recorded.

By 1965, French record companies had expanded their catalogues of Latin American folk music albums, in step with President Charles de Gaulle's efforts to create a "third bloc" with Latin America and other world regions that could challenge the international coalitions headed by the United States and USSR. Within this political conjuncture, Los Incas recorded one of their most influential albums, 1963's *Amérique du Sud* (South America). It contains the version of "El Cóndor Pasa" that, in 1970, would form the basis for Paul Simon and Art Garfunkel's megahit "El Cóndor Pasa (If I Could)" (Rios 2008, 157–62).

As explained in Chapter 2, the melody of "El Cóndor Pasa" had originally appeared as one of the movements in a 1913 Peruvian indigenista operetta (also called "El Cóndor Pasa") for which Daniel Alomía Robles crafted the music. Los Incas put their stamp on "El Cóndor Pasa," by fashioning an Andean conjunto arrangement of the kashua movement (Rios 2008, 159–162).[4] Los Incas' version differs substantially from Alomía Robles's 1913 setting of the same movement for symphonic orchestra, as well as the renditions for chamber orchestra and brass band that RCA-Victor recorded in Peru in 1917, and the piano reduction that Alomía Robles completed in the 1930s. Los Incas' 1963 take on "El Cóndor Pasa" intrigued Favre (Favre 1981, 11), who would record essentially the same arrangement of this popular number with Los Jairas in 1966.

Favre embarked on his second trip to Chile in August 1965, this time in the company of Violeta Parra. Santiago's La Peña de los Parra would be his main haunt for the rest of the year. A performance space of modest size, it was operated by Ángel and Isabel Parra, who had returned to Chile the year before. The venue's leftist and pan–Latin Americanist programming, combined with other novel aspects such as the minimal separation between performers and spectators, and informal ambience, distinguished La Peña de los Parra from conventional Chilean "folk music" locales.[5] In the first year of the peña's existence, the musical acts frequently juxtaposed genres and instruments from various Latin American countries within a single number or set, as an artistic expression of their utopic vision for a socially progressive and culturally united América (Rodríguez Musso 1988, 60–65; González Rodríguez, Rolle, and Olsen 2009, 228–31).

La Peña de los Parra would soon become the wellspring for Chilean nueva canción, a leftist artistic movement that would acquire its name in time for 1969's Primer Festival de la Nueva Canción Chilena (see González Rodríguez, Rolle, and Olsen

2009, 262–67, 371–435). A future pan–Latin Americanist hallmark of nueva canción, Andean folkloric music, already could be heard in the shows of La Peña de los Parra by the mid-1960s. Prior to this juncture, Chilean folkloric musicians had seldom played typical Andean musical instruments (e.g., kena, charango), or interpreted Andean genres (e.g., huayño). The Parra family's strong interest in the music of the Andes, stemming largely from their experiences performing alongside Los Incas and Los Calchakis at L'Escale and La Candelaria in Paris, played a major part in the nueva canción movement's adoption of the Andean conjunto as its preferred "indigenous" ensemble format (Rios 2008, 153–57).

Within a few months of her arrival in Santiago, Violeta Parra had secured the location for her own peña, La Carpa de la Reina. Unfortunately, tensions arose between her and Favre amid the lastminute preparations for its premiere on December 17, 1965 (Sáez 1999, 151–52). It was not the first time they had fought. Their relationship had always been volatile, because Parra's headstrong nature and strong temper often would cause her to clash with the laid-back Favre (Favre 1981; Oviedo 1990; Sáez 1999). But it was worse this time, and at one point she had actually thrown a rock at Favre that struck him in the back. Even he could not take it anymore and decided for his safety and sanity that they needed to spend some time apart. Fleeing Santiago to sort out his thoughts, he boarded a train northward, eventually reaching Antofagasta, and later Arica on the Chile-Peru border. After a few weeks, Favre headed back to Santiago to reconcile with Parra. The reunion was fleeting, though. Following another argument, she shockingly attempted to end her life, and it was at this point that Favre realized that he was in over his head. Ending the relationship, he took off once again, for a new adventure (Favre 1981, 34–60).

Heading to a place where he could experience firsthand the musical traditions of the Andes made sense to Favre. He selected Peru as his destination. When he stopped at the Peruvian embassy to inquire about the necessary paperwork, however, the surliness of the staff convinced him to consider other options. If not Peru, then how about Bolivia? His friendly reception at the Bolivian consulate contrasted strikingly with the poor attention he had gotten earlier. The Bolivian embassy officials not only were courteous to Favre and granted his request for travel documents, but also, prophetically, assured him that he would be "received very well" in their country (Favre 1981, 61–62). Bolivia it was, then, although how to get there was another matter. Short on cash, Favre ended up selling one of his few possessions of monetary value, his clarinet, to pay for the train fare to La Paz (Favre 1981, 61–62).

THE CREATION OF PEÑA NAIRA AND LOS JAIRAS

Once in La Paz city, Favre settled into the budget Hotel Italia and began thinking about how he was going to support himself, as he was almost penniless at this point. After giving the matter some consideration, and abandoning his original plan of working as a cameraman, he resolved to try his luck at making some money by playing his "Indian flute" (Favre 1981, 74). Of course, he would need contacts to navigate the city's musical opportunities, so he hatched the idea of reaching out to a radio station. While he was asking around about which one he should visit, the name Radio Méndez surfaced. El Show de los Sábados was always on the lookout for new talent, he learned. Before long, Favre introduced himself to its host, Micky Jiménez, who knew exactly the person Favre should meet to fulfill his quest of teaming up with a seasoned folkloric musician: Ernesto Cavour (Favre 1981, 74–90).

The next day Favre visited the charanguista's home in the working-class barrio of Ch'ijini, where Cavour let him see his collection of Bolivian musical instruments—which would form the basis of a museum still in operation in La Paz city as of 2020. Favre's Argentine-made kena immediately intrigued Cavour. It was constructed of hardier material, and thicker in body, than the all-bamboo Bolivian kenas with which Cavour was most familiar. The two men hit it off well and spent the afternoon making music together. They met up at the same place the following day for another session, this time joined by a close friend of Cavour's, guitarist Julio Godoy. Pleased with the rehearsals, Cavour reserved a slot for the ad hoc trio in the upcoming edition of El Show de los Sábados (Favre 1981, 74–90).

Following their radio debut (discussed at the beginning of this chapter), Favre went forward with his plan to launch a peña, having noticed that La Paz surprisingly lacked this type of venue. He scouted out potential sites and soon ended up at Galería de Arte Naira. Printing-press owner Luis "Pepe" Ballón and painter-sculptor Jorge Carrasco Núñez del Prado (a relative of celebrated indigenista sculptor Marina Núñez del Prado) managed this art gallery, which was located in Ch'ijini neighborhood on the cobblestoned and almost vertical Sagárnaga Street. Favre pitched his peña concept to Ballón, who expressed enthusiasm for the idea. Ballón unhappily pointed out, though, that Galería de Arte Naira was near insolvency (Clarín International [La Paz newspaper], Oct.–Nov. 1966). This news did not deter Favre. With his entrepreneurial skills, he was able to persuade fellow Swiss expatriates to donate the required start-up capital, with which he contracted prison inmates to build the wooden chairs and tables that would accommodate the clientele (Favre 1981, 81–86, 91–92).

His furniture requirements resolved, Favre now needed to book the musicians for Peña Naira's inauguration, which was scheduled for March 4, 1966. He most wished to secure the participation of a panpipe tropa. In his first days in La Paz, while wandering a few blocks from Hotel Italia to explore the city, he had serendipitously come across a group of sikuris playing music in the street (probably Los Choclos or Los Cebollitas). It made a huge impression on him. Favre was most accustomed, after all, to hearing Andean conjunto reworkings of highland indigenous music. "A revelation . . . so beautiful and powerful" that it made him "shiver" was how he would later remember this encounter with the panpipe ensemble (Favre 1981, 70).

Favre could easily contact a siku group at the shoeshining stands on Plaza Murillo, Cavour informed him, because members of Los Choclos worked there. Cavour also introduced Favre to his Salta festival comrades Las Imillas and Los Caminantes, along with a new figure in the La Paz music scene, solo guitarist Alfredo Domínguez (Favre

1981, 95–96). Domínguez had recently offered a recital of Bolivian and Argentine folk-loric music at Galería de Arte Naira, and thus was acquainted with its owners (*ED*, Dec. 30, 1965).

Los Choclos, Las Imillas, Los Caminantes, and Alfredo Domínguez agreed to take part in the debut performance of the peña. Favre's own ensemble had expanded into a quintet by then, with the addition of another friend of Cavour's, guitarist Mauro Cerruto, and one of Cavour's colleagues from the Ballet Folklórico Oficial, Percy Bellido, who played bombo legüero in the yet unnamed band (Arauco 2011, 65–67, 77).

With the lineup of musical acts now ready for the opening show, Favre began circu-lating invitations to "The Inauguration of Bolivia's First Folkloric Peña" (Peña Naira Invitation, Feb. 1966). His hand-drawn depictions of the Tiwanaku ruins adorn the Peña Naira placards that he posted around town, especially at hotels, to entice non–La Paz residents to catch the program (Julio Godoy, personal communication). Favre also made sure that local radio stations and newspapers did their part to build public excitement for the premiere (e.g., *Presencia*, Mar. 2, 1966). The propaganda campaign was successful; a sizable crowd attended the Friday evening unveiling of Peña Naira (*ED*, Mar. 5, 1966).

Besides the impressive musical lineup, and oddity of a kena player from Switzerland fronting a Bolivian folklore group (then simply called Conjunto de la Peña Naira), the uniqueness of the establishment accounts for much of the anticipation surrounding its debut. At the time in La Paz city, a range of nighttime entertainment spots pro-grammed Bolivian folkloric acts, even boîtes such as Night Club Tabú (Taboo) and Club 21 interspersed performances of national folkloric music among the striptease sketches that represented their starring attractions (e.g., *ED*, Jan. 23 and Feb. 13, 1966). None of these locales, though, billed themselves exclusively as folkloric music venues.

The setting also contributed to Peña Naira's appeal. Ch'ijini's identity as a cholo-mestizo neighborhood (see Chapter 5) reinforced the image of the peña as a place where one could experience typical Bolivian culture, while the venue's address on the first block of Sagárnaga Street, close to the Prado boulevard, made the locale easily accessible to paceños living in the city's more affluent central district—these factors also would play a major part in Sagárnaga Street's eventual development into the main tourism zone for urban La Paz. Peña Naira's connection to an art gallery, which besides showing paintings and sculptures occasionally hosted lectures on highbrow subjects such as "Art in India" and "What Is Expressionism?" (*ED*, Feb. 27, 1966), gave the peña an air of cultural sophistication that enhanced its attractiveness for its pre-dominantly elite and middle-class clientele.

When walking in the door of Peña Naira for the first time, patrons must have often been surprised by the small size of the locale. The peña accommodated only around forty people, who sat elbow to elbow on sloppily made and uncomfortable chairs at communal wood tables. For the décor, Favre placed candles and wine jugs on the benches, imparting an artsy touch that corresponded with the paintings that were hung on the walls. When customers arrived, the hosts informed them of the drink selection, which was limited to wine, and handed out the complimentary *pasankalla*, a large-kerneled, and tough to eat, local variety of caramelized popped corn. As the spectators snacked on the pasankalla, so close were they to the artists—no stage separated the performers from the audience—that the music must have drowned out most of the chewing sounds they were making.

The food and drink offerings at Peña Naira (which resembled the menu at La Peña de los Parra)[6] overtly juxtaposed signifiers of cosmopolitanism and nativism, in a manner that represented an innovative touch in the urban La Paz context. The city's establishments had rarely served pasankalla, because paceños classified it as a lowly street food. Wine, on the other hand, had an elite association, and at the time was mainly offered at locales that catered to the upper socioeconomic class (Julio Godoy, personal communication).

Thrilled by the positive reception at the peña's debut, Favre began planning for the following weekend of Friday and Saturday shows. He could do so in a more stable living arrangement now, because he had accepted Pepe Ballón's generous offer of a tiny, ground-floor residence in the building that housed the venue (Leni Ballón, personal communication). For this round of performances, Favre booked the same musicians who had taken part in the inauguration, with the addition of the Potosí group Los Chasquis (*ED*, Mar. 12, 1966). This ensemble, profiled in Chapter 6, had come to La Paz to audition for the folklore delegation that would compete in the second Salta festival.

Once again, Peña Naira sold out, leading a journalist to remark that the venue was "too small, given the number of people who attend this folkloric peña" (*ED*, Mar. 12, 1966). The locale was well on its way to becoming something far greater than Favre must have imagined it would be when it was just a figment in his mind's eye. To maintain audience interest, and attract repeat customers, he changed up the musical programming for the next few weeks. Los de Umala represented the main novelty. A tropa from La Paz's Aroma Province, the group was led by Umala Mayor Adolfo Salazar (who would join the Andean conjunto Los Laickas the next year). Los de Umala offered a spectacle of Andean indigenous musical traditions that rarely if ever had been heard in a paceño club environment. In their set at Peña Naira, the musicians played the siku, kena, tarka, and pinkillu, in the traditional tropa format (*ED*, Mar. 23 and Mar. 27, 1966).

In April 1966, Conjunto de la Peña Naira members Julio Godoy and Percy Bellido took a brief leave of absence from the ensemble, to participate in the second Salta festival. The Bolivian contingent also included Los Chasquis, Zulma Yugar, Los Caminantes, Mauro Núñez, K'auquita García, Los Hermanos Gutiérrez, Dúo Loría-Salinas, soprano Elizabeth Araníbar, concertina artist Sabino Orosco, La Diablada Ferroviaria de Oruro, Conjunto Chapaco (led by Nilo Soruco), and Manuel Cruz and Ramón Magne (of Los Cebollitas and Los Sikuris del Altiplano). The entire group performed at the Open Air Theater, and paid a visit to the residence of President Alfredo Ovando, before leaving for Argentina (*ED*, Apr. 10, 11, and 12, 1966). Once the Salta contest was underway, Bolivians heard the proceedings by tuning in to the broadcasts of Buenos Aires' Radio El Mundo, and in such numbers that Bolivia's radio stations suffered a noticeable decline in their usual audience share (*ED*, Apr. 24, 1966). In La Paz city, the public rooted so enthusiastically for the Bolivian delegation that it reminded Favre of how sports fans typically act when watching the Olympics (Favre 1981, 139).

The Bolivian team did not disappoint its supporters. For the second time running, the troupe won the greatest number of prizes, but now there was even more reason to celebrate. Whereas at the 1965 contest the Bolivian and Peruvian contingents had shared the Best Delegation Trophy, there was no doubt as to which delegation had most impressed the judges at the second edition, because the committee awarded the Grand Prize of Honor solely to the Bolivians (El Canto de América Vibró en Salta 1966, 23–25). Just how much this victory meant to people back home became evident to the troupe on the train ride home. As Sabino Orosco recalled (personal communication), after the delegation crossed the Argentina-Bolivia border, "people treated us like kings . . . in every train station, people forced us to come down from the vehicle and join them, they gave us all kinds of gifts, placed [Bolivian] flags on top of us." At the town of Viacha, one of their last stops before La Paz city, the locals essentially "kidnapped us, they wouldn't let us leave, made us dance and everything," causing such a delay in the itinerary that President Ovando sent a caravan of cars to escort them to his home, where they stayed until the next morning (Sabino Orosco, personal communication). A couple of days later, the Ovando regime hosted a reception for the delegation at the Palace of the Government (*ED*, May 4, 1966), as was becoming customary. Favre scheduled two of the recently crowned groups, Los Chasquis and Los Caminantes, for Peña Naira that weekend, thereby taking advantage of the publicity surrounding the Salta contingent (*Presencia*, May 4 and 7, 1966).

While Godoy and Bellido had been away in Argentina, Favre, Cavour, and Cerruto initially had carried on as a trio in La Paz. Before long, though, they became dissatisfied with the limitations of this condensed lineup. On the recommendation of Cavour, they recruited one of his neighbors in Ch'ijini, vocalist and radio jingle artist Edgar "Yayo" Joffré (Ernesto Cavour, personal communication). Joffré's facility with singing tunes with Aymara and Quechua lyrics, a skill that he had picked up in his childhood years in the La Paz town of Ayata (Muñecas Province), made him a good fit for the band. In terms of his professional musical background, Joffré had mainly performed in bolero groups, especially Cuarteto de Oro (e.g., *ED*, Feb. 27, 1962). Despite their focus on Caribbean-derived musical genres, Cuarteto de Oro also interpreted local criollo-mestizo genres, like most Bolivian bolero acts (Chapter 5). In 1964, for instance, Cuarteto de Oro had devoted an EP to "national" folkloric repertoire. Cavour was well aware of this release; he had supplied the charango accompaniment (Arauco 2011, 17).

In May 1966, soon after Godoy and Bellido had rejoined Conjunto de la Peña Naira, the sextet taped the EP *Folklore de Bolivia* (Naira EP 001). A self-financed, and entirely instrumental, release with four tracks, *Folklore de Bolivia* sold well in La Paz (Favre 1981, 142–44).[7] The recording, moreover, conferred additional publicity to Peña Naira, because the name of the locale was emblazoned on the front cover of the EP jacket.

The opening track, "Alborozo Colla" (Exuberant Andean Indian), would become a signature number for Favre. A technically challenging piece, it features octave leaps in the kena part, and abrupt shifts in tempo and genre (from yaraví to cueca to huayño). A Peruvian kena player, Antonio Pantoja,[8] composed "Alborozo Colla," as the credits acknowledge on *Folklore de Bolivia*. "Danza de la Platita" (The silver/money dance) is the sole original work on the EP. Favre and Cavour jointly authored the humorously labeled piece, in the hopes "it would make us lots of money" (Julio Godoy, personal communication). Godoy took Cavour's customary place as the charango player on this track, so Cavour could realize the second kena part that harmonizes in thirds with Favre's kena melody. The two remaining selections, "Dos Palomitas" (also known as "Manchay Puito") and "Auqui Auqui" (by Alberto Ruiz Lavadenz), had long been familiar to Bolivian audiences. Conjunto de la Peña Naira's rendition of "Auqui Auqui" closely follows the version that Conjunto 31 de Octubre recorded in the mid-1950s (Chapter 5), although Favre and Cavour play the melody as a kena duet (rather than as a flute solo).

Violeta Parra came back into Favre's life about a week after the release of *Folklore de Bolivia*. She visited him in La Paz, yearning to rekindle their love affair (Oviedo 1990, 104; Sáez 1999, 153–55). Favre welcomed her back and must have been excited for her to see his successful new enterprise, and anticipated that she would contribute to its popularity. Parra performed several times at Peña Naira, as a singer-guitarist, and also exhibited her paintings and other visual artwork at the venue (*ED*, May 20, 26, and 27, 1966; *La República*, May 22, 1966; *Presencia*, May 26 and June 1, 1966).

As someone who proudly identified as a socially conscious artist with communist sympathies, Parra would have noticed that the politicized music so characteristic of the shows of La Peña de los Parra and La Carpa de la Reina was largely absent from Peña Naira's programming. At the time, Bolivia and Chile's folkloric music movements diverged in their degree of politicization. The Chilean folklore scene had become polarized between leftist and conservative factions, as was true of Chilean society in general (Mularski 2014). Bolivia was not immune from this type of development. Indeed, the number of militantly leftist folklore musicians would rise in Bolivia as the decade progressed (as explored later in this chapter). Yet, in 1966, politicized folkloric music did not yet represent a major trend among La Paz criollo-mestizo musicians, a reflection of the relatively limited following that Bolivian radical-leftist parties then enjoyed in the country beyond the confines of the labor movement, when compared to the situation in Chile.

In early June 1966, Violeta Parra returned to Santiago with Favre, who stayed only briefly, and Los Choclos, who remained for a few weeks and played sets at La Carpa de la Reina (*Presencia*, June 1, 1966; Oviedo 1990, 104; Arauco 2011, 82–84). On behalf of Joffré, while Favre was in Santiago he purchased an Argentine-style bombo legüero, the preferred percussion instrument among Chilean folkloric musicians. Favre was soon back in La Paz and had reformed his group, but now they had a dilemma. Joffré, with his new bombo legüero, could serve as the lead singer *and* percussionist, rendering Percy Bellido's participation in the band unnecessary.

By early July, Bellido had gotten the message, as he was no longer in the ensemble. Guitarist Mauro Cerruto had left the group as well, to focus on his university studies (Arauco 2011, 80, 86).

With their quartet lineup finalized, Favre, Cavour, Godoy, and Joffré still had one unfinished piece of business, selecting a name for the band that was catchier than The Ensemble of Peña Naira. As they were weighing the pros and cons of various suggestions, Cavour, who had a mischievous sense of humor, and often chided his bandmates for their less than assiduous use of rehearsal time, blurted out "Los Jairas" (Aymara for "The lazy guys"). It sent them into a fit of laughter; no one thought that he was serious about the proposal. But serious he was, and the other members ultimately agreed to follow his lead (Arauco 2011, 87–89). They made their public debut as "Los Jairas" in the swanky space of Boîte Crillón in July 1966. The suits and ties that the group had recently worn at its performances perfectly matched this environment. However, Los Jairas donned striped ponchos and lluchus (*ED*, July 7, 1966), an outfit that the band would occasionally use instead of their usual suits and ties.

"EL LLANTO DE MI MADRE"

A couple of months after Los Jairas' premiere at Boîte Crillón, Conjunto Kollasuyo— which was still led by kenista Jaime Medinaceli—filled in for them at Peña Naira (*Presencia*, Sept. 3, 9, and 16, 1966). Los Jairas were in Cochabamba city at the time, for the second Lauro Festival of Bolivian Song. Held at Teatro Ópera, the competition lasted three days, during which time the contestants tried their utmost to impress the jury and also excite the public, who cheered for their favorite artists. When Los Jairas took the stage, the emcee could not help pointing out the pecularity of Favre's presence in a Bolivian folklore group, to which the audience responded loudly with a mix of applause and jeers (Favre 1981, 180–81).

With some trepidation, Los Jairas stepped up to the microphones and opened with Joffré's arrangement of a somber yaraví or triste, titled "El Llanto de Mi Madre" (The tears of my mother). The lyrics, which alternate between Quechua and Spanish, convey the immense sadness an indigenous boy feels when he learns about his mother's death. As a dark cloud approaches, he wonders if the impending rain represents her tears. Pleading with his mother to rest in peace, the boy, dropping to his knees, begs God to receive her in Heaven. He then entreats her to pray for him, and proclaims she will never be forgotten, because he will cry for her day and night.

The group attributed the poignant text to Juan Huallparrimachi Mayta. A quasi-mythical figure, ostensibly of cacique and/or Incan heritage, he is said to have been born in Potosí in the 1790s and died around 1814 while fighting on the patriot side in the Wars of Independence. Bolivian writers often characterize Huallparrimachi Mayta as the country's first indigenous poet, on the basis of a dozen or so Quechua-language poems of uncertain authorship that they nonetheless credit to him (see

Anaya de Urquidi 1947, 91–100; Lara 1960, 119–32; Nagy 1994–1995). "El Llanto de Mi Madre" draws most of its text from one of these poems, "Mamay" (Quechua for "My mother") (see Lara 1960, 130–31, 215)."[9]

Joffré set these verses of "Mamay" to a preexisting, simple-duple meter tune that exhibits some characteristics of Andean indigenous music. In the minor mode, the melody consists of two repeated sections (AABB form) that differ solely in their respective opening measures, in the vein of Conjunto 31 de Octubre's "Sicuris," Los Cebollitas' "Ese Vase de Cerveza" (see Chapter 5), and numerous Andean indigenous tropa pieces. Underlining the simplicity of the tune, the melody progresses mainly in stepwise quarter notes, and spans only a major sixth (see Example 7.1).[10] That "El Llanto de Mi Madre" is a yaraví would have bolstered its "indigenous" aura for the spectators assembled at Teatro Ópera, given the enduring, though erroneous, belief in Bolivian criollo-mestizo society that the genre's roots lie in the pre-Columbian harawi (see Paredes 1913, 187–88; Anaya de Urquidi 1947, 80; Lara 1960, 114–16).

Shortly after the contest, Los Jairas made a studio recording of "El Llanto de Mi Madre" for Lauro Records. This track likely approximates how Los Jairas had played the tune at Teatro Ópera. In the slow tempo that typifies Bolivian as well as Peruvian yaravís, it begins with a fifteen-measure introduction in which Cavour executes punteados (mainly in parallel thirds) on the charango, and then rasgueos; the latter technique establishes the home key of G minor. At this point Joffré enters with the melody, which he sings at a steady pace with no rubato. In the A and B sections, Joffré begins with lines from "Mamay" and then offers Spanish-language translations of the text, making the message clear to non-Quechua speakers. The most dramatic moment in Joffré's performance occurs at the start of the B section, because he shifts to a loud wailing tone on the words "Mamay" (my mother) and "Será" (will be).

After Joffré completes the melody, Favre takes it up on the kena. He starts the A and B sections in the same register as Joffré, but jumps one octave higher eight measures

EXAMPLE 7.1 Los Jairas, "El Llanto de Mi Madre," basic melody

later. Favre continues in the upper register on the sectional repeats. He eventually moves to the lower octave, though, drawing attention to the kena's timbral spectrum. Throughout his solo, Favre uses a pronounced vibrato (a legacy of his days as a Dixieland or trad-jazz clarinetist) that is reminiscent of the quavering sound of crying. The third iteration of the tune returns the spotlight to Joffré, who sings a new stanza, in Spanish. To conclude, Favre plays the melody on the kena again, this time while Joffré hums along at the interval of a third.

Favre's extended solo no doubt was meant to musically embody the romanticized image of an Andean Indian expressing his anguish through the sound of the kena. Criollo-mestizos have often associated this stereotype with the yaraví genre, and one tune in particular, "Manchay Puito/Dos Palomitas." Many Bolivian groups recorded this folklore standard in the 1960s, from Los Chasquis (Chapter 6), to the members of Los Jairas, in the band's original incarnation as Conjunto de la Peña Naira (as previously noted).

"Manchay Puito/Dos Palomitas" is closely tied to the Legend of Manchay Puito, a tragic story that vividly evokes the trope about the affective properties of Andean kena music. In most versions of this tale, the protagonists are a Catholic priest (of indigenous or mestizo descent) and an indigenous woman, who are engaged in a forbidden love affair that ends with her unexpected death while he is away. Tormented by grief upon learning of her passing, the priest frantically exhumes her body. And in a demented state, he makes the startling decision to create a musical instrument from one of her shinbones. The instrument he fabricates is a kena, and with it he vents his pain by playing mournful melodies. The macabre Legend of Manchay Puito would have been known to most of the audience at the 1966 Lauro festival, as they would have encountered it in school, or read the versions found in Mercedes Anaya de Urquidi's *Indianismo* (1947, 82), Jesús Lara's *La Literatura de los Quechuas* (1960, 116–19), or other Bolivian indigenista volumes.[11]

As their follow-ups to "El Llanto de Mi Madre" at the Lauro festival, Los Jairas performed two instrumentals, starting with Cavour's arrangement of the unattributed bailecito "Quisiera un Puñal" (I wish I had a dagger). They taped it a few weeks later, for the same Lauro EP that contains "El Llanto de Mi Madre" (Lauro CDLR 5094). "Quisiera un Puñal" showcases the energetic charango playing of Cavour, who interprets the melody with punteados and rasgueos, while Godoy and Joffré accentuate the hemiola cross-rhythms of the bailecito genre on the guitar and bombo legüero (Favre sits out on this piece). "Huayño de la Roca" represented their final selection. Favre had taught the tune to the group, after learning it by listening to Los Incas' *Amérique du Sud* (Julio Godoy, personal communication).[12] Los Jairas included this huayño as well on their 1966 Lauro EP. Favre interprets the melody of "Huayño de la Roca" on the kena, Cavour harmonizes on second kena, and Godoy and Joffré again function as the band's rhythm section on this track.

When they closed out their set at the contest, the spectators burst into chants, clamoring noisily for an encore of "El Llanto de Mi Madre" (Favre 1981, 181–83). The jury, too, was taken with the yaraví. Los Jairas walked away with the "Best Song" prize for "El Llanto de Mi Madre," and also received the "Best Ensemble" award (*ED*, Sept. 19, 1966). Sensing it had a hit on its hands, Lauro immediately offered a recording contract to Los Jairas. A photograph of the ensemble, dressed in their Andean folkloric outfits (i.e., ponchos and lluchus) and pretending to play their musical instruments, adorns the front cover of the ensuing three-track EP that Los Jairas recorded for the label. This release carries the descriptive title "Así Triunfaron Los Jairas en el Segundo Festival de la Canción Boliviana 1966" (That's how Los Jairas triumphed at the Second Festival of Bolivian Song 1966) (Lauro CDLR 5094).

The band also recorded its first full-length album, *Los Jairas*, for the Lauro label before the members returned to La Paz (Lauro LPLR 1049). This 1966 LP includes "El Llanto de Mi Madre" as well, although it is listed under the alternate title "Dos Amigos (El Llanto de una Madre)."[13] And instead of a photo of Los Jairas, one of an indigenous kena-kena tropa in fiesta attire appears on the front jacket of the album. Company owner Laureano Rojas must have believed this image would attract the interest of tourists, a market that he was seeking to tap into (Chapter 6). Consistent with this strategy, the opening track on *Los Jairas* is "El Cóndor Pasa," in a version that closely follows Los Incas' earlier arrangement on the 1963 album *Amérique du Sud*, which had been gaining favor in France (as Laureano Rojas surely knew).

Favre is the principal soloist on most of tracks on the 1966 LP *Los Jairas*, including "El Cóndor Pasa," "Alborozo Colla," "Llamerada" (in Conjunto 31 de Octubre's arrangement, with minor changes to the melody), and "Sicureada" (based on Conjunto 31 de Octubre's track "Sicuris," but with a new introduction). Cavour takes the spotlight on two selections: a bailecito medley (which encompasses "Quisiera un Puñal," Rolando Soto's "El Charanguerito," and Tito Yupanqui's "Chunquituy"), and Mauro Núñez's "Estudio para Charango" (Étude for charango). A vehicle for displaying the technical abilities of the charango soloist and unique sonorities of the instrument, Núñez's "Estudio para Charango" incorporates techniques that had not yet become common among Bolivian charanguistas, such as the classical guitar "tremolo effect" (which creates the illusion of a continuous melody and independent bass line), and the execution of triplet passages solely through the left-hand technique known as pull-offs or ligados. As he was much younger than Núñez, Cavour naturally drew inspiration from the musicianship and innovative compositions of the traveled charango master from Chuquisaca. Joffré, meanwhile, sings on two of the tracks on this album: "El Llanto de Mi Madre," and "Sarkaway." When he intones the melody of "Sarkaway," Cavour replicates it at the interval of a fifth on the charango, thereby producing the parallel-fifth harmony characteristic of indigenous tropa styles such as Kantus de Charazani music.

"El Llanto de Mi Madre" unquestionably was the LP's most popular number, a fact not lost upon the opportunistic owner of La Paz record company Discolandia, Miguel Dueri. Once Los Jairas had resumed their gig at Peña Naira, he incessantly pressured them to record the song at his studio. Favre explained to him several times that they could not do so, because the band had signed an exclusivity clause with Lauro Records that applied to the selections that they had recorded for the Cochabamba label. Dueri was undeterred, and went so far as to threaten them with the possibility that he would contract a different group to record a note-for-note copy of the hit yaraví. Faced with this unpleasant prospect, Favre, Cavour, Joffré, and Godoy eventually gave in to Dueri's demands in late October 1966. The result was the four-track EP *El Llanto de Mi Madre* (Naira EPN 001).[14] Despite their acquiescence to Dueri's threat, by the time they turned up at the studio, the Discolandia manager already had commissioned an ad hoc group to tape "El Llanto de Mi Madre" and was in the final stages of production. Singer Víctor Hugo Leaño and kenista Jaime Medinaceli were the artists who made this recording, which hit the market a few days before the release of Los Jairas' EP (Arauco 2011, 109–10, 112–13).

Laureano Rojas soon caught wind that Los Jairas had re-recorded "El Llanto de Mi Madre," and became so furious with them for violating their contract with Lauro Records that he initiated a lawsuit against the group. He even convinced the La Paz Police Department to issue a warrant for the arrest of Los Jairas, as a way of forcing the members to accede to the company's demands for monetary compensation. Unaware of Rojas's machinations, Favre found himself detained by the police and thrown in jail, where he remained for five days as the authorities searched for his bandmates. He received many visitors during his incarceration, including newspaper and radio reporters, and at one point Favre apparently embarked on a hunger strike (*Presencia*, Oct. 22 and 24, 1966; *ED*, Oct. 23, 1966).

Rojas's attempt to settle the score with Los Jairas backfired. The judge dismissed the charges, while the publicity that the incident generated boosted sales of the very recording that had so angered Rojas. Indeed, Los Jairas' *El Llanto de Mi Madre* EP would soon top the list of Bolivia's bestselling records for 1966 (Arauco 2011, 108, 118). The media hype benefited Peña Naira as well (Favre 1981, 201). The turnout surged and, in response, ads for the venue started to feature the phone number to call for reservations (e.g., *Presencia*, Nov. 4 and 11, 1966). Peña Naira was becoming the place to go and be seen at. In late November 1966, even the Vice President, Luis Adolfo Siles Salinas (half-brother of former President Hernán Siles Zuaso), along with his brother, Senator Jorge Siles Salinas, arrived for a Friday show (*ED*, Nov. 27, 1966; *Jornada*, Nov. 29, 1966).

Favre—who in a couple of years would ask the Vice President to be his best man at his wedding to Indiana Reque Terán (the daughter of a Bolivian general) (Arauco 2011, 259)—by then had acquired a new nickname that humorously alluded to his time in prison, *el gringo bandolero* (the gringo bandit). He also had begun mulling over the possibility of using this catchy sobriquet for the title of the next Los Jairas record, to further capitalize on the episode (see *ED*, Nov. 20, 1966). Joffré went one step further, by proposing that they insert Favre's handle into the name of a musical number.

And he knew just the song for this purpose, Ruiz Lavadenz's "Lappa Kummu" (Aymara for "Filthy, hunchbacked man"). The lyrics of this light-hearted huayño, in Aymara and grammatically awkward Spanish, parody a chola's tirade against a foreigner who had seduced her with empty promises. With the permission of the Ruiz Lavadenz family (Julio César Paredes Ruiz, personal communication), Joffré gave his modified version of the tune the title "El Gringo Bandolero," and to the closing refrain, added the nonsensical line "lero, lero, lero, lero, lero, lero, lero, lero, gringo bandolero!" Favre now had a theme song, which rapidly became one of the band's most requested numbers (Favre 1981, 206). Los Jairas taped it in June 1967 for the EP *El Gringo Bandolero* (Arauco 2011, 124). A photograph of a wistful-looking Favre behind prison bars, passing away the time with his ever-present cigarette in hand, graces the EP cover, an image that would cement into popular memory the unusual circumstances that had brought about his amusing moniker.

Sticking with the genre with which the band had made its name, Los Jairas over the next two years recorded a string of yaravís that take after "El Llanto de Mi Madre." Two of them, "Llanto del Olvido" (Tears of oblivion) and "A Vuestros Pies Madre" (I'm at your feet, Mother), even mimic the title of, and explore similar topics as, "El Llanto de Mi Madre." But of the yaravís that Los Jairas crafted to replicate the success of their first hit, their 1969 track "El Cisne" (The swan) enjoyed the greatest popularity (see *ED*, Jan. 12, 19, and 31, 1969; Feb. 2, 16, and 23, 1969; Mar. 30, 1969). Again, Joffré set a minor-mode tune to verses of a poem by a celebrated Bolivian writer, in this instance, Adela Zamudio (Discolandia 13066). The text closes with the line "I who have lived my life crying, wish to go to my death singing." It was a fitting finale for "El Cisne," given the commonly held belief that swans sing a mournful tune before they perish (i.e., swan song).

"Ollantay" is another yaraví that Los Jairas popularized in this period. With a Quechua text, and named after one of Peru's best-known indigenista theater works (Chapter 2), it is listed on the LP credits as an "ancestral Incan prayer" (Discolandia 13066). The composition actually dates from the late 19th or early 20th century, however. Peruvian musician Leandro Alviña authored it, under the title "Canto de la Ñusta" (Song of the Incan princess). From Cuzco, Alviña was an early figure of Peruvian indigenismo, in the fields of musical composition and music research (Romero 2016, 81). Los Jairas' hit recording of "Ollantay" thus reflects Peruvian indigenismo's lasting influence on the Bolivian folklore scene, as of course does the band's intepretation of "El Cóndor Pasa."

Los Jairas' yaraví repertoire played a critical role in launching the band to national prominence. These folkloric numbers had exceedingly minimal basis in Andean indigenous musical traditions, notwithstanding the yaraví's purported roots in the harawi, which suggests that the group's predominantly criollo-mestizo fan base had limited familiarity with rural highland musical expressions. Even among Bolivian folklore artists, many clung to the mistaken view that the yaraví represented a traditional rural indigenous genre. The criollo-mestizo ensemble Los Yaravís is a case in point. Configured as a siku tropa, the group was founded by La Paz university students in 1968 in time for the Primer Festival Folklórico Universitario Nacional (discussed in the section "University Students and the Folklore Movement") (*ED*, June 2, 1968). The members' choice of name for their indigenous-style panpipe *tropa*, "Los Yaravís," demonstrates that they assumed that indigenous ensembles of this type played the yaraví genre.

Los Jairas' audience certainly included people who previously had attended a state-sponsored "autochthonous" folklore festival, or village fiesta, and therefore had been exposed to Andean indigenous musical ensemble styles. For them, Los Jairas' deviation from indigenous musical conventions probably was not a major issue. They likely regarded Los Jairas's yaravís as improved or more "evolved" versions of the so-called source tradition, in much the same manner as, earlier in the century, the elite and middle-class often had extolled the "superior" artistry of Bolivian as well as Peruvian art-classical musical works of an indigenista character.

The political context within which Los Jairas' yaraví repertoire obtained such a positive reception must be taken into account as well. Using a strategy that the MNR had pioneered, though he carried it out with greater panache, President Barrientos boasted that his administration counted on "overwhelming peasant backing" (Mitchell 1977, 97–98). He also regularly deployed Andean indigenous militia forces to urban areas, purposely "raising the specter of multitudes of Indians marching against any civil or military factions that might try to unseat him" (Malloy and Gamarra 1988, 20). At one point Barrientos even proclaimed, ominously, that he was fully willing to "place himself at the head of the peasant militias to defend the progress of the National Revolution" (quoted in Mitchell 1977, 99). Through statements such as these, the President intentionally conjured up the specter of the resentful and bloodthirsty "Indian" who longed for the opportunity to annihilate Bolivia's criollos and mestizos once and for all.

The yaravís of Los Jairas evoked a highly contrasting array of tropes about Andean indigenous people, ones at odds with the sensationalized images of gun-toting Indians that Bolivian media outlets increasingly circulated in the Barrientos era. The sorrowful, resigned Indian figure portrayed in "El Llanto de Mi Madre" and its spin-off yaravís therefore would have been palatable for those who opposed the Barrientos regime and its Military-Indian Pact, and probably would also have appealed to criollo-mestizos who supported Barrientos yet found the administration's deployment of indigenous militias to be unsettling. As for Barrientos himself, "El Llanto de Mi Madre" was apparently to his liking. According to his friend and pastor, Father Miguel Ángel Kippez, the President grew so enamored of the yaraví that he learned to play the melody on the kena (Kippez 1992, 87–91). Regardless of the veracity of this anecdote, Barrientos certainly was known to appreciate Bolivian folkloric music (see Chapter 6). This aspect of his populism made a positive impression on many artists, including Cavour (personal communication), and Favre (1981, 218–20).

TO CHILE

In December 1966, a couple of months after Favre's spell in jail, Los Jairas traveled abroad for the first time. Their destination was Santiago, where the group had been scheduled as a headlining act for the week-long Festival de Festivales. Also among the participants was a rising star from Uruguay, singer-guitarist Daniel Viglietti, and a host of Chilean folklore artists and ensembles who would soon become major figures of nueva canción, such as Víctor Jara, the Parra family, Rolando Alarcón, Quilapayún, and Patricio Manns's Voces Andinas (Andean voices; Carrasco Pirard 1988, 107; González Rodríguez, Ohlsen, and Rolle 2009, 257, 365). Los Jairas pulled out their reliably popular hit "El Llanto de Mi Madre," and with this tune made a strong impression on the audience of Chilean folklore fans at the Caupolicán Theater (*ED*, Dec. 30, 1966).

The yaraví enthralled the festival's first-place winning ensemble, Quilapayún, who added it to their repertoire. The group's 1967 album, *Canciones Folclóricas de América* (Folk songs of the Americas), includes "El Llanto de Mi Madre," and their version of Cavour's bailecito medley for solo charango (Santander 1984, 213).[15] Founded in 1965, Quilapayún, whose name (Mapuche for "Three bearded men") referenced the leftist 1960s fashion of growing beards in the style of Ernesto "Che" Guevara and Fidel Castro (Carrasco Pirard 1988, 9–10), had only recently begun to interpret genres of Andean association, and play Andean wind and stringed instruments (González Rodríguez, Ohlsen, and Rolle 2009, 365). By the end of the decade, this facet of Quilapayún's musical production would represent an essential part of their identity.

Los Jairas fit in a few performances at La Peña de los Parra and La Carpa de la Reina before returning to Bolivia (*ED*, Jan. 8, 1966). It would be their last meeting with Violeta Parra, who committed suicide on February 5, 1967, with a revolver that she had purchased the year before in Bolivia (Sáez 1999, 164). Many writers have speculated about why she took her life. In most accounts (e.g., Oviedo 1990; Sáez 1999), Favre's breakup with her in late 1966 is given as one of the causes that provoked the bout of depression that led her to this tragic outcome. It has even been raised that because February 5 falls only one day after Saint Gilbert's feast day in the Roman Catholic calendar, the timing of Parra's final action might have represented a testimony of her love for Favre (Oviedo 1990, 109).

Violeta Parra's eerily titled 1967 album, *Las Últimas Composiciones de Violeta Parra* (The last, or latest, compositions of Violeta Parra), which was released a few weeks before her passing, contains several textual references to Favre, most clearly in the *rin* "Run Run Se Fue Pa'l Norte" (Run Run went northward).[16] While strumming a huayño-like rhythm on her Bolivian charango, Parra sadly recounts how when "Run Run"—one of her many nicknames for Favre—left her side to travel northward, she had no clue if he would ever return. Parra also accompanies herself with the charango on the *sirilla* "Gracias a la Vida" (Thanks to life).[17] In this evocative song, she expresses her appreciation for a life that has given her many gifts, from the "two eyes" that enable her to pick out "the man whom I love among the multitudes," to the "heart that flutters with excitement when I look deep into your light-colored eyes"— references to the blue-eyed Swiss kenista. And in the sirilla "Volver a los Diecisiete" (To be seventeen again), Parra, singing in a delicate and innocent tone, relates how love has made her feel like a girl of seventeen, despite having "lived a century," an apparent allusion to the almost twenty-year age gap separating her from the far younger Favre.

With the Chilean nueva canción movement's consolidation in the late 1960s and international dissemination in the 1970s, Violeta Parra's standing as a musician would belatedly reach new heights in the Americas, Europe, and beyond, while *Las Últimas Composiciones de Violeta Parra* would be widely hailed as a masterpiece. The album would also immortalize Parra's bond with el gringo Favre, a chapter in the tormented Chilean artist's life that Bolivians would find especially fascinating because it represented a rare instance in which an internationally famed musician professed a strong connection with a Bolivia-based artist. Their romantic relationship would particularly captivate the country's university students, a sector increasingly drawn in the coming years to the music of socially conscious folkloric musicians. In the short term, Favre's association with *la Violeta* spurred another round of Bolivian media attention for Los Jairas and Peña Naira, keeping them both in the limelight (e.g., *ED*, Feb. 10, 1967).

THE THIRD SALTA FESTIVAL

While Los Jairas were in Chile, a posting in *El Diario* informed Bolivians that the auditions for Salta's 3rd Festival Latinoamericano de Folklore would be underway soon (*ED*, Jan. 24, 1967). Once again, ex–Los Chalchaleros member José Antonio Saravia traveled from Salta to La Paz, to ensure Bolivia's participation in the event (*ED*, Mar. 1, 1967). Pulling together the money to cover the delegation's expenses, though, was proving to be a major challenge for the Comité Boliviano del Folklore (the entity tasked with this duty), so much so that in late March, it considered calling off the endeavor (*ED*, Mar. 26, 1967). Then, on the eve of the festival, President Barrientos saved the day by bestowing a personal check for 15,000 pesos to the troupe. With much fanfare, the First Lady hand-delivered it to the Ministry of Education of Fine Arts (*ED*, Mar. 29 and Apr. 1, 1967). With the financial matters taken care of, the Comité Boliviano del Folklore announced the roster of music-dance acts that it had selected for the festival: Los Laickas (Aymara for "The sorcerors"), Los Caballeros del Folklore (The gentlemen of folklore), Los Mayas (Aymara for "The number ones"), the Ballet Folklórico Nacional (led by Chela Urquidi), Alfredo Domínguez, Los de Umala, Los Carlos (a música oriental group from Beni), Dúo Moreira Rojas, and Isabel "Chaby" Valda and Los Kolke Llajta (Quechua for "City of silver") (*ED*, Mar. 29, 1967).

The next day, the Comité Boliviano del Folklore felt compelled to defend its omission of the "meritorious" Los Jairas from the Salta contingent (*ED*, Mar. 30, 1967). The presence of a "foreign" artist in the band made it ineligible, the committee explained (*ED*, Mar. 30, 1967). Also disqualifying Los Jairas from consideration was the fact that the group had not actually taken part in the auditions. Disregarding these matters, their fans had mounted a "campaign" to have the popular ensemble added to the delegation anyway (unknown La Paz newspaper, circa Apr. 1, 1967). In the end, Los Jairas played no part in the festival. Their first yaraví hit did, however; Potosí's Chaby Valda sang "El Llanto de Mi Madre" at the Salta contest, accompanied by her group Los Kolke Llajta (Fernández Coca 1994, 181).

Of the musical ensembles chosen for Bolivia's folklore delegation, Los Laickas shared the most in common stylistically with Los Jairas. Los Laickas founding members Tito Morlán, Jaime Lafuente, and Hugo Solares had a wealth of musical experience, acquired primarily by gigging as the bolero group Los Dandys (Chapter 5). Their decision to switch the thrust of their musical activities, from the bolero to Andean folkloric repertoire, had been for the express purpose of earning a spot on the Salta delegation (Jaime Lafuente and Tito Morlán, personal communications). The duo Los Mayas (later renamed "Los Payas"; Aymara for "The two") and Los Caballeros del Folklore (formed by ex-members of the zamba band Los Inti Huasi) similarly reinvented themselves as Bolivian folklore acts so that they could audition for the 1967 Salta festival (Edgar Pato Patiño and Jorge Molina of Los Caballeros del Folklore, personal communications). Once again, the possibility of taking part in the Festival Latinoamericano de Folklore thus had motivated soon-to-be influential Bolivian folkloric musicians to abruptly change their specializations from "foreign" to "national" music (see Chapter 6).

Los Laickas deliberately patterned their lineup and repertoire after those of Los Jairas (although unlike Los Jairas, Los Laickas always wore ponchos, as did most Bolivian Andean conjuntos of the late 1960s), becoming the first of many Andean conjuntos to take the Peña Naira house band as their main model. Recruiting a kena soloist represented an early challenge the group confronted. Musicians with this specialty remained scarce in Bolivia. They eventually found someone who could assume the role, the teenaged musician Hugo García from the nearby La Paz town of Palca, and were able to persuade him to join the ensemble. The final addition to the group was multi-instrumentalist Adolfo Salazar, who at the time also served as the guía of the tropa Los de Umala (Tito Morlán and Jaime Lafuente, personal communications).

Yaravís that conclude as huayños, often known as "yaraví-huayños," constituted the forte of Los Laickas; examples include "Plegaria del Indio" (Prayer of the Indian), "Lamento Aymara" (a slightly revised arrangement of "Plegaria del Indio"), "Sentimiento del Indio" (Sentiments of the Indian; by Hugo García), "Cantar Indio" (Indian song; by art-classical musician Eduardo Caba [profiled in Chapter 2]), and "Huayra Huayra" (Quechua for "Powerful wind"; by Raúl Shaw [this tune is discussed in Chapter 5]). Of these, Los Laickas' signature number was "Plegaria del Indio" (Jaime Lafuente, personal communication).

In two-part form, "Plegaria del Indio" begins as a ponderous yaraví, in simple-duple meter, and has a sparse musical texture, in the style of "El Llanto de Mi Madre." Whereas the Los Jairas hit implicitly references the caricature of a solitary Indian playing the kena, however, "Plegaria del Indio" presents it unambiguously. As Hugo García (the tune's composer) performs a plaintive kena melody, Morlán orates in Spanish, in a theatrically dramatic half-spoken, half-singing manner, these lines: "In the highest hills and mountains, one hears the vibrating wail of a kena. It is the Indian who offers his prayer, to the god of the hills, and to his adored Mother Earth." Then switching to Aymara, or vocables meant to suggest the language, Morlán launches into the main melody of "Plegaria del Indio." It prominently features rising fourths, an interval ubiquitous in Hollywood soundtrack depictions of Native American music, along with an accompanying isorhythmic pattern that US-produced films also commonly employ to sonically evoke "the Indian" (see Pisani 2005, 292–332). With a solemn-toned voice, Morlán sings the text with a slight trembling quality at the end of phrases, to reproduce the grief of an Andean Indian. The effect is reminiscent of Tito Yupanqui's exaggerated vocal mannerisms on Los Wara Wara's 1960 recordings of the yaraví "Thaya" (Chapter 5).

The second part of "Plegaria del Indio" follows huayño conventions. To mark this abrupt transition in genre, tempo, and mood, a few of the band members interject spontaneous-sounding shouts, apparently to rouse Hugo García, whose technically accomplished kena soloing dominates the rest of the track. "El Cóndor Pasa" contains similar musicians' banter, in the versions of the piece that Los Incas taped in France and Los Jairas recorded in Bolivia. The two-part structure of "Plegaria del Indio" also calls to mind Los Incas' and Los Jairas' interpretations of "El Cóndor Pasa," which commence with a slow-paced section (often labeled a yaraví, or Incan foxtrot), before speeding up to a huayño that presents new melodic material.

As the defending champion at the 3rd Festival Latinoamericano de Folklore, the Bolivian contingent opened the entertainment, with a set by Los Laickas, whose first number unsurprisingly was "Plegaria India." A música oriental group from Beni, Los Carlos, performed next, exposing the audience to the music-dance traditions of a non-highland area of Bolivia. Then Los de Umala shifted the focus back to the Andean region, with indigenous tropa pieces that included "Baile de las Llameros" (Dance of the llama herders) and "Danza de los Wititis" (*wititi* refers to an Aymara genre that is played with pinkillus). Bolivia's other music-dance acts also had the opportunity to take the stage on the first day of the festival (*Clarín* [Buenos Aires], Apr. 9, 1967).

The Bolivian folklore delegation thrilled their compatriots for the third time in a row, by winning five gold and six silver medals, along with three additional trophies. One of them, the Trofeo Güemes, was adorned with this inscription: "To the triumphant of America, for their authenticity" (*Presencia*, Apr. 26, 1967; *ED*, Apr. 27, 1967). Once the contingent had returned to La Paz, President Barrientos made sure they visited the Palace of the Government, so that he could honor their patriotism (*ED*, Apr. 27, 1967).

La Paz and Cochabamba record companies reacted quickly to the commercial opportunities that the latest edition of the Salta festival had given them, by releasing albums such as *Bolivia Triunfa en Salta* (Bolivia triumphs at Salta), *Bolivia Triunfa en Salta Vol. II, Ganadores del Segundo Festival Latinoamericano de Folklore* (Winners of the Second Latin American Folklore Festival), *Disco de Oro del Festival de Salta* (Gold Record from the Salta Festival), and *Los Laickas: Triunfadores en Salta y Sus Grandes Éxitos* (Los Laickas: Winners at Salta and their greatest hits). Even though Los Jairas had not been part of the Bolivian delegation, their recording of the huayño "La Cacharpaya" (The farewell) nonetheless appears on *Bolivia Triunfa en Salta Vol. II*, a testament to the group's high standing in the Bolivian folklore scene. "El Llanto de Mi Madre," meanwhile, represents one of the tracks on EMI ODEON's 1967 compilation of the outstanding performances at the third Salta festival, *América Canta en Salta*, in the "live" version of the yaraví with which Chaby Valda and Los Kolke Llajta had won accolades at the event.

THE REPERTOIRE OF LOS JAIRAS, 1966 TO 1969

As underscored in this chapter, Los Jairas' interpretive approach and instrumentation exhibited key similarities with those of Bolivian criollo-mestizo ensembles from earlier periods. The band's repertoire likewise shared important commonalities with the catalog of previous figures in the folklore movement, as it consisted overwhelmingly of standard criollo-mestizo genres.

On their recordings from 1966 to 1969, Los Jairas interpreted huayños, yaravís, cuecas, bailecitos, carnavales, taquiraris, morenadas, auqui auquis (or *doctorcitos*), llameradas, and cullawas. Paceño musicians had long considered each of these genres to represent folklore staples. The Andean indigenous imagery that Los Jairas elicited through the yaraví "Llanto de Mi Madre" and many of their other hits, meanwhile, recycled long-standing tropes of Bolivian and Peruvian indigenismo, and therefore reveal another way in which the music of Los Jairas represented a continuation of earlier artistic currents in the Bolivian folklore movement.

Los Jairas' "San Benito" (Saint Benedict), the opening track from the 1968 album *Bolivia con Los Jairas* (Campo LPS 004), is among their selections that breaks the most new ground, and anticipates future directions in Andean conjunto practices. Named after the patron saint for Afro-Bolivians, "San Benito" is a tundiqui (also known as *tuntuna* and *baile de los negritos*), an Andean criollo-mestizo genre that parodies Afro-Bolivian music-dance traditions. When Los Jairas recorded "San Benito," the tundiqui was not part of the Andean conjunto repertoire. From the 1990s onward, though, it would be an Andean conjunto favorite internationally, under the genre's newer name of "saya" or "caporal-saya," largely through the efforts of Cochabamba's superstar group Los Kjarkas (see Chapter 8: Postlude). Los Jairas' 1968 recording of the canción "El Solitario" (The solitary one) (Discolandia-Lyra LPL 13066)—by Chilean "neo-folklore" composer Guillermo "Willy" Bascuñan[18]—points to another forthcoming signature of Los Kjarkas, the pop ballad-style folkloric numbers in $\frac{6}{8}$ meter that the Cochabamba band astutely would brand as "chuntunquis" in the 1970s (also see Chapter 8: Postlude).

Besides "El Solitario," "El Condór Pasa," and "Alborozo Colla," Los Jairas incorporated other non-Bolivian compositions or arrangements into their repertoire. These selections, which are interspersed on the group's recordings, include the Peruvian fox incaico "Vírgenes del Sol," Argentine *vidalita* "Vidala de la Lluvia" (Vidala for the rain), Chilean *plegaria* "El Promesero" (The pilgrim), and Uruguayan *aire de bailecito* "Canción para Mi América" (Song for my America), to name a few examples.[19]

Los Jairas largely adhere to their default "Andean conjunto style" on every track that they recorded from 1966 to 1969, regardless of the genre. On the carnaval "Noche de Luna Llena" (Full moon night; by Susano Azogue Rivero) and taquirari "Carahuata" (by Edgardo Otero de la Vega), for instance, Favre solos on the kena while Cavour executes his customary charango rasgueos, imparting a western highland flavor to these eastern lowland classics. Los Jairas uses a highly similar approach on the tonada tarijeña "La Vidita" (collected by Nilo Soruco), even though Tarija musicians traditionally play the violin and guitar, rather than the kena and charango. From time to time, the band members make minor adjustments to their musical practices, usually by adding percussion instruments that are associated with the corresponding genre. Examples include Los Jairas' use of the *reco-reco* scraper on the tundiqui "San Benito," and *matraca* shaker on the morenada "Reyes Morenos" (Black kings). Yet even on these "Afro-Bolivian" tunes, Los Jairas highlight the kena, which perhaps needless to say, is not an instrument that either tundiqui or morenada musicians traditionally employed.

By performing a wide array of locally distinctive genres within the unitary musical style that characterizes the Andean conjunto tradition, Los Jairas artistically expressed a core tenet of MNR nationalist ideology, mestizaje, that is, the fusion of distinct cultural practices into a new form that theoretically united Bolivians across ethnic and regional lines. In this respect, Mexico's mariachi tradition represents a "national folkloric music" style that is comparable to the Andean conjunto practices of groups like Los Jairas. Since the mid-20th century, the mariachi repertoire has encompassed a variety of regional and popular music genres (e.g., *son jaliscience, huapango, polca*, son jarocho, bolero-ranchero), which the ensembles interpret without making major changes to their standard performance practices and instrumentation (see Sheehy 1997; Jáuregui 2007). In most other Latin American countries, in contrast, the primary form of "national music" has tended to center on a single genre, or genre-family (i.e., a single genre with many variants), rather than a musical style that incorporates numerous genres. Brazilian samba, Dominican merengue, Cuban son, Argentine tango, Ecuadorian pasillo, and Chilean cueca represent some examples of this more common Latin American scenario in the sphere of "national" popular or folkloric music (see Austerlitz 1997; Moore 1997; Vianna 1999; González Rodríguez, Rolle, and Olsen 2009; Wong 2012; Luker 2016).

In Mexico, the mariachi tradition is generally viewed as the embodiment of mestizaje, not primarily because of the repertoire's integration of distinct genres, but because the mariachi tradition itself is strongly associated with mestizo nationalism (see Mulholland 2007). Notably, mariachi music seldom references indigenous traditions in an overt manner, nor do the ensembles use musical instruments that Mexicans mainly identify with indigenous people. In the Andean conjunto tradition, in contrast, the instrumentation, majority of the repertoire, and associated imagery foregrounds signifiers of indigeneity, to such a great degree that it represents a defining characteristic of the musical style that Los Jairas played a major part in canonizing in Bolivia.

LOS JAIRAS AND THE PANPIPE

Although in the 1966–1969 period Los Jairas had not yet added the panpipe to their lineup, a number of the selections that they then performed allude musically or textually to Bolivia's most acclaimed rural indigenous panpipe tropa traditions, Los Sikuris de Italaque and Kantus de Charazani. The huayño "Alturas de Huallpacayu" (The heights of Huallpacayu), which Los Jairas recorded in 1967 and figures among their biggest hits, represents an early example (LPL 13051). Huallpacayu is the name of the mountain range that is located in close proximity to Italaque and that the province's residents regard as their most emblematic landmark. Through the title of this number, then, Los Jairas references Italaque, and by extension the famed indigenous siku groups associated with the area. Yet rather than incorporating stylistic aspects of the Sikuris de Italaque tradition, Los Jairas fuses two identifying markers of Kantus de Charazani music, its parallel-fifth panpipe harmonies, and the "bouncing ball" pattern that the drummers traditionally execute on the bombo to introduce kantus tunes.[20] In Los Jairas' reworking of these kantus hallmarks, the string players pluck single notes in parallel fifths, to the same rhythm as the bombo legüero. This passage commences "Alturas de Huallpacayu," and appears at various other spots in the song as well, functioning as an interlude. The next year, Los Jairas recorded another huayño that evokes Italaque, "El Imán de tus Ojos" (The magnetism of your eyes) (Campo LPS 004). This time, Favre's solo kena reproduces the stock introduction for Italaque sikuri music, a drawn-out passage that is typically played on the panpipes in unison and that progresses melodically in octaves and fourths (see Example 7.2).[21]

Also in 1968, Los Jairas started to collaborate with Los Choclos, a partnership that foreshadowed the panpipe's eventual centrality, musically and visually, in the Andean conjunto tradition. Los Jairas' second Discolandia album (issued in 1968; Lyra LPL 13066) includes their earliest joint recording with Los Choclos, the suitably

EXAMPLE 7.2 Italaque-style panpipe introduction

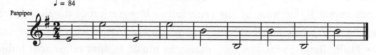

titled huayño "Zampoñas" (Panpipes). The track opens with Los Choclos imitating the passage that Sikuris de Italaque groups use to mark the beginnings and endings of pieces. Once Los Choclos completes the introduction, they drop out of the mix, to make way for Joffré to sing the melody to the accompaniment of Godoy's bass runs on the guitar and Cavour's charango strums. For the second pass, Cavour and Godoy again supply the accompaniment, but Los Choclos interpret the melody on their panpipes (tuned in unison and octaves), with which they insert a standard cadence for the "mestizo" zampoñada or sikuris genre (see Example 7.3). Cavour mimics this stock zampoñada passage with his charango, before Joffré enters for the second time. Continuing this alternation scheme, Los Choclos take the lead role on the fourth run through the melody. For the fifth and final rendition, Joffré and Los Choclos finally unite, to perform the huayño together. Instead of delivering the text, Joffré sings the vocables "La, lay."

Los Jairas were evidently pleased with "Zampoñas." Later in the same year, the group recorded an EP consisting of four huayños in which Los Choclos participate on every track. One of Los Jairas' most popular musical numbers, "Agüita de Phutina" (Waters of Phutina), appears on this release. From January to March 1969, this huayño remained on *El Diario*'s Top Ten chart for Bolivian music singles—at the very moment that Los Jairas' yaraví "El Cisne" was also topping the charts (*ED*, Jan. 12, 19, and 31; Feb. 2, 16, and 23; Mar. 30, 1969). By the year's end, La Paz musical acts as varied as the folklore band Los Caminantes and orquesta de jazz Delfín y su Combo had added "Agüita de Phutina" to their repertoire (*ED*, Mar. 4, 1969; *Hoy*, Nov. 24, 1969).

The Charazani Valley is the inspiration behind the huayño "Agüita de Phutina." In the opening line of the lyrics, Joffré extols the region's "refreshing waters of Phutina" (i.e., the thermal springs of Phutina River), while at a later point in the track, he states that he will "never be able to forget" the "woman from Charazani" whom he once loved. For the melody of "Agüita de Phutina," Los Jairas might have adapted a tune from the Kantus de Charazani repertoire, "Yaku Kantu" (Quechua for "Water song"). It is equally possible, though, that Charazani panpipe groups learned the melody by listening to Los Jairas' recording of "Agüita de Phutina."[22] In any case, in Bolivia and abroad, musicians and audiences have strongly associated "Agüita de Phutina" with the frequently exoticized Charazani Valley ("home of the mystical Kallawaya"), which at least partially accounts for the popularity this huayño has enjoyed in Bolivia and internationally among Andean conjunto fans.[23]

EXAMPLE 7.3 Los Jairas and Los Choclos, "Zampoñas," sikureada cadence

Los Choclos play the main melody of "Agüita de Phutina" in unison and parallel octaves, rather than in the harmonically richer polyphony of the kantus tradition, perhaps because the ensemble did not have access to a set of Charazani-style panpipes.[24] For the introduction, meanwhile, Los Choclos render the standard panpipe cadence in the Sikuris de Italaque tradition. Adding to the semiotic mix, Cavour, as he had done on "Zampoñas," repeatedly plucks a misti sikuri–style cadential passage on the charango, this time at almost every pause in Joffré's vocal line. "Agüita de Phutina," in sum, references the three panpipe tropa traditions most familiar to paceño criollo-mestizos: Sikuris de Italaque, Kantus de Charazani, and misti sikuri zampoñada. Standard elements of criollo-mestizo folkloric-popular music also appear on this selection, from the use of a powerful lead singer, to the guitar and charango accompaniment. The Los Jairas urban fan base no doubt found these aspects of the musical arrangement to be appealing as well.

Since the consolidation of Bolivian indigenismo in the 1920s and 1930s, paceño criollo-mestizo folkloric musicians often looked to indigenous panpipe tropa traditions for inspiration, especially Los Sikuris de Italaque. At the 1939 Concurso Popular de Arte Folklórico, for instance, two of the prizewinning estudiantinas, Kollasuyo and Inti-Karkas, impressed the judges with Italaque-themed instrumental pieces, "Aire Italaqueño" and "Kaluyo Italaqueño," respectively (Chapter 3). In the MNR period, circa 1960, Tito Yupanqui of Los Wara Wara recorded "Italaqueñita" for Mexico's Vanguard label, as a panpipe solo (Chapter 5)—over a decade and a half before zampoña soloists would become a standard feature of the Andean conjunto lineup (see Chapter 8: Postlude). As for the Kantus de Charazani tradition, few elite and middle-class paceños even knew it existed until the mid-1950s (see Chapters 2 and 4), and largely for this reason, musical or textual references to the kantus genre started to become common in La Paz criollo-mestizo folkloric music only in the mid-to-late 1960s. For another example of this more recent practice, in 1967 the paceño string band Amerindia announced in El Diario that their upcoming release would feature the piece "Kantus," although revealing their lack of knowledge about the genre's Charazani roots, they subtitled it "aire Italaqueño" (ED, Mar. 12, 1967).

Los Jairas were not the first La Paz–based criollo-mestizo group to collaborate with a siku tropa on a recording. Los Pregoneros had done so over ten years earlier, with Los Cebollitas on the 1956 release "Ese Vaso de Cerveza" (Chapter 5). Whereas the Los Pregoneros–Los Cebollitas partnership had not spurred a paceño musical trend of any consequence in the MNR years, however, the recordings that Los Jairas made with Los Choclos did have a significant impact on contemporaneous folklore acts. By 1969, Fidel Magno and Los Zampoñas del Huracán were putting out recordings that clearly took after the Los Jairas–Los Choclos formula, and in the same year, Los Rhupay taped their debut album, Music of Bolivia, which contains several tracks that integrate siku tropa music with vocals and charango. The musical activities of Los Rhupay and Magno-Los Zampoñas del Huracán, moreover, heralded the emergence of elite- and middle-class-affiliated urban siku tropas, and rise of the closely related música autóctona movement (as this chapter discusses at a later point).

TRÍO DOMÍNGUEZ-FAVRE-CAVOUR AND NEO-FOLKLORE

In the first year of Peña Naira's existence, Los Jairas, Los Choclos, Ernesto Cavour, and Alfredo Domínguez made up the core of the programming and as such largely defined the locale's artistic identity. Just as Los Jairas and Los Choclos eventually teamed up, Domínguez took the initiative to create musical partnerships with Favre and Cavour. In December 1966, at an exposition of his oil paintings at the venue, Domínguez played the bailecito "Campanitas de Cualquier Parte" (Bells from anywhere) with Cavour, and the yaraví "El Triste" (The sad one) with Favre (Arauco 2011, 168). By November 1967, Domínguez, Favre, and Cavour had begun to perform as a trio on "La Pastora" (The shepherdess) (Arauco 2011, 174), the composition that soon would be regarded as emblematic of the "neo-folklore" output of Trío Domínguez-Favre-Cavour.

Domínguez was the driving force behind this artistic project. Born and raised in the southern Potosí town of Tupiza, where his early musical experiences included a stint as first guitarist in a Trío Los Panchos–style cover band named Trío Los Panchitos, he had moved to La Paz in 1962. By then, he had taught himself to play, largely by ear, Spanish classical guitar standards such as those of Francisco Tárrega (e.g., tremolo piece "Recuerdos de la Alhambra" [Memories of the Alhambra]), and also had become adept at performing the solo guitar numbers of Argentine folklorists Eduardo Falú and Atahualpa Yupanqui (Arauco 2011, 59–64). Yupanqui's oeuvre in particular had a deep impact on Domínguez, shaping the style of "La Muerte del Indio" (The death of the Indian) and several of Domínguez's other works for unaccompanied guitar (*ED*, June 27, 1965).[25]

Violeta Parra represented another important influence on Domínguez. He saw her as a kindred spirit, because of her equal dedication to music and visual art. It was Parra who had convinced Domínguez, during her first visit to La Paz in 1966, not to limit himself to playing instrumental pieces, despite his initial lack of confidence in his singing abilities. Once he had agreed to follow her advice and embark on a career as a singer-guitarist-songwriter, Domínguez regularly found inspiration in the poetry of Parra's lyrics and her other writings (Herrada 1996, 65–72; Arauco 2011, 59–64).

After playing music together for about a year, in December 1967 the three artists recorded their first album as "Domínguez-El Gringo-Cavour" (*ED*, Dec. 10, 1967). This release, simply titled *Folklore*, consists mainly of Domínguez's compositions and arrangements (Campo CPS 002). They taped the LP at the studios of a recently established La Paz label, Campo, which promoted it as "a new expression of Bolivian folklore" (*Presencia*, Jan. 6, 1968). *Folklore* instantly found favor among La Paz's radio deejay association. The organization unanimously pronounced the album "The Record of the Year," only a few weeks after the LP had hit the market (*Presencia*, Jan. 6, 1968).

The band members obtained additional publicity by the end of the month. It was at this moment that the public became aware that the musical stylings of Domínguez, Favre, and Cavour would appear on the soundtracks of two soon-to-be released films: the Bolivian movie *Mina Alaska* (Alaska mine), and Argentine-Bolivian production *Crimen sin Olvido* (Unforgotten crime) (*Presencia*, Jan. 18 and 31, 1968). Favre and Domínguez would also have acting parts in *Crimen sin Olvido* (despite their negligible competence in this field), foreshadowing their cameos in Bolivian director Jorge Sanjinés's controversial 1969 film *Yawar Mallku* (briefly discussed in a later section).

The most popular number on *Folklore*, from the year of its release, to the Campo label's dissolution in 1986, and beyond, has been the opening track, "La Pastora" (record-label owner Jorge "Willy" Ocampo, personal communication). The melody that Favre plays on the kena in the A section (the piece is in AABB form) is highly unusual for a Bolivian folklore number, mainly because of its inclusion of microtonal intervals, which he executes via protracted falling and rising glissandos (Example 7.4). The other tracks on the album, in contrast, largely conform with criollo-mestizo genre conventions (e.g., melodic content, repetition schemes, rhythmic patterns, harmonic progressions), although the musicians perform these selections in a style more virtuosic than had been the norm in the field of Bolivian folkloric music. "La Pastora" also differs from the rest of the LP in that it is the sole selection in which all three musicians participate. Favre, for instance, appears on only two additional numbers: the duets "Coplas" (Couplets) and "El Triste." A yaraví, "El Triste" is based on the piece "Soncoiman" (named after a mountain in Jujuy, Argentina) that Los Incas had recorded in 1963 for *Amérique du Sud*.[26]

"Coplas" is a mournful song in strophic form, which Domínguez set in the traditional Tarija genre of the same name. His subdued vocals alternate with the sound of Favre's kena on the minor-mode melody, while Domínguez's guitar strums fill out the texture. The track "Rosendo Villegas Velarde" also features Domínguez singing. The Tupiza poet and playwright Gastón Suárez wrote the text, which he named after a fictional Andean indigenous character. In Quechua-inflected and grammatically incorrect Spanish, the lyrics of "Rosendo Villegas Velarde" are intended to illuminate the struggles of southern Bolivia's indigenous population. Backed by his guitar,

EXAMPLE 7.4 Trío Dominguez-Favre-Cavour, "La Pastora," kena melody for A section

Domínguez delivers the stanzas by using an unadorned melodic line and reedy timbre. His standard vocal approach, it is reminiscent of the straightforward singing style of Violeta Parra.

Whereas on Los Jairas' albums the guitarist (Julio Godoy) almost exclusively provides accompaniment, Domínguez uses the guitar as a solo instrument on eleven of the thirteen tracks on *Folklore*. On the unaccompanied guitar piece "Por la Quebrada" (On the mountain pass), Domínguez executes a gamut of techniques, ranging from percussive effects to tremolo passages. Equally impressive from a technical standpoint are the seven charango-guitar duets that he performs with Cavour. These duo numbers comprise most of the tracks on the album. Neither the charango or guitar parts remain at the center of attention for very long on these seven selections, because the spotlight repeatedly shifts between the two instruments (e.g., cueca tarijeña "En Fa, Sol, La, Si" [named after the solfège syllables], bailecito "Campanitas de Cualquier Parte"). Cavour plays one solo piece on the LP, "Punteado." It strongly resembles Mauro Núñez's "Estudio para Charango" (e.g., triplet passages played with a combination of right-hand punteado and left-hand ligados), which Cavour had recorded two years earlier with Los Jairas for their first LP.

The critical and popular acclaim that "La Pastora" received clearly influenced the direction that Domínguez, Cavour, and Favre took on their follow-up Campo release, *Folklore 2* (issued in December 1968; *ED*, Dec. 15, 1968). Instead of mainly featuring duets and only one trio, as had been the case on *Folklore*, the *Folklore 2* album contains seven trio numbers, with three duets and two solos rounding out the LP (Campo LPS 005). The melodic and rhythmic imprint of "La Pastora" is unmistakable on the opening tracks for the A and B sides, "Procesión" (Procession) and "Puna" (Highlands), respectively, and one additional selection, "Senda Nueva" (New path). Favre's drawn-out kena glissandos on "Puna" and "Senda Nueva" represent another similarity between these pieces and "La Pastora."

On the rin "Cerca del Cielo" (Close to heaven), which is one of two compositions by Violeta Parra that appear on *Folklore 2* (the other is the funereal song "El Rin del Angelito"), Favre once again produces kena glissandos in the style of "La Pastora." Interestingly, at various points on "Cerca del Cielo," the musicians shift from the galloping simple-duple-meter pulse of the huayño, to the sesquiáltera hemiola of the cueca. This rhythmic ambiguity is not present in Parra's original version of "Cerca del Cielo," nor is it characteristic of the Chilean rin genre. The trio "El Jilguero" (The goldfinch) and charango-guitar duet "Subida" (Rising) on *Folklore 2* take the principle of genre hybridity even further. It is often unclear if these pieces are huayños or bailecitos, because the musicians play the accompaniment patterns for both genres, at times simultaneously.

Apparently to stave off negative criticisms from purists who might disapprove of their unorthodox approach to folkloric music interpretation, Domínguez, Favre, and Cavour described their creative approach as "neo-folklore." Their use of this term, and the musical innovations associated with it, nevertheless generated spirited public discussion. *El Diario* invited Bolivia's leading folklore scholar, Julia Fortún, to weigh in. She made her views on the subject crystal clear in the sternly titled article that she submitted to the daily, "Neofolklore No Puede Existir" (Neofolklore cannot exist) (*ED*, Aug. 18, 1968). In the essay, Fortún maintains that only "expressions of past eras that are still being cultivated in the present" should be categorized as folklore, a criterion excluding neo-folklore, given that "the word neo means new." Offering further clarification of her perspective, Fortún states that "folklore is a spontaneous act, . . . free of any artifice . . . [or] preconceived notions" (*ED*, Aug. 18, 1968), in a pointed dig at the intellectualism of Domínguez. And with a tone of alarm, she contends that excessive stylization on the part of Bolivian folkloric musicians could have disastrous effects on typical local genres because these traditions might lose their characteristic "essence" (*ED*, Aug. 18, 1968).

On the other side of this debate was poet and literary critic Óscar Rivera Rodas. In his essays "Neo-Folklore" and "El Talento También Existe en el Folklore" (Talent also exists in folklore) (*Presencia*, June 2 and Sept. 1, 1968), in which he incorporates quotations from Favre, Cavour, and especially Domínguez, Rivera Rodas argues that their innovations promise to raise the quality of Bolivian folkloric music and therefore deserve nothing but praise. He was hardly an impartial observer, though. His poem "Padre Surco" (Furrowed father) appears on *Folklore 2*, in Domínguez's setting for solo voice and guitar. Yet Rivera Rodas was far from alone in supporting the artists' creative vision, considering the popularity that *Folklore* and *Folklore 2* enjoyed. The "neo-folklore" designation itself, however, seems to have been less well received at first among Bolivian folkloric musicians and audience members in La Paz (see *ED*, Sept. 15 and 22, 1968; *Hoy*, Mar. 7, 1969).

The neo-folklore label was not something that Domínguez, Favre, and Cavour had pulled out of thin air. As they knew, Chileans had been using this term since the mid-1960s to refer to artists who performed recently restored or reconstructed Chilean "folk" genres (especially the sirilla, rin, *cachimbo*, and *refalosá*) with polyphonic vocal arrangements that featured onomatopoeic imitations of the sounds of the guitar and bombo legüero (González Rodríguez, Rolle, and Olsen 2009, 337–56). Chile's leading neo-folklore groups, such as Los Cuatro Cuartos (The four fourths), borrowed extensively from the musical style of Los Trovadores del Norte and Los Huanca Hua (González Rodríguez, Rolle, and Olsen 2009, 337–56), who were protagonists of the "vanguardist" school in Argentina's folklore scene (Chamosa 2012, 160–63).

Instead of noting parallels with these developments, the members of "Trío Domínguez-Favre-Cavour"—as the group or artistic project came to be known—stressed that their music had little if anything in common with that of Los Cuatro Cuartos or Los Trovadores del Norte, whose output they dismissed as being insufficiently traditional (e.g., *Presencia*, Sept. 1, 1968).[27] In any case, Bolivians and Chileans certainly attached the neo-folklore tag to different musical trends in the late 1960s. Whereas Chileans employed this descriptor for vocally oriented artists who sang polyphonic arrangements of revived genres, Bolivians mainly associated "neo-folklore" with the predominantly instrumental music of "Trío Domínguez-Favre-Cavour."[28]

In the Americas, sales of commercial "folk music" recordings experienced a major upsurge in the 1960s, and as a consequence, folkloric-popular music artists increasingly felt the need to distinguish themselves from their many competitors, invariably steering some to introduce musical innovations. Predictably, these innovations provoked heated debates over the rightful place of creavitity in folkloric music performance and composition, pitting traditionalists against those who championed experimentation. Academically trained folklore researchers such as Fortún tended to frown upon the interpretive approaches that in their estimation deviated too radically from "the tradition." The broader public, particularly youths of elite and middle-class background, however, frequently expressed keen interest in the artists who pushed the boundaries of folkloric musical conventions (for the Argentine case, see Chamosa 2012, 152–81). Bolivia's neo-folklore trend, and the debates that it provoked among local artists, fans, and scholars, therefore was not a phenomenon unique to the country.

The 1960s also represented the decade when record companies around the globe began to devote more resources to constructing and marketing "new" musical forms for teenagers and young adults. This capitalist strategy fostered the consolidation of modern-day notions of "youth culture," such as the idea that it is natural for young people to exhibit musical preferences that highly contrast with those of older adults (see Taylor 2016, 40–42, 66–69). The emergence of *nueva ola* (new wave), the designation that Latin Americans often used in this period to characterize the local rock music current (see Pacini Hernandez, Fernández-L'Hoeste, and Zolov 2004), is tied to this marketing tactic. The nueva ola trend of the 1960s also presents some parallels with Bolivian neo-folklore.

When the Campo label released *Folklore 2* in late 1968, La Paz city boasted many nueva ola bands. Some of the most popular were Los Bonny Boy Hots, Los Black Byrds, Four Star, Los Grillos (The crickets), The Donkeys, and Loving Dark's (Basualdo Zambrana 2003, 12–28). The folklore numbers of Trío Domínguez-Favre-Cavour contrasted of course with the rock music styles that these nueva ola groups played.[29] But when the trio's members spoke passionately about their creative artistry, something they were known to do, their rhetoric mirrored that of nueva ola acts. That the ensemble primarily interpreted original works constituted another similarity with nueva ola practices (especially those of Latin American superstar artists). Trío Domínguez-Favre-Cavour's identification with the "neo" prefix, meanwhile, framed their brand of folkloric music as "cutting edge" and thereby differentiated it from the "old-fashioned style" of previous generations of Bolivian folklore artists—in a manner that also paralleled how Chilean nueva canción artists set themselves apart from the more conservative strands in Chile's folklore movement (see González Rodríguez, Rolle, and Olsen 2009, 371–435). The trio's customary performance attire, which consisted of casual clothing (e.g., sweaters), further underscored the ensemble's distinction from more traditional Bolivian folkloric acts. Without a doubt, the neo-folklore identity of Trío Domínguez-Favre-Cavour contributed to the group or project's popularity among Bolivian youths of elite and middle-class background, as the members of this sector, like their counterparts elsewhere, gravitated toward the musical styles that they envisioned as forward-looking or "modern."

By 1969, Bolivians were commonly applying the term "neo-folklore" not only to Trío Domínguez-Favre-Cavour, but also to Los Jairas, in large part because newspaper writers, the public, and even other artists frequently conflated the two bands (see Arauco 2011, 193, 196–200). Favre and Cavour playing in both ensembles of course contributed to this state of affairs. So did the fact that Trío Domínguez-Favre-Cavour alternated sets with Los Jairas, and that the two groups toured together (Arauco 2011, 193, 196–200). Like the case with Trío Domínguez-Favre-Cavour, Los Jairas' association with "neo-folklore" bolstered their image as a hip folklore act and consequently made them more appealing to the younger crowd. The quasi-leftist associations that Los Jairas started to acquire in 1967 contributed as well to the band's popularity among this sector.

UNIVERSITY STUDENTS AND THE FOLKLORE MOVEMENT

Domínguez and Los Jairas gave one of their earliest joint recitals outside of their usual Peña Naira gig in April 1967. The setting was the Paraninfo Universitario (main assembly hall) of Bolivia's flagship public university, La Paz's Universidad Mayor de San Andrés, or UMSA. Domínguez played "Por la Quebrada" and two additional solo guitar works, as well as duets with Favre, Cavour, Joffré, and Godoy. Los Jairas offered a set of eight numbers that included the crowd favorites "El Llanto de Mi Madre" and "Alborozo Colla" (*Presencia*, Apr. 4, 1967; Arauco 2011, 170).

The recital constituted a personal victory for Xavier Díaz Torres. As the student representative for cultural events, he had lobbied the school's officials for permission to use the Paraninfo Universitario as the venue for folkloric music performances, only to be frustrated when his requests were denied time and time again. In response to his entreaties, UMSA rector Carlos Terrazas had habitually retorted, "You cannot convert the Paraninfo into a *chichería*!" (Xavier Díaz Torres, personal communication). In Terrazas's view, the assembly hall represented a hallowed space reserved for important events in the academic calendar like commencement and therefore an inappropriate site for programs featuring musical traditions that might be heard in chicherías—drinking establishments selling chicha (maize beer) that catered primarily to the working class.

Eventually, Díaz Torres somehow convinced UMSA officials to acquiesce to the petition.[30] His next move, then, was to select the musicians for the show. Consistent with his Trotskyist leanings and affiliation with the Bolivian Communist Party, Díaz Torres was intrigued with *canción comprometida*, that is, politically engaged song, and around this time even had written a research paper on the subject (Xavier Díaz Torres, personal communication). Bolivian folklorists whose music conveyed radical-leftist messages, such as Nilo Soruco, thus naturally appealed to him. So would the repertoire of singer-guitarist Benjo Cruz when he appeared on the La Paz scene a couple of years later.[31] But because it had been such a struggle for Díaz Torres to obtain approval from UMSA authorities for the 1967 recital, he trod carefully. In the end, he programmed Domínguez and Los Jairas, no doubt because their appeal cut across the growing divide in Bolivian society between leftist and conservative-reactionary factions.

The Barrientos government's authoritarianism, strong alliance with the United States, and violent repression of the labor movement (including clandestine executions of union leaders) by then had galvanized the left, with university students by and large joining this bloc (Dunkerley 1984, 124). One shocking incident that steered many students to commit themselves to the opposition occurred in June 1967 in the mining town of Llallagua, Potosí. In the early morning hours following the feast day of Saint John the Baptist (June 23)—which marks the winter solstice in the southern hemisphere—the military opened fire on half-awake and still-sleeping mine workers who had gone on strike, resulting in a massacre termed La Noche Triste de San Juan (The sad night of Saint John). Outraged by this violent action, UMSA students denounced Barrientos and Ovando as "enemies of the people" and proclaimed that the university represented an autonomous space, free from state control, to which the regime replied in belligerent fashion, with "much use of tear gas and the occupation of the campus" (Dunkerley 1984, 149).

A few months before the tragedy unfolded in Llallagua, Barrientos had declared a state of emergency, after learning that a foreign guerilla contingent had slipped into the country. Its leader was Che Guevara. The Argentine revolutionary and former right-hand man of Fidel Castro had arrived with a plan, to plunge Bolivia into such violent strife that it would trigger a South American revolution comparable in international scope to the Vietnam War (Anderson 1997, 703–4). He chose an isolated area of Santa Cruz, in the province of Vallegrande, for his base of operations. From March to October 1967, Bolivia's US-trained Rangers regiment combed through the region's Ñancahuazú jungle, looking for the insurgents. When they finally apprehended Guevara, he remained in their custody for only a day, because Barrientos had ordered his swift execution (Debray 1975, 150–57; Dunkerley 1984, 134–54). Ending the charismatic revolutionary's life did not terminate his influence, however. Worldwide, the left elevated *El Che* to the rank of a martyr, and before long a romanticized image of a bereted, long-haired Guevara circulated that especially resonated with idealistic university students (Casey 2009). Bolivian students were no exception (see Vásquez Diaz 1968; Siles del Valle 1997).

Peña Naira was under state surveillance when Guevara was killed in the tiny village of La Higuera on October 9, 1967. Barrientos officials had been keeping tabs on the venue ever since they had discovered a live recording of a Peña Naira show among the confiscated possessions of Haydeé Tamara Bunke, aka Tania la Guerillera (Leni Ballón, personal communication). An undercover agent of German-Argentine ancestry who worked for the Cuban government, Bunke went by the alias "Laura Gutiérrez Bauer" in her Bolivian assignment. She fought alongside Guevara in Santa Cruz's Vallegrande Province and died in a hail of bullets while trying to escape from an ambush on August 31, 1967. Bunke had entered the country in late 1964. After settling down in La Paz, she befriended Julia Fortún, who hired her for a position at the Department of Folklore (Gálvez Rodríguez 2003, 38–41, 732). For part of her duties with the bureau, Bunke attended Compi's inaugural Concurso Regional de Danzas Autóctonas, where by chance she was able to chat briefly with Barrientos and Ovando. She also visited Colquencha (home of Los Chajes de Colquencha; Chapter 6) and other La Paz villages to document fiesta traditions. Bunke even traveled with the Bolivian folklore delegation to the first edition of Salta's Latin American Folklore Festival (Rodríguez Ostria 2010, 97–99).

Before joining the insurgents in Vallegrande, Bunke had been a frequent presence at Peña Naira, where no one had suspected her true identity and mission (Leni Ballón and Ernesto Cavour, personal communications). Nevertheless, once the military had seized Bunke's "Peña Naira tape," a cloud of suspicion began to surround the venue, particularly its owner, Pepe Ballón, whose membership in the Bolivian Communist Party had long been widely known. In October 1967, Bolivian state authorities took action against Ballón, by arresting him for (allegedly) passing information to the guerillas. He spent a few weeks in jail, until his name was cleared (Leni Ballón, personal communication).

The intrigue henceforth linked to Peña Naira imparted a quasi-leftist aura to the locale's primary musical act, the largely apolitical Los Jairas. In the final weeks of Guevara's ill-fated Bolivian campaign, Favre had been in Chile, to reconnect with Ángel and Isabel Parra. While there, he taped the LP *Ángel Parra y el Tocador Afuerino* (Arauco 2011, 142–43). Favre's continued ties with the politically outspoken Parra family bolstered Los Jairas' growing association with the left, in particular for Bolivian university students, for whom this relationship added to the band's mystique (Xavier Díaz Torres, personal communication). It must be underscored, though, that the members of Los Jairas were not known to express strong political views at the time.

After Favre returned to La Paz from Santiago, a group of UMSA students, who in all likelihood had attended the recital that Los Jairas and Alfredo Domínguez presented on the campus earlier in the year (discussed at the start of this section), convinced the Swiss kenista along with Domínguez to head the prize committee for the university's inaugural folkloric music contest, the Primer Festival Folklórico Universitario. Under the auspices of the College of Architecture, Urban Studies, and Plastic Arts, the festival took place at the Paraninfo Universitario from late October to the early weeks of November 1967 (*ED*, Oct. 26, Nov. 8 and 15, 1967). It thus transpired in the tense political climate following the Bolivian military's capture and execution of Guevara and his guerrilla force in Vallegrande.

Students from every UMSA unit participated in the Primer Festival Folklórico Universitario. Those from the Medical School, though, went home with the most medals, including the first-place trophy for ensembles, which the jury awarded to Los Huiñay (Quechua for "The eternals"). Dressed in striped ponchos with matching lluchus—the most commonly used outfit among Bolivian folkloric groups of the late 1960s, Los Huiñay configured itself as an indigenous siku tropa, although on a smaller scale. The group had just four members, of whom three played the siku. The remaining musician kept the beat on the bombo but did not additionally perform on the panpipe (see *ED*, Nov. 15 and Dec. 10, 1967). The ensemble therefore had only one complete ira-arca siku pair, leaving the third sikuri without a partner and limited to doubling the notes on about half of the tune. All in all, Los Huiñay would have sounded thin, lopsided, and light years away from the dense sound that is characteristic of indigenous sikuri music.

The prize committee nonetheless appreciated the group's efforts, and must have hoped that other UMSA students would eventually focus on typical Andean indigenous musical styles. Of the many ensembles that took part in the Primer Festival Folklórico Universitario, Los Huiñay was the sole musical act that used the tropa format. The group also represented one of urban La Paz's earliest siku tropas to be formed by musicians of elite or upper-middle-class socioeconomic background, anticipating by at least a year the founding of the UMSA sikuris Los Yaravís, and peña act Los Zampoñas del Huracán (discussed in a later section).

Los Collanos (The Kollas/Andeans) of the Architecture School earned the runner-up prize in the ensemble category, with a lineup that was almost identical to that of Los Jairas; a kena player, a charanguista, and a guitarist constituted Los Collanos. In the contest for soloists (open to vocalists and instrumentalists), meanwhile, César Espada (Industrial Engineering) won first place for his charango set, beating out a future national star of the charango scene, William Ernesto Centellas (Architecture). Singer Norah Zapata (Economics) netted third place in the soloist competition, for her take on "El Llanto de Mi Madre" and other numbers (*ED*, Nov. 8 and 15, 1967).

UMSA students staged a more ambitious festival the next year, one with a national scope and over 150 musical acts, the Primer Festival Folklórico Universitario Nacional (*ED*, June 2, 16, 21, and 23, 1968; *Los Tiempos*, June 18, 1968). The ten-member siku tropa Los Yaravís took part, in the hopes that they would match Los Huiñay's first-place finish in the 1967 contest. The name "Los Yaravís," as previously noted, reveals that the group mistakenly thought that indigenous panpipe ensembles traditionally played the yaraví genre. The name that the members chose for their musical act also reflects the influence of Los Jairas. Yaravís figured so prominently in Los Jairas' repertoire that the popularity of the genre had noticeably increased in Bolivia. For another example of this phenomenon, in 1967, one year after Los Jairas had premiered "El Llanto de Mi Madre" at the 2nd Lauro Festival of Bolivian Song, the duo Los Ídolos (The idols) won the top award at the third edition of the contest with the yaraví "Añoranzas" (Nostalgias). Invoking the stereotype of Andean indigenous music that the yaraví genre is most associated with, the text of "Añoranzas" opens with this line: "The Indian with his burden, plays this lament on his kena" (*ED*, Oct. 15, 1967; Fernández Coca 1994, 135).

To the disappointment of Los Yaravís, the jury members for the Primer Festival Folklórico Universitario Nacional favored groups whose instrumentation closely emulated those of Los Jairas and Trío Domínguez-Favre-Cavour. The first-place winner in the ensemble category, Cochabamba's Los Inti Wara (Quechua for "Morning sun"), in fact modeled its lineup after that of Los Jairas (Mario Hugo Romero of Los Inti Wara, personal communication). Oruro's Los Huankara (*huankara* is an alternate spelling for wankara) received the runner-up trophy in the same category, for playing the cueca tarijeña "En Fa, Sol, La, Si"—a staple for Trío Domínguez-Favre-Cavour. The inclusion of a kena soloist contest in the festival (won by Cochabamba's Daniel Guerra) also reveals the mark of Los Jairas and Trío Domínguez-Favre-Cavour, and more specifically of Favre. As the most famous Bolivia-based kenista of the time, Favre represented the main inspiration for criollo-mestizo musicians who took up the instrument during the folklore boom (various, personal communications).

Raúl Ibargüen, in his capacity as the secretary of the student organization that coordinated the Primer Festival Folklórico Universitario Nacional, the Federación Universitaria Local, declared that the winning ensemble would soon be traveling to Bulgaria for the IX World Festival of Youth and Students for Peace and Friendship (*ED*, June 14, 1968). He knew full well that the Barrientos government would never permit the students to visit the Socialist Bloc, in light of the regime's alliance with the US and the president's anti-communist rhetoric (see Dunkerley 1984, 129, 153, 358). Instead of representing a realistic scenario, then, Ibargüen's announcement expressed the student body's leftist affiliation and was meant to provoke the administration. The next year, undeterred by the state's escalating crackdown on political protests, La Paz university students used poetry recitation and musical performance to give voice to their political views at the Primer Festival de Música y Poesía de Protesta (*Hoy*, Aug. 9, 1969). Powerfully delivered Bolivian folkloric numbers with unambiguously leftist lyrics dominated the proceedings at this event (organizer Xavier Díaz Torres, personal communication).

Prior to the late 1960s, Bolivian university students had not been so closely aligned with the left. Nor had they been heavily involved in the folklore movement. From now on, however, it would be commonplace for Bolivian young adults to adopt leftist positions and express this political orientation through their involvement with folkloric music as performers or fans. Many other countries in the Americas and elsewhere of course experienced this type of musical-political development in the late 1960s as well as 1970s.

It was also at this time that Andean conjuntos started to become part of campus life in multiple Latin American countries, a trend that with the main exception of Bolivia, can be directly linked to the influence of Chilean nueva canción. In Peru, Ecuador, Colombia, and Mexico, for instance, the first wave of locally based Andean conjuntos took inspiration primarily from Chilean bands such as Quilapayún and Inti-Illimani. Like the case in Chile, in each of these countries, leftist-oriented university students represented the principal audience for Andean conjunto music, to such an extent that the Andean conjunto tradition became highly identified with this sector of the population in the late 1960s and 1970s, and often retained this association into the 1980s (see Oliart and Lloréns 1984; Arana 1988; Zolov 1999, 225–33; Peralta 2003; González Rodríguez, Rolle, and Olsen 2009; Tucker 2013; Katz-Rosene 2015).

In Bolivia, in contrast, university students were only one, and not even the primary, part of the fan base for Andean conjunto music in the 1960s and 1970s. This particularity of the scene had many contributing factors. Perhaps most significantly, Bolivians categorized local bands of this variety as "national" folklore acts, a designation that widened the appeal of the music that these ensembles interpreted to a broad spectrum of society, even to nationalists of politically conservative inclinations. This scenario seldom occurred in other Latin American countries. Outside of Bolivia, the public mainly identified Andean conjuntos with leftist pan–Latin Americanism (especially in the 1970s), which in turn tended to limit the audience for Andean conjunto music to those who embraced or expressed sympathy for leftist political positions.

It is worth underscoring that whereas in most Latin American countries Andean conjuntos introduced and popularized typical genres and instruments of the Southern Andean region (e.g., huayño, kena, charango), this was not the case in Bolivia. Bolivian artists and audiences had long been familiar with criollo-mestizo folklorizations of highland indigenous music and dance traditions. Andean conjunto music, as performed by Bolivian groups like Los Jairas, shared much in common with earlier forms of Bolivian música folklórica nacional, something that greatly facilitated the Andean conjunto format's canonization in the late 1960s and 1970s as the preeminent lineup for Bolivian national folkloric-popular music bands.

THE EXPANSION OF THE PEÑA SCENE

Around 1967, La Paz university students created a new paceño tradition, the "peña universitaria," which was the name they gave to folklore shows held on the UMSA campus or nearby locales that mainly featured performances by the student body (e.g., *ED*, Nov. 26 and Dec. 10, 1967). Some students took the initiative to transplant their music and/or dance acts to one of the commercially oriented peñas located in the downtown. In August 1967, for instance, four UMSA undergraduates, each of whom pursued a different field of study, landed a gig for their folkloric dance troupe at a recently inaugurated paceño venue, Peña Kori Thika (*ED*, Aug. 20, 1967).

It was the second peña to be established in La Paz city. Opened for business by July 1967 (*ED*, July 14, 1967), Peña Kori Thika (Quechua for "Golden flower") took after Peña Naira, from its refreshment selection (at first similarly restricted to wine) and complimentary pasankalla, to the musical programming. For the house band, the owners contracted Los Caminantes. Ever since Pepe Murillo and Carlos Palenque had started to issue recordings as the duo Los Caminantes, following their performances at the first Salta festival, the group had been one of Bolivia's most popular folkloric music acts. By 1967, Los Caminantes had expanded to a trio, with the addition of singer and bombo legüero player Reynaldo "Tito" Peñarrieta, who was Palenque's former bandmate in the Argentine-style zamba group Los Inti Huasi (Pepe Murillo and Tito Peñarrieta, personal communications). A few months after the unveiling of the peña, Murillo, Palenque, and Peñarrieta purchased the venue and took over its daily operations (*ED*, Nov. 10, 1967).

Peña Naira and Peña Kori Thika had plenty of competition in urban La Paz within a couple of years. By 1969, Peña Incahuasi (Quechua for "House of the Inca"), Peña Pachamama (Quechua for "Mother Earth"), Peña Kori Inti (Quechua for "Golden sun"), Peña El Tambo (named after the Inca Empire's roadside storage facilities), Peña Tiahuanaco (alternate spelling for Tiwanaku), and Peña Restaurant Copacabana were in business in the city (*ED*, Aug. 25, Oct. 27, 1967; *ED*, May 31, 1968; *Hoy*, Jan. 9, Aug. 1, 1969), to name only those peñas that advertised in *El Diario* and *Hoy*.[32] Los Escudos (The coats of arms), despite being founded as a German restaurant and beer hall in 1968, by the end of the decade had become known in La Paz mainly for its Bolivian folklore spectacles (owner Betty Abdala, personal communication). Peñas soon sprouted up in other urban centers. The first of these, Peña Ollantay, opened in Cochabamba city in 1969 (*ED*, Feb. 12, 1969). In the coming years, its impact on folkloric musical trends in Cochabamba would be akin to Peña Naira's for La Paz.

The rising number of foreign tourists in La Paz, who were usually on their way to or from the Macchu Picchu ruins of Cuzco, contributed to the growth of the peña scene. The Dirección Nacional de Turismo spearheaded the Barrientos government's attempts to boost Bolivia's share of the international tourist market. For part of its early efforts, in 1965 the bureau staged Cochabamba's Primer Festival Folklórico Nacional, and Compi's Primer Concurso Regional de Danzas Autóctonas (Chapter 6). In 1967—or "International Tourist Year," as a United Nations initiative designated it (Urquizo Sossa 1973, 92)—the Dirección Nacional de Turismo once again showcased indigenous music-dance traditions, this time at the Primer Festival Interprovincial de Folklore. President Barrientos attended the event, which coincided with Day of the Indian and took place at La Paz's Coliseo Cerrado, a convenient setting for tourists (foreign as well as Bolivian) who were staying at a hotel in the downtown. Sikuris de Italaque, Kantus de Charazani, Chajes de Colquencha, Laquitas de Compi, and other tropa styles of the La Paz region were represented at the festival. In the intermissions, Alfredo Domínguez, Los Laickas, Las Imillas, Los Caballeros del Folklore, and Los Payas interpreted their usual numbers, notwithstanding the festival's "provincial" or "indigenous" theme (*ED*, Aug. 2, 3, and 5, 1967). Los Jairas also participated in Dirección Nacional de Turismo–sponsored events. In 1967, the band figured among the musical acts that the government agency programmed for the "homage to International Tourist Year" convened at Hotel La Paz (*ED*, Dec. 13, 1967).

Despite the conspicuous presence of foreign tourists and other non-Bolivian patrons at La Paz peñas in the mid-to-late 1960s (e.g., embassy personnel, expatriate community; Favre 1981, 119), Bolivians made up most of the customers, because the foreign contingent remained small in number (for tourism statistics, see Urquizo Sossa 1973, 105). For Bolivians from other regions who were visiting La Paz, spending an evening at a peña would have represented a novel experience in this period. A typical show featured an Andean conjunto, a siku tropa, a vocal duo (or trio), a charango soloist, and a singer-guitarist. Musical acts that specialized in the regional traditions of the eastern lowlands, northern Potosí, or Tarija often rounded out the lineup at peñas. Overall, the programming called to mind what Bolivians would have encountered in the MNR years at state-sponsored folklore company productions such as *Fantasía Boliviana*, though on a smaller scale and in a more intimate setting.

As the next three sections detail, the Bolivian peña scene's expansion in the late 1960s and early 1970s spurred the creation of numerous musical acts whose folklorization practices adhered to the conventions that Peña Naira had helped to establish for this type of venue. A prime performance context for música folklórica nacional, Bolivian peñas thus enacted a crucial role in propagating and canonizing the varieties of musical expression that these locales most commonly programmed, especially Andean conjuntos and urban-based panpipe ensembles.

NEW ANDEAN CONJUNTOS

Los Jairitas, or "The Little Jairas," was among of the earliest Andean conjuntos to be born at Peña Naira. The group's name signaled its identity as a Los Jairas cover band, and the members' youth; each musician was under fifteen years of age when the ensemble debuted in 1967 (*ED*, Oct. 22, 1967).[33] The next year, Ricardo Mendoza (kena) and Basilio Huarachi (charango) left the band to found Los Chaskas (discussed later on).

A second version of The Little Jairas, one with even younger members, then came into existence. José Mendoza (Ricardo Mendoza's cousin), Eddy Meneses, and José Rodríguez formed this latest incarnation of the ensemble (*ED*, May 12 and June 9, 1968). The three friends, all under ten years old, resided in the building that housed Peña Naira. Rodríguez and José Mendoza shared tiny ground-floor apartments with their mothers, with whom they eked out a livelihood selling candies, cigarettes, and other small items near the doorway facing Sagárnaga Street. The boys idolized Los Jairas and absorbed all they could learn from them. Cavour helped Mendoza figure out the charango fingerings for "Manchay Puito/Dos Palomitas" and "Huayño de la Roca," while Favre (as previously noted, he also lived on the premises of Peña Naira) taught Rodríguez how to play the most challenging kena parts in "El Cóndor Pasa" and "Alborozo Colla." To further encourage Rodríguez, Favre graciously bestowed him one of his own prized kenas (José Rodríguez, José Mendoza, and Marcelo Peña, personal communications).

With neighborhood pal and occasional Los Jairitas member Marcelo Peña, in the mid-1970s Rodríguez and Mendoza would form the group that definitely established their reputations as accomplished folklore artists in the La Paz music scene: José, Joselo y Marcelo. A virtuosic and mainly instrumental trio created on the grounds of Peña Naira, this musical act patterned itself after, and interpreted many of the hits of, Trío Domínguez-Favre-Cavour (José Rodríguez, José Mendoza, and Marcelo Peña, personal communications).

Los Nairas (founded in 1969) is another Andean conjunto that made its name at Peña Naira. Often billed as "the emulators of Los Jairas" (e.g., *Hoy*, Nov. 6, 1970), the group exclusively played the music of the superstar ensemble. Founder Hugo Loza, who lived in the same neighborhood as Peña Naira and was a classmate of Los Jairitas' original charanguista, Basilio Huarachi, mastered Cavour's charango style so expertly that when Los Jairas and Trío Domínguez-Favre-Cavour were forced to replace Cavour in the early 1970s, Loza was the obvious choice to fill this important role (Hugo Loza, personal communication). One of Los Nairas' earliest performances to take place outside of the peña setting occurred at the Coliseo Cerrado in 1969, as part of a musical extravaganza that paid homage to the six-year anniversary of deejay Micky Jiménez's still popular El Show de los Sábados (*ED*, Aug. 16, 1969). The slate of acts included a second Andean conjunto, Los Chaskas, which by this time had become one of Bolivia's most highly acclaimed ensembles, especially among the younger crowd.

The fashionably long and unruly hairstyles that the musicians sported matched the ensemble's catchy name of "Los Chaskas," or "The guys with the messy hair." Only a year into their trajectory, a writer for *Hoy* underscored the band's sizable fan base: "There is no other group as popular in Bolivia. And this is not an exaggeration" (*Hoy*, Dec. 20, 1969). Ex–Los Jairitas members Ricardo Mendoza and Basilio Huarachi established the group in 1968 with Percy Bellido and Gualberto Valenzuela; Miguel Ibañez joined them by 1969 (*Hoy*, Mar. 19, 1969).[34] For Bellido, Los Chaskas afforded a second chance at being in the limelight. After all, he had been the bombista for Conjunto de la Peña Naira, until Yayo Joffré took his spot. Between his stints in the two ensembles, Bellido had become adept at singing in falsetto, in the style of Javier Pantaleón of the Argentine folklore group Los Cantores del Alba (The singers of dawn) (Percy Bellido, personal communication). Los Chaskas lead vocalist Gualberto Valenzuela, meanwhile, began his musical career as a bolerista in Trío Los Danubios, and took inspiration from the vocal harmonies of Mexico's Los Tres Diamantes (The diamonds) when arranging Los Chaskas' characteristic three-part vocal lines (Gualberto Valenzuela, personal communication).

By integrating these sonically compatible features of "Mexican" and "Argentine" musical styles, while cultivating a youthful image, Los Chaskas arrived at a winning formula. This approach constituted a major trend among Bolivian Andean conjuntos in the 1970s, not only in La Paz, but also in Cochabamba. Throughout this period, Los Chaskas often performed at Cochabamba's Peña Ollantay, and in doing so, influenced a number of folkloric musical acts in the Cochabamba scene—which would become the home base for many of Bolivia's most popular Andean conjuntos in the 1980s (see Chapter 8: Postlude).

Los Sumac Huaynas represents one of the earliest La Paz bands who unmistakably resembled Los Chaskas, from their polyphonic vocal harmonies with prominent falsetto lines, to their hippy-style fashion sense. This Andean conjunto, which was active in the peña's scene by 1969 (*Hoy*, June 7 and 20, 1969), scored a hit in 1970 with "Cueca del Guerrillero" (cueca of the guerilla). University students especially liked this politically themed number (Los Sumac Huaynas member Andrés Fossati, personal communication).

Los Sumac Huaynas did not select a name for themselves that accentuated their image as modern folklorists, unlike what Los Chaskas had done. Instead, they recycled one from a classic Bolivian group, the "old Los Sumac Huaynas" (member Andrés Fossati, personal communication), that is, the plucked-string band that had accompanied Las Kantutas, Las Hermanas Tejada, and numerous other folklore acts on Radio Illimani in the 1940s (Chapter 3). In a similar vein, around 1970 José Rodríguez and José Mendoza took a respite from Los Jairitas to play in the short-lived Andean conjunto Nina Inti (José Rodríguez and José Mendoza, personal communications), which they named after Luciano Bustíos's long-defunct indigenista choir (Chapter 2). And in the mid-1970s, singer-guitarist Julio César Paredes Ruiz (and future member of Savia Andina [Chapter 8: Postlude]) branded his Andean conjunto as "Lyra Incaica," in homage to the indigenista estudiantina Lira Incaica that his grandfather, Alberto Ruiz Lavadenz, had performed and recorded with in the 1920s and 1930s (Julio César Paredes Ruiz, personal communication).

Besides inspiring the newer generations, veteran paceño musicians actively participated in the peña shows of La Paz, especially those who in the 1950s had formed part of musical acts whose interpretive approaches anticipated future hallmarks of the Andean conjunto tradition. In 1967, Conjunto Kollasuyo's charanguista, K'auquita García, struck out on his own with Conjunto Melódico La Paz, an Andean conjunto that he founded with his son and two former bandmates from the estudiantina Huiñay Inti (*ED*, Mar. 5, Apr. 9 and 23, 1967). José Aramayo Martínez—the bombo legüero player for Conjunto 31 de Octubre and kena soloist for Armando Valdéz y su Conjunto Andino (Chapter 5)—revived his musical career as well (José Aramayo Martínez, personal communication). With guitarists Miguel Butrón and Gastón Valdivia, and charango player Abdón Cameo, Aramayo Martínez formed Los Amigos del Folklore (The friends of folklore). This group, in which Aramayo Martínez served as the kena soloist, performed at Peña Kori Thika soon after the venue's debut (*ED*, July 15, 1967). The duo Los Wara Wara (Tito Yupanqui, Pepa Cardona) similarly took advantage of the opportunities on hand for musicians at the peñas of La Paz, and even played sets at Peña Naira (e.g., *ED*, June 29, 1967). Although Los Wara Wara was not an Andean conjunto, the group's performance practices and repertoire had much in common with, and in the 1950s had foreshadowed, defining characteristics of the Andean conjunto musical style (Chapter 5).

CHARANGO SOLOISTS, AND PANPIPE TROPAS

Charango soloists also started to become a more familiar sight in the La Paz music scene in the late 1960s, largely as a result of the proliferation of peñas. Heeding the example of Peña Naira, where Cavour's technically impressive and invariably humorous solos represented a mainstay of the entertainment, Peña Kori Thika offered the charango stylings of Mario Gallardo (e.g., *Presencia*, Jan. 19, 1968), yet another former member of Los Inti Huasi who recently had changed his focus to Bolivian folkloric music. The early wave of charanguistas who played solo sets at La Paz's peñas also included Abdón Cameo (of Los Amigos del Folklore) and Sucre's Florencio Oros, both of whom recorded albums in this period that highlighted their formidable musicianship on the instrument (*ED*, Jan. 29 and Nov. 12, 1967). Mauro Núñez's innovative charango compositions could be heard on the peña stage, too, as interpreted by his devoted student and fictive nephew Carlos Eduardo Vásquez, who went by the pseudonym "Maurito" or "The Little Mauro" (e.g., *Hoy*, Dec. 3, 1969). From the 1970s onward, a large number of Bolivian charango soloists would cut their teeth as folklore interpreters at the peñas of La Paz (see Cavour 2001, 250–82).

With the exception of Los de Umala, indigenous tropas would seldom participate in the peña scene until the mid-1970s. It was then that Los Chajes de Colquencha, over ten years after they had tasted glory at the first Salta festival, began performing in the circuit (e.g., *ED*, May 7, 1976; Apr. 1, 1977; June 9, 1978). When a Kantus de Charazani tropa from the town of Kaata presented several shows at Peña El Tambo in 1969, then, it represented a rare occurrence for the time (*ED*, Mar. 29, Mar. 30, and Apr. 8, 1969). The Charazani group had made the journey to La Paz city so that Jorge Sanjinés's motion picture company *Ukamau* (Aymara for "That's how it is") could film their scenes in *Yawar Mallku* (Quechua for "Blood of the condor"). An example of the leftist social-realism current, this polemical movie features untrained indigenous actors from Kaata, who speak their lines in Quechua.[35] The music of a Kantus de Charazani tropa can be heard in *Yawar Mallku*, as well as the solo guitar playing of Alfredo Domínguez and kena passages of Gilbert Favre (Domínguez and Favre also had cameo acting parts in the film).

From 1966 to 1969, Los Choclos, Los Cebollitas, and Los Sikuris del Altiplano largely monopolized the siku tropa niche in the peña scene. By the early 1970s, though, the number of urban La Paz panpipe ensembles had significantly expanded. A new cohort of sikuris of blue-collar background had emerged in the city, mainly in response to the prospects of employment at peñas (siku artist Héctor Quisbert, personal communication). Los Kori Sikus (Quechua for "The golden panpipes"), Los Wara Waynas (Aymara for "The young stars"), Kori Inti (Quechua for "Golden sun"), and Los Ch'uspitas (named after the pouch that indigenous people use to carry coca leaves) are some examples of these new groups (*Hoy*, May 15, May 22, June 6, and Oct. 9, 1970). Around the same time, all-female siku tropas started to have a presence in peña shows. The pioneers were Ch'ijini's Las Tunkawaris (Aymara for "The ten vicuñas"), and Oruro city's Las Kory Majtas (Aymara for "The golden youths") (*Hoy*, Feb. 3, Feb. 9, July 2, and Nov. 20, 1969).[36]

Los Zampoñas del Huracán broke new ground as well, as one of Bolivia's first siku bands of criollo-mestizo (rather than cholo-mestizo) membership that regularly performed at peñas (*Hoy*, Jan. 3 and 17, 1969). Raúl Lizárraga and René Machicado, at the time high school students residing with their parents in the middle-class neighborhood of Obrajes, created the group in 1968, with several additional members of the

Lizárraga clan. To pick up the style of indigenous sikuris, they attended fiestas in the village of Mocomoco (located near Italaque), where the Lizárraga family had relatives among the vecino residents. After many rehearsals, Los Zampoñas del Huracán debuted at a small venue on Sagárnaga Street that was stationed not far from Peña Naira (Raúl Lizárraga and René Machicado, personal communications). By 1969 or 1970, they had teamed up with Fidel Magno, who was then studying for a law degree at UMSA (Fidel Magno, personal communication). A vocalist and charango player, Magno represented his university at the second edition of the Festival Folklórico Universitario Nacional (*ED*, Aug. 14, 1969).

With Magno as their frontman, Los Zampoñas del Huracán recorded their biggest hit in the early 1970s, the morenada "La Mariposa" (The butterfly). The sikuris' collaborations with Magno recalled Los Jairas' earlier partnership with Los Choclos, because in both cases, a vocalist and siku tropa took turns realizing the melody while a charanguista rapidly strummed chords in the background. That Magno and Joffré had been raised in the same town, Ayata, added to the parallels between the two artistic projects. Los Zampoñas del Huracán and Magno paid tribute to the La Paz village when they recorded the huayño "Ayata," which appears on the four-track EP containing "La Mariposa."

Los Rhupay (Quechua for "Rays of the sun") was founded in La Paz city around the same time as Los Zampoñas del Huracán, and its members likewise combined the siku tropa with charango and vocals. The first recording of Los Rhupay, the 1969 album *Folk Music of Bolivia*, has several examples of this practice (e.g., "La Cacharpaya del Indio" [The farewell of the Indian]). It also includes tracks in which the ensemble plays the tarka, pinkillu, and kena-kena in the tropa format (Discolandia SLC 13892). The English title of the LP suggests, and liner notes make even clearer, that Discolandia marketed *Folk Music of Bolivia* mainly to foreigners—a strategy similar to that of Capital Records with Raúl Shaw Moreno y Los Peregrinos' 1957 LP *Music of Bolivia* (Chapter 5).

In a parallel with the bolerista musical style of Shaw and his band, Los Rhupay's singers execute three- and four-part harmonies on *Folk Music of Bolivia*. This vocal practice of course also resembled that of Argentine folklore bands. Los Rhupay members Mario Gutiérrez and Agustín "Cacho" Mendieta had ample experience with Argentine folkloric music, from their time in the Argentine-style ensemble La Tropilla del Achalar (Cacho Mendieta, personal communication). In contrast, Hery Cortéz of Los Rhupay started off his artistic career as a performer of boleros and other romantic-themed songs, in the musical act Elsita Navarro y Los Melódicos (Hery Cortéz, personal communication).

It was Los Rhupay's tropa selections, however, that caught the most attention in the Bolivian folklore scene. To be sure, Los Choclos and Los Cebollitas had been using the tropa configuration in the urban La Paz context for quite some time by then. But no doubt because of Los Rhupay's higher social standing, steady output of full-length albums, and other factors (e.g., the band members managed Peña Naira for a few months in 1971), the ensemble would be heralded by ensuing generations of

Bolivian folklorists as the origin of the urban-based música autóctona movement. As the name "música autóctona" implies, the criollo-mestizo artists who lead this current seek to faithfully reproduce the sonic characteristics of a diverse array of rural indigenous tropa traditions (Céspedes 1984, 228–31). In the 1970s and 1980s, Grupo Aymara (founded in 1973), Awatiñas (Aymara for "Those who protect"; founded in 1974), Boliviamanta (Quechua for "In Bolivia"; founded in 1978), and Kollamarka (Aymara for "Kolla City"; founded in 1979) would gain renown at home and abroad for their música autóctona repertoire, which built on the artistic line of Los Rhupay.

NON-PACEÑO MUSICAL ACTS

Since the establishment of La Paz's peñas, folklorists specializing in the music-dance forms of other regions of the country, in particular the eastern lowlands, northern Potosí, and Tarija, have often enhanced the programming. In the mid-to-late 1960s, the taquiraris and carnavales of Beni's Los Taitas, Santa Cruz's Trío Oriental, and many other visiting camba groups contrasted with the Andean-associated repertoire that predominated in the peña scene of La Paz, but would not have been considered novel. After all, these música oriental genres had been part of paceño musical life for a few decades (Chapter 3). Most La Paz residents had less familiarity with the "folk music" of Tarija, though, and thus listened with greater curiosity to the cuecas tarijeñas, coplas, and *chapaquedas* that Tarija's Los Cantores del Valle, Los Montoneros de Méndez, and Los Embajadores del Guadalquivir sang to the accompaniment of guitars and violin at peña shows in La Paz. Equally attention-grabbing were northern Potosí acts such as Los Laimes, Los Curmis, and Los de Alonso de Ibañez, who, following in the footsteps of Los Chasquis, recreated Andean indigenous musical styles of their home region for paceño audiences (*ED* and *Hoy*, 1966–1970).

In the MNR era, Urquidi's Academia de Danzas and Ballet Folklórico Oficial had similarly presented folkloric enactments of regionally distinctive music-dance traditions. These state-sponsored companies had seldom featured artists from regions other than La Paz, however, because paceños comprised almost the entirely of their cast. The local peña scene, in contrast, granted a space to non-paceño folklorists, and gave them the incentive to stylize their regional expressive practices in accordance with the aesthetic preferences of mainstream urban criollo-mestizo audiences. The peña circuit of La Paz thus not only fostered the major currents in música folklórica nacional, but also played a part in the development of regional folklore movements outside of the La Paz region.

Non-Bolivian artists frequently provided additional musical variety at La Paz peña shows. In 1969, three years after Violeta Parra's presentations of music and visual art at Peña Naira, Inti-Illimani became the second Chilean folklore act to perform in the scene. At this early stage in the group's trajectory (the band was founded in 1967), the members "passion was Andean music, especially Bolivian music" (Jorge Coulón of Inti-Illimani, personal communication). This explains why they adopted an indigenista-style ensemble name that referenced the Illimani mountain and the Incas' worship of the sun, and imagined their 1969 trip to La Paz as akin to "making a pilgrimmage to Mecca" (Jorge Coulón, personal communication). In their stay in La Paz, the musicians played at Peña Kori Thika and other spots, purchased a tropa of sikus, and recorded their first full-length album (Jorge Coulón, personal communication; *ED*, Feb. 6, 7, and 14, 1969). In keeping with the pan–Latin Americanism of the nueva canción movement, they titled the release *Si Somos Americanos* (If we are Americans), and musically expressed this stance with a repertoire of Chilean, Bolivian, Ecuadorian, and Argentine genres (Cifuentes 1989, 23).

Although touring Chilean ensembles occasionally stopped in La Paz, Argentine musicians represented the majority of visiting non-Bolivian artists who performed at the peñas of La Paz as well as Cochabamba in the late 1960s and 1970s. Within a few years of the birth of Peña Naira, Los Fronterizos, Los Cantores de Quilla Huasi, Los Cantores del Alba, Los Tucu Tucu, Los de Salta, and Horacio Guarany interpreted their characteristic zambas, chacareras, and other typical Argentine genres at Bolivian peña shows (e.g., *ED*, Nov. 16 and Dec. 28, 1967; Apr. 4 and 7, Nov. 22, 1968; *ED*, Mar. 1, 1969; *Hoy*, May 29, 1969). Bolivian fans of Argentine folkloric-popular music thus now had regular opportunities to catch performances by the leading exponents of the movement. Local "Argentine-style" cover bands that focused on this repertoire—a cohort that included Cochabamba's Los Kjarkas (Chapter 8: Postlude)—accordingly saw the demand for their musical production noticeably decline. The members often turned their attention to other musical expressions, usually Bolivian "national folklore." Yet Argentina's folklore movement remained a point of reference for Bolivian folkloric artists, because most of them continued to borrow interpretive approaches from their more famous Argentine counterparts. Indeed, one effect of the Bolivian peña scene's expansion in the late 1960s and early 1970s is that for the first time, superstar Argentine folklore artists came into regular contact with Bolivian musicians, which deepened the influence that the Argentine folklore movement exerted on the practices of Bolivian criollo-mestizo folklore artists.

EUROPE BECKONS

The late 1960s represents a defining conjuncture not only for Bolivia's folkloric music movement, but also for the emergence of a major European market for Andean-associated music. The "folk" musical expressions of the Andes, primarily as interpreted by Los Incas and Los Calchakis, experienced unprecedented interest in Europe in the aftermath of the May 1968 strikes, demonstrations, and riots that erupted in Paris and shook France's political foundations. Many Europeans who backed the uprisings viewed Che Guevara as their New Left idol and admired his decision to foment "the revolution" in one of the exceedingly few countries in the Americas with an indigenous-majority population. Even though the site that Guevara elected for his Bolivian campaign, Santa Cruz's Vallegrande Province, is not located in the altiplano and musicians from the area do not typically play the kena or zampoña, all the same, for many Europeans the music of the Andean highlands became associated with the final exploits of El Che, an odd turn of events that greatly increased the commercial possibilities for Andean folklore artists on the European stage (Rios 2008, 163–73, 181).

The Andean music boom that was developing overseas constituted a golden opportunity for Bolivian musicians. The first contingent of Bolivian folkloric artists to make their way to Europe for this purpose commenced the journey in early 1969. By November, the troupe, branded as Bolivia Andina and composed of various ensembles (e.g., Los Chasquis, Los de Umala), had given concerts in Spain, Belgium, and The Netherlands (Bolivia Andina 1970, 20–23). To the misfortune of the artists, as they were preparing for their upcoming recitals in France and Italy, the entourage's unscrupulous promoter took off with their money, forcing the Bolivia Andina delegation to head home prematurely (Willy Loredo of Los Chasquis, personal communication).

Los Jairas and Domínguez left for Europe in September 1969, after considering this plan of action for at least two years (*ED*, Feb. 4 and June 25, 1967; *Hoy*, Dec. 29, 1968). A Discolandia employee had recently given them a signal that the timing was right for this endeavor, in a newspaper article in which this person noted that the company had received inquiries from France for the recordings of Los Jairas (*Hoy*, Feb. 12, 1969). The band needed a sponsor to pay for the trip, though. Using his savvy networking skills, Favre persuaded the Swiss director of the Simon I. Patiño Foundation—managed by the descendants of the Bolivian tin baron—to fund the group's airplane tickets to the first stop, Switzerland (Ernesto Cavour, personal communication). Before they took off for Europe, Cavour put the finishing touches on his method book for kena soloists, which complemented his previously issued and soon-to-be classic manual for charango players (*ED*, Aug. 23, 1969). Then, with a series of concerts that opened in Santa Cruz and culminated with shows in La Paz, Los Jairas and Domínguez bid farewell to Bolivia (*Presencia*, Aug. 4, 9, 16, and 23, 1969).

With Geneva as their new home base, Los Jairas and Domínguez spent much of the next four years on the road, to and from their engagements, most of which took place in Switzerland and France, although they also performed in Belgium, West Germany, England, and the USSR (personal collection of newspaper clippings, Ernesto Cavour). In Bolivia, the newspapers kept the artists in the public eye by running numerous stories about their exploits (e.g., *Hoy*, Apr. 25, 1971; Oct. 5, 1972; Mar. 8, 1973). These reports invariably characterized Los Jairas and Domínguez's musical experiences in Europe as "triumphs," similarly to how, in previous decades, Bolivian journalists had depicted the artistic activities abroad of José María Velasco Maidana, Las Kantutas, Las Hermanas Tejada, Raúl Shaw Moreno y Los Peregrinos, and the *Fantasía Boliviana* troupe.

About four months into Los Jairas and Domínguez's European stay, in January 1970 Columbia Records issued Paul Simon and Art Garfunkel's album *Bridge over*

Troubled Water. Its single "El Cóndor Pasa (If I Could)"—dubbed over Los Incas' 1963 track—quickly reached the top of the charts in multiple countries around the globe. In response, almost every France-based Latin American music artist recorded a version of "El Cóndor Pasa," usually as the album's title track or opening number. French pop vocalists Maurice Dulac and Marianne Mille reproduced the spirit of the Simon-Garfunkel–Los Incas formula, with their guerilla-themed reworkings of Tito Yupanqui's panpipe solo "Italaqueñita" (which Los Calchakis had recorded in 1967 as "Quiaqueñita"; Chapter 5), and the Peruvian fox incaico "Vírgenes del Sol." On these 1970 hits, which Dulac and Mille titled "Dis à Tons Fils" (Tell your son) and "Libertad" (Liberty), respectively, the duo sings the melody while France's Pachacamac or Los Chacos accompany them with kenas, charangos, guitars, and bombo legüero. Also in 1970, Greek vocalist and then-French resident Nana Mouskouri scored an international hit with another version of "Italaqueñita," the contemplative "Open your Eyes" (Rios 2008, 164–65, 167–68). As for Los Jairas and Domínguez, in 1970 alone they jointly recorded five albums with French record labels; these releases almost exclusively feature their repertoire from the 1966–1969 period (Arauco 2011, 262–64).

It was at this juncture that Los Jairas' members began to play the panpipe on recordings. On the 1970 track "El Imán de tus Ojos" (they had first recorded this huayño, without sikus, in 1968), for instance, Cavour, Favre, Joffré, and Godoy realize the melody with their panpipes in tropa style (albeit with only two sets of sikus), to the accompaniment of overdubbed charango, guitar, and bombo legüero (Evasion LP 110). In the European setting, the ensemble could not rely on Los Choclos to supply the siku parts as they previously had for selections such as "Zampoñas" and "Agüita de Phutina." That by 1970 Los Calchakis and other Europe-based Andean folkloric music groups had already integrated the zampoña into their line-ups in all likelihood also encouraged Los Jairas to follow suit. In another modification to their previous practice, Los Jairas no longer used suits and ties, as they exclusively wore ponchos and other highland indigenous regalia at their performances in Europe.

Los Jairas had selected an advantageous moment to embark on their European sojourn. They could have chosen a better time to disband, though. In August 1973, at a festival in the United Kingdom, Los Jairas played their last show with their original lineup—albeit with charanguista Hugo Loza (of Los Nairas) in the place of Cavour (Arauco 2011, 265–66).[37] A few weeks later, on September 11, Chilean military forces overthrew Salvador Allende's leftist government. Inti-Illimani and Quilapayún unexpectedly found themselves stranded in Europe, where over the next decade and a half they would become high-profile advocates for the ouster of General Pinochet's dictatorship and restoration of Chile's democracy. The cause of these nueva canción acts earned widespread sympathy in Europe, while their many tours and recordings spurred another wave of interest there for Andean conjunto music (Rios 2008, 169–73). The latter development benefited the next cohort of Bolivian criollo-mestizo folklore artists who traveled to Europe, and it offered additional motivation for aspiring as well as established Bolivian musicians to form Andean conjuntos rather than other types of ensembles.[38]

As this chapter has detailed, Los Jairas' rapid climb to the summit of the Bolivian folkloric music scene transpired within a conjuncture that was highly favorable for them. Proactively and skillfully, the ensemble took full advantage of the opportunities available to local musical acts in the boom years of the folklore movement, and in doing so catapulted to national stardom, and set into motion the Andean conjunto's establishment as Bolivia's preeminent criollo-mestizo ensemble format for the interpretation of música folklórica nacional.

Key to Los Jairas' success in the Bolivian folklore field is that their musical practices adhered to long-standing conventions. The repertoire of Los Jairas, after all, centered on staple Andean criollo-mestizo genres (e.g., yaraví, huayño, cueca, bailecito), while the group's interpretive approach aligned with the nationalist ideologies of mestizaje and indigenismo and moreover shared important stylistic continuities with the folklorization practices of earlier generations of Bolivian criollo-mestizo musical acts (e.g., Lira Incaica, Conjunto 31 de Octubre). At the same time, though, Los Jairas were strongly identified with the major new developments in the folklore scene, such as the emergence of peñas, and debate surrounding neo-folklore. For Bolivian audiences of this period, consequently, the musical style of Los Jairas constituted a "traditional" form of national music that also had "contemporary" associations, a potent mix of signifiers that is often present in national musics with mass appeal. From the 1970s onward, Bolivia's leading Andean conjuntos would display "modern" signifiers in a far more overt manner through their music, with a prime example being Los Kjarkas (Chapter 8: Postlude).

In historical studies that examine the rise and canonization of national "folkloric" or "popular" musics, the role that the state enacted in the process is typically addressed, and oftentimes also the influence of foreign artistic currents or markets. This book has given ample attention to both factors. From the Bolivian folklore movement's beginnings in the early 20th century, to its boom decade of the 1960s, state agencies and officials regularly provided logistical and financial support for criollo-mestizo-led musical activities that framed Andean rural indigenous music as the roots of "national culture." In so doing, the Bolivian state fostered a significant shift in how mainstream urban society imagined the most characteristic musical expressions of the nation, which in turn made it possible for Los Jairas and other local groups in this mold to eventually canonize the Andean conjunto. As for the influence that foreign artistic currents or markets had in shaping Bolivian national music, this book has uncovered numerous instances in which La Paz's leading folkloric musicians incorporated key practices and ideas from non-Bolivian musical scenes. Contrary to Bolivia's image internationally as a bastion of culturally isolated and timeless Andean traditions, from the 1920s to 1960s Bolivia's folkloric music movement developed in close dialogue with transnational or cosmopolitan musical trends radiating primarily from Peru, Argentina, Chile, Mexico, and France, as this book has shown.

NOTES

1. The previous year (1965), Favre had used the pseudonym "El Tocador Afuerino" on an EP that he recorded in Chile with Violeta Parra. A Chilean expression, "afuerino" can be translated either as "outsider" or "foreigner." It was one of the nicknames that Violeta Parra gave to Favre (Favre 1981, 27–28).

2. The only other detailed publication on Los Jairas is María Antonieta Arauco's 2011 book *Los Jairas y el Trío Domínguez, Favre, Cavour: Creadores del Neofolklore en Bolivia (1966–1974)*, which largely consists of reproductions of newspaper clippings.

3. Besides the releases of Los Hermanos Ábalos, Los Incas and Los Calchakis most likely obtained "Andean" repertoire from the albums of other well-known Argentine folklore acts, such as Edmundo Zaldívar y Su Conjunto, and Margarita Palacios y Los Coyas.

4. Five years before Los Incas taped "El Cóndor Pasa" for the 1963 LP *Amérique du Sud*, another Paris-based band, Ricardo Galeazzi's short-lived L'Ensemble Achalay, recorded a slightly different arrangement of the piece for the 1958 LP *Musique Indienne des Andes*. The charango player heard on this track is Jorge Milchberg, who later joined Los Incas and re-recorded "El Cóndor Pasa" for the release *Amérique du Sud* (Rios 2008, 160–61).

5. In the 1950s and 1960s, Chilean folklore artists often borrowed ideas and musical practices from their Argentine counterparts (see Rodríguez Musso 1988, 60–61; González Rodríguez, Rolle, and Olsen 2009, 345, 417, 447–49). It is likely, then, the folklore peñas of Buenos Aires—in existence since the Peronist 1940s (see Chamosa 2010, 175–77)—served as one of the models for La Peña de los Parra.

6. Initially, La Peña de los Parra had similarly restricted its refreshment service to wine, while the only food served was empanadas (González Rodríguez, Ohlsen, and Rolle 2009, 229).

7. None of the tracks on *Folklore de Bolivia* showcase the vocals of Yayo Joffré, perhaps because he had only recently become a member of Conjunto de la Peña Naira.

8. The trajectory of Peruvian kena soloist Antonio Pantoja intersects with the career of Mauro Núñez. Both musicians formed part of Yma Sumac and Moisés Vivanco's folklore troupe for the 1942 trip to Buenos Aires, and elected to remain in the Argentine capital once the company had fulfilled its engagements there. Pantoja's authorship of "Alborozo Colla," meanwhile, appears to date from the 1950s (Pantoja 1958, 41).

9. Joffré was not the first person to set the poem "Mamay" to music. Potosí artist Felipe V. Rivera crafted a version decades earlier, which he titled "Diusllaguan" (Quechua for "Only with God"). Listed as a triste, it appears in his 1937 songbook *Último Cancionero de Felipe V. Rivera y Su Conjunto Típico Boliviano* (Arauco 2011, 114). Around 1960, Oruro estudiantina 14 de Junio played another yaraví setting of "Mamay." The group later recorded it as "Sentimiento Indio" (Sentiments of the Indian) (Arauco 2011, 114).

10. In Peru, yaravís usually exhibit the sequiáltera hemiola, which underscores the genre's probable origin as a criollo or mestizo musical expression. In Bolivia, though, for unknown reasons, the genre has usually been performed in simple-duple meter (e.g., $\frac{2}{4}$).

11. Juana Manuela Gorriti's 1851 short story *La Quena* (The kena) contains an early account of the Legend of Manchay Puito. According to literature scholar Keith Richards, Gorriti "adapted material" from Garcilaso de la Vega's 17th-century volume *Royal Commentaries of the Incas* (Richards 1999, 21–22; see Gruszczyńska-Ziólkowska 1995, 89–98). From Salta, Argentina, Gorriti moved to Bolivia in her youth and eventually married President Manuel Isodoro Belzú (term in office: 1848–1855). She later settled in Lima. While there, Gorriti met Peruvian

indigenista author Ricardo Palma, who incorporated the Manchay Puito Legend into one of his most famous works, the collection *Tradiciones Peruanas* (Peruvian traditions) (Richards 1999, 21–22).

12. Los Incas, in turn, had been introduced to the melody of "Huayño de la Roca" through a field recording that French kenista Guillaume de la Rocque or "Guillermo de la Roca" had lent them. The album's cover and liner notes were so badly faded, though, that none of the members of Los Incas could read the title of the piece. So as a show of appreciation to their friend and occasional band mate, they named the tune "Huayño de la Roca" (Carlos Ben-Pott of Los Incas, personal communication).

13. By then, Julia Fortún had convinced Los Jairas that "Dos Amigos" (Two friends) was the correct name of the preexisting melody of "El Llanto de Mi Madre" (Arauco 2011, 104).

14. The EP *El Llanto de Mi Madre* also includes "Huayño de la Roca," the irreverently named auqui auqui "Señor Lebudo" (Mister dummy), and Cavour's solo charango piece "Elisa." In the 1980s, Cavour would record an expanded version of "Elisa," titled "Mis Llamitas" (My little llamas). It would become a charango classic.

15. Two years later, Los de Salta also recorded "El Llanto de Mi Madre" (*Hoy*, May 22, 1969). This Argentine folkloric group then enjoyed a massive following in Bolivia.

16. Derived from the Scottish reel, the rin is a simple-duple-meter Chilean genre that seems to have first taken root on the island of Chiloé. Violeta Parra played a major role in reviving the genre, and "invented" many of the performance conventions that artists have since used to interpret it (González Rodríguez, Rolle, and Olsen 2009, 391–92).

17. In compound-duple meter, the sirilla genre is a Chilean variant of the Spanish seguidilla. Like the rin, the sirilla likely originated in Chiloé, and was revived or reinvented by Violeta Parra (González Rodríguez, Rolle, and Olsen 2009, 339–40).

18. For a discussion of the Chilean and Bolivian "neo-folklore" currents, see the section "Trío Domínguez-Favre-Cavour and Neo-Folklore" that appears later in this chapter.

19. In 1969, Los Jairas devoted almost the entirety of an album to non-Bolivian genres. It includes examples of the Venezuelan *joropo*, Mexican son jarocho, Paraguayan galopa, Colombian bambuco, and other music-dance forms (Lyra LPL 13094).

20. Kantus de Charazani groups have been using this "bouncing ball" drum pattern to initiate panpipe tunes since at least the 1950s. In 1955, the kantus tropa from Niño Korin that earned accolades at the III Festival de Música y Danza Nativa (see Chapter 4) executed this characteristic introduction, as documented in the field recording *Bolivian Folk Music Festival, La Paz, Bolivia, 1955* (AFC 1961/010). As of 2020, Kantus de Charazani tropas continue to use this stock introduction.

21. On ethnologist Bernard Keiler's 1947 field recordings (*Bernard Keiler Collection of Bolivian Recordings* AFC 1950/009), Italaque siku tropas perform the same stock introduction and cadence that, as of 2020, ensembles of the region still employ.

22. Sometime between 1965 and 1973, Louis Girault made a field recording of a Kantus de Charazani group's rendering of "Yaku Kantu." This track, which melodically is very similar to Los Jairas' "Agüita de Phutina," appears on the 1987 UNESCO album *Bolivia, Panpipes: Syrinx de Bolivie* (AUVIDIS D 8009). Given the ambiguous dating of the field recording, it is conceivable that a kantus group adapted Los Jairas's 1969 version of "Agüita de Phutina," and renamed it "Yaku Kantu."

23. On the 1974 album *Los Mejor de Los Jairas* (The best of Los Jairas), "Agüita de Phutina" is the second track (the first is "El Llanto de Mi Madre," under its alternate title "Dos Amigos"), a placement that accurately reflects its popularity. Around 1980, the Andean conjunto Savia

Andina (profiled in Chapter 8: Postlude) recorded another popular version of "Agüita de Phutina." For a discussion of Savia Andina's instrumental rendition, see Rios 2012: 12–13.

24. In 1956, Antonio González Bravo had criticized Los Choçlos for using their customary, parallel octave and unison set of "misti sikuri" panpipes when they played the kantus piece "Surimana" in the folkloric theater production *Bolivia Indiana* (Chapter 5).

25. For transcriptions of many of Domínguez's solo guitar pieces, see Fernando Ardúz Ruiz's 1997 collection *Música Boliviana para Guitarra* (Bolivian music for guitar).

26. L'Ensemble Achalay seems to have been the first Paris-based group to record the yaraví "Soncoiman." It appears on their 1958 LP *Musique Indienne des Andes*.

27. Despite the Trío Domínguez-Favre-Cavour's professed disapproval of Chilean neo-folklore, in 1968 Los Jairas recorded a composition that formed part of this current, Willy Bascuñan's "El Solitario." For a discussion of Bascuñan's artistic trajectory in relation to the Chilean neo-folklore trend, see González Rodríguez, Rolle, and Ohlsen (2009, 342–44).

28. Bolivian music scholars recently have expanded the definition of the term "neo-folklore," though, to the point that it encompasses a much wider variety of post-1960s folk-loric music currents in the Bolivian scene (e.g., Sánchez Patzy 2014b).

29. Paceño nueva ola bands of this period sometimes played folkloric standards, how-ever. In 1967, for instance, Los Bonny Boy Hots recorded "La Diablada," "Vírgenes del Sol," and the Bolivian fox incaico "Nevando Está/Khunuskiwa (Snowing, it is)" (*ED*, Feb. 19 and Dec. 10, 1967). This practice would become more common in Bolivia's rock music scene in the next decade. The group Wara (founded in 1973) represented the vanguard of this trend in the 1970s as well as 1980s. On their albums, the music often shifts from heavy metal music, to indigenous-style tropa pieces (Basualdo Zambrana 2003, 40–42; Sánchez Patzy 2017, 230–36).

30. Los Jairas and Alfredo Domínguez's 1967 recital at the UMSA's Paraninfo Universitario was not the first folklore-themed concert to take place there. In 1963, Trío Cochabamba (charango soloist Julio Lavayén, and guitarists David Milán and Jorge Arteaga) had per-formed in the space (*ED*, Aug. 10, 1963). In the intervening years between Trío Cochabamba's 1963 recital and the concert that Los Jairas and Domínguez offered in 1967, though, the Paraninfo Universitario apparently did not program any Bolivian folkloric musical acts (see *ED*, Sept. 24, 1967).

31. Nilo Soruco, a Tarija folkloric musician and Bolivian Communist Party member, was known by 1967 for his leftist repertoire (Fuentes Rodríguez 2001, 71–83). Singer-guitarist Benjamin Cordeiro or "Benjo Cruz" emerged on the La Paz scene in 1969, after having lived for a time in Argentina. He quickly gained a following among Bolivian university students as an outspoken leftist musician (*ED*, Feb. 5 and Apr. 22, 1969; *Hoy*, Apr. 23, 1969). In 1970, Cruz joined a guerrilla group, the Ejercito de Liberación Nacional (Army of national liberation), with whom he lost his life in a skirmish with the military in the La Paz town of Teoponte (Assmann 1971).

32. According to Arauco (2011, 151–52), by 1969 Peña Inkawara, Peña de Obrajes, Peña Curmi, and Peña Union also were in operation in the city of La Paz.

33. Again emulating Los Jairas, Los Laickas spawned a juvenile spin-off, Los Laickitas. The group performed at Peña Tiahuanaco and other venues in the late 1960s (*ED*, Sept. 8, 1968; *Hoy*, Jan. 11 and Feb. 11, 1969; Jaime Lafuente, personal communication).

34. Besides his activities in this period with Los Chaskas, Miguel Ibañez formed part of another folklore act, Los Trovadores de Bolivia (The troubadours of Bolivia). Originally a bolero trio, Los Trovadores de Bolivia adopted the Andean conjunto format in 1966, although the ensemble retained its configuration as a trio rather than the far more customary quartet

setup. For their performance attire, the band members dressed in tarabuqueño-style ponchos (e.g., *ED*, Oct. 29, 1966; Mar. 24, 1968), that is, in outfits inspired by those that indigenous people traditionally wear in Chuquisaca's Yamparáez Province (see Chapter 6). Popular with the public, Los Trovadores de Bolivia also earned the praise of music critics (e.g., *Hoy*, Jan. 29, 1969; Mar. 5, 1969).

35. The plot of *Yawar Mallku* tells the sordid tale of the Peace Corps' (alleged) sterilization of unwitting indigenous Bolivian women in the name of "modernization." The film caused such an uproar, that in a few years the Bolivian state indefinitely expelled the Peace Corps (FEDAM 1999, 148–57; Sánchez H. 1999, 83–84).

36. In September 1968, the all-female panpipe group Las Kory Majtas competed in Cochabamba's Festival Lauro de la Canción Boliviana, in which they earned first place in the categories of "instrumental ensemble" and "dress" (*ED*, Sep. 15, 1968). The next month, Las Kory Majtas performed siku music at the Palace of the Government for President Barrientos, who in appreciation awarded the group's director, Alfredo Solíz Bejar, a gold medal in the shape of a panpipe (personal collection of Alfredo Solíz Bejar).

37. Cavour had returned to La Paz in 1971. Three years later, he would take over the operations of Peña Naira with singer-guitarist Luis Rico. The venue would continue to serve as a proving ground for folklore artists, until it closed in 1996 (see Arauco 2011, 344–46). Joffré, meanwhile, formed a new "Los Jairas" soon after the original group's dissolution. It similarly featured a Swiss kenista, Ivan Serf (Arauco 2011, 322–32). Around the same time, Favre and his friend Jean Vidaillac founded the Swiss-French Andean music group Los Gringos (Jean Vidaillac, personal communication). In 1977, Favre returned to La Paz with the ensemble, with which he played at Peña Naira and recorded the Campo album *El Gringo Bandolero* (*Hoy*, Jan. 14 and 30, 1977; *ED*, Mar. 12, 1977). As for Godoy and Domínguez, in the 1970s they settled in Geneva and devoted their artistic energies to solo guitar performance (Julio Godoy, personal communication). Domínguez passed away in 1980, while Favre succumbed to lung cancer in 1998.

38. Bolivian musicians and audiences have seldom credited Chilean nueva canción artists for expanding the European market for Andean folkloric ensembles, however. Instead, Bolivians regularly have leveled the charge of cultural appropriation against them, as well as against Argentine and even Peruvian folkloric artists who interpret Andean-associated genres that Bolivians have tended to regard as solely Bolivian (see Rios 2014).

8

POSTLUDE

LOS RHUPAY WAS the first Bolivian folklore group to settle in Europe after Los Jairas. They arrived in France in 1973, with new members Ricardo Mendoza and Basilio Huarachi (both formerly of Los Jairitas and Los Chaskas) (*Hoy*, July 5, 1974; Hery Cortéz of Los Rhupay, personal communication). Stylistically, Los Rhupay made adjustments for their stay abroad. They had distinguished themselves over the last five years in La Paz with their tropa renditions of música autóctona, but in the European setting the group adopted the Andean conjunto format. It was, after all, what Europeans expected of artists who played the music of the Andes, ever since Los Incas and Los Calchakis' breakthrough albums of the 1960s. Los Rhupay's new orientation is evident on the 1976 LP *Los Rhupay: Folklore de Bolivia*—the debut release for Hamburg's Eulenspiegel label (rebranded as the "world music" company ARC Music in 1983).[1] The group soon returned its focus to música autóctona, however, probably to stand out from the local competition.[2] Europe had become a major destination for Bolivian and non-Bolivian Andean conjuntos, particularly ad hoc acts. Established groups also tried their luck in the major cities of Western Europe in the mid-to-late 1970s, including Bolivia's Savia Andina, Los Masis, Los Kusis, Los Aransayas, and Los Awatiris (*Última Hora*, Sept. 9, 1975; *ED*, May 4, 1976; *Hoy*, Dec. 5, 1976; *ED*, Mar. 6 and Dec. 30, 1977).

The possibility of performing on the European stage enticed many Bolivian musicians to dedicate their energies to the Andean conjunto style, although it was not the only, or often the primary, factor that led them to take this course of action. The

Panpipes & Ponchos. Fernando Rios, Oxford University Press (2020). © Oxford University Press.
DOI: 10.1093/oso/9780190692278.001.0001.

Bolivian audience for Andean conjunto music expanded considerably in the 1970s and 1980s (particularly in the country's urban centers in the Andean highland and valley regions, but far less so in rural areas as well as non-Andean regions such as the eastern lowlands), creating openings for new ensembles to tap the local market. Savia Andina and Los Kjarkas seized the opportunity. Their trajectories share many parallels: both ensembles recorded their first albums in 1976, attained superstar status in the 1980s, and, as a testament to their enduring popularity in Bolivia, have continued to offer concerts as of 2019.

For the original members of Savia Andina—wind specialist Alcídes Mejía, charanguista Eddy Navía, guitarist Julio César Paredes Ruiz, and bombo legüero player Óscar Castro—the early months of the group's existence were especially eventful. In May 1976, Savia Andina served as the warm-up band for a famed Spanish singer of romantic music, none other than Julio Iglesias, at his shows in La Paz. They clearly impressed him, because afterwards Iglesias offered the young folklorists the chance of a lifetime. He was about to embark on a tour of Spain and France that would culminate with a concert at Paris's esteemed Olympia Hall, and asked Savia Andina if they would like to be his opening act at these prestigious engagements. Without hesitation they accepted this exciting prospect (*ED*, May 4, 1976; *Hoy*, Aug. 14 and 29, 1976; Julio César Paredes Ruiz and Alcídes Mejía, personal communications).

While in Spain for the 1976 tour with Julio Iglesias, Savia Andina recorded the album *Ritmos y Canciones del Altiplano* (Rhythms and songs of the high plain) (CBS 1056). The next three years the quartet taped a string of LPs with non-Bolivian labels that established Mejía and Navía as virtuoso instrumentalists. Staples of the Andean conjunto repertoire appear on the albums the group released from 1976 to 1979, including "El Cóndor Pasa," "Vírgenes del Sol," "Alborozo Colla," "Urubamba" (a cueca by Jorge Milchberg of Los Incas), and "Chokolulu" (a "danza incaica" by La Paz composer Ismael Zeballos; Chapter 3), as well as many new compositions and arrangements, such as Navía's "Danza del Sicuri" (Panpiper's dance) and danza incaica "Regreso del Inca" (Return of the Inca); Mejía's yaraví "Raza de Bronce" (Bronze race) and danza incaica "Incallajta" (Home of the Inca); and unattributed huayño "Poncho Color Viento" (Poncho, the color of wind). At this juncture, instrumentals made up almost the entirety of the repertoire of Savia Andina, recalling the early releases of Los Jairas, and primary output of Trío Domínguez-Favre-Cavour.[3]

Whereas Favre had limited himself to the kena, however, Mejía was equally adept at executing technically demanding solos on the Andean panpipe (e.g., "Poncho Color Viento"), specifically, on a modified version of the siku that amalgamated the ira and arca pairs, so that one player could realize the full diatonic scale on a single panpipe. Zampoña soloists had been uncommon in Bolivia prior to the mid-1970s. Reflecting this state of affairs, in a 1976 La Paz newspaper article that discussed Savia Andina (*ED*, May 5, 1976), the journalist highlighted "the novelty of using two panpipe registers simultaneously."

Through the efforts of Mejía and many other Andean panpipe soloists active in the late 1970s and early 1980s (e.g., Gastón Guardia of Los Kjarkas, Peña

Naira house musician Ramiro Calderón, Yayo Joffré of the "new" Los Jairas, France-based Argentine artist Uña Ramos of Los Incas and Urubamba), the zampoña became an indispensable component of the Andean conjunto lineup in Bolivia and abroad, a position that the instrument retains to the present. Since the 1970s, moreover, the panpipe has been synonymous with the Andean conjunto tradition, musically and visually, so much so that it has usurped the status formerly occupied by the kena.

The Andean panpipe's far more distinctive image undoubtedly facilitated this development. The kena, after all, resembles many other types of flutes that are used around the world, whereas the zampoña belongs to the less common instrument family of the panpipe. The range of sounds that Andean conjunto wind soloists generate on the zampoña, from breathy (which for many fans evokes the sound that the wind makes in the Andes mountains) to staccato, combined with the instrument's more unique timbre compared to the kena, has played a major role as well in cementing the zampoña's post-1970s prominence in the Andean conjunto tradition.[4]

In the 1980s, Savia Andina's mass appeal increased dramatically in Bolivia, following lead singer Gerardo Arias's addition to the group, which ushered in a more vocally oriented phase for the ensemble. Also a guitarist, Arias was previously known to Navía and Castro. The three musicians had grown up together in Potosí city and, for a time in the 1960s, played in a rock band there, Los Rebeldes (The rebels). Yet again, the core members of a prominent Bolivian criollo-mestizo folklore ensemble thus started their musical careers as performers of a non-Bolivian genre.[5]

With this revamped lineup, Savia Andina scored major hits in 1980 with the kaluyo "K'alanchito" (Quechua for "Unclothed child"; author unattributed), and classic huayños "El Minero" (The miner; by Jaime Medinaceli; see Chapter 5) and "A Los Bosques" (To the forests; by Alberto Ruiz Lavadenz; see Chapter 3). Arias sings his lines in a subdued manner on these selections, with few changes in volume, in the style of easy-listening Latin American and US pop musicians. The group's ensuing albums feature a number of tracks in this vein, such as the 1982 hit "¿Por Qué Estás Triste?" (Why are you sad?; by Gerardo Arias), interspersed with their customary instrumental showpieces.

Navía and Mejía parted ways with Savia Andina in the early 1990s, marking the end of the ensemble's heyday. The band has remained active as of 2019, though, with the recurring incorporation of new members. Yet whereas Savia Andina's time in the spotlight faded as the 1990s progressed, Los Kjarkas were able to sustain their high level of popularity in Bolivia over the same period, and even into the following decades.

The Hermosa brothers Gonzalo, Wilson, and Castel, along with Edgar Villarroel, founded Los Kjarkas in the late 1960s in Cochabamba city, as an Argentine-style folkloric group.[6] They gradually shifted their repertoire to local criollo-mestizo genres, fitting a familiar pattern for Bolivian bands that originally specialized in Argentine zambas (see Chapters 6 and 7). The members of Los Kjarkas, meanwhile, regularly changed from the late 1960s to mid-1970s (at one point, future Savia Andina founder Alcides Mejía played the kena and zampoña in Los Kjarkas). The main constant was Gonzalo Hermosa, who led the group and composed most of the tunes they played. His brothers Ulises (a composer like Gonzalo) and Elmer (a lead vocalist) joined the ensemble in the mid-1970s.[7] By then, Los Kjarkas had fully transitioned from an Argentine-style folkloric group, to an Andean conjunto that focused on Bolivian genres.

Consistent with their new identity as a Bolivian folklore act, Los Kjarkas replaced their Argentine bombo legüero with the wankara, because the members regarded it as a more authentically Bolivian, as well as indigenous, drum. Another instrument that Los Kjarkas added to their lineup was the *ronrroco*, a large-sized or baritone charango. At concerts, Elmer Hermosa usually strums chords on the ronrroco, which fill out the middle register of the string section, that is, in between the parts that the sole charanguista and several guitarists perform. As for the kena and zampoña, Los Kjarkas feature them prominently, in the usual Andean conjunto style (i.e., as the primary solo instruments, regardless of the regional or ethnic associations of the genre being performed). Since the 1990s, the group has also employed the services of a trap-set drummer and electric bassist. The musicians who play these instruments, though, are considered unofficial members of the ensemble.

The influence of *balada latinoamericana* (Latin American ballad)—the post-1960s Latin American iteration of the bolero tradition—permeates the music of Los Kjarkas, especially their chuntunqui songs. On these numbers, lead singer Elmer Hermosa displays his dynamic range, expressive vibrato, ability to sustain long notes, and other emotive effects (e.g., "Siempre He De Adorarte" [I will always love you]; "Sin Ella" [Without her]; "Puedo Vivir Sin Tu Amor" [I can live without your love]). This version of the chuntunqui has almost nothing in common with the genre of the same name that Chuquisaca musicians have traditionally performed at Christmastime.[8]

Set in a moderately paced § meter, Los Kjarkas' chuntunquis feature choral refrains and harmonic progressions of the type that are commonly found in mainstream popular music worldwide, while the lyrics explore the subject of romantic love. Designating these romantic-themed songs as "chuntunquis" has proven to be a masterstroke for Los Kjarkas, because it has led many Bolivian folklore fans to believe that these numbers are rooted in a traditional local genre—one that few non-Chuquisaca residents had even heard of until Los Kjarkas netted their earliest chuntunqui hits in the 1970s. In the 1980s, this new form of the chuntunqui became an Andean conjunto staple for Bolivian bands, as well as for non-Bolivian groups of this variety.[9]

The repertoire of Los Kjarkas extends well beyond the chuntunqui, as it encompasses an array of folkloric music-dance expressions. These include the primary genres that Los Jairas interpreted in the mid-to-late 1960s (e.g., huayño, cueca, bailecito, taquirari, carnaval; the prime exception is the yaraví),[10] along with post-1970s Andean conjunto adaptations of Bolivian entrada (folkloric parade) traditions, such as the tinku (e.g., "Imillitay" [Quechua for "Little girl"]), tobas (e.g., "Hombres de la Selva" [Men of the jungle]), and caporal-saya (e.g., "Llorando Se Fué" [She left, weeping]). The tinku, in its nationally popular criollo-mestizo folkloric version, is a fanciful rendering of the indigenous music-dance styles that accompany ritual battles in northern Potosí (these events are also called tinkus) (Solomon 1997, 527–36; Abercrombie 2003, 204–5). The tobas tradition, meanwhile, enacts Amazonian Bolivian expressive practices in a manner that has little basis in the actual indigenous genres of the region (Sánchez Patzy 2014c, 857–60).[11]

Los Kjarkas' caporal-sayas represent some of their most popular songs, and therefore the genre merits a more extended discussion. The group labels these musical selections as "sayas," to the frustration of Afro-Bolivians. For the members of this numerically minuscule sector of Bolivia's population, "saya" refers to their community's most emblematic music-dance expression, in which singers perform in call-and-response fashion to the accompaniment of rhythmic figures that the percussionists realize on three types of drums (*asentador, cambiador,* and *gangengo*) and a bamboo scraper (*cuancha*) (Templeman 1998, 435–37). Stylistically, the Afro-Bolivian saya does not bear even the slightest resemblance to the "sayas" that Los Kjarkas interpret, something that Afro-Bolivian musicians and activists have repeatedly stressed in public forums since the 1980s (Templeman 1998, 440–42).

A traditional Andean criollo-mestizo parade form that caricatures Afro-Bolivian expressive practices, and in which the participants usually are in blackface, constitutes the actual musical basis for the caporal-sayas of Los Kjarkas. This genre has been known variously in Bolivia as tundiqui, tuntuna, and baile de los negritos (Sánchez Patzy 2017, 178–79; Roper 2019, 382, 388–90). In 1969, Los Jairas adapted it to the conventions of the Andean conjunto style and thereby became the first group to do so. The result, "San Benito," which they labeled a "tundiqui," is the opening track on the 1968 LP *Bolivia con Los Jairas* (Chapter 7). Chile's Inti-Illimani heard the tune in their visit to La Paz the next year and soon added it to their repertoire. In the following decade, the traveled nueva canción group would often perform the tundiqui, as "Fiesta de San Benito" (Salinas 2013, 34).

In the meantime in Bolivia, the popular Andean conjunto Los Payas—Octavio Cordero and Freddy Zuaso had originally formed the group as a duo folklore act to compete in the third Salta festival (Chapter 7)—made the genre a specialty in the 1970s. Unlike Los Jairas, though, Los Payas generally preferred the descriptor "tuntuna" (see Maidana 2011, 120, 122–27). By the 1980s, a new version of the tundiqui or tuntuna had taken the Bolivian entrada scene by storm, *danza de los caporales* (dance of the slave drivers), which employs flashier dance steps and different outfits, and does not involve the use of blackface. It also became commonplace in the 1980s for Bolivian criollo-mestizo folklorists to term the musical element of the caporales genre as "saya" (Templeman 1998, 440–42; Sánchez Patzy 2017, 178–79; Roper 2019, 390–92).

Los Kjarkas' earliest caporal-saya composition, "Llorando Se Fué," appears on their sixth album, the 1982 release *Canto a la Mujer de Mi Pueblo* (Song for the woman of my people) (Lauro LPLR 1408). The genre had a minimal presence in the Andean conjunto repertoire at the time, a situation that would remain unchanged until the early 1990s. Notably, even though Los Kjarkas taped seven full-length albums from 1983 to 1990, they recorded only three additional caporal-sayas over that period. It was the *lambada* catching fire in "world beat" circles in 1989, sparked by the Brazilian-African-French band Kaoma's unauthorized recasting of the "Llorando Se Fué" melody in their signature lambada tune (titled simply "Lambada") (see Céspedes 1993), that motivated Los Kjarkas and most other Andean conjuntos to devote greater attention to the caporal-saya, to the point that it became a staple genre (Sánchez Patzy 2017, 152). In another development related to the world-beat industry's fetishization of Afro-diasporic music, in the 1990s Bolivian caporal-saya lyrics increasingly referenced the genre's (dubious) Afro-Bolivian roots; the texts of Los Kjarkas' hits "Mi Samba, Mi Negra" (1992), "Negrita" (1993), "El Ritmo Negro" (1994), and "Saya Morena" (1997) exemplify this practice. The music videos that Los Kjarkas made for these selections invoke another highly problematic world-beat trope, the supposed inherent sexuality of Afro-diasporic music and dance traditions.

For much of the career of Los Kjarkas, the ensemble's stylistic fusion of "traditional" and "modern" signifiers—most readily apparent in their chuntunqui and caporal-saya songs—has allowed them to reach a broad demographic of fans in which young adults constitute a sizeable part. Predictably, the "modern" facets of the ensemble's music (e.g., its baladista tendencies) have often been met with disapproval among traditionally minded music critics and folklore artists (see Leichtman 1989, 39–40; Guardia 1994, 168–82; Bigenho 2002, 228; Sánchez Patzy 2017, 127). The charge of inauthenticity that they frequently have leveled at Los Kjarkas has done little to dampen the public's enthusiasm for the band and its musical productions, however.

Bolivian musicians, too, generally have not been deterred by these criticisms, as a large number of groups look to Los Kjarkas as their primary model. Proyección (Projection) was among the earliest to do so. Originally known as Proyección-Kjarkas, this popular Cochabamba band emerged around 1979, under the mentorship of Gonzalo Hermosa, and at first mainly performed his compositions and those of his brother Ulises (Ariel Villazón of Proyección, personal communication). Proyección began to concentrate on new repertoire in the mid-1980s (e.g., the 1984 hit huayño "No Vuelvo a Amar" [I'll never love again]; composed by Ramiro de la Zerda of Fortaleza), although their performance style and instrumentation retained the strong influence of Los Kjarkas. Soon thereafter, Proyección adopted a slogan that from this point onward would appear on their album covers: "la nueva expresión del folklore de Bolivia" (the new expression of the folklore of Bolivia). Back in 1967, Campo record company had used essentially the same phrase to promote the debut LP of Trío Domínguez-Favre-Cavour (Chapter 7), likewise to brand the artists' interpretive approach and artistic vision as forward-looking or modern.

As the 1980s advanced, Cochabamba displaced La Paz as the headquarters for Bolivia's most admired Andean conjuntos, due to the popularity of Los Kjarkas and its local offshoots in the valley city. Cochabamba's Fortaleza (Fortress) underwent a transformation analogous to, and contemporaneous with, that of Proyección. Led by ex–Los Kjarkas member Ramiro de la Zerda, Fortaleza started off as a Los Kjarkas cover band in the late 1970s, before forging a distinct identity by focusing on de la Zerda's compositions (Ramiro de la Zerda, personal communication). Grupo Amaru (named after Túpaj Amaru II, the 18th century Andean indigenous leader; see Chapter 1) represents another well-known Cochabamba group that since the 1970s has largely followed the artistic line of Los Kjarkas (e.g., vocal approach, repertoire, instrumentation).

Los Kjarkas' influence is not limited to Cochabamba musical acts, though. La Paz's Jach'a Mallku (Aymara for "Great leader"; founded in 1985), Oruro's Llajtaymanta (Quechua for "In my homeland"; founded in 1986), and Chuquisaca's Bonanza (founded in 1990) also have drawn heavily from the style of Los Kjarkas, to name only a few well-known post-1980s Bolivian Andean conjuntos based elsewhere in the country. Since the 1990s Los Kjarkas has been a major point of reference as well for non-Bolivian Andean folkloric-popular musicians, especially Peruvian artists (see Mendoza 2000, 210–12; Ferrier 2010, 37–39; and Tucker 2013, 128; for the Ecuadorian case, see Meisch 2002, 141; for Colombia, see Katz-Rosene 2015, 70, 77).

In 2014, the Cochabamba group Ch'ila Jatun rose to the pinnacle of the Bolivian music scene, after having earned plaudits for their performance of the huayño "Boquita de Miel" (Mouth of honey) at the Festival Internacional de la Canción held in Viña del Mar, Chile.[12] The band's pedigree piqued the Bolivian public's early curiosity about them. Founded in 2005 by sons and nephews of Los Kjarkas, Ch'ila Jatun carries on their legacy of folkloric numbers with amorous texts. The progeny of Los Kjarkas' first vocalist Elmer Hermosa, Jonathan Hermosa, sings lead, while the director is Gonzalo "Junior" Hermosa (as of 2019, the band has three additional members of the Hermosa family: Huáscar, Ulises "Junior," and Luis). The group's musical style and repertoire unsurprisingly resembles that of Los Kjarkas. Ch'ila Jatun has revamped its original look, however. Since the 2010s, the musicians wear casual street clothes in the style of rock stars or a boy band, whereas they had originally dressed in matching white and black shirts that were adorned with the same Tiwanaku patterns seen on Los Kjarkas' characteristic ponchos.[13] Differentiating Ch'ila Jatun further from their illustrious forebears, the group's electric bassist and drum-kit player are full-fledged band members rather than invited artists.

Ch'ila Jatun's carefully fashioned image as a modern folklore act represents the predominant trend among Bolivian Andean conjuntos established since 2010. By reaching out to teenagers and young adults through their romantically-themed folkloric numbers, hip image, and elaborately produced music videos, this cohort of recently formed ensembles—which besides Ch'ila Jatun includes Pasión Andina (Andean passion), Kharua (Aymara for "Llama"), Tiempo Bolivia (Bolivian time), and many other bands—has played an essential role in preserving the Andean conjunto's standing as Bolivia's most emblematic ensemble configuration for the performance of national folkloric-popular music among the current generation.[14]

NOTES

1. For information on the labels Eulenspiegel and ARC Music, see "Interview with Horst Tubbesing" (http://www.cluas.com/music/features/tubbesing.htm).

2. Besides Los Rhupay, the Hamburg ensemble Ukamau (founded by ex-Los Rhupay member Hery Cortéz) and Paris-based Boliviamanta (led by La Paz musicians Julio and Carlos Arguedas) carved a niche in the European setting with their música autóctona repertoire. Established in the late 1970s, Ukamau and Boliviamanta remained active in the European scene in the following decades.

3. The trio José, Joselo y Marcelo (briefly discussed in Chapter 7) began performing at La Paz venues around the same time as Savia Andina (mid-1970s), and likewise gained recognition for their virtuosic instrumentals. Many other Bolivian Andean conjuntos have focused on technically challenging instrumental repertoire, such as La Paz's Rumillajta (founded around 1980).

4. Among Bolivian folkloric musicians, there is little agreement over which artist or ensemble was most responsible for the solo panpipe's addition to the Andean conjunto lineup in the 1970s, while they tend to give Favre the credit for popularizing the kena's usage in the post-1960s Bolivian criollo-mestizo folkloric scene.

5. For further discussions of Savia Andina, see Céspedes 1984, 233–34; Leichtman 1989, 37–39; Rios 2012, 12–13; and Sánchez Patzy 2017, 96–97, 124–26.

6. My overview of Los Kjarkas' career draws from the accounts in Céspedes (1993), Guardia (1994, 119–190), and Sánchez Patzy (2017, 115–20, 124, 147–48). The band members have offered various translations of the Quechua word "kjarkas," from "Pre-Spanish fortresses built by the Inca" (see Céspedes 1993, 58), to "earthquakes" (see http://www.loskjarkas.com.bo/web/index.php; Sánchez Patzy 2017, 116–17).

7. From the early 1980s to mid-1990s, when Los Kjarkas scored many of their biggest hits, charango player Fernando Torrico and guitarist Edwin Castellanos (both of whom originally played in Proyección-Kjarkas) were core members of the group. Since 2002, Japanese musician Makoto Shishido has filled the role of Los Kjarkas' principal charanguista (see Bigenho 2012, 116–17).

8. In a four-part series posted on Youtube, Proyección's Ariel Villazón demonstrates that the "Los Kjarkas version" of the chuntunqui lacks the musical characteristics of the original Chuquisaca tradition (https://www.youtube.com/watch?v=6TRSxlpMMmc). For more information on both iterations of the chuntunqui genre, see Sánchez Patzy 2014a.

9. As Chapter 7 notes, Los Jairas' performance practices on their 1968 recording of Chilean neo-folklore composer Willy Bascuñan's canción "El Solitario" bear a strong resemblance stylistically to the interpretive approach that Los Kjarkas adopted in the 1970s on chuntunquis.

10. As of 2019, Los Kjarkas' sole yaraví track ("Pachamama") appears on their first album (issued in 1976). The genre fell from favor in the Bolivian folklore scene within a few years of this release, perhaps in light of the growing popularity of other musical forms such as the chuntunqui.

11. Bolivia's folkloric parade tradition (i.e., the entrada) underwent major expansion in the 1970s, and since then has functioned as a key performance context within which artists update folkloric genres as well as create new ones (see Albó and Preiswerk 1986; Mendoza 1996; Guss 2006; Abercrombie 2003; Martin-Frost 2009, 42–45, 128–46).

12. The ensemble name "Ch'ila Jatun," Quechua for "Small big ones," is a tongue-in-cheek reference to the members' tender age when they formed the band, and their familial relationship to Los Kjarkas (see http://www.chilajatun.bo/historia.html).

13. Four decades before Ch'ila Jatun and the group's contemporaries in the Bolivian scene would set aside their ponchos for "modern" outfits, Los Chaskas and many other popular Bolivian Andean conjuntos of the 1970s had presented themselves as "cool" by wearing trendy clothing of the time, such as close-fitting shirts and bell-bottom pants. In the 1980s, though, most Bolivian Andean conjuntos returned to wearing ponchos.

14. Since the 1970s, Bolivian music education has also helped to enshrine the Andean conjunto's status as the preeminent national folkloric-popular music ensemble (Martin-Frost 2009: 119–28). In the sphere of state politics, meanwhile, Bolivia has undergone a series of major shifts since the late 1960s, from the right-wing military dictatorships of the 1970s and early 1980s, to the democratically elected neoliberal regimes that governed from 1985 to 2006, to the successive left-wing administrations of President Evo Morales and the MAS party (Movimiento al Socialismo; Movement toward Socialism) (2006–2019). Needless to say, illuminating how Bolivian folkloric musical trends articulated with state projects and ideologies over this fifty-year period (1970–2019) is beyond the scope of this postlude chapter.

References

Abercrombie, Thomas. 2003. "Mothers and Mistresses of the Urban Bolivian Public Sphere: Postcolonial Predicament and National Imaginary in Oruro's Carnival." In *After Spanish Rule: Postcolonial Predicaments of the Americas*, edited by Mark Thurner and Andrés Guerrero, 176–220. Durham, NC, and London: Duke University Press.

Acevedo Raymundo, Saúl. 2003. *Los Sikuris de San Marcos: Historia del Conjunto de Zampoñas de San Marcos*. Lima, Peru: Saúl Acevedo Raymundo.

Alarcón, J. Ricardo, ed. 1925. *Bolivia en el Primer Centenario de Su Independencia*. New York: University Society.

Albó, Xavier, and Matías Preiswerk. 1986. *Los Señores del Gran Poder*. La Paz, Bolivia: Centro de Teología Popular, Taller de Observaciones Culturales.

Albó, Xavier. 2008. "The 'Long Memory' of Ethnicity in Bolivia and Some Temporary Oscillations." In *Unresolved Tensions: Bolivia, Past and Present*, edited by John Crabtree and Laurence Whitehead, 13–34. Pittsburgh: University of Pittsburgh Press.

Albro, Robert. 1998. "Introduction: A New Time and Place for Bolivian Popular Politics." *Ethnology* 37, no. 2: 99–115.

Alcaldia Municipal La Paz. 1953. *Catalogo de la Primera Exposición de Folklore y Etnografía de la Región Norte del Departamento de La Paz, Zona Charazani*. La Paz, Bolivia: Alcaldia Municipal La Paz.

Aldunate viuda de Azero, Angélica. 1994. *Recopilacíon de Villancicos*. La Paz, Bolivia: Kraft S. R. L.

Alejo, Benjamin. 1925. "Notas para la Historia del Arte Musical en Bolivia." In *Bolivia en el Primer Centenario de Su Independencia*, edited by J. Ricardo Alarcón, 357–61. New York: University Society.

Álvarez García, Francisco. 2011. "Medio Siglo de Teatro Boliviano." In *500 Años de Teatro en Bolivia: Testimonios y Reflexiones desde el Siglo XVI al XX*, edited by Carlos Cordero Carraffa. La Paz, Bolivia: SPC Impresores.

"¡América Canta en Salta! Primer Festival Latinoamericano de Folklore." 1965. Special issue, *Folklore*, no. 93 (May).

Anaya de Urquidi, Mercedes. 1947. *Indianismo*. Buenos Aires, Argentina: Sociedad Editora Latino-Americana, Soc. de Resp. Ltda.

Anderson, Jon Lee. 1997. *Che Guevara: A Revolutionary Life*. New York: Grove Press.

Andreu Ricart, Ramón. 1995. *Estudiantinas Chilenas: Origen, Desarrollo y Vigencia (1884–1955)*. Santiago, Chile: FONDART.

Antezana, Luis, and René Zavaleta Mercado, eds. 1983. *Bolivia, Hoy*. Mexico City, Mexico: Siglo Veintiuno Editores.

Arana, Federico. 1988. *Roqueros y Folcloroides*. México City, Mexico: Editorial Joaquín Moritz.

Arauco, María Antonieta. 2011. *Los Jairas y el Trío Domínguez, Favre, Cavour: Creadores del Neo-Folklore en Bolivia (1966–1973)*. La Paz, Bolivia: All Press Labores Gráficos.

Araujo, Samuel. 1999. "The Politics of Passion: The Impact of Bolero on Brazilian Musical Expressions." *Yearbook for Traditional Music* 31: 42–56.

Ardúz, Fernando. 1997. *Música Boliviana para Guitarra*. Barcelona, Spain: Casa Beethoven.

Arnade, Charles. 1970. *The Emergence of the Republic of Bolivia*. New York: Russell & Russell.

"El Arte en los Sindicatos." 1956. Brochure. No publisher.

Arze Aguirre, René Danilo. 1979. *Participación Popular en la Independencia de Bolivia*. La Paz, Bolivia: Organización de los Estados Americanos.

Assman, Hugo. 1971. *Teoponte: Una Experiencia Guerrillera*. Oruro, Bolivia: Centro "Desarrollo Integral."

Austerlitz, Paul. 1997. *Merengue: Dominican Music and Dominican Identity*. Philadelphia: Temple University Press.

Auza León, Atiliano. 1985. *Historia de la Música Boliviana*. La Paz, Bolivia: Editorial Los Amigos del Libro.

Auza León, Atiliano. 1989. *Simbiosis Cultural de la Música Boliviana*. La Paz, Bolivia: Producciones CIMA.

Baily, John. 1994. "The Role of Music in the Creation of an Afghan National Identity, 1923–1974." In *Ethnicity, Identity, and Music: The Musical Construction of Place*, edited by Martin Stokes, 45–60. Oxford, Providence: Berg.

Barragán, Rossana. 1990. *Espacio Urbano y Dinámica Étnica*. La Paz, Bolivia: HISBOL.

Barragán, Rossana. 2011. "The Census and the Making of a 'Social Order' in Nineteenth-Century Bolivia." In *Histories of Race and Racism: The Andes and Mesoamerica from Colonial Times to the Present*, edited by Laura Gotkowitz, 113–33. Durham, NC: Duke University Press.

Bastien, Joseph. 1978. *Mountain of the Condor: Metaphor and Ritual in an Andean Ayllu*. Prospect Heights, IL: Waveland Press.

Basualdo Zambrana, Marco. 2003. *Rock Boliviano: Cuatro Décadas de Historia*. La Paz: Plural Editores.

Bauman, Richard. 1992. "Folklore." In *Folklore, Cultural Performances, and Popular Entertainments*, edited by Richard Bauman, 29–40. Oxford: Oxford University Press.

Becerra, Rogers. 1959. *Tratado Histórico Sobre el Origen y Significado de las Danzas de la Música Beniana*. La Paz, Bolivia: Editorial Inti.

Becerra, Rogers. 1990. *Reliquias de Moxos*. La Paz, Bolivia: Empresa Editora PROINSA.

Becerra, Rogers. 1998. *Orígenes de la Música del Carnaval Cruceño*. Santa Cruz, Bolivia: Fondo Editorial Gobierno Municipal Santa Cruz de la Sierra.

Becerra, Rogers. 2003. *Introducción a La Cultura Musical*. Santa Cruz, Bolivia: Cooperativa Rural de Electrificación.

Becerra, Rogers. n.d. "Balance General sobre el Movimiento Musical en Bolivia." Unpublished manuscript.

Bedregal de Conitzer, Yolanda, and Antonio González Bravo. 1956. *Calendario Folklórico del Departamento de La Paz*. La Paz, Bolivia: Honorable Municipalidad de La Paz, Dirección General de Cultura.

Béhague, Gérard. 1979. *Music in Latin America: An Introduction*. Englewood Cliffs, NJ: Prentice-Hall.

Béhague, Gérard. 1991. "Reflections on the Ideological History of Latin American Ethnomusicology." In *Comparative Musicology and Anthropology of Music: Essays on the History of Ethnomusicology*, edited by Bruno Nettl and Philip Bohlman, 56–68. Chicago: University of Chicago Press.

Béhague, Gérard. 2006. "Indianism in Latin American Art-Music Composition of the 1920s to 1940s: Case Studies from Mexico, Peru, and Brazil." *Latin American Music Review* 27, no. 1: 28–37.

Beltrán, Augusto. 1956. *Carnaval de Oruro*. Oruro, Bolivia: Editorial Universitaria.

Beltrán, Augusto. 1962. *El Carnaval de Oruro y Proceso Ideológico e Historia de los Grupos Folklóricos*. Oruro, Bolivia: Edición del Comité Departamental de Folklore.

Berrocal, Esperanza. 2002. "Ricardo Viñes and the Diffusion of Early Twentieth-Century South American Piano Literature." PhD diss., Catholic University of America.

Bigenho, Michelle. 2002. *Sounding Indigenous: Authenticity in Bolivian Music Performance*. New York: Palgrave Macmillan.

Bigenho, Michelle. 2005. "Making Music Safe for the Nation: Folklore Pioneers in Bolivian Indigenism." In *Natives Making Nation: Gender, Indigeneity, and the State in the Andes*, edited by Andrew Canessa, 60–79. Tucson: University of Arizona Press.

Bigenho, Michelle. 2006. "Embodied Matters: Bolivian Fantasy and Indigenismo." *Journal of Latin American and Caribbean Anthropology* 11, no. 2: 267–93.

Bigenho, Michelle. 2012. *Intimate Distance: Andean Music in Japan*. Durham, NC: Duke University Press.

Bolivia Andina: The Most Beautiful Folklore in the World. 1970. La Paz, Bolivia: Promociones Culturales.

Brading, David. 1988. "Manuel Gamio and Official Indigenismo in Mexico." *Bulletin of Latin American Research* 7, no. 1: 75–89.

Bridikhina, Eugenia, Horacio Vera Cossío, Sergio Rojas, Bernardo Mikjhael Mamani Iñiguez, et al., eds. 2009. *Fiesta Cívica: Construcción de lo Cívico y Políticas Festivas*. La Paz, Bolivia: Instituto de Estudios Bolivianos (IEB).

Briggs, Charles. 1996. "The Politics of Discursive Authority in Research on the Invention of Tradition." *Cultural Anthropology* 11, no. 4: 435–69.

Brill, William Handforth. 1967. *Military Intervention in Bolivia: The Overthrow of Paz Estenssoro and the MNR*. Washington, DC: Institute for the Comparative Study of Political Systems.

Browman, David. 2007. "La Sociedad Arqueológica de Bolivia y su Influencia en el Desarrollo de la Práctica Arqueológica en Bolivia." *Nuevos Aportes* 4: 29–54.

Brun, Percy. 2000. *Rendición Imposible: Radio Fides; 60 Años de Lucha por la Modernidad (1939–1999)*. La Paz, Bolivia: Grupo Fides.

Buchanan, Donna. 2006. *Performing Democracy: Bulgarian Music and Musicians in Transition*. Chicago: University of Chicago Press.

Buechler, Hans. 1980. *The Masked Media: Aymara Fiestas and Social Interaction in the Bolivian Highlands*. The Hague, Netherlands: Mouton.

Buechler, Hans, and Judith Marie Buechler. 1971. *The Bolivian Aymara*. New York: Holt, Rinehart and Winston.

Caamaño, Roberto. 1969. *La Historia del Teatro Colón, 1908–1968, Vol. II*. Buenos Aires, Argentina: Editorial Cinetea.

Caballero Farfán, Polcarpo. 1988. *Música Inkaika: Sus Leyes y Su Evolución Histórica*. Cuzco, Peru: Comité de Servicios Integrados Turístico Culturales Cusco, 1988.

Canessa, Andrew. 2006. "Todos Somos Indígenas: Towards a New Language of National Political Identity." *Bulletin of Latin American Research* 25, no. 2: 241–63.

Canessa, Andrew. 2007. "Who Is Indigenous? Self-Identification, Indigeneity, and Claims to Justice in Contemporary Bolivia." *Urban Anthropology and Studies of Cultural Systems and World Economic Development* 36, no. 3: 195–237.

"El Canto de América Vibró en Salta." 1966. Special issue, *Folklore*, no. 119 (May).

Cárdenas, Jenny. 1986. "El Impacto de la Guerra del Chaco en la Música Boliviana (Música Criollo-Mestiza: Resurgimiento de una Identidad Cultural de Interpelación)." Bachelor's thesis. Universidad Mayor de San Andrés.

Cárdenas, Jenny. 2015. *Historia de los Boleros de Caballería: Música, Política y Confrontación Social en Bolivia*. La Paz, Bolivia: Estado Plurinacional de Bolivia, Ministerio de Culturas y Turismo.

Cárdenas Tabares, Fabio, and Jorge Valencia Caro. 1972. *Corporación Boliviana de Turismo y Políticas Generales para el Desarrollo Turístico de Bolivia: Agosto a Octubre de 1972; Tomo I*. La Paz, Bolivia: Organización de los Estados Americanos, División de Fomento Turismo.

Carrasco Pirard, Eduardo. 1988. *Quilapayún: La Revolución y las Estrellas*. Santiago, Chile: Las Ediciones de Ornitorrinco.

Casey, Michael. 2009. *Che's Afterlife: The Legacy of an Image*. New York: Vintage Books.

Castro Riveros, Alan. 2016. "Vida y Obra de Sergio Suárez Figueroa." *Ciencia y Cultura* 37: 107–28.

Cavour, Ernesto. 1994. *Instrumentos Musicales de Bolivia*. La Paz, Bolivia: Producciones CIMA.

Cavour, Ernesto. 2001. *El Charango, Su Vida, Costumbres y Desventuras*. La Paz, Bolivia: Producciones CIMA.

Cavour, Ernesto. 2003. *Diccionario Enciclopédico de los Instrumentos Musicales de Bolivia*. La Paz, Bolivia: Producciones CIMA.

Cejudo Velázquez, Pablo. 1966. *Colorista del Collao: Una Biografía de Italaque y del Pintor Leonardo Flores*. La Paz, Bolivia: Talleres Gráficos Bolivianos.

Cerruto, Karina. 1996. *Crónicas Históricas Documentadas*. La Paz, Bolivia: Editorial Juventud.

Céspedes, Augusto. 1966. *El Presidente Colgado*. Buenos Aires, Argentina: Editorial J. Alvarez.

Céspedes, Gilka Wara. 1984. "New Currents in 'Música Folklórica' in La Paz, Bolivia." *Latin American Music Review* 5, no. 2: 217–42.

Céspedes, Gilka Wara. 1993. "'Huayño,' 'Saya,' and 'Chuntunqui': Bolivian Identity in the Music of Los Kjarkas." *Latin American Music Review* 14, no. 1: 52–101.

Chamosa, Oscar. 2010. *The Argentine Folklore Movement: Sugar Elites, Criollo Workers, and the Politics of Cultural Nationalism, 1900–1955*. Tucson: University of Arizona Press.

Chamosa, Oscar. 2012. *Breve Historia del Folclore Argentino, 1920–1970: Identidad, Política y Nación*. Buenos Aires, Argentina: Edhasa.

Chesterton, Bridget María, ed. 2016. *The Chaco War: Environment, Ethnicity, and Nationalism.* New York: Bloomsbury Academic.

Choque, Roberto. 1986. *La Masacre de Jesús de Machaca.* La Paz, Bolivia: Ediciones Chitakolla.

Christoforidis, Michael. 2017. "Serenading Spanish Students on the Streets of Paris: The International Projection of Estudiantinas in the 1870s." *Nineteenth-Century Music Review* 14, no. 2: 1–14.

Cifuentes, Luis. 1989. *Fragmentos de un Sueño: Inti-Illimani y la Generación de los 60.* Santiago, Chile: Ediciones Logos.

Contreras, Manuel. 2003. "A Comparative Perspective on Education Reforms in Bolivia: 1950–2000." In *Proclaiming Revolution: Bolivia in Comparative Perspective*, edited by Merilee Grindle and Pilar Domingo, 259–88. London: Institute of Latin American Studies.

Cordero, Julio. 2004. *Estudio Archivo Cordero: Bolivia 1900–1961.* Madrid, Spain: Editorial Casa de América y Turner.

Cornejo Díaz, Marcela. 2012. *Música Popular Tradicional del Valle del Chili.* Lima, Peru: Theia.

Coronel Quisbert, Cristobal. 1997. *Radio Illimani: El Proceso de la Revolución Nacional (1950–1960).* Bachelor's thesis, Universidad Católica Boliviana.

Coronel Quisbert, Cristobal. 2013. *Ondas Que Provocan: Radio Illimani, los Estados y el Nacionalismo.* La Paz, Bolivia: Editorial Gente Comun, Edición Limitada.

Costa Ardúz, Rolando. 1996. *Monografía de la Provincia Camacho.* La Paz, Bolivia: Prefectura del Departamento de La Paz.

Cristelli, Silvia. 2004. "Bolivia en el Primer Centenario de Su Ceguera: La Centralidad de la Cultura Visual en el Proceso de Construcción de la Identidad Nacional." *Anuario de Estudios Bolivianos, Archivisticos y Bibliograficos* 10: 251–69.

Crónica del Primer Centenario de la República, 1825–1925, Bolivia. 1926. La Paz, Bolivia: n.p.

Cuba, Simón, and Hugo Cuba. 2007. *Boliviana 100% Paceña: La Morenada.* La Paz, Bolivia: Universidad Mayor de San Andrés.

Davies, Nigel. 1995. *The Incas.* Niwot: University of Colorado Press.

Debray, Régis. 1975. *Che's Guerrilla War.* Translated from French by Rosemary Sheed. Harmondsworth, UK: Penguin Books.

Demelas, Marie-Danielle. 1981. "Darwinismo a la Criolla: El Darwinismo Social en Bolivia, 1809–1910." *Historia Boliviana* 1, no. 20: 55–82.

d'Harcourt, Marguerite, and Raoul d'Harcourt. 1959. *La Musique des Aymara sur les Hauts Plateaux Boliviens.* Paris: Musée de l'homme.

d'Harcourt, Marguerite, and Raoul d'Harcourt. 1990 (1925). *La Música de los Incas y Sus Supervivencias*, translated from French by Luis Alberto Suárez. Lima, Peru: Occidental Petroleum Corporation of Peru.

De la Cadena, Marisol. 2000. *Indigenous Mestizos: The Politics of Race and Culture in Cuzco, Peru, 1919–1991.* Durham, NC: Duke University Press.

De la Quintana, Raúl, and Ramiro Duchén. 1986. *Radio Illimani: Los Primeros Años de Su Historia (1933–1937).* La Paz, Bolivia: CIMA.

De la Quintana, Raúl. 1999. *Aproximación al Catálogo Bio-Bibliográfico de la Radiodifusión Boliviana.* La Paz, Bolivia: Producciones CIMA.

Dent, Alex. 2009. *River of Tears: Country Music, Memory, and Modernity in Brazil.* Durham, NC: Duke University Press.

Dueñas, Pablo. 1993. *Historia Documental del Bolero Mexicano.* Mexico City, Mexico: Asociación Mexicana de Estudios Fonográficos, A.C.

Dunkerley, James. 1984. *Rebellion in the Veins: Political Struggle in Bolivia, 1952–1982.* London: Verso.

Dunkerley, James. 2007. *Bolivia: Revolution and The Power of History in the Present, Essays by James Dunkerley.* London: Institute for the Study of the Americas.

Dunkerley, James. 2013. "The Bolivian Revolution at 60: Politics and Historiography." *Journal of Latin American Studies* 45, no. 2: 325–50.

Earle, Rebecca. 2007. *The Return of the Native: Indians and Myth-Making in Spanish America, 1810–1930.* Durham, NC: Duke University Press.

Eguino, Fenelón. 1906. *Breves Notas sobre la Música Indígena en Bolivia.* Buenos Aires Argentina: Imprenta de G. Kraft.

Favre, Gilbert. 1981. *Mémoires d'un Gringo.* n.p.

FEDAM. 1999. *El Cine de Jorge Sanjinés.* Santa Cruz, Bolivia: Fundación para la Educación y Desarrollo de las Artes y Media.

Feldman, Heidi. 2006. *Black Rhythms of Peru: Reviving African Musical Heritage in the Black Pacific.* Middletown, CT: Wesleyan University Press.

Fellman Velarde, Jose. 1954. *Víctor Paz Estenssoro: El Hombre y la Revolución.* La Paz, Bolivia: Editorial Don Bosco.

Fellman Velarde, Jose. 1955. *Álbum de la Revolución Nacional: 128 Años de Lucha por la Independencia de Bolivia.* La Paz, Bolivia: Subsecretaria de Prensa, Informaciones y Cultura.

Fernández, Celina. 2005. *Los Panchos.* Madrid, Spain: Ediciones Martínez Roca.

Fernández Coca, Víctor. 1994. *35 Años de Folklore Marcando la Soberania Patria.* Cochabamba, Bolivia: Lauro Records.

Fernández Terán, Roberto. 2002. "Prensa, Radio e Imaginario Boliviano Durante la Guerra del Chaco (1932–1935)." In *La Música en Bolivia: De la Prehistoria a la Actualidad*, edited by Wálter Sánchez Canedo., 209–48. Cochabamba, Bolivia: Fundación Simon I. Patiño.

Ferrier, Claude. 2010. *El Huayno con Arpa: Estilos Globales en la Nueva Música Popular Andina.* Lima, Peru: Ponitificia Universidad Católica del Perú.

Field, Thomas C. 2014. *From Development to Dictatorship: Bolivia and the Alliance for Progress in the Kennedy Era.* Ithaca, NY: Cornell University Press.

Fiol, Stefan. 2017. *Recasting Folk in the Himalayas: Indian Music, Media, and Social Mobility.* Urbana: University of Illinois Press.

Fortún, Julia. 1957. *Manual para la Recolección de Material Folklórico.* La Paz, Bolivia: Ministerio de Educación, Departmento de Folklore.

Fortún, Julia. 1961. *La Danza de los Diablos.* La Paz, Bolivia: Ministerio de Educación y Bellas Artes, Oficialía Mayor de Cultura Nacional.

Fuentes Rodríguez, Luis. 2001. *Nilo Soruco Arancibia.* Salta, Argentina: Editorial MILOR.

Gálvez Rodríguez, William. 2003. *El Guerrillero Heroico: Che en Bolivia.* Vizcaya, Spain: Status Ediciones.

García Corona, Leon. 2015. "Mexico's Broken Heart: Music, Politics, and Sentimentalism in the Bolero." PhD diss., University of California, Los Angeles.

Gelbart, Matthew. 2007. *The Invention of "Folk Music" and "Art Music": Emerging Categories from Ossian to Wagner.* Cambridge: Cambridge University Press.

Gildner, Matthew. 2012. "Indomestizo Modernism: National Development and Indigenous Integration in Postrevolutionary Bolivia, 1952–1964." PhD diss., University of Texas–Austin.

Gildner, Matthew. 2013. "Andean Atlantis: Race, Science and the Nazi Occult in Bolivia." *The Appendix* 1, no. 2. http://theappendix.net/issues/2013/4/andean-atlantis-race-science-and-the-nazi-occult-in-bolivia.

Giordano, Santiago, and Alejandro Mareco. 2010. *Había Que Cantar: Una Historia del Festival Nacional de Folklore de Cosquín*. Cosquín, Argentina: Comisión Municipal de Folklore.

Giraudo, Laura, and Stephen E. Lewis. 2012. "Introduction: Pan-American Indigenismo (1940–1970), New Approaches to an Ongoing Debate." *Latin American Perspectives* 39, no. 5: 311.

Gobierno Municipal de la Ciudad de La Paz Oficialia Mayor de Cultura. 1993. *Primera Exposición Histórica del Disco Fonográfico Paceño: Casa Municipal de la Cultura "Franz Tamayo" del 19 al 30 de Octubre de 1993*. La Paz, Bolivia: Gobierno Municipal de La Paz, Oficialía Mayor de Cultura, Esquina Cultural Paceña.

Gonzales, Michael J. 2009. "Imagining Mexico in 1921: Visions of the Revolutionary State and Society in the Centennial Celebration in Mexico City." *Mexican Studies* 25, no. 2: 247–70.

González, Anita. 2010. *Afro-Mexico, Dancing between Myth and Reality*. Austin: University of Texas Press.

González Bravo, Antonio. 1936. "Sicus." *Boletín Latino Americano de Música* II: 253–57.

González Bravo, Antonio. 1937. "Kena, Pincollos y Tarkas." *Boletín Latino Americano de Música* III: 25–32.

González Bravo, Antonio. 1938. "Trompeta, Flauta Traversa, Tambor y Charango." *Boletín Latino Americano de Música* IV: 167–75.

González Bravo, Antonio. 1948. "Música, Instrumentos y Danzas Indígenas." In *La Paz en su IV Centenario 1548–1948, Vol. III*, 403–23. La Paz, Bolivia: Edición del Comité Pro IV Centenario 1948.

González Bravo, Antonio. 1949. "Clasificación de los Sicus Aymaras." *Revista de Estudios Musicales* 1, no. 1: 92–101.

González Bravo, Antonio. 1956. "El Modo Pentatónico en la Música Nacional." *Khana* II, nos. 17–18: 34–40. Originally published in 1925 in *Revista Inti*.

González Bravo, Antonio. 1957. "En Torno a la Escuela de Warisata." *Khana* V, nos. 25–26: 92–97. Originally published in 1939.

González Bravo, Antonio. 1958. "Italaque." *Khana* VI, nos. 27–30: 228–33.

González Bravo, Antonio. 1961a. "Generalidades y Ciertos Detalles de Fabricación en Algunos Instrumentos Musicales Indígenas Bolivianos." *Archivos Bolivianos de Folklore* 1: 57–63.

González Bravo, Antonio. 1961b. "Medio Siglo de Vida Musical." *Khana* VIII, no. 35: 92–105.

González Ríos, Yolanda, and Jóse González Ríos. 1998. *Cerrito de Huacsapata: Estudiantinas y Música Puneña del Sigle XX*. Cusco, Peru: Editorial Edmundo Pantigozo.

González Rodríguez, Juan Pablo. 2005. "The Making of a Social History of Popular Music in Chile." *Latin American Music Review* 26: 248–72.

González Rodríguez, Juan Pablo, and Claudio Rolle. 2005. *Historia Social de la Música Popular en Chile, 1890–1950*. Santiago, Chile: Ediciones Universidad Católica de Chile.

González Rodríguez, Juan Pablo, Oscar Ohlsen, and Claudio Rolle. 2009. *Historia Social de la Música Popular en Chile, 1950–1970*. Santiago, Chile: Ediciones Universidad Católica de Chile.

Gordillo, José M. 2000. *Campesinos Revolucionarios de Bolivia: Identidad, Territorio y Sexualidad en el Valle Alto de Cochabamba, 1952–1964*. La Paz, Bolivia: PROMEC/Universidad de la Cordillera/Plural Editores/UMSS.

Gotkowitz, Laura. 2007. *A Revolution for Our Rights: Indigenous Struggles for Land and Justice in Bolivia, 1880–1952*. Durham, NC: Duke University Press.

Gotkowitz, Laura. 2011. "Introduction: Histories of Race and Racism in the Andes and Mesoamerica." In *Histories of Race and Racism: The Andes and Mesoamerica from Colonial Times to the Present*, edited by Laura Gotkowitz, 1–53. Durham, NC: Duke University Press.

Gould, Jeffrey. 1998. *To Die in This Way: Nicaraguan Indians and the Myth of Mestizaje, 1880–1965*. Durham, NC: Duke University Press.

Grindle, Merilee, and Pilar Domingo, eds. 2003. *Proclaiming Revolution: Bolivia in Comparative Perspective*. London: Institute of Latin American Studies.

Gruszczyńska-Ziólkowska, Anna. 1995. *El Poder del Sonido: El Papel de las Crónicas Españolas en la Etnomusicología Andina*. Cayambe, Ecuador: Ediciones Abya-Yala.

Guardia, Marcelo. 1994. *Música Popular y Comunicación en Bolivia: Las Interpretaciones y Conflictos*. Cochabamba, Bolivia: Universidad Católica Boliviana.

Guss, David. 2000. *The Festive State: Race, Ethnicity, and Nationalism as Cultural Performance*. Berkeley: University of California Press.

Guss, David. 2006. "The Gran Poder and the Reconquest of La Paz." *Journal of Latin American and Caribbean Anthropology* 11, no. 2: 294–328.

Hafstein, Valdimar. 2018. *Making Intangible Culture: El Condor Pasa and Other Stories from UNESCO*. Bloomington: Indiana University Press.

Hagedorn, Katherine. 2001. *Divine Utterances: The Performance of Afro-Cuban Santería*. Washington, DC: Smithsonian Institution Press.

Harris, Olivia. 1995. "Ethnic Identity and Market Relations: Indians and Mestizos in the Andes." In *Ethnicity, Markets, and Migration in the Andes: At the Crossroads of History and Anthropology*, edited by Brooke Larson and Olivia Harris, with Enrique Tandeter, 351–90. Durham, NC: Duke University Press.

Hayes, Joy Elizabeth. 2000. *Radio Nation: Communication, Popular Culture, and Nationalism in Mexico, 1920–1950*. Tucson: University of Arizona Press.

Hellier-Tinoco, Ruth. 2011. *Embodying Mexico: Tourism, Nationalism and Performance*. New York: Oxford University Press.

Herrada, Nivardo. 1996. "Alfredo Domínguez o El Hombre 'Discreto.'" *Taquipacha* no. 4, 65–72.

Himpele, Jeffrey. 2008. *Circuits of Culture: Media, Politics, and Indigenous Identity in the Andes*. Minneapolis: University of Minnesota Press.

Hutchinson, Sydney. 2009. "The Ballet Folklórico de México and the Construction of the Mexican Nation through Dance." In *Dancing across Borders: Danzas y Bailes Mexicanos*, edited by Olga Nájera-Ramírez, Norma E. Cantú, and Brenda M. Romero, 206–55. Urbana: University of Illinois Press.

Ichuta Ichuta, Gerardo. 2003. "Sikuris de la Tradición Misti." *Reunión Anual de Etnología* XVI: 123–37.

Itier, César. 2000. *El Teatro Quechua en al Cuzco, Vol. II*. Lima, Peru: Institut Français d'Études Andines.

Izikowitz, Karl. 1935. *Musical and Other Sound Instruments of the South American Indians: A Comparative Ethnographical Study*. Göteborg, Sweden: Elanders Boktryckeri Aktiebolag.

Jáureguí, Jesús. 2007. *El Mariachi: Símbolo Musical de México*. Mexico City, Mexico: Santillana Ediciones Generales, S.A. de C.V.

John, Sándor. 2009. *Bolivia's Radical Tradition: Permanent Revolution in the Andes*. Tucson: University of Arizona Press.

Karush, Matthew B. 2017. *Musicians in Transit: Argentina and the Globalization of Popular Music*. Durham, NC: Duke University Press.

Katz-Rosene, Joshua. 2015. "Discourse in Música Latinoamericana Cultural Projects from Nueva Canción to Colombian Canción Social." *Volume! La Revue des Musiques Populaires* 11, no. 2: 65–83.

Kippez, Miguel Ángel. 1992. *René Barrientos Ortuño ("El Hombre")*. Cochabamba, Bolivia: Impresiones Poligraf.

Klein, Herbert. 1969. *Parties and Political Change in Bolivia, 1880–1952*. London: Cambridge University Press.

Klein, Herbert. 1992. *Bolivia: The Evolution of a Multi-Ethnic Society*. New York: Oxford University Press.

Knight, Alan. 2003. "The Domestic Dynamics of the Mexican and Bolivian Revolutions." In *Proclaiming Revolution: Bolivia in Comparative Perspective*, edited by Merilee Grindle and Pilar Domingo, 54–90. London: Institute of Latin American Studies.

Knudsen, Jerry. 1986. *Bolivia, Press and Revolution, 1932–1964*. Lanham, MD: University Press of America.s

Koegel, John. 2002. "Crossing Borders: Mexicana, Tejana, and Chicana Musicians in the United States and Mexico." In *From Tejano to Tango: Latin American Popular Music*, edited by Walter Aaron Clark, 97–125. New York: Routledge.

Kuenzli, Gabrielle. 2010. "Acting Inca: The Parameters of National Belonging in Early Twentieth-Century Bolivia." *Hispanic American Historical Review* 90, no. 2: 247–81.

Kuenzli, E. Gabrielle. 2013. *Acting Inca: Identity and National Belonging in Early Twentieth-Century Bolivia*. Pittsburgh: University of Pittsburgh Press.

Kuon Arce, Elizabeth, Rodrigo Gutiérrez Viñuales, Ramón Gutiérrrez, and Graciela María Viñuales. 2009. *Cuzco-Buenos Aires: Ruta de Intelectualidad Americana (1900–1950)*. Lima, Peru: Universidad de San Martín de Porres, Fondo Editorial.

Langevin, André. 1990. "La Organización Musical y Social en el Conjunto de Khantu." *Revista Andina* 8, no. 1: 113–37.

Lara, Jesús. 1960. *La Literatura de los Quechuas: Ensay y Antología*. Cochabamba, Bolivia: Editorial Canelas.

Larson, Brooke. 2003. "Capturing Indian Bodies, Hearths and Minds: 'El Hogar Campesino' and Rural School Reform in Bolivia, 1920s–1940s." In *Proclaiming Revolution: Bolivia in Comparative Perspective*, edited by Merilee S. Grindle and Pilar Domingo, 181–209. London: Institute of Latin American Studies.

Larson, Brooke. 2004. *Trials of Nation Making: Liberalism, Race, and Ethnicity in the Andes, 1810–1910*. Cambridge: Cambridge University Press.

Larson, Brooke. 2011. "Forging the Unlettered Indian: The Pedagogy of Race in the Bolivian Andes." In *Histories of Race and Racism: The Andes and Mesoamerica from Colonial Times to the Present*, edited by Laura Gotkowitz, 134–56. Durham, NC: Duke University Press.

Lehman, Kenneth. 1999. *Bolivia and the United States: A Limited Partnership*. Athens: University of Georgia Press.

Leichtman, Ellen. 1989. "Musical Interaction: A Bolivian Mestizo Perspective." *Latin American Music Review* 10, no. 1: 29–52.

Limanksy, Nicholas. 2008. *Yma Sumac: The Art behind the Legend*. New York: YBK Publishers.

Lloréns Amico, José. 1983. *Musica Popular en Lima: Criollos y Andinos*. Lima, Peru: Instituto de Estudios Peruanos.

López, Rick. 2006. "The Noche Mexicana and the Exhibition of Popular Arts: Two Ways of Exalting Indianness." In *The Eagle and The Virgin: Nation and Cultural Revolution in Mexico, 1920–1940*, edited by Mary Kay Vaughn and Stephen Lewis, 95–118. Durham, NC: Duke University Press.

Lora, Guillermo. 1977. *A History of the Bolivian Labour Movement, 1848–1971*. Edited and abridged by Laurence Whitehead. Translated from Spanish by Christine Whitehead. Cambridge: Cambridge University Press.

Luker, Morgan. 2016. *The Tango Machine: Musical Culture in the Age of Expediency*. Chicago: University of Chicago Press.

Luna Muñoz, Manuel. 1993. *De Juglares, Trovadores, Tunos y Estudiantinas*. Santiago, Chile: Editorial Cercom.

Macedo Juárez, Ángel. 2006. *Historia del Conjunto de Sikuris del Barrio Mañazo*. Puno, Peru: Editorial Universal E.I.R.I.

MacLean y Esteros, Jorge. 1926. *Crónica de las Fiestas del Primer Centenario de Bolivia*. Lima, Peru: n.p.

Maidana, Freddy. 2011. *La Danza de los Caporales*. La Paz, Bolivia: Nexo Print.

Malloy, James M. 1970. *Bolivia: The Uncompleted Revolution*. Pittsburgh: University of Pittsburgh Press.

Malloy, James M. 1971. "Revolutionary Politics." In *Beyond the Revolution: Bolivia since 1952*, edited by James M. Malloy and Richard S. Thorn, 111–56. Pittsburgh: University of Pittsburgh Press.

Malloy, James M., and Eduardo Gamarra. 1988. *Revolution and Reaction: Bolivia, 1964–1985*. New Brunswick, NJ: Transaction Books.

Martin-Frost, Ladona. 2009. "Pedagogy and Politics in Bolivian Music Education at the End of Neoliberal Reform." PhD diss., University of Illinois at Urbana-Champaign.

Martín Sárraga, Félix O. 2014. "La Fígaro, Estudiantina Más Viajera del Siglo XIX." Accessed July 2, 2017. http://tunaemundi.com.

McCann, Bryan. 2004. *Hello, Hello Brazil: Popular Music in the Making of Modern Brazil*. Durham, NC: Duke University Press.

McDowell, John. 2010. "Rethinking Folklorization in Ecuador: Multivocality in the Expressive Contact Zone." *Western Folklore* 69, no. 2: 181–209.

Meisch, Lynne. 2002. *Andean Entrepreneurs: Otavalo Merchants and Musicians in the Global Arena*. Austin: University of Texas Press.

Mendoza, Jesús. 1996. "La Tradicional Entrada Folklórica de Urkupiña." *Taquipacha*, no. 4, 31–45.

Mendoza, Zoila. 2000. *Shaping Society through Dance: Mestizo Ritual Performance in the Peruvian Andes*. Chicago: University of Chicago Press.

Mendoza, Zoila. 2008. *Creating Our Own: Folklore, Performance, and Identity in Cuzco, Peru*. Durham, NC: Duke University Press.

Ministerio de Asuntos Campesinos. 1965. *Primer Festival Cívico Folklórico del Niño Campesino*. La Paz, Bolivia: Ministerio de Asuntos Campesinos/Departamento de Relaciones Públicas.

Ministerio de Educación y Bellas Artes. 1961a. *Revista del Consejo Nacional de Arte 1*. La Paz, Bolivia: Oficialia Mayor de Cultura Nacional.

Ministerio de Educación y Bellas Artes. 1961b. *Revista del Consejo Nacional de Arte 2*. La Paz, Bolivia: Oficialia Mayor de Cultura Nacional.

Mintz, Amanda. 2015. "Reading Nicaraguan Folklore through Inter-American Indigenismo, 1940–1970." *Latin American and Caribbean Ethnic Studies* 9, no. 3: 197–221.

Mitchell, Christopher. 1977. *The Legacy of Populism in Bolivia: From the MNR to Military Rule*. New York and London: Praeger Publishers.

Molina, Juan Alberto B. 1986. *El Libro de Cosquin: Crónica del Festival Nacional de Folklore, 1961–1985*. Córdoba, Argentina: Editorial El Oeste.

Moore, Robin. 1997. *Nationalizing Blackness: Afrocubanismo and Artistic Revolution in Havana, 1920–1940*. Pittsburgh: University of Pittsburgh Press.

Moreno Rivas, Yolanda. 1989. *Historia de la Música Popular Mexicana*. Mexico City, Mexico: Editorial Patria, S.A. de C.V.

Morris, Nancy. 2014. "New Song in Chile: Half a Century of Musical Activism." In *The Militant Song Movement in Latin America: Chile, Uruguay, and Argentina*, edited by Pablo Vila, 19–44. Lanham, MD: Lexington Books.

Mularski, Jedrek. 2014. *Music, Politics, and Nationalism in Latin America: Chile during the Cold War Era*. Amherst, NY: Cambria Press.

Mulholland, Mary Lee. 2007. "Mariachi, Myths and Mestizaje: Popular Culture and Mexican National Identity." *National Identities* 9, no. 3: 247–64.

Mullo Sandoval, Juan. 2014. *La Estudiantina Quiteña*. Quito, Ecuador: Instituto Iberamericano del Patrimonio Natural y Cultural (IPANC) de la Organización del Convenio Andrés Bello.

Nagy, Silvia. 1994–1995. "Juan Wallparrimachi: El Poeta de la Ausencia." *Bolivian Studies* 5, no. 1: 31–59.

Oblitas Poblete, Enrique. 1954. "Informe Sobre la Provincia Bautista Saavedra: Aspectos Folklóricos, Ethnográficos y Arqueológicos." *Khana* III, nos. 5–6: 57–73.

Oblitas Poblete, Enrique. 1957. "Surimana: Leyenda Callawaya Dramatizada." *Khana* V, no. 2: 1–34.

Oblitas Poblete, Enrique. 1963. *Cultura Callawaya*. La Paz, Bolivia: Talleres Gráficos Bolivianos.

Oliart, Patricia, and José Llorens. 1984. "La Nueva Canción en el Perú." *Comunicación y Cultura* 12: 73–82.

Olson, Laura. 2004. *Performing Russia: Folk Revival and Russian Identity*. New York: Routledge Curzon.

Ortíz, Pablo Marcial. 2004. *El Trío Los Panchos: Historia y Crónica*. San Juan, Puerto Rico: Editora Corripio.

Oviedo, Carmen. 1990. *Mentira Todo lo Cierto: Trás la Huella de Violeta Parra*. Santiago, Chile: Editorial Universitaria.

Pacini Hernandez, Deborah, Héctor D. Fernández-L'Hoeste, and Eric Zolov. 2004. *Rockin' las Américas: The Global Politics of Rock in Latin/o America*. Pittsburgh: University of Pittsburgh Press.

Pagaza Galdo. 1960–1. "El Yaraví." *Folklore Americano* 8–9: 75–141.

Pantoja, Antonio. 1958. *Método para Quena*. Buenos Aires, Argentina: Publicaciones Musical Tempo.

Paredes, M. Rigoberto. 1898. "Monografía de las Provincia de Muñecas." *Boletín de la Sociedad Geográfica de La Paz* 1, no. 2: 1–54.

Paredes, M. Rigoberto. 1913. "El Arte en la Altiplanicie." *Boletín de la Sociedad Geográfica de La Paz* 11, no. 2: 151–220.

Paredes, M. Rigoberto. 1949. *El Arte Folklórico de Bolivia*. La Paz, Bolivia: Talleres Gráficos Gamarra.

Paredes Candia, Antonio. 1966. *La Danza Folklórica en Bolivia*. La Paz, Bolivia: Ediciones Isla.

Paredes Candia, Antonio. 1967. *La Vida Ejemplar de Antonio González Bravo*. La Paz, Bolivia: Ediciones Isla.

Paredes Candia, Antonio. 1984. *La Danza Folklórica en Bolivia*. La Paz, Bolivia: Editorial Gisbert y Cía.

Parejas, Alcides. 1999. *El Carnaval Cruceño a Través del Tiempo*. Santa Cruz, Bolivia: Editorial La Hoguera.

Party, Daniel. 2012. "'Un Pequeño Defecto': El Bolero de Lucho Gatica entre sus Fans y la Crítica." In *El Lenguaje de las Emociones: Afecto y Cultura en América Latina*, edited by Mabel Moraña and Ignacio Sánchez Prado, 227–42. Madrid, Spain: Vervuert Iberoamericana.

Pedelty, Mark. 1999. "The Bolero: The Birth, Life, and Decline of Mexican Modernity." *Latin American Music Review* 20, no. 1: 30–58.

Pekkola, Sari. 1996. *Magical Flutes: Musical Culture and Music Groups in a Changing Bolivia.* Lund, Sweden: Lund University Press.

Peña Bravo, Raúl. 1971. *Hechos y Dichos del General Barrientos.* n.p.

Peñaloza, Luis. 1963. *Historia del Movimiento Nacionalista Revolucionario, 1941–1952.* La Paz, Bolivia: n.p.

Peralta, Hernán. 2003. "Nueva Canción: La Crónica de las Luchas del Movimiento Social Ecuatoriano." MA thesis, Universidad Andina Simón Bolívar, Sede Ecuador.

Pérez, Elizardo. 1962. *Warisata, La Escuela-Ayllu.* La Paz, Bolivia: n.p.

Pérez Bugallo, Ruben. 1993. *Catálogo Ilustrado de Instrumentos Musicales Argentinos.* Buenos Aires, Argentina: Ediciones del Sol.

Picard, Michel. 1990. "'Cultural Tourism' in Bali: Cultural Performances as Tourist Attraction." *Indonesia* 49: 37–74.

Pisani, Michael. 2005. *Imagining Native America in Music.* New Haven, CT: Yale University Press.

Platt, Tristan. 1982. *Estado Boliviano y Ayllu Andino.* Lima, Peru: Instituto de Estudios Peruanos.

Ponce Valdivia, Omar Percy. 2008. *"De Charango a Chillador: Confluencias Musicales en la Estudiantina Altiplánica."* Magister en Artes con Mención en Musicología. Universidad de Chile.

Portorrico, Emilio. 2004. *Diccionario Biográfico de la Música Argentina de Raíz Folklórica.* Buenos Aires, Argentina: E. P. Portorrico.

Pruden, Hernán. 2012. "Cruceños into Cambas: Regionalism and Revolutionary Nationalism in Santa Cruz de la Sierra, Bolivia (1935–1959)." PhD diss., Stony Brook University.

Qayum, Seemin. 2002. "Nationalism, Internal Colonialism and the Spatial Imagination: The Geographic Society of La Paz in Turn-of-the-Century Bolivia." In *Studies in the Formation of the Nation State in Latin America*, edited by James Dunkerley, 275–98. London: Institute of Latin American Studies.

Qayum, Seemin. 2011. "Indian Ruins, National Origins: Tiwanaku and Indigenismo in La Paz, 1897–1933." In *Histories of Race and Racism: The Andes and Mesoamerica from Colonial Times to the Present,* edited by Laura Gotkowitz, 159–78. Durham, NC: Duke University Press.

Ramón y Rivera, Luis Felipe. 1953. *El Joropo: Baile Nacional de Venezuela.* Caracas, Venezuela: Ministerio de Educación.

Raphael, Alison. 1990. "From Popular Culture to Microenterprise: The History of Brazilian Samba Schools." *Latin American Music Review* 11, no. 1: 73–83.

Rendón Marín, Héctor. 2009. *De Liras a Cuerdas: Una Historia Social de la Música a Través de las Estudiantinas; Medellín, 1940–1980.* Medellín, Colombia: Universidad Nacional de Colombia, Sede Medellín, Facultad de Ciencias Humanas y Económicas.

Reyes Zárate, Raúl. 2017. "El Sindicato de Vendedores de Periódicos de La Paz, 1936–2016." *Historia* 38: 97–129.

Richards, Keith. 1999. *Lo Imaginario Mestizo: Aislamiento y Dislocación de la Visión de Bolivia de Néstor Taboada Terán.* La Paz, Bolivia: Plural Editores/CID.

Rios, Fernando. 2008. "La Flûte Indienne: The Early History of Andean Folkloric-Popular Music in France and Its Impact on Nueva Canción." *Latin American Music Review* 29, no. 2: 145–89.

Rios, Fernando. 2012. "The Andean Conjunto, Bolivian Sikureada and the Folkloric Musical Representation Continuum." *Ethnomusicology Forum* 21, no. 1: 5–29.

Rios, Fernando. 2014. "They're Stealing Our Music: The Argentínísima Controversy, National Culture Boundaries and the Rise of a Bolivian Nationalist Discourse." *Latin American Music Review* 35, no. 2: 197–227.

Ritter, Jonathan. 2002. "Siren Songs: Ritual and Revolution in the Peruvian Andes." *British Journal of Ethnomusicology* 11, no. 1: 9–42.

Rivera Cusicanqui, Silvia. 1986. *Oprimidos Pero No Vencidos: Luchas del Campesinado Aymara y Qhechwa de Bolivia, 1900–1980*. Geneva, Switzerland: Instituto de Investigaciones de las Naciones Unidas para el Desarrollo Social.

Rivera de Stahlie, Teresa. 1995. *Música y Músicos Bolivianos*. La Paz, Bolivia: Los Amigos del Libro.

Rivera de Stahlie, Teresa. 2003. *El Ballet en Bolivia: Relatos de las Primeras Bailarinas*. Madrid, Spain: Editorial Música Mundana Maqueda, S.L.

Rockefeller, David. 1999. "There Is a Culture Here: Spectacle and the Inculcation of Folklore in Highland Bolivia." *Journal of Latin American and Caribbean Anthropology* 3, no. 2: 118–49.

Rodríguez Musso, Osvaldo. 1988. *La Nueva Canción Chilena: Continuidad y Reflejo*. Havana, Cuba: Ediciones Casa de las Américas.

Rodríguez Ostria, Gustavo. 2011. *Tamara, Laura, Tania: Un Misterio en la Guerrilla del Che*. Buenos Aires, Argentina: Editorial del Nuevo Extremo S.A.

Rojas Foppiano, Gilberto. 1991. *Semblanza Artística Sentimental y Humana de un Compositor: Gilberto de Bolivia*. La Paz, Bolivia: Ministerio de Educación y Cultura.

Rojas Rojas, Orlando. 1989. *Creadores de la Música Boliviana*. La Paz, Bolivia: Producciones Cima.

Romero, Raúl. 2002. "Panorama de los Estudios sobre Música Andina en el Perú." In *Sonidos Andinos: Una Antología de la Música Campesina del Perú*, edited by Raúl Romero and Rosa Alarco, 11–70. Lima, Peru: Pontificia Universidad Católica de Perú, Instituto Riva-Agüero, Centro de Ethnomusicologia Andina.

Romero, Raúl. 2016. "Music Research in South America." In *A Latin American Reader: Views from the South*, edited by Javier León and Helena Simonett, 75–93. Urbana: University of Illinois Press.

Romero Kuljis, Regina. 2016. "Significados de los Qanthus como Elemento de Resistencia Cultural y Construcción del Espacio Social en Charazani, Niño Corín, Chajaya y Chullina de la Provincia Bautista Saavedra." BA thesis, Universidad Mayor de San Andrés.

Rommen, Timothy, and Daniel T. Neely. 2014. *Sun, Sea, and Sound: Music and Tourism in the Circum-Caribbean*. New York: Oxford University Press.

Roper, Danielle. 2019. "Blackface at the Andean Fiesta: Performing Blackness in the Danza de Caporales." *Latin American Research Review* 54, no. 2: 381–97.

Rossells, Beatriz. 1996. *Caymari Vida: La Emergencia de la Música Popular en Charcas*. Sucre, Bolivia: Corte Suprema de Justicia de la Nación.

Rossells, Beatriz. 1997a. *Lola Sierra del Beni*. La Paz, Bolivia: Ministerio de Desarrollo Humano, Secretaría de Asuntos de Suntos Etnicos, de Genero y Generaciones.

Rossells, Beatriz. 1997b. *Gladys Moreno: La Canción Enamorada*. La Paz, Bolivia: Ministerio de Desarollo Humano, Secretaría de Asuntos de Suntos Etnicos, de Genero y Generaciones.

Rossells, Beatriz. n.d. "Una Familia Singular en la Música Popular de La Paz: Los Bravo, entre el Siglo XIX y XX." Unpublished manuscript.

Rossells, Beatriz, and Osvaldo Calatayúd. 2009. *Carnaval Paceño y Jisk'a Anata: Proyecto la Fiesta Popular; Espacio de Continuidades, Creación y Recreación; Exploración de un Fenomeno Paceño Esencial.* La Paz, Bolivia: Instituto de Estudios Bolivianos.

Rowe, William, and Vivian Schelling. 1991. *Memory and Modernity: Popular Culture in Latin America.* London: Verso.

Sáez, Fernando. 1999. *La Vida Intranquila: Violeta Parra, Biografía Esencial.* Santiago, Chile: Editorial Sudamericana.

Salazar Mostajo, Carlos. 1997. 3rd ed. *Warisata Mia! Y Otros Articulos Polemicos.* La Paz, Bolivia: Librería Editorial "Juventúd."

Salinas, Horacio. 2013. *La Canción en el Sombrero: Historia de la Música de Inti-Illimani.* Santiago, Chile: Catalonia.

Salles-Reese, Verónica. 1997. *From Viracocha to the Virgin of Copacabana: Representation of the Sacred at Lake Titicaca.* Austin: University of Texas Press.

Salmón, Josefa. 1997. *El Espejo Indígena: El Discurso Indigenista en Bolivia, 1900–1956.* La Paz, Bolivia: Plural.

Sanabria, Hernando. 1964. *Música Popular de Santa Cruz: Los Mejores 25 Carnavales de la "Guardia Vieja."* Santa Cruz, Bolivia: Universidad Gabriel René Moreno.

Sánchez C., Wálter. 1994. *Aires Criollos: Música, Interpretes y Compositores de Cochabamba.* Cochabamba, Bolivia: Honorable Municipalidad de Cochabamba.

Sánchez C., Wálter. 1995. "Aires Nacionales de la Tierra: Criollos, Indios y Mestizos en las Imágenes Auditivas de lo Boliviano." *Reunión Anual de Etnología* 2: 77–96.

Sánchez C., Wálter. 1996. "Nacionalismo y Folklore: Indios, Criollos y Cholo-Mestizos." *Taquipacha*, no. 4, 53–64.

Sánchez-H., José. 1999. *The Art and Politics of Bolivian Cinema.* Lanham, MD, and London: Scarecrow Press.

Sánchez Huaringa, Carlos Daniel. 2013. *La Flauta de Pan Andina: Los Grupos de Sikuris Metropolitanos.* Lima, Peru: Fondo Editorial de la Universidad Nacional Mayor de San Marcos.

Sánchez Patzy, Mauricio. 2014a. "Chuntunqui." In *Bloomsbury Encyclopedia of Popular Music of the World, Volume IX, Genres: Caribbean and Latin America*, edited by David Horn and John Shepherd, 193–95. London and New York: Bloomsbury.

Sánchez Patzy, Mauricio. 2014b. "Neofolklore (Bolivia)." In *Bloomsbury Encyclopedia of Popular Music of the World, Volume IX, Genres: Caribbean and Latin America*, edited by David Horn and John Shepherd, 536–41. London and New York: Bloomsbury.

Sánchez Patzy, Mauricio. 2014c. "Tobas." In *Bloomsbury Encyclopedia of Popular Music of the World, Volume IX, Genres: Caribbean and Latin America*, edited by David Horn and John Shepherd, 857–61. London and New York: Bloomsbury.

Sánchez Patzy, Mauricio. 2017. *La Ópera Chola: Música Popular en Bolivia y Pugnas por la Identidad Social.* La Paz, Bolivia: Plural Editores.

Sánchez Patzy, Radek. 2014. *Felipe V. Rivera, Un Puente Fecundo: Música Andina en las Fronteras.* Buenos Aires, Argentina: Ministerio de Cultura de la Nación.

Sanjinés, Javier C. 2004. *"Mestizaje" Upside-Down: Aesthetic Politics in Modern Bolivia.* Pittsburgh: University of Pittsburgh Press.

Santamaría-Delgado, Carolina. 2014. *Vitrolas, Rocolas y Radioteatros: Hábitos de Escucha de la Música Popular en Medellín, 1930–1950.* Bogotá, Colombia: Editorial Pontificia Universidad Javeriana.

Santander, Ignacio. 1984. *Quilapayún.* Madrid, Spain: Ediciones Jucar.

Schwartz-Kates, Deborah. 2002. "The Popularized Gaucho Image as a Source of Argentine Classical Music, 1880–1920." In *From Tejano to Tango: Latin American Popular Music*, edited by Walter Aaron Clark, 3–24. New York: Routledge.

Scruggs, T.M. 1998. "Nicaraguan State Cultural Initiative and 'the Unseen Made Manifest.'" *Yearbook for Traditional Music* 30 (1998): 53–73.

Scruggs, T. M. 1999. "'Let's Enjoy as Nicaraguans': The Use of Music in the Construction of a Nicaraguan National Consciousness." *Ethnomusicology* 43, no. 2: 297–321.

Seoane, Carlos. "Velasco Maidana, José María." *Grove Music Online. Oxford Music Online.* Oxford University Press. Accessed January 19, 2016. http://www.oxfordmusiconline.com. proxy-um.researchport.umd.edu/subscriber/article/grove/music/29127.

Shaw, Víctor. 2007. *Cuando Tú Me Quieras: Raúl Shaw Moreno, Semblanzas.* La Paz, Bolivia: SPC Impresores S.A.

Sheehy, Daniel. 1997. "Popular Mexican Musical Traditions: The Mariachi of West Mexico and the Conjunto Jarocho of Veracruz." In *Music in Latin American Culture: Regional Traditions*, edited by John M. Schechter, 34–79. New York: Schirmer Books.

Shesko, Elizabeth. 2015. "Mobilizing Manpower for War: Toward a New History of Bolivia's Chaco Conflict, 1932–1935." *Hispanic American Historical Review* 95, no. 2: 299–334.

Siekmeier, James. 2011. *The Bolivian Revolution and the United States, 1952 to the Present.* University Park: Pennsylvania State University Press.

Sierra, Luis. 2013. "Indigenous Neighborhood Residents in the Urbanization of La Paz, Bolivia, 1910–1950." PhD diss., Binghamton University, State University of New York.

Siles del Valle, Juan Ignacio. 1997. *La Guerrilla del Che y la Narrativa Boliviana.* La Paz, Bolivia: Plural Editores.

Smale, Robert. 2010. *"I Sweat the Flavor of Tin": Labor Activism in Early Twentieth-Century Bolivia.* Pittsburgh: University of Pittsburgh Press.

Smith, Carol. 1996. "Myths, Intellectuals, and Race/Class/Gender Distinctions in the Formation of Latin American Nations." *Journal of Latin American and Caribbean Anthropology* 2, no. 1: 148–69.

SODRE. 1956. *II Festival Internacional de Cine Documental y Experimental: Mayo-Junio de 1956.* Montevideo, Uruguay: S.O.D.R.E.

Solomon, Thomas. 1997. "Mountains of Song: Musical Constructions of Ecology, Place and Identity in the Bolivian Andes." PhD diss., University of Texas, Austin.

Solomon, Thomas. 2014. "Performing Indigeneity: Poetics and Politics of Music Festivals in Highland Bolivia." In *Soundscapes from the Americas: Ethnomusicological Essays on the Power, Poetics, and Ontology of Performance*, edited by Donna Buchanan, 143–63. Farnham, UK: Ashgate.

Soruco, Nilo. 1994. *Como Gato Panza al Sol.* Tarija, Bolivia: n.p.

Soruco, Ximena, Wilfred Plata, and Gustavo Medeiros. 2008. *Los Barones del Oriente: El Poder en Santa Cruz Ayer y Hoy.* Santa Cruz, Bolivia: Fundación Tierra—Regional Oriente.

Soux, Maria Eugenia. 1992. "La Música en la Ciudad de La Paz: 1845–1885. Bachelor's thesis. Universidad de San Andrés. La Paz, Bolivia.

Soux, Maria Eugenia. 1997. "Música de Tradición Oral en La Paz: 1845–1885." *DATA, Revista del Instituto de Estudios Andinos y Amazónicas*, no. 7, 219–47.

Soux, Maria Eugenia. 2002. "Música e Identidad: La Ciudad de La Paz durante el Siglo XIX." In *La Música en Bolivia: Desde la Prehistoria a la Actualidad*, edited by Wálter Sánchez C., 249–68. Cochabamba, Bolivia: Fundación Simón I. Patiño.

Stefanoni, Pablo. 2012. "Jano en los Andes: Buscando la Cuna Mítica de la Nación; Arqueólogos y Maestros en la Semana Indianista Boliviana de 1931." *Revista Ciencia y Cultura* 29: 51–81.

Stefanoni, Pablo. 2015. *Los Inconformistas del Centenario—Intelectuales, Socialismo y Nación en una Bolivia en Crisis (1925–1939)*. La Paz, Bolivia: Plural Editores.

Stephenson, Marcia. 1999. *Gender and Modernity in Andean Bolivia*. Austin: University of Texas Press.

Stevenson, Robert. 1968. *Music in Aztec and Inca Territory*. Berkeley: University of California Press.

Stobart, Henry. 2006. *Music and the Poetics of Production in the Bolivian Andes*. Aldershot, UK: Ashgate.

Stobart, Henry. 2014. "Staging Sound: Acoustic reflections on Inca Music, Architecture and Performance Spaces." In *Inca Ushnus: Landscape, Site and Symbol in the Andes*, edited by Frank Meddens, Colin McEwan, Katie Willis, and Nicholas Branch, 133–46. London: Archetype Publications.

Stutzman, Ronald. 1981. "El Mestizaje: An All-Inclusive Ideology of Exclusion." In *Cultural Transformations and Ethnicity in Modern Ecuador*, edited by Norman Whitten, 45–94. Urbana: University of Illinois Press.

Susz, Pedro. 1997 *Cronología del Cine Boliviano (1897–1997)*. La Paz, Bolivia: Fundación Cinemateca Boliviana.

Taborga, Carlos. 1948a. "Provincia Camacho." In *La Paz en su IV Centenario 1548–1948, Vol. I*, 245–271. La Paz, Bolivia: Edición del Comité Pro IV Centenario.

Taborga, Carlos. 1948b. "Provincia Larecaja." In *La Paz en Su IV Centenario 1548–1948, Vol. I*, 351–86. La Paz, Bolivia: Edición del Comité Pro IV Centenario.

Taylor, Timothy. 2016. *Music and Capitalism: A History of the Present*. Chicago: University of Chicago Press.

Terceros, Armando and Alex Parada. 1989. *Libro de Oro de los Interpretes de la Música Cruceña*. Santa Cruz, Bolivia: n.p.

Terceros, Armando. 2006. *Libro de Oro de los Autores, Compositores e Interpretes de la Música Oriental*. Santa Cruz, Bolivia: UNAGRO.

Téllez, Rodolfo. 1998. *Legislación Turística de Bolivia*. La Paz, Bolivia: Industrias Graficas Acuarela Ltda.

Templeman, Robert. 1994. "We Answer Each Other: Musical Practice and Competition among Kantus Panpipe Ensembles in Bolivia's Charazani Valley." MA thesis, University of Illinois at Urbana-Champaign.

Templeman, Robert. 1998. "We are People of the Yungas, We are the Yungas Race." In *Blackness in Latin America and the Caribbean: Social Dynamics and Cultural Transformations*, edited by Norman Whitten and Arlene Torres, 426–44. Bloomington: Indiana University Press.

Thomson, Sinclair. 2002. *We Alone Will Rule: Native Andean Politics in the Age of Insurgency*. Madison: University of Wisconsin Press.

Tomlinson, Gary. 2009. *The Singing of the New World: Indigenous Voice in the Era of European Contact*. Cambridge: Cambridge University Press.

Toranzo, Carlos. 2008. "Let the Mestizos Stand Up and Be Counted." In *Unresolved Tensions: Bolivia, Past and Present*, edited by John Crabtree and Laurence Whitehead, 35–50. Pittsburgh: University of Pittsburgh Press.

Torres, Eleazar. 2007. *Estudiantinas Venezolanas*. Caracas, Venezuela: Fundación Vicente Emilio Sojo, Instituto de Musicología.

Torres, George. 2002. "The Bolero Romántico: From Cuban Dance to International Popular Song." In *From Tejano to Tango: Latin American Popular Music*, edited by Walter Aaron Clark, 151–71. New York: Routledge.

Torres, Norberto. 2006. *Mauro Nuñez: Para el Mundo*. Sucre, Bolivia: Editorial Tupac Katari.

Trigo O'Connor d'Arlach, Eduardo. 1999. *Conversaciones con Víctor Paz Estenssoro*. La Paz, Bolivia: Comunicaciones El Pais, S.A.

Tucker, Joshua. 2013. *Gentleman Troubadours and Andean Pop Stars: Huayno Music, Media Work, and Ethnic Imaginaries in Urban Lima*. Chicago: University of Chicago Press.

Turino, Thomas. 1984. "The Urban-Mestizo Charango Tradition in Southern Peru: A Statement of Shifting Identity. *Ethnomusicology* 28, no. 2: 253–69.

Turino, Thomas. 1993 *Moving Away from Silence: Music of the Peruvian Altiplano and the Experience of Urban Migration*. Chicago: University of Chicago Press.

Turino, Thomas. 2000. *Nationalists, Cosmopolitans, and Popular Music in Zimbabwe*. Chicago: University of Chicago Press.

Turino, Thomas. 2003. "Nationalism and Latin American Music: Selected Case Studies and Theoretical Considerations." *Latin American Music Review* 24, no. 2: 169–209.

Turino, Thomas. 2008a. *Music as Social Life: The Politics of Participation*. Chicago: University of Chicago Press.

Turino, Thomas. 2008b. *Music in the Andes: Experiencing Music, Expressing Culture*. Oxford: Oxford University Press.

Urban, Greg, and Joel Sherzer. 1991. *Nation-States and Indians in Latin America*. Austin: University of Texas Press.

Urquizo Sossa, Carlos. 1973. *Breve Ensayo en Torno a la Teoria del Turismo*. La Paz, Bolivia: H. Municipalidad de La Paz.

Valcárcel, Luis. 1981. *Memorias*. Lima, Peru: Instituto de Estudios Peruanos.

Valencia, Américo. 1983. *El Siku Bipolar Altiplánico Vol. I: Los Sikuris y Pusamorenos*. Lima, Peru: Artex E.I.R.L.

Valeriano Thola, Emmo E. 2004. *Origen de la Danza de los Morenos*. La Paz, Bolivia: n.p.

Varallanos, José. 1988. *El Cóndor Pasa: Vida y Obra de Daniel Alomía Robles*. Lima, Peru: Talleres Gráficos.

Vargas, Fernando. 2010. *Wara Wara: La Reconstrucción de una Pelicula Perdida*. La Paz, Bolivia: Plural Editores.

Vásquez Diaz, Rubén. 1968. *Bolivia a La Hora del Che*. Mexico City, Mexico: Siglo XXI Editores.

Vega, Carlos. 1953. *La Zamacueca (Cueca, Zamba, Chilena, Marinera): La Zamba Antigua*. Buenos Aires, Argentina: J. Korn.

Vega, Carlos. 1962a. "El Yaraví." *Folklore*, no.15, 42–46.

Vega, Carlos. 1962b. "El Triste." *Folklore*, no.16, 42–45.

Vega, Carlos. 1962c. "El Triste." *Folklore*, no. 17, 42–45.

Vellard, Jehan, and Mildred Merino. 1954. "Bailes Folklóricos del Altiplano." In *Travaux de L'institut Francais d'Études Andines, Tome IV*, edited by Jehan Vellard and Milfred Merino, 59–132. Lima, Peru: Études sur le lac Titicaca, V and VI.

Veniard, Juan María. 1986. *La Música Nacional Argentina: Influencia de la Música Criolla Tradicional en la Música Académica Argentina*. Buenos Aires, Argentina: Ministerio de Educación y Justicia, Secretaría de Cultura, Instituto Nacional de Musicología Carlos Vega.

Veniard, Juan María. 2000. *Aproximación a la Música Académica Argentina*. Buenos Aires, Argentina: Ediciones de la Universidad Católica Argentina.

Ventocilla, Eleodoro. 1969. *Barrientos*. Lima, Peru: Ediciones Nuevo Mundo.

Vianna, Hermano. 1999. *The Mystery of Samba: Popular Music and National Identity in Brazil*. Chapel Hill: University of North Carolina Press.

Wade, Peter. 2000. *Music, Race, and Nation: Música Tropical in Colombia*. Chicago: University of Chicago Press.

Wahren, Cecilia. 2014. "Raza, Nación y Folklore: La Representación del Indio en la Construcción de la Identidad Nacional Boliviana (1899–1933)." Master's thesis, Universidad de San Andrés-Buenos Aires.

Weismantel, Mary. 2001. *Cholas and Pishtacos: Stories of Race and Sex in the Andes*. Chicago: University of Chicago Press.

Whitehead, Laurence. 2003. "The Bolivian National Revolution: A Twenty-First Century Perspective." In *Proclaiming Revolution: Bolivia in Comparative Perspective*, edited by Merilee S. Grindle and Pilar Domingo, 25–53. London: Institute of Latin American Studies.

Wong, Ketty. 2012. *Whose National Music? Identity, Mestizaje, and Migration in Ecuador*. Philadelphia: Temple University Press.

Wood, Grant. 2014. *Agustín Lara: A Cultural Biography*. Oxford: Oxford University Press.

Young, Kevin. 2017. *Blood of the Earth: Resource Nationalism, Revolution, and Empire in Bolivia*. Austin: University of Texas Press.

Zavaleta Mercado, René. 1986. *Lo Nacional-Popular en Bolivia*. Mexico City, Mexico: Siglo Veintiuno Editores.

Zolov, Eric. 1999. *Refried Elvis: The Rise of the Mexican Counterculture*. Berkeley: University of California Press.

Index